CAMBRIDGE LIBRARY COLLECTION

Books of enduring scholarly value

European History

This series includes accounts of historical events and movements by eye-witnesses and contemporaries, as well as landmark studies that assembled significant source materials or developed new historiographical methods. It covers the social and political history of continental Europe from the Renaissance to the end of the nineteenth century, and its broad range includes works on Russia and the Balkans, revolutionary France, the papacy and the inquisition, and the Venetian state archives.

A History of Greece

A participant in the Greek struggle for independence alongside Lord Byron, the philhellene George Finlay (1799–1875) lent his support to the newly liberated nation while diligently studying its past. The monographs he published in his lifetime covered the history of Greece since the Roman conquest, spanning two millennia. His two-volume *History of the Greek Revolution* (1861) is reissued separately in this series. Edited by the scholar Henry Fanshawe Tozer (1829–1916) and published in 1877, this seven-volume collection brought together Finlay's histories, incorporating significant revisions. Notably, Finlay gives due consideration to social and economic factors as well as high politics. Volume 5 covers the history of Greece under Ottoman and Venetian rule from 1453 to 1821. Finlay gives an overview of the political and military organisation of the Ottoman empire, touching also on the social conditions of the Greeks. He argues that growing national consciousness set the stage for Greek independence.

Cambridge University Press has long been a pioneer in the reissuing of out-of-print titles from its own backlist, producing digital reprints of books that are still sought after by scholars and students but could not be reprinted economically using traditional technology. The Cambridge Library Collection extends this activity to a wider range of books which are still of importance to researchers and professionals, either for the source material they contain, or as landmarks in the history of their academic discipline.

Drawing from the world-renowned collections in the Cambridge University Library and other partner libraries, and guided by the advice of experts in each subject area, Cambridge University Press is using state-of-the-art scanning machines in its own Printing House to capture the content of each book selected for inclusion. The files are processed to give a consistently clear, crisp image, and the books finished to the high quality standard for which the Press is recognised around the world. The latest print-on-demand technology ensures that the books will remain available indefinitely, and that orders for single or multiple copies can quickly be supplied.

The Cambridge Library Collection brings back to life books of enduring scholarly value (including out-of-copyright works originally issued by other publishers) across a wide range of disciplines in the humanities and social sciences and in science and technology.

A History of Greece

*From Its Conquest by
the Romans to the Present Time,
B.C. 146 to A.D. 1864*

VOLUME 5:
GREECE UNDER OTHOMAN
AND VENETIAN DOMINATION

GEORGE FINLAY
EDITED BY H.F. TOZER

CAMBRIDGE
UNIVERSITY PRESS

CAMBRIDGE
UNIVERSITY PRESS

University Printing House, Cambridge, CB2 8BS, United Kingdom

Cambridge University Press is part of the University of Cambridge.
It furthers the University's mission by disseminating knowledge in the pursuit of
education, learning and research at the highest international levels of excellence.

www.cambridge.org
Information on this title: www.cambridge.org/9781108078375

© in this compilation Cambridge University Press 2014

This edition first published 1877
This digitally printed version 2014

ISBN 978-1-108-07837-5 Paperback

HISTORY OF GREECE.

FINLAY.

a

𝔏𝔬𝔫𝔡𝔬𝔫

MACMILLAN AND CO.

PUBLISHERS TO THE UNIVERSITY OF

𝔒𝔵𝔣𝔬𝔯𝔡

A

HISTORY OF GREECE

FROM ITS

CONQUEST BY THE ROMANS TO THE PRESENT TIME

B.C. 146 TO A.D. 1864

BY

GEORGE FINLAY, LL.D.

A NEW EDITION, REVISED THROUGHOUT, AND IN PART RE-WRITTEN,

WITH CONSIDERABLE ADDITIONS, BY THE AUTHOR,

AND EDITED BY THE

REV. H. F. TOZER, M.A.

TUTOR AND LATE FELLOW OF EXETER COLLEGE, OXFORD

IN SEVEN VOLUMES

VOL. V

GREECE UNDER OTHOMAN AND VENETIAN DOMINATION

A.D. 1453 — 1821

Oxford

AT THE CLARENDON PRESS

M DCCC LXXVII

CONTENTS.

CHAPTER II.

The Naval Conquests of the Othomans in Greece.—A.D. 1453-1684.

CHAPTER III.

Social Condition of the Greeks until the Extinction of the Tribute of Christian Children.—A.D. 1453-1676.

CHAPTER IV.

History of the Venetian Domination in Greece.—A.D. 1684-1718.

CHAPTER V.

**The Causes and Events which prepared the Greeks for Independence.
A.D. 1718–1821.**

CHRONOLOGY.

1397. Bayezid I. establishes the timariot system in Thessaly.
1453. Mohammed II. repeoples Constantinople.
   ,, Re-establishes the Orthodox Greek Church.
1454. Insurrection of Albanian population in the Morea.
1456. Mohammed II. defeated at Belgrade.
1458. Walls of Constantinople repaired, and Castle of Seven Towers built.
1459. Servia annexed to the Othoman empire.
   ,, Amastris taken from the Genoese.
1460. Mohammed II. conquers the Morea.
   ,, Athens annexed to the Othoman empire.
1461. Conquest of empire of Trebizond.
1462. Mytilene annexed to Othoman empire.
1463. Argos occupied by Othoman troops.
   ,, War with Venice.
1466. Athens taken by Venetians, and abandoned.
1467. 17th January, death of Skanderbeg at Alessio.
1469. Earthquake at Santa Maura, Cephalonia, and Zante.
1470. Conquest of Negrepont.
1475. Kaffa and Tana taken from the Genoese.
1477. Croïa surrenders to the Othomans.
1479. Peace between Mohammed II. and Venice.
   ,, Zante and Cephalonia taken by Mohammed II. from Leonard Tocco, despot of Arta.
1480. Othoman army defeated at Rhodes.
1481. Death of Mohammed II.
1484. Venice restores Cephalonia to Bayezid II., and pays a tribute of five hundred ducats annually for Zante.
1489. Catherine Cornara cedes Cyprus to Venice.
1492. Jews expelled from Spain by Ferdinand and Isabella.

1494. Andrew Palaeologos, son of Thomas, despot in the Peloponnesus, cedes his rights to it and to the Byzantine empire to Charles VIII. of France, but that cession not being accepted within the stipulated time, in

1498. He cedes his rights to Ferdinand and Isabella of Spain.

1500. Bayezid II. takes Lepanto, Modon, Coron, and Durazzo, from Venice.

1501. Mohammedans expelled from Spain if they refuse to be baptized.

1502. Peace between Bayezid II. and Venice. The republic cedes Santa Maura to the Sultan, but retains Cephalonia.

1509. Great earthquake at Constantinople.

1510. Walls of Constantinople repaired.

1512. Bogdan, Prince of Moldavia, becomes tributary to Sultan Selim I.

1515. Great fire at Constantinople.

1516. Vallachia pays an annual tribute of six hundred Christian children to the sultan.

1522. Conquest of Rhodes by Suleiman I.

1526. Vienna besieged.

1535. First public treaty of alliance between the Othoman empire and the King of France.

,,   Supremacy of the Othoman navy in the Mediterranean.

1537. Defeat of the Othomans at Corfu.

,,   Barbarossa takes Paros, Skyros, Patmos, and Stympalea.

1540. Treaty of peace between Suleiman I. and Venice. The republic cedes Monemvasia and Nauplia to the Sultan.

1563. Great inundation, caused by rain, at Constantinople.

1565. Othoman expedition against Malta defeated.

1566. Chios and Naxos annexed to the Othoman empire.

,,   Rebellion of the Janissaries.

1570. Morescoes, descendants of Mohammedans in Spain, driven to rebellion by persecution.

1571. Conquest of Cyprus by Othomans.

,,   15th of October, battle of Lepanto.

1572. Tunis taken by Don Juan of Austria.

1573. Treaty of peace between the Othoman empire and Venice.

1574. Tunis retaken by the Othoman fleet.

1591. Thirty thousand workmen employed to construct a canal at Nicomedia.

1593. First commercial treaty between the Sultan and England.

1600. Rebellion of the Janissaries.

1609. Final expulsion of the Morescoes from Spain by Philip III.

1614. Maina compelled to pay haratch.
1622. Great rebellion of Janissaries and Sipahis against Sultan Othman II.
1624. Cossacks plunder the shores of the Bosphorus.
„ Piracy prevalent in the Mediterranean.
1632. Great rebellion of troops at Constantinople.
1642. Great earthquake at Constantinople.
„ Corsairs and pirates continue their ravages in the Archipelago.
1645. Othoman troops invade Crete.
1648. Earthquake at Constantinople.
1650. New island rises out of the sea at Santorin.
1653. Great earthquake at Constantinople.
1656. Great insurrection at Constantinople.
1669. Conquest of Crete completed by capitulation of Candia. Treaty of peace between the Othoman empire and Venice.
„ Foundation of the official power of the Phanariots by the rank conceded to Panayotaki of Chios, dragoman of Achmet Kueprili.
1670. Subjugation of Maina. Forts of Zarnata, Porto Vitylo, and Passava, armed and garrisoned by Turks.
1671 to 1684. Corsairs and pirates infest the coasts and islands of Greece and Asia Minor in great numbers.
1672 and 1673. Mainates emigrate to Apulia and Corsica.
1675. Disputes of the Greeks and Catholics concerning the possession of the Holy Places at Jerusalem.
1683. Siege of Vienna by Kara Mustapha.
1685. The Venetians commence the conquest of the Morea. Morosini takes Coron.
1687. Athens taken by Morosini. Parthenon ruined.
„ Plague in the Venetian army.
„ Great fire at Constantinople.
1688. Defeat of Morosini at Negrepont.
1690. Earthquake at Constantinople.
1692. Fire at Constantinople.
1699. Peace of Carlovitz.
1711. Defeat of Peter the Great. Treaty of the Pruth.
1712. Commencement of Phanariot domination in Moldavia.
1715. Re-conquest of the Morea by Ali Kumurgi.
1716. Commencement of Phanariot domination in Vallachia.
1718. Peace of Passarovitz.
1719. Great fire and earthquake at Constantinople.
1720. Treaty of perpetual peace between Turkey and Russia.

1736 to 1739. Marshal Munich's campaigns against the Crimea and Turkey.

1739. Treaty of Belgrade.

1740. Great fire at Constantinople.

1741. Fire at Constantinople.

1746. Fire at Constantinople.

1751. Piracies on the coast of Maina and in the Archipelago.

„ Tumult of Greeks at Constantinople against the Patriarch and the Phanariots.

1754. Great earthquake at Constantinople.

1755. Great fire at Constantinople.

1761. First treaty between Turkey and Prussia.

„ Persecution of Catholic Armenians at Constantinople.

1764. Insurrection of Greeks in Cyprus.

1766. Earthquake at Constantinople.

1767. Great fires at Constantinople and at Pera.

1770. Great fire at Constantinople.

„ Russian invasion of the Morea.

„ Sphakiots compelled to pay haratch.

1774. Treaty of Kutchuk Kainardji.

1787. War of Suliots with Ali Pasha of Joannina.

„ Russian privateering in the Archipelago.

1792. Treaty of Yassi.

1797. Ionian Islands surrendered to France by the Treaty of Campo Formio.

„ Ali Pasha massacres the Christian Albanians of Chimara.

1800. Russia cedes the continental dependencies of the Ionian Islands, Parga, Prevesa, etc., to Turkey.

„ Establishment of the Ionian republic.

1807. Russia cedes the Ionian Islands to France by the treaty of Tilsit.

1815. Ionian republic placed under the protection of Great Britain by the treaty of Vienna.

1819. Parga delivered to Turkey by Great Britain.

1821. Commencement of the Greek Revolution.

HISTORY OF GREECE

UNDER

OTHOMAN AND VENETIAN DOMINATION.

CHAPTER I.

THE POLITICAL AND MILITARY ORGANIZATION OF THE OTHOMAN EMPIRE, BY WHICH THE GREEKS WERE RETAINED IN SUBJECTION. A.D. 1453–1684.

Measures of the Othoman conquerors to consolidate their domination.—Position of the Greeks in the Othoman empire.—Extent of the empire.—Degradation of the Greek population.—Stability of the Othoman power.—Its institutions. —Tribute-children.—Ulema.—First class of institutions: those derived from the Koran.—Second class: those derived from the Seljouk empire.—Third class: those peculiar to the Othoman government.—Kanun-namé of Moham- med II.—Administrative divisions.—Defective administration of justice.— Nizam Djedid of Mustapha Kueprili, A.D. 1691.—Finances.— Haratch.—Com- mercial taxes.—Land-tax.—Depreciation of the currency.—Project of exter- minating the Christian subjects of the Sultan.—Improvement in the Othoman administration.—Murder authorized by an organic law of the empire.— Othoman army.—Feudal militia.—Janissaries.—Regular cavalry.—Sipahis. —Tribute of Christian children.—Irregular troops.—Christian troops and auxiliaries.—Decline of the administrative system.—Venality.—Wealth.— Discipline long maintained in the army.

THE conquest of Greece by Mohammed II. was felt to be a boon by the greater part of the population. The government of the Greek emperors of the family of Palaeologos, of their relations the despots in the Morea, and of the Frank princes and Venetian signors, had for two centuries rendered Greece the scene of incessant civil wars and odious oppression. The Mohammedan government put an end to the injustice of the petty tyrants, whose rapacity and feuds divided, impoverished, and depopulated the country[1]. When Mohammed II. annexed the Peloponnesus and Attica to the Othoman empire, he deliberately exterminated all remains of the existing aristocracy, both Frank nobles and Greek archonts, and introduced in their place a Turkish aristocracy, as far as such a class existed in his dominions. The ordinary system of the Othoman administration was immediately applied to the greater part of Greece, and it was poverty, and not valour, which exempted a few mountainous districts from its application.

Saganos Pasha was appointed by Mohammed II. governor of the Morea and the duchy of Athens, but garrisons of the sultan's regular troops were stationed in a few of the strongest fortresses, under officers independent of the pasha's authority. The general defence of the country and the maintenance of order among the inhabitants was intrusted to Saganos, who was intrusted with complete control over the revenue necessary for that purpose. The arbitrary power of the pasha, and the license of the regular garrisons, were restrained by the timariot system. The feudal usages, which the earliest Othoman sultans had inherited with their first possessions in the Seljouk empire, were introduced by Mohammed II. into Greece, as the natural manner of retaining the rural population under his domination. Large tracts of land in the richest plains having reverted to the government as belonging to the confiscated estates of the princes and nobles, a certain proportion of this property was divided into liferent fiefs, which were conferred on veteran warriors who had merited rewards by distinguished service. These fiefs were called timars, and consisted of a life-interest in lands, of which the Greek and Albanian cultivators sometimes remained in possession of the exclusive right of cultivation within determined limits, and under the obligation of paying a fixed revenue, and performing certain services for the Mussulman landlord. The timariot was bound to serve the sultan on horseback with a number of well-appointed followers, varying according to the value of his fief. These men had no occupation, and no thought but to perfect themselves in the use of their arms, and for a long period they formed the best light cavalry in Europe. The

---

[1] Stephen, king of Bosnia, in a letter to Pope Pius II., says, 'Turcae in agrestes mitem animum ostendunt.' Gobellinus, *Pii II. Pont. Max. Comm*, Franc. 1614, p. 298.

timars were granted as military rewards, and were not hereditary while the system continued to exist in its ancient purity.
The veteran soldiers who held these fiefs in Greece were bound
to the sultan by many ties.   They looked forward to advancement to the larger estates called ziamets, or to gaining the
rank of sandjak-beg, or commander of a timariot troop of
horse.   This class was consequently firmly attached to the
central authority of the Othoman sultan, and constituted a
check both on the ambitious projects and local despotism of
powerful pashas, and on the rebellious disposition of the Christian population.   The rich rewards granted by Mohammed II.
to his followers drew numerous bands of Turkoman and
Seljouk volunteers to his armies from Asia Minor, who came
to Europe, well mounted and armed, to seek their fortunes as
warlike emigrants.   His brilliant conquests enabled him to
bestow rich lands on many of these volunteers, while their own
valour gained for them abundant booty during his unceasing
wars.   Many of these adventurers were established in Greece
after its conquest, and they were always ready to take the
field against the Christians, both as a religious duty and as a
means of acquiring slaves, whom, according to their qualifications, they might send to their own harems, to their farms, or
to the slave-market.   The timariots of the Othoman empire,
like the feudal nobility of Europe, required a servile race to
cultivate the land.   Difference of religion in Turkey created
the distinction of rank which pride of birth perpetuated in
feudal Europe.   But the system was in both cases equally
artificial ; and the permanent laws of man's social existence
operate unceasingly to destroy every distinctive privilege
which separates one class of men as a caste from the rest of
the community, in violation of the immutable principles of
equity.   Heaven tolerates temporary injustice committed by
individual tyrants to the wildest excesses of iniquity; but
history proves that Divine Providence has endowed society
with an irrepressible power of expansion, which gradually
effaces every permanent infraction of the principles of justice
by human legislation.   The laws of Lycurgus expired before
the Spartan state, and the corps of janissaries possessed more
vitality than the tribute of Christian children.

The Turkish feudal system was first introduced into
Thessaly by Bayezid I., about the year 1397, when he sent

Evrenos to invade the Peloponnesus. He invested so large a number of Seljouk Turks with landed estates, both in Macedonia and Thessaly, that from this period a powerful body of timariots was ever ready to assemble, at the sultan's orders, to invade the southern part of Greece[1]. Murad II. extended the system to Epirus and Acarnania, when he subdued the possessions of Charles Tocco, the despot of Arta; and Mohammed II. rendered all Greece subject to the burden of maintaining his feudal cavalry. The governmental division of Greece and the burdens to which it was subjected, varied so much at different times, that it is extremely difficult to ascertain the exact amount of the timariots settled in Greece at the time of Sultan Mohammed's death. The number of fiefs was not less than about 300 ziamets and 1600 timars[2].

Along with the timariot system, Mohammed II. imposed the tribute of Christian children on Greece, as it then existed in the other Christian provinces of his empire. A fifth of their male children was exacted from the sultan's Christian subjects, as a part of that tribute which the Koran declared was the lawful price of toleration to those who refused to embrace Islam[3].

---

[1] Chalcocondylas, pp. 53, 232, 234, edit. Par. Ἐπιδιδόασι μὲν οὗτοι οἱ χῶροι πρός γε πολεμίων.

[2] The number is thus stated in various accounts:—

		Ziamets.	Timars.
The Sandjak of Morea .	. . . .	109	342
.. ..	Negrepont . . .	12	188
.. ..	Thessaly, that is Palaeopatra and Tricala	60	344
.. ..	Epakto	13	287
.. ..	Karlili, that is Acarnania and Aetolia	11	119
.. ..	Joannina	62	345
		267	1625

Estimating the force of the ziamets at 15 men, and of the timars at 2, this would furnish 7250 cavalry.

When Crete was conquered, it was divided into 3 sandjaks.

		Ziamets.	Timars.
Candia	. . . .	8	1400
Khanea	. . . .	5	800
Retymos	. . . .	4	350
		17	2550
Rhodes	. . . .	5	71
Mytilene	. . . .	4	83

The islands and maritime districts subject to the jurisdiction of the captain pasha were obliged to maintain a number of galleys.

[3] Sale's *Koran*, chap. ix. vol. i. p. 224. 'Fight against those who forbid not what God and his prophet have forbidden, and who profess not the true religion of those unto whom the Koran has been delivered, until they pay tribute, and they be reduced low.' D'Ohsson, *Tableau général de l'Empire othoman; Code militaire*, c. ii. vol. v. p. 79.

By these measures the last traces of the political institutions
and legal administration, which the Greeks derived from the
Roman Caesars, the Byzantine emperors, or the Frank princes,
from the code of Justinian, the Basilika of Leo, or the assize
of Jerusalem, were all swept away. Greece was partitioned
among several pashas and governors, all of whom were under
the orders of the beglerbeg of Roumelia, the sultan's commander-in-chief in Europe. The islands and some maritime
districts were at a later period placed under the control of the
captain pasha. The Greeks, as a nation, disappear from history; but they had long laid aside the once glorious name of
Hellenes and called themselves Romans[1]. No instances of
patriotic despair ennobled the records of their subjection. A
dull uniformity marks their conduct and their thoughts. Byzantine ceremony and orthodox formality had already effaced
the stronger traits of individual character, and extinguished
genius. Othoman oppression now made an effort to extirpate
the innate feelings of humanity. Parents gave their sons to be
janissaries, and their daughters to be odalisques[2].

The history of the Othoman government during the period
when its yoke bore heaviest on the Greeks, deserves to be
carefully studied, if it were only to institute a comparison
between the conduct of the Mussulmans, and the manner in
which the most powerful contemporary Christian states treated
their subjects. Unless this comparison be made, and the condition of the rayah in the sultan's dominions be contrasted
with that of the serf in the holy Roman empire of the Germans, and in the dominions of the kings of France and Spain,
the absolute cruelty of the Othoman domination would be
greatly overrated. The mass of the Christian population

---

[1] Until the commencement of the Greek revolution the name of Hellenes was
forgotten, that of Graikoi little used, and that of Romaioi universal.

[2] [The harassing life of the Greeks, owing to Latin barons, Turkish pirates, and
Byzantine officials, was surely enough to quench 'patriotic despair,' without its
being necessary to refer everything to the degeneracy of the people. The author
has himself pointed out, elsewhere, that it was the crushing character of Mohammed II.'s policy which caused the Greeks to acquiesce in the payment of the tribute
of their children (vol. iv. p. 266), though at the commencement of chap. iii. of this
volume he speaks of this acquiescence as ' the strongest proof of the demoralization
of the Hellenic race.' The feelings of the Greeks at the time of the capture
of Constantinople are well portrayed
in the poem entitled ' A Lament for Constantinople' (Θρῆνος τῆς Κωνσταντινουπό-
λεως), which is to be found (among other places) in Dr. Wagner's *Mediaeval Greek
Texts*, published for the Philological Society (pp. 141-170). The description
of the enslaving of the citizens (lines 194-223) is extremely pathetic. ED.]

engaged in agricultural operations was allowed to enjoy a far
larger portion of the fruits of their labour, under the sultan's
government, than under that of many Christian monarchs.
This fact explains the facility with which the sultans of Constantinople held millions of Christian landed proprietors and
small farmers in submissive bondage to a comparatively small
number of Mohammedans in the European provinces of their
empire. Indeed, the conquest of the Greeks was completed
before the Othoman government had succeeded in subduing a
considerable part of the Seljouk Turks in Asia Minor, and for
several centuries the Mussulman population in Asia proved far
more turbulent subjects to the sultans than the orthodox Christians in Europe. Mohammed II., and many of his successors,
were not only abler men than the Greek emperors who preceded them on the throne of Byzantium, but they were really
better sovereigns than most of the contemporary princes in the
West. The Transylvanians and Hungarians long preferred
the government of the house of Othman to that of the house
of Hapsburg ; the Greeks clung to their servitude under the
infidel Turks, rather than seek a deliverance which would
entail submission to the Catholic Venetians. It was therefore
in no small degree by the apathy, if not by the positive good-
will of the Christian population, that the supremacy of the
Sublime Porte was firmly established from the mountains of
Laconia to the plains of Podolia and the banks of the Don.
So stable were the foundations of the Othoman power, even on
its northern frontier, that for three centuries the Black Sea was
literally a Turkish lake. The Russians first acquired a right
to navigate freely over its waters in the year 1774[1].

After the conquest of Constantinople, the Othomans became the most dangerous conquerors who have acted a part
in European history since the fall of the western Roman
empire. Their dominion, at the period of its greatest extension, stretched from Buda on the Danube to Bussora on the
Euphrates. On the north, their frontiers were guarded against
the Poles by the fortress of Kamenietz, and against the Russians by the walls of Azof ; while to the south the rock of Aden
secured their authority over the southern coast of Arabia,

---

[1] By the ninth article of the treaty of Kainardji. By the third article of the
treaty of Belgrade in 1739, Russia was bound not to build any ships of war,
and not to maintain any fleet, even in the Sea of Azof.

invested them with power in the Indian Ocean, and gave them the complete command of the Red Sea. To the east, the sultan ruled the shores of the Caspian, from the Kour to the Tenek ; and his dominions stretched westward along the southern coast of the Mediterranean, where the farthest limits of the regency of Algiers, beyond Oran, meet the frontiers of the empire of Morocco. By rapid steps the Othomans completed the conquest of the Seljouk sultans in Asia Minor, of the Mamlouk sultans in Syria and Egypt, of the fierce corsairs of northern Africa, expelled the Venetians from Cyprus, Crete, and the Archipelago, and drove the Knights of St. John of Jerusalem from the Levant, to find a shelter at Malta. It was no vain boast of the Othoman sultan, that he was the master of many kingdoms, the ruler of three continents, and the lord of two seas.

For three centuries the position of the Greek race was one of hopeless degradation. Its connection with the old pagan Hellenes was repudiated by themselves, and forgotten by other nations[1]. The modern Greeks continued to be prouder of having organized the ecclesiastical establishment of the orthodox hierarchy than of an imaginary connection with an extinct though cognate society, which had once occupied the highest rank in the political and intellectual world, and created the literature of Europe. The modern identification of the Christian Greeks with the pagan Hellenes is the growth of the new series of ideas disseminated by the French Revolution. At the time when ecclesiastical orthodoxy exerted its most powerful influence on the Greeks as a people, they were content to perpetuate their national existence in the city of Constantinople, in a state of moral debasement not very dissimilar from the position in which Juvenal describes their ancestors at Rome[2]. The primates and the clergy acted as

---

[1] [The question of the nationality claimed by the Greeks of this period seems rather a question of names. To the uneducated classes ancient Greeks and ancient Romans were equally unknown, and it would be more accurate to say that they were unacquainted with, than that they 'repudiated' their connection with the Hellenes. But the educated, though they called themselves Ῥωμαῖοι, and looked to the Byzantine empire as the stock from which they sprang, were not altogether forgetful of a connection with the ancient people whose language they used ; as the Author implies, when in chap. iv. of this volume he says of the Athenians in the time of Morosini that they 'pretended to represent the countrymen of Pericles.' ED.]

[2] Ingenium velox, audacia perdita, sermo
Promptus et Isaeo torrentior : ede quid illum
Esse putes? quem vis hominem secum attulit ad nos;
(Juv. iii. 73–75.)
is quite as correct a description of the nobles of the Phanar who served the

agents of Turkish tyranny with as much zeal as the artists
and rhetoricians of old had pandered for the passions of their
Roman masters.   On the other hand, the slavery of the Greeks
to the Othomans was not the result of any inferiority in
numerical force, material wealth, and scientific knowledge.
The truth is, that the successes of the Othoman Turks, like
those of the Romans, must be in great part attributed to their
superiority in personal courage, individual morality, systematic
organization, and national dignity.   The fact is dishonourable
to Christian civilization.   After the conquest of Constantinople, the Greeks sank, with wonderful rapidity, and without
an effort, into the most abject slavery.   For three centuries
their political history is merged in the history of the Othoman
empire.   During this long period, the national position, for
evil and for good, was determined by the aggregate of vice
and virtue in the individuals who composed the nation.   Historians rarely allow due weight to the direct influence of
individual conduct in the mass of mankind on political
history.   At this period, however, the national history of
the Greeks is comprised in their individual biography.   Because
they were destitute of virtue as individuals, they were contemptible as a nation.

The power and resources of the Othoman empire, at the
time when the Sultans of Constantinople were most dreaded
by the Western Christians, were principally derived from the
profound policy with which the Turkish government rendered
its Christian subjects the instruments of its designs.   It gave
to its subjects a modicum of protection for life and property,
and an amount of religious toleration which induced the
orthodox to perpetuate their numbers, to continue their labours
for amassing wealth, and to prefer the domination of the sultan
to that of any Christian potentate.   In return, it exacted a
tithe of the lives as well as of the fortunes of its subjects.
Christian children were taken to fill up the chasms which
polygamy and war were constantly producing in Mussulman
society, and Christian industry filled the sultan's treasury with
the wealth which long secured success to the boldest projects
of Othoman ambition.   No accidental concourse of events
could have given permanence to a dominion which maintained

Othoman administration, as it was of the Rhetor who flattered the senators
and proconsuls of imperial Rome.

its authority with the same stern tyranny over the Seljouk Turk, the Turkoman, the Kurd, the Arab, and the Moorish Mussulman, as it did over the Greek, the Albanian, the Servian, the Bulgarian, the Vallachian, and the Armenian Christian. An empire whose greatness has endured for several centuries, must have been supported by some profound political combinations, if not by some wise and just institutions. Accidental accumulations of conquest, joined together by military force alone, like the empires of Attila, Genghis Khan, and Timor, have never attained such stability.

The Othomans exhibit the last example of a barbarous tribe intruding itself among civilized nations and forming a new nation in countries already densely peopled. It is true, that the great Turkish race, of which they were an offset, has always been one of the most numerous on the earth, and the Seljouk Turks had for three centuries formed a considerable part of the population of Asia Minor. But hitherto the Turks had exercised very little influence either in retarding or accelerating the progress of European civilization.

At the commencement of the fourteenth century the Othomans were a nameless tribe, whose leader Othman transferred his own name to his scanty band of followers. His father Ertogrul entered the Seljouk empire with a tribe numbering only 400 tents. Othman founded an empire, and in a short time the tribe of Ertogrul expanded into a great nation. The history of the Othomans offers some striking points of resemblance with that of the Romans. The legends of Romulus, of Numa the legislator, of Tarquin the Proud, and of the destruction of Rome by the Gauls, find a parallel in the foundation of an empire by Othman, in the legislation of Orkhan, in the character of Bayezid the Thunderer, and in the temporary extinction of the Othoman government by Timor the Great. The marvels of Othoman history have a grandeur in the simple truth that requires no aid from legendary ornament. Our aversion to the enduring results of Othoman institutions and conquests has sought gratification by depreciating the power of those institutions, and treating the mighty victories of the sultans as accidental and prosaic events. Our fathers feared and hated the Othomans too much to judge them fairly, and our prejudices still offer some obstacles to our contemplating with equanimity the marked superiority which they displayed in politics and war over Christian nations for more than two centuries. The Hellenic race in ancient times divided the inhabitants of the globe into Greeks and barbarians. The Othomans separated the inhabitants of their empire into Mussulmans and infidels. The division marks both intellectual and political progress.

The peculiar institutions which characterize the Othoman empire were first introduced by Orkhan. About the year 1329, Christian orphans, whose parents had been slain, were collected together, and schools for educating young slaves in the serai were formed. This was the commencement of a systematic education of Christian children, and of the corps of janissaries. Murad I. gave both measures that degree of systematic regularity, by which the tribute of Christian children afforded a permanent supply of recruits to the sultan's army and to the official administration. Hence Murad, rather than his father Orkhan, has been generally called the founder of the janissaries [1]. The political institutions of the empire were extended and consolidated by Mohammed II. After the conquest of the empires of Constantinople and Trebizond, he published his Kanun-namé, or legislative organization of the Othoman empire. In the reign of Suleiman I., called by the Mussulmans the Legislator and by the Christians the Magnificent, the Othoman power attained its meridian splendour. The death of the Grand-Vizier, Achmet Kueprili, in the year 1676, during the reign of Mohammed IV., marks the epoch of its decline. Yet the decay of its strength was not without glory. In the year 1715 it inflicted a mortal wound on Venice, its ancient rival, by reconquering the Morea; and at the peace of Belgrade, in 1739, it frustrated the combined attacks of its most powerful enemies, by baffling the projects of Russia, and obtaining terms which were dishonourable to Austria.

A slight sketch of the Othoman government at the end of the reign of Mohammed II. will be sufficient to place the relation of the Greeks to the dominant race and to the central administration in a clear light. This relation underwent very little change as long as the original institutions of the empire

---

[1] Hadji Khalfa fixes the establishment of the janissaries, and Saadeddin that of the sipahis, in the year of the Hegira 730 = A.D. 1329. Compare Hammer, *Staatsverfassung und Staatsverwaltung des Osmanischen Reichs*, i. 52–56. Christian writers, and even some Turkish, consider Murad I. their founder.

remained unaltered. During this period the records of the
Greeks are of very little historical value; indeed, they are so
destitute of authenticity on public affairs, that they can only
be trusted when they can be confronted with the annals of
their masters. It is by the influence which the Othoman
government exercised on European politics that Greece finds
a niche in the history of the sixteenth and seventeenth centuries, and it is by the influence the Greek Church exercised
on Muscovite civilization that the national importance was
preserved.

The power of systematic organization, as distinct from the
pedantry of uniform centralization, was never more conspicuous
than in the energy of the Othoman administration. The
institutions of Orkhan infused vigour into the Othoman tribe
by forming a central administration, and organizing a regular
army in immediate dependence on the person of the sultan.
The administration of the Othoman power became in this
way a part of the sultan's household, and the Sublime Porte,
which formed the emblem of the political existence of the
empire, was called into active operation, without any direct
dependence on Turkish nationality. The conquering race
was never allowed a share of political power in the sultan's
government, however great the privileges might be which they
were allowed to assume in comparison with the conquered
Christians.

The strength of the Othoman empire during the most
flourishing period of the sultan's power reposed on the house-
hold troops he composed from the children of his Christian
subjects. A tribute of male children was collected from
Christians in the conquered provinces; and it was paid by the
Greeks with as much regularity, and apparently with as little
repining, as any of the fiscal burdens imposed on them.
These tribute-children form the distinctive feature of the
Othoman administration, as compared with the preceding
Turkish empire of the Seljouks of Roum or of Iconium[1].
They were carefully educated as Mussulmans, and their con-
nection with their master the sultan, as household slaves, was
always regarded in the East as more close, and even more

---

[1] The caliphs of Bagdad and the sultans of Egypt had also guards composed
of slaves, and those of the sultans of Egypt were called Bahairiz. Joinville,
Histoire de St. Louis, p. 55, observ. 77, edit. Ducange; Pachymeres, i. 116.

honourable to the individual, than the connection of a subject
to his sovereign, where the tie was not strengthened by a
relationship of family, or at least of tribe. We find the same
social relation between the slave and the master existing
among the Jews at the earliest period of their national history. No stranger could partake of the passover, but the
servant that was bought for money could eat thereof. The
foreigner and the hired servant were nevertheless excluded
from the family festival [1]. The tribute-children, who were fed
in the sultan's house and were members of his household,
supplied the Othoman emperors with an official administration and a regular army, composed of household slaves, as
ready to attack the Seljouk and Arab sovereigns, though they
were Mohammedans, as they were to assail the Greeks and
the Servians, who were Christians.

We must not, however, conclude that the sovereignty of the
sultan, even when aided by this powerful instrument, was
entirely without restraint. The ministers of the Mohammedan religion, as interpreters of the civil and ecclesiastical law,
had a corporate existence of an older date than the foundation of the Othoman power. This corporation, called the
Ulema, possessed political rights, recognized throughout
every class of Mohammedan society, independent of the
sultan's will, and the power of the sultan was long restrained
by the laws and customs of which the Ulema was the representative and the champion. But in the long struggle between
a despotic central authority and class privileges, supported
only by local interests and prejudices, the victory at last
remained with the sultan, and the Ulema no longer exerts
any very important restraint on the political action of the
Othoman government. Corruption, which is the inseparable
attendant of despotic power, gradually rendered the principal
interpreters of the dogmas of Islam the submissive instruments of the sultan's will, and the power of the Ulema over
public opinion was thus undermined.

The institutions of the Othoman empire range themselves
in three classes : 1. Those which were derived from the
text of the Koran, and which were common to all Mohammedan countries from the times of the Arabian caliphs ;
2. Those civil and military arrangements connected with

---

[1] Exod. xii. 43.

property and local jurisdiction which prevailed among the Seljouk Turks in Asia Minor; and 3. The peculiar institutions of the Othoman empire which grew up out of the legislation of Orkhan and successive sultans.

The evils inflicted on society by the absolute power over the lives and property of all Mohammedans, except the members of the Ulema, with which the laws of Mahomet invest the sultan, form the staple of the history of Islam. And when the arbitrary nature of the administration of justice inherent in the constitution of the Ulema becomes a concomitant of the despotic power of the sovereign, it is not surprising that, in Mohammedan countries, there has always been as little security for the property of individuals as there has been protection for political liberty. The authority which the Ulema possesses of extracting rules of jurisprudence for the decision of particular cases from the religious precepts of the Koran, opens an unlimited field for judicial oppression. The acknowledged imperfection of the administration of justice prevents the law from being regarded with due respect ; and hence arises that ready submission to a despotic executive which characterizes all Mohammedan countries, for the power of the sovereign is considered the only effective check on the corruption of the Ulema. The sentiments of justice in the hearts of the people are also weakened by the laws of marriage, by the social relations which arise from the prevalence of polygamy, and by the immunity from all control enjoyed by the harem. The heads of families become invested with an arbitrary and despotic power at variance with the innate feelings of equity, and the moral responsibility which is the firmest basis of virtue in society is destroyed. The primary institutions which prevail wherever Mahomet has been acknowledged as the prophet of God, are, despotic power in the sovereign, an arbitrary administration of civil law, and an immoral organization of society. This is so striking, that every student of Turkish history feels himself puzzled in his attempts to solve the problem of ascertaining what were the good impulses of the human heart, or the sagacious policy of a wise government, by which these demoralizing influences were counteracted, and the Othoman empire raised to the high pitch of power and grandeur that it attained.

The second class of institutions which exerted a prominent influence on the Othoman government, consisted of the civil and military usages and customs of the Seljouk population of Asia Minor. The feudal institutions of the Seljouk empire continued to exist long after the complete subjection of its provinces to the Othoman sultan; and the wars of the national or feudal militia of Asia Minor with the central administration and the regular army at Constantinople, form an important feature in the history of the Othoman empire. The large irregular military force which marched under the sultan's banner, along with the regular army of janissaries and sipahis, even in the European wars, consisted principally of Seljouk feudatories enrolled in Asia Minor. The administration of the sultan's dominions has always presented strange anomalies in its numerous provinces, among the Mohammedan as well as among the Christian population. As in the Roman and the British empires, various races of men, and the followers of different creeds, lived intermingled in great numbers, and were allowed to retain those peculiar laws and usages that were closely interwoven with the thread of their social existence. This freedom from the administrative pedantry of centralization has saved the Othoman empire from the crime of becoming the exterminator of the races it has subdued. The sultans only interfered with the laws and customs of each conquered people in so far as was necessary to insure their submission to the Sublime Porte and render their resources available to increase the wealth and power of the Othoman empire.

It was the policy of the sultan to maintain constantly an isolated position, overlooking equally all the various nations in his empire, whether they were Mohammedan or Christian. This policy produced, in some respects, as direct an opposition between the Seljouk population of Asia Minor and the Othoman officials of the central administration, as it did between the dominant Mohammedans and the subject Christians in Europe. The sultan employed his household slaves as the agents of the executive government. The imperial officials, both civil and military, were consequently a distinct and separate race of men from the great body of the Mohammedan population of the empire, and this distinction was more galling to the proud Seljouk feudatory in Asia than to the Othoman landlord who had recently obtained the grant of an estate in Europe. The ties which connected the imperial officials with the Mussulman population were few and weak, while the bonds which united them to the sultan's person and government, as children of his household and slaves of his Sublime Porte, were closely interwoven with all their feelings and hopes. No sentiments of patriotism united the Seljouk Turk and the Syrian Arab to the Othoman government; while, on the other hand, no kindred sympathies, and no sense of national responsibility, restrained the rigour of the despotism exercised by its officials. Religious bigotry, and the community of interest arising out of a long career of conquest, inspired all the Mohammedan subjects of the sultan with one object, whenever war was proclaimed against a Christian state. The Seljouk feudatories and the Bedouin sheiks were then as eager for plunder and the capture of slaves as the janissaries. Even during the time of peace, the Seljouks on the Asiatic coast were compelled to stifle their aversion to the Othoman administration by the necessity of watching every movement of the Christian population. But the persevering opposition of the Seljouk population in the interior of Asia Minor to the government of the sultan fills many pages of Turkish history for two centuries after the conquest of Constantinople; and this opposition must be constantly borne in mind by those who desire to understand the anomalies in the administration of the Othoman empire and in the social position of its Turkish inhabitants[1]. Many relics of the former anomalies in the Othoman empire were visible at the beginning of the present century, which have now disappeared. The late Sultan Mahmoud II. swept away the last traces of the Seljouk feudal system, by exterminating the deré-beys, the ruins of whose castles still greet the traveller in many of the most sequestered and picturesque valleys in the Asiatic provinces. Much of the local vigour of the Mohammedan population was then extinguished; and how far the force of the empire has

---

[1] It would require a long explanatory dissertation to cite the proofs of these statements in detail, for the corruption introduced into the Othoman administration before the end of the sixteenth century had so mixed up the abuses in the regular army with those in the feudal militia, that the causes of the rebellions in Asia were often very complicated, and their origin often appears to have been accidental, in spite of the deep-rooted discontent.

been increased by centralizing its energies in the administrative establishments at Constantinople, is a problem which still waits for its solution.

The third class of Othoman institutions gave the empire its true historical character and distinctive political constitution. They had their origin in the legislation of Orkhan, and they grew under the fostering care of his successors, who persevered in following the direction he had marked out to them, until the work was completed by Mohammed II. the conqueror of the Greek race. Orkhan made the household of the sovereign the basis of the government of the Othoman dominions, as it had been of the imperial administration in the Roman empire. He assigned to the organization of the army and the civil and financial administration an existence perfectly independent of the people. The great political merit of Orkhan's institutions was, that they admitted of extension and development as the bounds of the empire were enlarged and the exigencies of the administration increased. Accordingly, we find Murad I. so far extending his father's regulations for recruiting the regular army from the tribute of Christian children, as to have obtained from some Turkish historians the honour of being called the founder of the corps of janissaries [1]. At length when Mohammed II. had completed his conquests, he turned his attention to the civil government of his vast empire. In all his plans for the administration of his new conquests, he made the institutions which Orkhan had bequeathed to the Othoman government the model of his legislation, and his Kanun-namé, consequently, is a collection of administrative ordinances, not an attempt to frame a code of civil laws. True to the spirit of Orkhan's theory of government, he constituted the sultan's palace the centre of political power, and its gate the spot to which his subjects must look for protection and justice. To the world at large the Sublime Porte was the seat of the sultan's government, and only the sultan's slaves could enter within its precincts to learn the sovereign's will in his own presence.

Mohammed II. was one of those great men whose personal conduct, from their superiority of talent and firmness of purpose, modifies the course of public events, when it is granted to them,

---

[1] *Annales Turcici, a Joanne Leunclavio latine translati*, p. 248, edit. Venet.

as it was to him, to exercise their influence during a long and successful reign. Though he ascended the throne at the age of twenty-one, his character was already formed by the education he had received. An enemy who knew him personally, and had the most powerful reasons to hate him, acknowledges that, with all the fire and energy of youth, he possessed the sagacity and the prudence of old age[1]. The palace of the sultan, where the young princes of the race of Othman received their education amidst tribute-children selected on account of their superior talents and amiable dispositions, was for several generations an excellent public school. No reigning family ever educated so many great princes as the house of Othman. When the intellect was strong and the disposition naturally good, the character was developed at an early age by the varied intercourse of the tribute-children and their instructors. In this society the young sultan Mohammed, whom nature had endowed with rare mental and physical advantages, learned the art of commanding himself, as well as others, by his desire to secure the esteem and attachment of the youths who were the companions of his amusements, and who were destined to become the generals of his armies and the ministers of his cabinet. Mohammed II. made it the duty of the sultan to preside in person over the whole government. For many years he was the real prime-minister, for he retained in his own hands the supreme direction of all public business after the execution of the grand-vizier Khalil. The succeeding grand-viziers only acted as commanders-in-chief of the army and principal secretaries of state for the general administration, not as vicegerents of the sultan's power. From the time of Murad I. to the taking of Constantinople, the usages and customs of the Othoman tribe still exercised some influence over the public administration, and the office of grand-vizier had been hereditary in the family of Djenderelli. Khalil was the fourth of this family who filled the office, and with him the political influence of the Othoman tribe expired. The project of Khalil had been to create an acknowledged power in the hands of the grand-vizier, as protector of the peaceable subjects of the empire, independent of the military power and the military classes. His avarice, as much as his ambition, induced him to

---

[1] Phrantzes, 93, edit. Bonn.

use his hereditary authority to control the operations of the army. His conduct awakened the suspicion of Mohammed II., who detected his intrigues with the Greeks; and forty days after the conquest of Constantinople, Khalil was beheaded at Adrianople. Several of the grand-viziers of Mohammed II. were men of great ability. Like the sultan, they had been educated in the schools of the imperial palace. The ablest of all was Mahmoud Pasha, whose father was a Greek and his mother an Albanian. He was a man worthy to rank with Mohammed II. and with Scanderbeg [1].

The successors of Mohammed II. pursued the line of policy he had traced out, and followed the maxims of state laid down in the Kanun-namé with energy and perseverance for several generations. They were men both able and willing to perform the onerous duties imposed on them. For two centuries and a-half—from Othman to Suleiman the Legislator—the only sultan who was not a man of pre-eminent military talent was Bayezid II.; yet he was nevertheless a prudent and accomplished prince. All these sovereigns directed in person the government of their empire, and the council, composed of the great officers of state and of viziers of the bench, was held in their presence.

The administrative fabric of the government was divided by Mohammed II. into four branches : 1. The Executive, the chief instruments of which were the pashas ; 2. The Judicial, embracing the Ulema, under the control of the kadiaskers, but subsequently presided over by the grand mufti ; 3. The Financial, under the superintendence of the defterdars ; and, 4. The Civil department, under the direction of the nishandjis or imperial secretaries. The grand-vizier, who was the chief of the pashas, exercised a supreme control over the whole government ; while the pashas, each in his own province, commanded the military forces, maintained the police, watched over the public security, and enforced the regular payment of all taxes and imposts. The kadiaskers, or grand judges of Asia and Europe, were, in the time of Mohammed II., the administrative chiefs of the judicial and religious establishments on the different sides of the Bosphorus. They named the cadis or inferior judges. But in the reign of Suleiman the Great, the

---

[1] Hammer, *Histoire de l'empire Othoman,* iii. 168.

grand mufti was vested with many of the functions previously exercised by the kadiaskers, who were rendered subordinate to this great interpreter of the law. A supreme defterdar acted as minister of finance, and directed that important branch of state business which, in all long-established and extensive empires, ultimately becomes the pivot of the whole administration. The sultan's private secretary was the chief nishandji, who performed the duty of principal secretary of state. His office was to affix the toghra (toura) or imperial cipher to all public acts, and to revise every document as it passed through the imperial cabinet.

Such was the general scheme of the administration as it was arranged by Mohammed II.; and though it was reformed and improved by Suleiman the Legislator, it remained in force until the commencement of the present century. But when the indolence and incapacity of the sultans left the irresponsible direction of public affairs in the hands of their grand-viziers, those ministers exercised the despotic power of their masters in the most arbitrary manner.

The administration of justice and that of finance are the two most important branches of government in civilized society, because they come hourly into contact with the feelings and actions of every subject. The organization of both these departments has always been singularly defective in the Othoman empire. The manner in which justice was dispensed to the subjects of the sultan—whether Mussulman or Christian— whether in the tribunal of the cadi or the court of the bishop —was so radically vicious as to render all decisions liable to the suspicion and generally to the imputation of venality. The consequence was that corruption pervaded the whole frame of society; there was an universal feeling of insecurity, and a conviction that candour and publicity were both attended with individual danger. The want of morality and self-reliance, which is made the reproach of the subjects of the Othoman empire, and from which hardly a portion of the dominant race was exempt, can easily be traced to this defect in their social position. In all historical investigations we ought constantly to bear in mind the observation of Hume, that all the vast apparatus of government has for its ultimate object the distribution of justice [1]. The executive power, and

---

[1] Hume's *Essays*, 'On the Origin of Government.'

C 2

the assemblies which form a portion of the legislative, ought both, in a well-constituted state, to be subordinate to the law. The fashionable phrase of modern constitutions, that every citizen is equal before the law, is a mockery of truth and common sense in all states where there is one set of laws or regulations for the government and its officials, and another for the mass of people as subjected to that government. Until neither rank, nor official position, nor administrative privileges can be pleaded as a ground of exceptional treatment by the agents of the executive in matters of justice, there can be no true civil liberty. The law must be placed above sovereigns and parliaments as well as above ministers and generals.

No such principles of government ever entered into the minds of the Othoman Turks. The Mohammedan jurisprudence declares distinctly that there is a different civil law for the believer in Islam and for the infidel. It pronounces that the Koran confers privileges on the true believer from which all others are excluded. The Mohammedan law, therefore, was founded on principles of partial, not of universal application, and it has maintained a perpetual struggle with the natural abhorrence of injustice which God has implanted in the human heart. Even the Mussulman population of the Othoman empire was not insensible to the instability of their legal position as a dominant race, where the mass of the population was of a different religion. They always felt that their power in Europe was based on maxims of law and policy which rendered its duration uncertain. The Mohammedans in Europe always contemplated the probability of their being one day expelled from countries where they appeared as foreign colonists and temporary sojourners, and looked forward to a period when they should be compelled to retreat into those Asiatic lands where the majority of the inhabitants followed the faith of Mahomet. Hence resulted the nervous anxiety displayed by the Mussulmans to convert the Christian population of the sultan's dominions. The true believers considered that this was the only manner by which it was possible to confer on the followers of a different religion an equality of civil rights, and they felt that this equality could alone give stability to their government. Several of the ablest statesmen in the Othoman empire declared, that until the Mohammedan religion was embraced by all the sultan's subjects, the government could neither be secure nor equitable. They fully acknowledged the danger of treating the Christians under their dominion with systematic injustice, and they endeavoured to palliate the evil they could not eradicate. The necessity of protecting the Christians against oppression was recognized by Mohammed II., and the patriarch of Constantinople was appointed the agent for the Greek nation at the Sublime Porte for this purpose. But the first legislative enactments for the declared object of protecting the Christian subjects of the sultan against official and Mussulman oppression, by investing them with a guarantee in their own personal rights, were dated in the year 1691. These imperial ordinances were promulgated by the grand-vizier Mustapha Kueprili, called the Virtuous, and were termed the Nizam-djedid, or New System. Governors of provinces, pashas and other officials, were commanded to treat the Christians with equity. They were strictly prohibited from exacting any addition to the haratch or capitation-tax, or to any of the imposts as fixed by the laws of the empire, under the pretext of local necessities. The intention of the Othoman government had always been to leave the collection and administration of the funds destined for local purposes in the hands of the inhabitants of the locality. This attempt of Mustapha the Virtuous to sanction the right of Christians to demand protection against Mussulman injustice, under Mohammedan laws, produced very little practical effect in ameliorating the lot of the Greeks[1]. The Othoman administration was about this period invaded by a degree of corruption, which left all the sultan's subjects, both Mussulman and Christian, exposed to the grossest injustice. It required many social changes in the East before any progress could be made in the task of levelling the barriers which separated the dominant religion from the faith of the subject people. The difference was too great to be effaced by legislative enactments alone.

The imperfection of the financial administration in the Othoman government assisted the vices of the judicial system

---

[1] Hammer, *Histoire de l'empire Othoman*, xii. 306, 322.

in accelerating the decline of the empire. In all countries, the manner in which the permanent revenues of the state are levied, exerts an important effect on the national prosperity. A small amount of taxation may be so collected as to check the accumulation of national wealth, and hinder the people from adopting fixed habits of industry, while a large amount may be imposed in such a way as to form a very slight check on the progress of a nation. The taxes in the Othoman empire were not so injurious from their amount, as from the way in which they were imposed and collected. The Mohammedans were exempt from many burdens which fell heavy on the Jews and Christians; and as often happens with financial privileges, these exceptions proved ultimately of very little advantage to the class they appeared to favour.

The great financial distinction between the followers of Islam, or the true believers, and the rayahs or infidel subjects of the sultan, was the payment of the haratch or capitation-tax. This tax was levied on the whole male unbelieving population, with the exception of children under ten years of age, old men, and priests of the different sects of Christians and Jews. The maimed, the blind, and the paralytic were also exempted by Moslem charity. This payment was imposed by the Koran on all who refused to embrace the Mohammedan faith, as the alternative by which they might purchase peace. The Othomans found it established in the Seljouk empire, and, as they were bound by their religious precepts, they extended it to every country they conquered. In the reign of Suleiman the Legislator, this tax yielded a revenue of seventeen millions of piastres, while the whole revenue of the empire only amounted to twenty-seven millions, or about £6,000,000 sterling [1].

A duty levied alike on imports and exports amounted to two and a half per cent. when the goods were the property of a Mohammedan, but to five per cent. when they belonged to a Christian or Jewish subject of the Porte. This moderate duty enabled the commerce of the Othoman empire to flourish greatly during the sixteenth and seventeenth centuries [2].

[1] D'Ohsson, *Tableau de l'empire Othoman*, vii. 237; Hammer, *Histoire*, vi. 510.
[2] Turkish merchants were numerous at Ancona, Venice, and Ragusa In the year 1522 the Venetian ambassadors to the Papal see estimated the amount

Though the commercial duties levied on the infidels were double the amount of those paid by the Mohammedans, they were in reality so moderate, that the difference was easily compensated by closer commercial relations with foreign merchants in distant countries, and by greater activity and economy. The Christians, consequently, preserved the greater share of the trade of Turkey in their hands. And as both Christians and Jews were excluded from war and politics, they turned their whole attention to trade. The different members of the same family dispersed themselves in various cities of the empire, in order that they might collect cargoes for exportation with the greatest facility, and personally superintend their distribution at the ports of consumption in the most economical manner. In an age when guarantees for personal honesty were not easily obtained beyond the circle of family ties, and extensive credit required to be replaced by personal attendance, the Greeks made their family connections a substitute for the privileges of corporations and guilds in the commercial cities of western Europe. Another circumstance favoured the trade of the non-Mussulman population of the Othoman empire. Venality and rapacity have always been prominent characteristics of the Othoman financial system. The Christian population of the East had been disciplined to every species of financial extortion for many ages by the Greek emperors. In fiscal measures the Othomans were the pupils of the Byzantine system, and the officials of the Porte soon perceived that the privilege of paying smaller duties placed the interests of the Mussulman trader in opposition to the interests of the imperial fisc. The custom-house officers were taught to favour that trade which brought the largest returns to the imperial treasury, and to throw obstacles in the way of commercial dealings which bore the character of individual privileges injurious to the sultan's revenue. The import and

---

of business of single Turkish and Greek traders at 500,000 ducats annually, and it is said with emphasis, that there were always numerous Turkish vessels at anchor in the port. Ranke, *History of the Popes*, 97, 101. The Turks had also a hostelry for themselves, and large warehouses (the fondaco), at Venice. Marin, viii. 155. Mohammed II., in the treaty he concluded with Scanderbeg in 1461, inserted a clause in favour of Othoman traders. See the letter of Mohammed to Scanderbeg; Barletius, 192; and Reusner, *Epist. Turcicae*, i. 213: 'Ut mercatores et negotiatores nostri regnum tuum cum mercimoniis suis ubique permeent atque percurrant.'

export duties formed one of the principal branches of the sultan's revenue, and we have already observed that the nature of the Othoman government prevented the existence of much sympathy between the great bulk of the Mohammedan landlords or cultivators of the soil and the agents of the sultan's administration. The policy of throwing obstacles in the way of the commercial operations of the Turks gradually gained strength, until the Mussulman landlord was content, in order to save time and avoid collision with the government officials, to sell his produce to rayah merchants, who in this way gained possession of the greater part of the trade of the empire[1]. At a later period, the privileges conceded by commercial treaties to the subjects of foreign nations introduced a change in the commercial position of the Christian subjects of the Porte, which was extremely injurious both to the wealth and moral character of the Greek traders. From this period the history of Othoman commerce becomes a record of privileges granted to foreigners, and of fraudulent schemes adopted by the rayahs to share in these privileges, or to elude their effect. The government strove to indemnify itself for these frauds by unjust exactions, and the native traders employed corruption and bribery as the most effectual protection against the abuses of tyrannical authority. The letter of the law and the legitimate duties served only as the text for an iniquitous commentary of extortions and evasions.

The land-tax, however, was the impost which bore heaviest on the industry of the whole agricultural population, without distinction of religion or race. This tax consisted of a fixed proportion of the annual produce, generally varying from a tenth to a third of the whole crop. Almost all the countries which fell under the domination of the Mohammedans were in a declining state at the time of their conquest. This was as much the case with Syria, Egypt, Persia, and Northern Africa in the seventh century, as it was with the Greek empires of Constantinople and Trebizond, and the principalities of Athens and the Morea, in the fifteenth. In such a state of society, communications are becoming daily more confined,

---

[1] Rayah was the name given by the Othomans to all subjects who paid haratch.

and it is consequently more easy for the cultivator to pay a determinate proportion of his crop than to make a fixed payment in money. Thus, the worst possible system of taxation was established in the dominions of the Mohammedan conquerors as a boon to their subjects, and was received with satisfaction. All the land in the Othoman empire was subjected to this tax, whether it was held by Mohammedans or infidels. The evil effect of this system of taxation in repressing industry arises in great measure from the methods adopted to guard against fraud on the part of the cultivator of the soil. He is not allowed to commence the labours of the harvest until the tax-gatherer is on the spot to watch his proceedings; and he is compelled to leave the produce of his land exposed in the open air until the proportion which falls to the share of the government is measured out and separated from the heap. Where the soil is cultivated by a race of a different religion from the landlord, it becomes the interest of the landlord to combine with the tax-collector, or to become himself a farmer of the revenue, and then every act of tyranny is perpetrated with impunity. Throughout the whole Othoman empire all agricultural industry is paralyzed for at least two months annually; the cultivators of the soil being compelled to waste the greater portion of their time in idleness, watching the grain on the threshing-floors, seeing it trodden out by cattle, or else winnowing it in the summer breezes; for immemorial usage has prescribed these rude operations as the surest guarantees for protecting the government against frauds on the part of the peasant. This barbarous routine of labour is supposed to be an inevitable necessity of state, and consequently all improvements in agriculture are rendered impracticable. The evils inherent in the system of exacting the land-tax in the shape of a determinate proportion of the annual crop, have produced a stationary condition of the agricultural population wherever it has prevailed. It arrested the progress of Europe during the middle ages, and at the present day it forms the great barrier to improvement in the Othoman empire and the Greek kingdom [1].

---

[1] The author of this work is practically acquainted with the difficulty of making any agricultural improvements under this system. He wasted much money and time before he fully perceived the impossibility of one individual

Another evil arising from this mode of levying the tax on the soil is, that it induces the government to weaken the rights of property, and thus, in the hope of increasing the annual revenue of the state, capital is excluded from seeking a permanent investment in land. Even under the Roman empire, a similar policy caused some degree of insecurity to the landed proprietor, whose arable land was not sufficiently protected by the law, if it remained uncultivated. For, by the Roman jurisprudence, the occupier who tilled the land belonging to another person, if he maintained his occupation for a year, acquired a right of occupancy, leaving the real proprietor only the power of regaining possession of his land by an action at law, which he had to carry on against the possessor in order to establish his right of property. It is evident that this transference of possession to the squatter who could obtain the undisturbed occupancy for a single year, was an element of insecurity in all landed property. The laws of Great Britain are based on very different principles from those of Rome. The rights of property are always considered too sacred to be tampered with for fiscal purposes; mere possession confers no right to land. The Othoman legislation has adopted the policy of the Roman law, and it considers the loss which might accrue to the state from the land remaining uncultivated as a greater evil than the injury inflicted on society by unsettling the rights of property. The Othoman law allowed any person to cultivate arable land which was left uncultivated by its proprietor beyond the usual term of fallow, even though the proprietor might desire, for his own profit, to retain it for pasture. The possession of arable land could only be retained by keeping it in constant cultivation, according to customary routine. Capital, under such circumstances, could not be invested in land with security or profit. A barrier was raised against agricultural improvements, and the population engaged in cultivating the soil was condemned to remain in a stationary condition[1].

---

contending against general regulations and the habits they produce. In a pecuniary point of view, he found cultivating the soil of Greece even more unprofitable than writing its history.

[1] D'Ohsson, *Tableau de l'empire Othoman; Code politique*, v. 21. These principles have been acted on by the Phanariot statesmen of the Greek kingdom, as well as by the members of the sultan's divan. Mavrocordatos, when minister of finance during the Bavarian regency, issued a circular, in which he says, 'that every spot where wild grass for the pasture of cattle grows is national property,' and that the

Another vice of the financial administration of the Othoman empire tended to annihilate the wealth of its subjects. This was the depreciation of the metallic currency; and it was so great, that it appears alone sufficient to explain the decline which has taken place in the resources and population of the sultan's dominions during the last two centuries. It happened repeatedly, that when the amount of specie in the imperial treasury was found inadequate to meet the demands on the government, the sultan's ministers supplied the deficiency by adulterating the coinage. Perhaps no administrative measures in the Othoman empire have produced more poverty, or have more rapidly undermined the resources of the people and the strength of the government, than this mode of defrauding the sultan's subjects of their property. The Byzantine emperors preserved their coinage unaltered in its standard for seven centuries; and there can be no doubt that this wise conduct contributed greatly to the stability of society and to the duration of that empire. On the other hand, the Greek emperors of the house of Palaeologos appear to have been constantly tampering with the coinage. But no government ever carried the depreciation of its coinage to such a degree as the Othoman. The asper was long the unit of Turkish monetary enumeration. Originally it was a silver coin, representing the miliaresion of the Byzantine empire, and ten were equal in value to a gold sequin or byzant. At the accession of Selim I., after an interval of only thirty-one years, the size of the asper, and the relative value of silver to gold, were so much diminished that fifty-four of the new aspers were equal to a Venetian sequin, which passed current for fifteen of the old aspers. The aspers of the time of Mohammed II. may, however, be supposed to have lost a considerable portion of their original weight by attrition. In the reign of Suleiman the Legislator, the sequin passed current for sixty aspers[1]; but about the middle of the sixteenth century that sultan issued a coinage so debased by alloy as to raise the value of the sequin to ninety aspers. From that

government of Greece, like that of the Sublime Porte, recognizes the principle that there can be no property in the soil, except the exclusive right of cultivation vested in private individuals. This will be found quoted in my pamphlet entitled, *The Hellenic Kingdom and the Greek Nation*, published in 1836, p. 64.

[1] Compare Ducas, 109; vol. iii. of this work, p. 491 *note;* Leunclavius, *Pandect. Hist. Turc.* 404.

period the deterioration of the Othoman coinage proceeded with accelerated speed in each successive reign. In the commercial treaty with England, concluded in the year 1675, the value of the dollar was fixed at eighty aspers, but when the treaty of Carlovitz was signed in the year 1699, German and Venetian dollars were already valued at one hundred and twenty aspers. At the accession of the present sultan, the value of the Venetian sequin was about six thousand aspers. The asper, however, has long been a mere nominal monetary division[1].

The Greeks found the line of separation which the Koran draws between the infidels and the true believers much more galling than the other Christian subjects of the sultan. They could not forget that they had been a dominant race when they were conquered by the Mohammedans; and even their pride could not conceal the fact that they were numerically superior to the Othomans in all the European provinces of the empire. The memory of lost power and former wealth was kept alive by some knowledge of Hellenic literature, and an unbounded confidence in their own merits as members of the only orthodox ecclesiastical hierarchy. These feelings have always rendered the Greeks as unquiet subjects as their inordinate selfishness has rendered them oppressive masters. The moral and political condition of the Greek race, during two thousand years, proves that neither classical knowledge nor ecclesiastical orthodoxy can supply the want of those qualities necessary to infuse morality into a corrupted society. Their system of education was evidently much inferior to that adopted by their Turkish masters for the education of the Christian children collected by the tribute and compelled to embrace Mohammedanism. These apostates

---

[1] Hammer, *Histoire*, vii. 235, xii. 311 ; Hertslet's *Commercial Treaties*, ii. 367. The asper is one-third of a para. The name *gurush* (piastre) was at first given to Spanish dollars. Turkish piastres were first coined in the reign of Mustapha III., and were equal in value to half a Spanish dollar, or perhaps only to half a Venetian dollar. called Arslani, or Lion dollars, from the Lion of St. Mark on their reverse. The Othoman government often increased the extent of its injustice by refusing to receive the base money it issued. Frederick the Great of Prussia appears to have copied this policy when he coined base money for the share he had received in the partition of Poland, which he made a legal tender from a Prussian to a Pole, but which no Pole could compel a Prussian to receive back. We have lately seen the English sovereign pass at Constantinople for 200 piastres, which is equal to 24,000 aspers. Compare the depreciation of Roman money in the reign of Gallienus mentioned in vol. i. *Greece under the Romans*, p. 437.

displayed a degree of activity, intelligence, honesty, and self-respect rarely found among their brethren whose education remained under the superintendence of Greek pedants and orthodox priests. Accordingly we find that many Greeks of high talent and moral character were so sensible of the superiority of the Mohammedans, that even when they escaped being drafted into the sultan's household as tribute-children, they voluntarily embraced the faith of Mahomet. The moral superiority of Othoman society must be allowed to have had as much weight in causing these conversions, which were numerous in the fifteenth century, as the personal ambition of individuals [1].

The number of the Christian subjects of the sultan in Europe filled the minds of several sultans with alarm, and the desire of increasing the number of the true believers became a measure of policy as well as of religion. The Koran, however, forbids the forced conversion of adults who believe in the revelations of Moses or of Jesus. The divan sought in vain for plans of conversion that promised any success in overcoming the national and religious attachments of the Christians, whose persevering opposition to Mohammedanism could not be concealed. At last the extermination of the whole orthodox population was suggested as the only means of eradicating the canker which was devouring the heart of the empire. In the breast of a bigoted tyrant the suggestions of political necessity were allowed to silence every sentiment of humanity and sound policy. The very bases of the Othoman power—the tribute of Christian children, and the revenues paid by the parents of these children—were in danger of being destroyed. But, fortunately for the Christians, Selim I. commenced his project of putting an end to all religious differences in his dominions by exterminating heresy among the Mohammedans. About forty thousand Shiis or sectaries of Ali were massacred by his orders in the year 1514 [2]. This monstrous act of barbarity was surpassed in Christian Europe, more than half a century later, by the massacre of St. Bartholomew's Eve

---

[1] Mohammed, vizier of Mohammed II., Mahmoud, grand-vizier, cousin of George, Protovestiarios of Trebizond, Khass Murad, of the family of Palaeologos, and Esaï Bey, were all Greeks. Ismael was a Sclavonian, and Carego a Servian. Hammer, iii. pp. 161, 169, 179.

[2] Hammer, *Histoire*, iv. 175.

(22nd August 1572). A despot who could murder heretics
in cold blood was not likely to have any compunction in
exterminating those whom he regarded as infidels. To
complete his project for establishing unity of faith in his
empire, Selim at last ordered his grand-vizier to exterminate
the whole Christian population of his dominions, and to
destroy all Christian churches. Orthodox and Catholics,
Greeks and Armenians, were alike condemned to death[1].
With great difficulty the grand-vizier, Piri Pasha, and the
mufti Djemali, succeeded in persuading Selim to abandon
his diabolical project[2]. The Christians in the East were
fortunate in escaping the treatment which the Catholics of
the West had inflicted on the Albigenses. Time had
improved the general condition of society. A Mohammedan
high-priest in the sixteenth century was more deeply sensible
of the feelings of humanity and true charity than the head of
the Latin Church in the thirteenth.

Nevertheless, the project of exterminating the Christians
was revived at subsequent periods. Sultan Ibrahim was
anxious to carry it into effect in the year 1646. The chief
of the hierarchy again refused to sanction the cruelty. He
declared that the laws of Mahomet forbid the issue of such
a fetva, for the Koran prohibits the murder of men who
have laid down their arms and consented to pay tribute to
the true believers. Although the grand mufti might have
found it impossible to convince the sultan of the injustice

---

[1] In judging the conduct of the sultan, who was a man of singular ferocity,
we must recollect the spirit and the maxims of the times, even among Christians.
That humane and amiable sovereign, Isabella of Castille, signed the edict for the
expulsion of the Jews from her dominions in 1492, and in 1502 she, and her
husband, Ferdinand of Aragon, expelled their Mohammedan subjects from Spain,
'in order to drive God's enemies from the land which He had delivered into their
hands.' Many exiles driven from Christendom by both these persecutions settled
in the Othoman empire, where their descendants still flourish. The severities
meditated by the passion of individual tyrants in Turkey fell short of the cruelties
actually perpetrated by popes, inquisitors, kings, and judges, in almost every
Christian state. Mohammedan history offers no parallel to the advice given by
the Archbishop of Valencia to Philip III. of Spain, so late as the year 1602. He
recommended selling the children of the Moriscos in Spain, as an act of mercy on
their souls, and a holy measure for bringing a large sum of money into the king's
treasury. Watson's *Philip III.* i. 415; Prescott's *Ferdinand and Isabella*, Pt. 2.
c. 7. [A large number of the Jews who migrated to Turkey, when they were
expelled from Spain by Ferdinand and Isabella, settled in Salonica. Of the sixty
thousand inhabitants of that city (some authorities estimate the population as high
as seventy-five thousand), from thirty-five to forty thousand are Jews; and most
of these still speak among themselves a debased form of Spanish. ED.]

[2] Hammer, *Histoire*, iv. 364.

of his proposed measure, he was able to demonstrate its impolicy. By referring to the registers of the haratch, he showed Ibrahim that a very large part of the revenues of the empire were paid by the Christian population. In the capital alone their number amounted to two hundred thousand, and throughout the whole empire they were the most docile tax-payers [1].

The progress of civilization among the Turks, and the abhorrence of injustice which is innate in the human heart, gradually induced some of the most eminent Othoman statesmen to adopt measures for improving the position of the sultan's Christian subjects. We cannot doubt that they contributed by their influence to accelerate the abolition of the tribute of Christian children, even though we can trace its cessation directly to other political causes. In the year 1691, the grand-vizier, Mustapha Kueprili, issued the regulations, already mentioned under the name of the Nizam-djedid, for securing to the Christians legal protection against official oppression [2]. Since that period the Othoman government has made several attempts to reconcile the legislation of the Koran with an equitable administration of justice to its subjects; but, until very recently, these attempts proved ineffectual to protect the Christians against the Mohammedans. The possibility of ultimately rendering Christians and Mohammedans equal in the eye of the law, under an Othoman sultan, admits of doubt, and the project is not viewed with much favour either by Christians or Mohammedans. It is quite as violently repudiated by the Greeks as by the Turks. As far as regards Arabs and Armenians, the possibility is readily admitted; but both the Othomans and the Greeks aspire at being a dominant race. As the Othoman government has grown more moderate in its despotism, the Greek subjects of the sultan have risen in their demands. They now assume that their orthodoxy is irreconcilable with Othoman domination; and they believe that it is the duty of all Christian powers to labour for their deliverance from a yoke

---

[1] Hammer, *Histoire*, xii. 306, 322; *Staatsverfassung und Staatsverwaltung*, i. 331. Yet as late as the year 1722, the grand mufti declared that it was the duty of the orthodox to exterminate heretics. To infidels he was more mild, but he said that, when their lives were spared, they ought invariably to be reduced to slavery. Hammer, *Histoire*, xiv. 92.

[2] Above, p. 21.

to which they submitted with unexampled docility for four centuries. The rivalry of the Greeks and Othomans produces a hatred which is much more deeply rooted than the mere aversion caused by the religious differences of the other Christians and Mohammedans in the empire. The victory, in the struggle between the Greeks and Othomans, can only be gained by political wisdom and military power. The religious differences of the other races may be separated from their political interests by a wise and equitable dispensation of justice to all the subjects of the sultan, without distinction of rank, of race, or of faith, and by the adoption of a system of free communal administration equalizing financial burdens.

It must not be supposed that the institutions of the Othoman empire have respected the principles of justice in regulating the rights of the Mohammedans any more than in governing the Christians. The legality of murder, when that crime has appeared necessary to secure the public tranquillity and remove the chances of civil wars, has been established as an organic law. Mohammed II., after citing in his Kanun-namé the opinion of the Ulema that the Koran authorizes the murder of his brothers by the reigning sultan, adds this injunction, 'Let my children and grandchildren be dealt with accordingly[1].' In a government where inhumanity and immorality were so publicly proclaimed to be grounds of legislation, it was natural that political expediency should become the only practical rule of conduct. But in order to act energetically on maxims so abhorrent to human feelings, it was also necessary for the government to create its own instruments. This could only be effected by educating a body of officials, and forming an army, whose members were completely separated from the rest of the sultan's subjects. It was absolutely requisite for the sultan to possess ministers and troops who were slaves of his Sublime Porte—men without family or nation—men who had as few ties to connect them with the dominant Mohammedan as with the subject Christian population of the empire. This desideratum was supplied by the institution of the tribute-children. These little Christians were reared to form

---

[1] Hammer, *Staatsverfassung und Staatsverwaltung,* i. 98.

the first regular troops of the Othoman sultans, and soon grew into a standing army.

This foundation of the Othoman army was laid by Orkhan, whether from his own impulse, or at the suggestion of his brother Aladdin, who acted as his prime-minister, or in consequence of the advice of Kara Khalil, his most intimate counsellor, is uncertain, and not of much historical importance. The organization of the tribute-children was improved and the numbers of the regular troops were increased by Murad I.; but even in the victorious reign of Mohammed II. the Othoman regular army was small when compared with the armies which the continental sovereigns of Europe consider it necessary to maintain at the present day, even during periods of profound peace. The whole military force of this sultan probably never exceeded seventy or eighty thousand fighting-men, and of these the regular infantry or janissaries amounted only to twelve thousand, and the regular cavalry to about ten thousand. The great numerical difference between the forces of the Othoman sultans at this period, and of the European sovereigns at present, must be in some degree attributed to the financial moderation of the Othoman government during the early period of the empire. It was this financial moderation, coming as a relief after the rapacity of the Greek emperors, which made the Greeks hug their chains; and it forms a strong contrast to the excessive financial burdens and constant interference with individual liberty which characterizes the system of administration in modern centralized states. The Othoman government required its troops principally in warfare. Even during the worst periods of Turkish tyranny, the Porte showed no disposition to intermeddle with every act of the local administration, which was often intrusted to its Christian subjects. The military forces of the empire consisted of different troops, which owed their existence to a variety of circumstances, and whose origin dates from very different times. It was the admirable organization of these troops, the great military talents of the generals who commanded them, and the indefatigable superintendence of every administrative detail by the sultans themselves, not the number of the troops, which so long rendered the Othoman armies superior to the military forces of contemporary Christian sovereigns. For a considerable time after the conquest of Constantinople the sultan possessed the only regular army of any importance in Europe.

The Greek race had been easily held in subjection by small bodies of men even before their conquest by the Othomans. The Crusaders, who conquered the Byzantine empire, and the Franks, the Venetians, and the Genoese, who ruled in Greece, in Asia Minor, and in the islands of the Archipelago, were far inferior in numbers to the subject Greeks. The Othomans were originally less numerous, but the sultans connected the interests of all the Turks with the extension of the empire, by conferring on them many of the privileges of a dominant race. The first and greatest was common to all Mohammedans. They were reputed to be born soldiers (askery), while non-Mohammedans were called merely burghers (beledy), and were incapable of entering the army[1].

The military force was divided into many bodies, organized at various periods by different governments, and on opposite systems. But from the period of the restoration of the power of the Othoman sultans by Mohammed I., after the dominion of Timor's successors in Asia Minor was overthrown, the troops of the Othoman empire may be classed under the heads of regulars, or those permanently receiving pay from the sultan, and irregulars, or those who were bound only to temporary service in time of war. The latter class, as has been already observed, existed long before the foundation of the Othoman government. It was composed of the proprietors of landed estates, who had owed military service for their possessions, either to the Seljouk sultans of Roum (or Iconium), or to the emirs who established themselves as sultans when that empire declined, and who were ultimately conquered by the house of Othman. This feudatory system formed the earliest military organization of Othman's own possessions, and its sphere was extended by his successors, who continued to grant new fiefs in all the subsequent conquests of the Othoman armies[2]. On the other hand, the aristocracy, which this system created, was circumscribed in its authority, and deprived of the power of controlling the sultan through its territorial influence, by the superior military organization of the slaves of the Porte. The tribute-children received, from their education and or-

---

[1] D'Ohsson, *Tableau de l'Empire Othoman*, Code religieux, vol. ii. p. 268.
[2] These fiefs were sipahiliks, timars, ziamets, and begliks.

ganization, an existence so completely separated from the old feudal militia, that they formed a complete counterpoise to the Seljouk nobility both in the cabinet and the camp. Thus, we find Sultan Mohammed II. in command of an army consisting in part of Seljouk nobles and Mohammedan gentlemen, like the armies of contemporary Christian monarchs in western Europe, and in part of a regular force of infantry, cavalry, artillery, and engineers, not unlike the invincible troops of ancient Rome, or the modern armies of civilized nations. In this way the sultans were able to take the field with a corps of janissaries, whose exploits have rivalled the deeds of the Roman legions, and with a host of irregular cavalry of matchless excellence, equal to that of the Parthians.

The janissaries formed the best portion of the regular infantry. They were the first-fruits of the institution of the tribute-children. At the conquest of Constantinople their number only amounted to twelve thousand, but in the reign of Suleiman the Legislator it had already attained forty thousand. The first blow which weakened the strength of this redoubtable corps was struck by its own members. When the janissaries rebelled, at the accession of Selim II. in 1566, they changed the original constitution of their corps by forcing the sultan to concede to them the right of enrolling their children as recruits to fill up vacancies[1]. At an early period they had not been allowed to marry, but this privilege had been afterwards conceded as a favour to those who distinguished themselves by their services, or who were stationed for a length of time in garrison. After their original organization underwent the change consequent on the introduction of hereditary succession, the numbers of the corps rapidly increased. At the accession of Mohammed III. in 1598, upwards of one hundred thousand janissaries were found inscribed on the rolls[2]. Until the reign of Murad III., A.D. 1574-95, the majority of the corps had consisted of tribute-children, supplied by the Christian provinces of the empire. The original constitution of these troops excluded all Mohammedan citizens from the body. Its members were required to be slaves, reared as an offering to the Prophet, and their education taught them to regard their

---

[1] *Relationi di Giovan Francesco Morosini*, quoted by Ranke in *The Othoman Empire*, 'Military Forces,' p. 19 (Kelly's Translation).
[2] D'Ohsson, *Tableau de l'Empire Othoman*, vii. 333, 8vo. edit.

dedication to the propagation of the Mohammedan religion as
their highest privilege, while their strict discipline rendered
them the best soldiers in the world for more than two centuries.
If we estimate the value of their education by the strength of
its influence on their minds throughout their lives, we are
compelled to concede to it the highest praise. Few men have
ever fulfilled the duties they were taught to perform in a more
effectual manner. The Jesuits in South America were not
more successful missionaries of Christianity than the janissaries
were of Mohammedanism in Christian Europe. Fortunately
it is the nature of despotism to accelerate the corruption even
of those institutions which increase its power, and the janissaries suffered the fate of every body whose privileges are at
variance with the principles of justice and those great laws of
human progress which impel the mass of mankind towards improvement. After the year 1578, the number of janissaries'
children entitled to enter the corps became so great that the
tribute-children were regarded by the veterans with jealousy.
On the other hand, the insubordination which the corps often
displayed, even under such warlike sultans as Selim I. and
Suleiman the Great, alarmed their more feeble successors, and
caused them to adopt the policy of weakening the military
strength of a body that threatened to rule the empire. The
tribute-children were no longer placed in its ranks, nor was the
tribute itself exacted with the former strictness, for the Christian population began to be regarded as more useful to the
state as tax-payers than as breeders of soldiers. The Turkish
population in Europe had now increased sufficiently to supply
the Porte with all the recruits required for the army. When
the position of the janissary became hereditary, the corps was
soon transformed into a military corporation, which admitted
into its ranks only the children of janissaries or born Mussulmans. The pay and privileges of the members of this militia
were so great that it became the habit of the sultan, the
officers of the court, and the ministers of the empire, to reward
those whom they favoured by introducing them into some of
the odas or battalions of the janissaries. At last, during the
reign of Mohammed IV. (A.D. 1649–1687), the tribute of Christian children ceased to be exacted. Indeed, for some time
before the formal abolition of the tribute, a comparatively
small number of children had been torn from their families,

and these had been employed as household servants of the
sultan and of powerful pashas[1]. Nearly about the same time,
the depreciation of the Turkish money reduced the pay of the
janissaries to such a pittance that it was insufficient to maintain a family in the capital, and married janissaries were
allowed to eke out their means of subsistence by keeping
shops and following trades. Their places in the corps, therefore, generally devolved on men bred to their father's occupation, and the celebrated army of tribute-children sank
into a militia of city traders, possessing only sufficient military
organization to render them formidable to their own government and to the peaceful inhabitants of the empire[2].

The regular cavalry was also originally composed of tribute-
children. In the time of Mohammed II. it was divided into
three distinct bodies, and consisted of ten thousand men.
The sipahis acquired the same pre-eminence among the
cavalry which the janissaries held among the infantry, and
their seditious conduct rendered them much sooner trouble-
some to the government[3]. The organization and discipline of
the regular cavalry, indeed, was modified at an early period
by the continual grants of fiefs which were conceded to its
members. From this circumstance, and from its frequent
seditions, the corps underwent many modifications, and ceased
to be recruited from the tribute-children at an earlier period
than the janissaries. The spirit of Seljouk feudalism and of
nomadic life always exercised a powerful influence among
the cavalry of the Othoman armies; but it is not necessary to
enter into any details on this subject, as it produced no very
marked effect on the relations between the sultan's government and his Christian subjects.

During the most flourishing period of the Othoman empire
the tribute of Christian children supported the whole fabric of
the sultan's power, and formed the distinguishing feature of

---

[1] Rycaut, *Present State of the Othoman Government*, book iii. chap. 7; Ranke,
Othoman Empire, p. 20.

[2] Compare the various statements in D'Ohsson, *Tableau de l'Empire Othoman*,
vii. 364; Marsigli. *Stato Militare*, i. 87; Rycaut, *Present State*, book iii. chap. 6.
Rycaut, speaking of the food and clothing of the janissaries in the latter half of
the seventeenth century, says, 'So their bellies are full and their backs are warm,
and in all points they are better provided than the tattered infantry which are to
be seen in most parts of Christendom.'

[3] The term sipahi or spahi was subsequently given to the lowest class of
timariots, and in that sense it is generally used. It originated in the practice of
rewarding the regular sipahis with these fiefs.

the political and military administration of the Sublime Porte. This singular tribute was first exacted from the Greek race as a tithe on the increase of the male population set apart for the glory and edification of Mohammedanism—just as the Anglican ecclesiastical establishment exacts the tithe-pig from the Catholics of Ireland for the benefit of the State Church of the British empire. There is nothing more startling in the long history of the debasement of the Greek nation, which it has been my melancholy task to record, than the apathy with which the Greeks submitted to this inhuman imposition. It seems to us wonderful to find a people, which even at the lowest ebb of their political fortunes preserved no inconsiderable degree of literary culture, displaying an utter indifference to the feelings of humanity, yet clinging to local interests and selfish prejudices, both civil and religious, with desperate energy. While their heads were hot with bigotry, their hearts were cold to the sentiments of philanthropy, and almost without a struggle they sank into the lowest depths of degradation to which a civilized race has ever fallen. The Turkish race never made much progress in colonizing Europe, even though the provinces of the Greek empire were almost depopulated at the time of the conquest. Had the Greeks, therefore, resisted the payment with any degree of national vigour, they might have saved their national honour from a stain which will remain as indelible as the glories of ancient Greece are enduring. Some sentiments of humanity and an ordinary degree of courage would have sufficed to prevent the Othoman Turks from acquiring the military renown that surrounds the power of the sultans with a halo of glory. Extermination ought to have been preferable to the dishonour of breeding recruits to extend the sway of Mohammedanism. And the value of Greek orthodoxy in directing the moral feeling of Christians must in some degree be estimated by the fact that for two centuries the Greek population, though completely under the guidance of the orthodox clergy, continued to pay this tribute without much repining. Mohammed II. secured the services of the higher clergy by restoring an orthodox patriarch at Constantinople, and employed the hierarchy of the Greek church as an instrument of Othoman police.

The history of this tax is worthy of attention. The Mohammedan law authorizes, or rather commands, every Mussulman

to educate all unbelieving children who may have legally
fallen under his power as true believers, but it strictly prohibits the forced conversion of any who have attained the age
of puberty[1]. The Koran also gives one-fifth of the booty.
taken in war to the sovereign. The Seljouk sultans had
generally either sold their share of the spoil, commuted it
for a payment in money, or else filled their palaces with
concubines and pages, in virtue of this privilege. The project
of converting this claim into a means of strengthening the
executive power was due to Orkhan, and its organization as
the source of recruiting the regular army to Murad I., as we
have already mentioned. Several sovereigns had previously
formed armies of purchased slaves, in order to secure the command over a military force more obedient and susceptible of
stricter discipline than the native militia of their dominions.
In the sixth century, Tiberius II., Emperor of the East, when
he wished to restore the discipline of the Roman armies,
formed a corps of fifteen thousand heathen slaves, whom
he purchased and drilled to serve as the nucleus of a standing
army unconnected with the feelings of the people, and un-
tainted with the license of the native soldiers. But this attempt
to introduce slavery as an element of military power in Christian society failed[2]. The system was adopted with more
success by the caliphs of Bagdad and the sultans of Cairo.
The Turkish guards of the Abassids, and the Circassian slaves
of the Mamlouk kings, were the best troops among the
Mohammedans for several ages. It is true, they soon proved
more dangerous to their sovereigns than the national militia :
nevertheless it was reserved for the Othoman sultans to found
an empire on the strength of a subject-population and the
votaries of a hostile religion. The plan required a constant
supply of recruits of the early age which admitted of com-
pulsory conversion to Islam.

The tribute of Greek children being once established, officers
of the sultan visited the districts on which it was imposed,
every fourth year, for the purpose of collecting that proportion
of the fifth of the male children who had attained the requisite

---

[1] 'If God had so willed it, every man who liveth on the earth would have
believed. Wouldst thou be so mad, O mortal, as to seek to compel thy fellow-
creatures to believe ? No ; the soul believeth not unless by the will of God.'

[2] *See* vol. i., *Greece under the Romans*, p. 301.

age. All the little Greeks of the village, between the ages of six and nine, were mustered by the protogeros, or head man of the place, in presence of the priest, and the healthiest, strongest, and most intelligent of the number were torn from their parents, to be educated as the slaves of the Porte[1]. It is not for history to attempt a description of the agony of fathers, nor to count the broken hearts of mothers caused by this unparalleled tax, but it offers a pathetic subject of tragedy to a modern Euripides. The children were carried to Constantinople, where they were placed in four great colleges, to receive the training and instruction necessary to fit them for the part they were afterwards to perform in life. Those who were found least fitted for the public service were placed in the families of Othoman landed proprietors in Bithynia; those of inferior capacity were employed as slaves in the serai, as gardeners and guards of the outer courts of the palaces. But the greater number were trained and disciplined as soldiers, and drafted into the corps of janissaries and sipahis of the regular cavalry; while those who displayed the most ability, who promised to become men of the pen as well as of the sword, were selected to receive a better education, and destined for the highest offices in the administration[2]. Never

---

[1] The city of Constantinople was exempt from the tribute; an exemption probably granted by the conqueror in order to facilitate the assembly of a numerous Greek population within its walls, but which was used by the Greeks as an argument to prove that the city had surrendered on capitulation. *Historia Patriarchica*, p. 167, edit. Bonn; and in Crusius, *Turco-Graecia*, p. 162. When L'Isle Adam surrendered Rhodes to Suleiman in 1522, one of the articles of the capitulation was, that the Greeks of Rhodes were not to be compelled to supply tribute-children to the Porte. Fontanus, *De Bello Rhodio*, in Lonicerus, i. 425, 8vo. edit.; *Négociations de la France dans le Levant,* i. 92; Vertot, ii. 522.

[2] Chalcocondylas says (p. 121) that the janissaries had reached the number of ten thousand in the reign of Murad II. His description of the education of the Christian children by the Othomans applies rather to those carried off at the first conquest of a province, than to the children of the regular tribute. For the importance attached to this institution see the various collections relating to Turkish history in the sixteenth century. Lonicerus, i. 77, 217, 8vo. edit.; Sansovino, 33, 80; Knolles, *A Brief Discourse of the Greatness of the Turkish Empire,* vol. ii. 982, 6th edit. The practice of filling the highest offices from those who were educated as tribute-children, secured them so long a preference, that Osman Pasha was not appointed grand-vizier in 1582, merely because he was a Turk by birth. It was argued that he could not be so devoted to the sultan's interest as if he had been a young infidel saved from perdition. Hammer, *Histoire,* vii. 125. Mahmoud Pasha, who was twice grand-vizier of Mohammed II., and a scholar and poet as well as a warrior, was a child of tribute from Greece. Ali Pasha, the grand-vizier of Suleiman the Great, who is praised by Busbequius, was also a child of tribute. Hammer, *Histoire,* vi. 147. In 1515 Selim I. imposed a tribute of six hundred children on Nagul Bessaraba, prince of Vallachia. Hammer, iv. 220, who quotes Engel, *Geschichte der Walachei,* 98.

TRIBUTE-CHILDREN.

was a more perfect instrument of despotism created by the hand of man. Affection and interest alike bound the tribute-children to the personal service of the sultan; no ties of affection, and no prejudices of rank or of race, connected them with the feudal landed interest, nor with the oppressed subjects of the empire [1]. They were as ready to strike down the proudest descendant of the Seljouk emirs, or the Arab who boasted of his descent from the Prophet, as they were to go forth against the Christian enemies of the sultan and extend the domain of Mohammedanism. The Turks formed a dominant race in the Othoman empire, but the tribute-children were a dominant class even among the Turks. Mankind has never witnessed a similar instance of such wise combinations applied to such bad ends, and depraved by such systematic iniquity. It is, however, manifestly a law of Providence, that immorality and injustice have a direct effect in developing the principles of decay in political communities. And history is continually recording facts which demonstrate how the infinite wisdom of God connects the decay and death of communities with moral causes. Time can alone determine whether it is possible so far to eradicate the seeds of immorality and injustice from political institutions, as to secure a permanent duration to any earthly community. But it is evident that it can only be attainable by an unceasing vigilance in the path of reform, individual as well as national; no principle of conservatism can produce this desirable condition of society. The temporal fortune of individuals often escapes the consequences of iniquity, for the physical decay of man is not directly connected with moral deterioration; vice, therefore, appears to enjoy impunity in many cases, unaffected both by the sense of moral responsibility, and by the fear of the judgment to come. But the deviations of governments from moral laws inevitably bring retributive justice on the State. The history of the Othoman empire affords a striking illustration of this truth. In no case did injustice so directly confer strength and dominion, and in none did it ever more evidently produce decline and ruin.

The irregular troops of the Othoman empire were composed chiefly of feudal cavalry. This militia existed in the Seljouk

---

[1] Knolles, *General History of the Turks,* i. 207.

empire before the ancestors of Othman entered Asia Minor. Its constitution placed it more under the control of the central authority, and caused it to be less influenced by class prejudices and the interests of an armed nobility, than the feudal chivalry of the West. Until the time of Suleiman the Legislator, the timars or cavalry fiefs were granted only for life; and it was rare for the son to obtain his father's grant of land, which was usually conferred on some veteran as a reward for long service in the field, or for distinguished valour and capacity. This militia was divided into three classes, according to the extent of the fiefs. First in rank were the Sandjak-begs, who were bound to bring into the field more than twenty well-armed followers on horseback. But many of this class possessed such extensive fiefs that they mustered several thousand horsemen. The second class was the Ziams, who were bound to take the field with from four to nineteen mounted followers, and who may be compared to the holders of knights'-fees in feudal Europe. The third class was called Timariots, and might be bound to take the field alone, or with as many as three followers. It is not necessary to notice the anomalies which were admitted into the system. The right of hereditary succession was respected in many districts where the great Seljouk nobles and Turkoman chiefs had voluntarily submitted to the Othoman government; and several of these great chieftains, at the commencement of the present century, could still boast of a princely authority, which dated from an older period than the dynasty of Othman. But in the case of the ordinary timariots, ziams, and sandjak-begs, the classes remained always too disconnected, and the right of hereditary succession never received the universal acknowledgment necessary to admit of the formation of a territorial aristocracy.

As long as the mass of Mussulman society in the Othoman empire was pervaded by a military spirit, and new conquests annually brought an increase of wealth, in the shape of captive slaves and grants of fiefs, the timariots and begs rushed eagerly to war with well-appointed followers, in order to secure a large share of the spoil. The harems were often filled with Russian, Polish, and Austrian ladies, and a great part of Hungary was parcelled out in fiefs. But when the conquests of the sultans were arrested, and many successive campaigns were required to defend the territory already conquered, it often happened that the holders of the smaller fiefs found their resources completely exhausted. Some were compelled to eke out their contingents with grooms and pipe-bearers, mounted on baggage-mules; and others abandoned the army, sacrificed their fiefs, and became cultivators of the soil to gain a livelihood. Before the time of Suleiman, a timariot who joined the army with a single follower, brought into the field a companion well-armed and mounted, who stood by his side in danger, and shared his booty in success; but before a century had elapsed, many of the ziams joined the army with contingents, in which grooms, pipe-bearers, domestic servants, and cooks were mustered to complete their masters' following[1]. Such militia was inefficient in the time of war, and it continued to be a means of wasting the resources of the country in time of peace; for these men being privileged to bear arms, would neither attend to agricultural pursuits, nor to any of the duties of landed proprietors. The personal nature of the tenure by which they held their estates prevented their devoting any portion of their annual revenues to improvements promising a distant return. Hence we find the land occupied by Othoman proprietors becoming less productive, in each successive generation, the buildings on it becoming more dilapidated; and from age to age a visible decline in the numbers of the Mohammedan population of the empire begins to be observed. At the present day the traveller in Asia Minor is often struck by finding a long-deserted mosque in the vicinity of a cemetery, adorned with numerous marble tombs, surrounded by a tract of country where there is now no human habitation; and fallen bridges and ruined caravanserais indicate the existence of a degree of activity and prosperity in past times which has long ceased in the Othoman empire. A just and inexorable law of society appears to have doomed the Turkish race to extinction in Europe and Asia Minor, unless it resign its privileges as a dominant people, and place itself on an equality with the other races who inhabit the sultan's dominions.

The feudal institutions of the Othoman empire, as they

---

[1] Rycaut, in the preface to his *History of the Turks from* 1679, says, ' Whilst I was in the camp with them, I found the timariots very poor, so that they stole from each other their bridles, saddles, lances, and other necessaries of war, and would excuse themselves by saying, that they could not do otherwise in so long a war, of more than three years.'

departed much less from the natural order of society than those of Western Europe, had a longer duration when transplanted into the Greek provinces. Those of the Latin empire of Romania disappeared in the third generation, but those of the Othoman empire survived almost to our own times. The latest traces of the system were swept away by the Sultan Mahmoud II., when he destroyed the Deré-beys, who were the last surviving element of Seljouk society[1]. He has often been accused of an erroneous policy in not endeavouring to reinvigorate and restore the institutions of his Mohammedan subjects in Asia Minor. Those, however, who are familiar with the changes which time has made in the state of property in the East, know well that it would have been no less futile than to attempt restoring the feudal system in France or Germany. The military organization of the Mohammedan landed proprietors had passed away as irrevocably as that of our Christian knights and barons.

Besides the feudal militia, the armies of the sultan received a considerable addition of irregular troops from the numerous bodies of soldiers maintained by the pashas in their respective governments. Some remarkable instances of the immense numbers of armed followers maintained in the households of great officers of the empire during the reign of Suleiman the Legislator deserve notice as illustrations of the state of society at the acme of the Othoman power. The defterdar Iskender Tchelebi, who was put to death in the year 1535, had upwards of six thousand slaves, consisting chiefly of captives torn from their parents at an early age, many of whom were of Greek origin. These slaves were educated in his household in a manner not very dissimilar to that adopted in the serai of the sultan for the tribute-children. The greater part was in due time formed into bodies of troops, and served in the Othoman armies ; many received a learned education, and were trained to enter the political and financial departments of the administration. The superiority of their education is proved by the fact, that when they passed into the

---

[1] Lord Byron has an allusion to the feudal system of Turkey in the *Bride of Abydos.*

> 'We Moslems reck not much of blood ;
> But yet the line of Karasman,
> Unchanged, unchangeable, hath stood
> First of the bold Timariot bands
> That won and well can keep their lands.'

sultan's household after their master's execution, several rose to the highest offices of the State, and no less than seven of these purchased slaves of Iskender Tchelebi attained the rank of vizier. Mohammed Sokolli, the celebrated grand-vizier of Suleiman at the time of that great sultan's death, was one of the number. The celebrated Barbarossa, who died in 1544, left two thousand household slaves; and the widow of Mohammed Sokolli possessed nine hundred slaves, all of Christian parentage, in the year 1582[1].

It would be difficult to enumerate all the anomalies that existed in the military forces of the Othoman empire. They varied in different provinces, and in the same province, from age to age[2]. It is only necessary here to notice those deviations from the general system which influenced the Greek population. The Porte found it often advisable to adopt different arrangements in Europe, where the majority of its subjects were Christians, from those established in Asia Minor, where the Mohammedan population was all-powerful. One remarkable deviation from the law which reserved all military power as an exclusive privilege of the true believers is to be found in the employment of Christian troops by various sultans. It was commenced by Orkhan himself, when he laid the foundations of the Othoman power. Motives of policy induced him to make every effort to secure the support of the Greek mountaineers of Bithynia (whose military spirit is often vaunted by the Byzantine historians), in order to oppose them to the Seljouk emirs in his vicinity. Orkhan, consequently, formed a corps of Greeks, consisting of one thousand cavalry and one thousand infantry[3]. When his son, Murad I., however, had increased and improved the corps of janissaries, these Christian troops were only employed in collecting the taxes and the tribute of Christian children. Still, even at later periods, after it was recognized as a law of the empire that Mohammedans alone should bear arms, the Christians

---

[1] Hammer, *Histoire*, v. 224, 388; vii. 157.

[2] The practical method of maintaining military efficiency and strict discipline, without the martinet's love of uniformity, gave a pleasing variety to the punishments in the army. The janissaries received their bastinado on the buttocks, as their feet were in constant requisition for the performance of their service; but the sipahis received their punishment on the soles of their feet, for when lifted on their horses they could still keep their place in the ranks.

[3] Compare Pachymeres, i. 129, and Hammer, *Staatsverfassung und Staatsverwaltung*, i. 53.

continued to act both as pioneers and as auxiliaries. Ibrahim, the grand-vizier of Suleiman, employed them as gendarmes for the protection of the unarmed rayahs against the disorderly conduct of the Turkish irregulars[1]; and Christians were generally admitted to form a portion of the contingents of Servia and Albania. Indeed, down to the commencement of the Greek revolution, a Christian gendarmerie was maintained by the Porte in the mountain districts of Macedonia, Epirus, and Greece ; and at the present day, Albanian Christians are serving with the Othoman armies on the banks of the Danube[2]. Besides the troops furnished by the immediate subjects of the sultan, large contingents of Christians from the tributary states have borne an important part in the Othoman wars from the earliest periods of their history. The defeat of Bayezid I. by Timor at Angora is generally attributed by native historians to the flight of the Servian auxiliaries[3].

The military strength of the Othoman empire began to decline from the period when the sultans ceased to take the field at the head of their armies. The absolute power necessary to imprint energy on every movement of its complicated administration could not be safely intrusted to the grand-vizier, so that even the most effeminate of the sultans, who lived secluded in the harem, and associated almost exclusively with women and eunuchs, frequently controlled the acts of the divan, and rendered the arrangements of the government subservient to the intrigues of the palace. Another evil followed which soon produced incalculable demoralization in the public service. When the

---

[1] D'Ohsson, *Tableau de l'Empire Othoman,* vii. 385 ; Hammer, *Histoire,* vii. 356; compare also *Staatsverfassung,* i. 171, and ii. 276.

[2] [This was evidently written at the commencement of the Crimean war, and must refer to the Mirdite tribe, who are all Roman Catholics, and twelve hundred of whom, under their independent chieftain, Bib Doda, fought for the sultan as auxiliaries in the campaign on the Danube. ED.]

[3] By the first treaty between the Othomans and the Servians in 1375 or 1376, Lazaros, kral of Servia, engaged to furnish Murad I. with an auxiliary corps of one thousand cavalry, besides paying one thousand lb. of silver annually as tribute. The second treaty between Stephen of Servia and Bayezid I. was concluded in 1389. Ducas, 6 ; Hammer, *Histoire,* i. 295. The Servian auxiliary corps was subsequently increased to two thousand men, when Bayezid was making every effort to meet Timor. This number has been magnified into twenty thousand, and doubtless the whole numbers of the armies of Timor and Bayezid have been exaggerated in the same proportion. It is singular to find how readily historians adopt fables in place of truth.

sultans ceased to hold constant communication with the military and civil servants of the Porte, they lost the power of judging of their merits. Viziers were enabled to advance their personal adherents over the heads of the ablest administrators and bravest soldiers in the empire; and favourites reared in the palace could easily, by securing the favour of the sultan or the chief of the eunuchs, obtain the highest offices in the State, without possessing any of the qualifications required for the performance of its duties. The Othoman empire followed the usual steps of other despotisms in its progress from corruption to decline; and the selection of ignorant and unsuitable ministers, generals, and admirals was facilitated by the fatalism of the Mohammedans. The populace, who judged the grand-viziers and highest dignitaries of the empire rather by their individual temper and personal conduct than by the policy of their administration, often showed dissatisfaction at the measures of those grand-viziers who had enjoyed the highest reputation before entering on office. The apparent contradiction between the behaviour of the ablest men in different circumstances and positions, at last induced the people to infer that human intelligence alone was insufficient to guide a sovereign in selecting fit ministers. The religious element was always powerful in the Mohammedan population; and it became the feeling of the people that it was better to trust in God than in man. It was a sincere confidence in that divine protection which had raised the Othoman empire to its unexampled pitch of power and glory that gave currency to the popular saying,—'Where God gives an employment, He bestows the qualities it requires.'

There was one evil in the Othoman administration which could only be restrained by the constant personal attention of the sultan. Venality was, from an early period, the prevalent vice in the civil and judicial administration of the empire. Yet, though the interest of the sovereign was directly opposed to this inherent vice of the administration, avarice induced many sultans to become participators in its fruits, and the court became as deeply tainted with the corruption as the government. The practice of the sovereign receiving a present whenever he conferred an office, gradually introduced the system of selling every office to the highest bidder. The venality of the Othoman officials was great even before the taking of Constantinople. The avarice of Khalil, the grand-vizier of Mohammed II., is notorious, and it cost him his life. Before one half of the reign of Mohammed II. had elapsed, the patriarchs of Constantinople purchased their rank by paying a sum of money to the Porte [1]. Khotshibeg, who wrote a work on the causes of the decline of the Othoman empire, dates its decay from the time of Suleiman the Legislator, and attributes it to the great increase of venality which then took place [2]. Rustem, the grand-vizier of Suleiman, dropped the veil which had concealed the extent of this corruption in the general administration. He openly put up every office for sale at a fixed price, and declared publicly that money was the object most eagerly sought for by the Porte. To increase the public revenues of the State, he farmed the taxes to Jews and Greeks. By his venality and exactions Rustem accumulated a fortune of two hundred thousand gold ducats of annual revenue [3]. In a state of society where riches were all powerful, his example was irresistible. The two other causes of decline indicated by Khotshibeg are, the habit adopted by Suleiman of absenting himself from the ordinary meetings of the divan, which were held four times every week, and of naming his personal favourites to the highest offices in the State, without their having acquired the experience requisite for the performance of their duty by a long and active career of service. The nomination of Ibrahim, the grand-falconer of Sultan Suleiman, to the office of grand-vizier, accelerated the decline of the administrative organization.

After the reign of Suleiman, justice grew every day more venal. Judicial offices were as openly sold as administrative ; and, except when the army was engaged in active service, all promotion, even in the military service, was obtained by the payment of a bribe. The veteran janissaries languished, forgotten or neglected, in the frontier garrisons of Buda and Bagdad ; while the sons of shopkeepers in the capital, and the followers of pashas, whose public duties had been confined to

---

[1] *Historia Patriarchica*, in Crusius, *Turco-Graecia*, 124.
[2] He wrote during the reign of Murad IV., A.D. 1623-40. Hammer, *Histoire*, vi. 281.
[3] Hammer, *Histoire*, vi. 284.

police service—to maintaining order in the markets, to guarding the persons of foreign ambassadors, or standing sentinel at the city gates—were allowed to purchase the highest military commands. This corruption soon became incurable, for it pervaded the whole body of the Othoman officials, who, as we have already observed, formed a class of men too completely separated from the mass of the population to be under the influence of its moral sympathies. The conviction of the members of the government that they were not amenable to public opinion, and owed no responsibility to the people, very naturally led to the exactions and oppressions which render Turkish history a continual record of revolts and rebellions. There was no hope of punishing the iniquities of a pasha, except by the arbitrary action of the sultan's power. It was necessary to slay the accused, for to obtain his condemnation by any tribunal which could take cognizance of his crimes was almost hopeless. The suffering people had little hope of redress, if compelled to bring their complaints before the divan, for every member of that body felt that he was himself exposed to similar accusations. The condition of the sultan's Christian subjects bore a strong resemblance, in this point, to that of the Roman provincials in the time of the republic, who had no great chance of redress when they sought for justice against the tyrannical and oppressive conduct of a proconsul, as their complaints required to be laid before a senate in which proconsuls possessed an overwhelming influence. Yet, we must not condemn the Othoman empire in the time of Suleiman without comparing the state of its administration with that of contemporary Christian governments. The sale of offices was then very general in Europe, and we find it adopted by the papal court, towards the end of the sixteenth century, as a regular method of recruiting the finances. The abuse was carried quite as far by the pope as by the sultan[1]. It was the inherent defects in the judicial administration of the Mohammedans which rendered the venality of public employments more injurious to the State at Constantinople than at Rome. This abuse, however, had no inconsiderable effect in producing the degraded social condition of the papal dominions existing at the present day.

---

[1] Ranke, *History of the Popes in the Sixteenth and Seventeenth Centuries* (Kelly's Translation), 102, 118.

In the reign of Suleiman the Great, the wealth of the
Othoman empire far exceeded that of any other European
state. The annual income of the sultan was generally estimated at 12,000,000 ducats, while the revenues of Charles
V., from all his wide-extended dominions, never exceeded
6,000,000 ; yet the Netherlands and the richest parts of Italy
were included in the Spanish empire [1]. At that period many
parts of Asia Minor, Macedonia, and Thrace, which are now
almost deserted, were cultivated by an active population.
Venice drew large supplies of wheat from the Othoman dominions, and during the greater part of the two centuries which
followed the conquest of Constantinople, both the Othoman
and the Greek population of the empire increased considerably. It was not until the middle of the seventeenth century
that the incessant extortions of the pashas, who became
partners with the farmers of taxes in their pashalics, en-
croached so far on the accumulated capital of the preceding
period as to diminish the resources, and, ultimately, the
numbers of the population [2].

As the power of the Othoman empire reposed on its military
strength, the internal decay of the government produced little
change on its position, with reference to the Christian states of
Europe, until the number and discipline of its troops were
sensibly diminished. It was long before this happened. In
the moral conduct of the soldiers and in the public police of

---

[1] Hammer, *Histoire*, vi. 510; Ranke, *Spanish Empire*, chap. 4. Our Henry
VII., A.D. 1509, left a treasure of £1,800,000. Hallam, *Constitutional History*,
i. 12. Hume (c. xxxvii.) says the revenues of England in the time of Mary were
about £300,000. Hallam (*Middle Ages*, i. 265) gives an estimate of the forces of
the European powers in 1454, and of their revenues in 1415, which prove how
little authentic information on these subjects can be extracted even from contemporary historians.
[2] It would be impossible to give a complete account of the financial resources
and monetary condition of the Othoman empire, without more accurate information than we possess concerning the quantity of the precious metals which was
annually put in circulation from the produce of the mines in the sultan's dominions
during the latter half of the fifteenth and the early part of the sixteenth centuries.
The sum must have been considerable, with reference to prices, at that period.
In Europe, very productive mines were worked in Macedonia, Servia, and
Bosnia ; and in Asia, those of Bakyr Kuresi, near Ineboli, had yielded large
revenues to the emirs of Sinope, and those of Gümüsh Khaneh to the emperors
of Trebizond, while various productive silver mines were worked in the mountains which extend from Angora to Tokat, separating the ancient Galatia from
Paphlagonia and Pontus. Besides this, several very rich mines of copper and
lead afforded large returns, and these metals were often exported in considerable quantities to Western Europe, as well as to Syria, Egypt, and Northern
Africa.

the army, a Turkish camp, until a late period, displayed a marked superiority over the military forces of contemporary Christian sovereigns. This superiority was one of the most efficient causes of the long career of victory of the Othoman armies. Before the sultan's armies entered on a campaign, the regular troops, janissaries, sipahis, and artillerymen, received a part of their pay in advance, that they might purchase the necessaries required before taking the field. During the campaign they were paid with regularity, and the strictest discipline was maintained on the march, in order to insure the establishment of markets at every halt and the attendance of numerous suttlers in the camp. Of their superiority in military science we have also many testimonies[1].

We possess two remarkable testimonies in favour of the order and discipline which prevailed at the head-quarters of Othoman armies by Christian writers, well acquainted with the Turkish troops, and neither of them favourably disposed towards the Othoman government. There is an interval of two centuries between the periods at which they wrote, and both were eye-witnesses of the facts they describe. The first was the Greek Chalcocondylas, who lived in the middle of the fifteenth century; the other was the Englishman Rycaut, who resided in Turkey in the latter half of the seventeenth. Chalcocondylas, in describing the invasion of the Morea by Sultan Murad II., in the year 1445, praises the discipline of the Othoman army as incomparably superior to that of contemporary Christian powers. He mentions that it secured ample supplies in the camp-markets by paying regularly and liberally for provisions, and by this means relieved the commanders from the necessity of detaching large bodies of men to forage. The historian says that he had never heard of armies in which such order was preserved. Though the suttlers were accompanied by immense trains of mules, laden with provisions and stores of every kind, there was no confusion. A spot was assigned for their tents, and the soldiers always found a

---

[1] *Négociations de la France dans le Levant*, i. 566, 567. 'Les Turcs, ayant, par merveilleuse habileté et expertise, parachevé leurs fortifications non loin du camp.' And 'Le Marquis du Guast visitant Nice et regardant les ouvrages des Turcs, s'emerveilloit tellement de leur artifice à drécir remparts, qu'il confessoit que nos gens luy sembloit de beaucoup inférieurs en telles choses auprès des barbares.' This was in 1543, when the Sultan Suleiman sent troops to Marseilles to defend France against her invaders.

E 2

well-stocked market in the vicinity of the camp[1]. It is true
these suttlers derived as large a part of their profits from
the slave-trade and from the purchase of the soldiers' booty,
as from the sale of supplies to the troops. Accordingly, when
the number of captives made in war decreased, and the slave-
trade became less profitable in the Othoman camps, the
difficulty of supplying the troops was considerably increased.
Still, the viziers regarded it as the first of their military duties
to see that their soldiers were well supplied, and that discipline
was strictly enforced.

Sir Paul Rycaut, who resided in the Othoman empire for
eighteen years, seven of which he passed at Constantinople as
secretary of the English ambassador, and eleven at Smyrna
as consul, describes the army of the grand-vizier, which he
visited at Belgrade in the year 1665, in the following words:
'In the Turkish camp no brawls, quarrels, or clamours are
heard; no abuses are committed on the people by the march
of the army; all is bought and paid for with money as by
travellers that are guests at an inn. There are no complaints
of mothers of the rape of their virgin daughters, no violences
or robberies offered to the inhabitants; all which order tends
to the success of their armies, and to the enlargement of their
empire[2].'

While this system of military discipline was enforced as
a means of increasing the efficiency of the regular army, the
peaceful provinces of the empire were exposed to be plundered by pashas and their households when travelling to their
governments, almost as if they were inhabited by a hostile
population. Every great officer had a right to demand lodging
and provisions at the charge of the districts through which he
passed on the public service. This right became a source of
incredible exactions, as the venality of the imperial officials
increased with constant impunity. We may form some faint
idea of the extent to which the oppression of the sultan's
officers was carried by calling to mind the extortions exercised
under the authority of the royal prerogative of purveyance in
feudal England, after it was recognized to be the country in

---

[1] Chalcocondylas, p. 182, edit. Par. *See* above, vol. iv. *Mediaeval Greece*, p. 250.
[2] Rycaut, *The Present State of the Othoman Empire*, book iii. ch. xi. See also *Relation d'un Voyage fait au Levant*, in Thevenot, *Voyages*, edit. Amst., i. 225; 'Comme
ils païent fort exactement ce qu'ils prennent, et ne font aucun desordre, ni ne
volent par la campagne, on apporte tout au camp comme à un marché ordinaire.'

which the best protection for individual property had been established. We find, even as late as the reign of James I., the English parliament declaring, that though the king's prerogative of purveyance had been regulated by not less than thirty-six statutes, still the royal purveyors imprisoned men for refusing to surrender their property, lived at free quarters, and felled wood without the owner's consent[1]. The abuses which originated in the right of every petty officer in Turkey to claim lodging and provisions, at the expense of the town or village at which he might find it convenient to halt, became at last so great a burden to the agricultural population near some of the principal roads, that the villagers abandoned their dwellings, and emigrated to the most secluded valleys in the mountains[2].

But long after the immediate vicinity of most of the great highways had been depopulated by the exactions of pashas and tax-gatherers, discipline continued to be strictly enforced at the head-quarters of the armies of the Othoman empire. As late as the year 1715, when the grand-vizier (Ali Kumurgi) conquered the Morea from the Venetians, the exactitude with which the Turkish cavalry paid for the fodder, which was brought to the camp from a distance and sold at a high price, excited the wonder of Monsieur Brue, the French interpreter of the embassy at Constantinople, who accompanied the expedition[3]. But after that period even the discipline of the Othoman armies in the field declined with great rapidity.

---

[1] Hallam's *Constitutional History of England*, i. 223. The tyrannical abuse of the prerogative of purveyance, though restrained by Magna Charta, was not abolished until the reign of Charles II.; 12 Car. II., c. 24.

[2] Several examples of the abuses caused by the license of official travellers will be found in Otter's *Voyage en Turquie et en Perse*, in 1734, vol. i. pp 47, 54, 68. Yet Otter praises the good order and excellent police which then existed at Constantinople, a city of 800,000 inhabitants. p. 9.

[3] *Journal de la Campagne que le Grand-Vizier Ali Pasha a faite en 1715 pour la Conquête de la Morée*, original MS. in the Author's possession, purchased at a sale of Oriental MSS in Paris in 1843. M. Brue, a relation of Voltaire, is mentioned in the *History of Charles XII.*, livre v. Some notices concerning him will be found in the *Nouvelle Revue Encyclopédique*, Fevrier 1847 ; *Journal inédit de Galland*. The fact cited in the text is noted by M. Brue as a justification of the high price at which barley for his horses is charged in his accounts. [Brue's Journal was published at Paris by Thorin in 1870 by Mr. Finlay's permission from this MS. with the title which is given above. The facts here referred to are to be found on pp 98, 107. The subsequent references to this work are made to this edition. It is written in the form of a diary, and though the style is brief and dry, its simplicity and faithfulness occasionally produce a graphic effect. From a military point of view the features of the country are well described, but classical sites are noticed in a very cursory way. ED.]

From the preceding sketch of the military establishments of the Othoman empire, it is evident that the conquests of the sultans were the result of a wise organization, and of a system of education which formed a superior class of soldiers, much more than from any overwhelming superiority of numbers.

Such were the most prominent features of the government to which the Greeks were subjected for several centuries. Yet, with all the vices of the sultans' administration, and though the lives and property of the rayahs were valued chiefly in proportion as they contributed to supply the sultan with recruits for his army and money for his treasury, it may be doubted whether any contemporary Christian government would have treated an alien and heretical race, which it had conquered, with less severity and injustice.

CHAPTER II.

THE NAVAL CONQUESTS OF THE OTHOMANS IN GREECE.
A.D. 1453–1684.

Decline of the Greek population during this period.—Effects of the Othoman conquest —Extent of country inhabited by the Greek race which remained under the domination of the Latin Christians after the conquest.—Conquest of Mytilene.—Venetian war, A. D. 1463–1479.—Conquest of the dominions of Leonardo di Tocco.—Venetian war, A. D. 1499–1502.—Conquest of Rhodes. —Invasion of the Morea by Andrea Doria.—Venetian war, A.D. 1537–1540.— Conquest of Chios.—Extinction of the duchy of Naxos.—Conquest of Cyprus. —Battle of Lepanto, A.D. 1571.—State of the Greek population, A.D. 1573–1644.—Maritime warfare, and piracies in the Grecian seas.—Knights of Malta.—Knights of St. Stefano, and navy of Tuscany.—Exploits of the Othoman navy.—Depopulation of the coasts of Greece by the maritime expeditions of the Christian powers.—Ravages of the Cossacks in the Black Sea.—War of Candia, A.D. 1645–1669.—Subjugation of Maina.—Apostasy of Christians.

DURING the period of more than two centuries which elapsed from the conquest of Constantinople to the conquest of the Morea by the Venetians, the Greek nation declined both in civilization and numbers. The Hellenic race had never fallen so low in the social scale at any previous period of its history. It may possibly have incurred greater danger of extermination in its native regions, during the dark age which followed the Sclavonian colonization of the Peloponnesus at the end of the sixth century; but at that time, though the valleys of the Spercheus and the Eurotas, and the plains of Thebes, Sparta, and Olympia, were occupied by Sclavonian invaders, the principal cities of Greece, the islands in the Grecian seas, and a large part of western Asia were still densely inhabited by a numerous and wealthy Greek population, whose commercial activity, municipal administration, and social organization, joined to the advantages

resulting from the accumulation of capital, during a long
series of ages, in public works, rendered the Byzantine empire
for centuries the most civilized portion of the world. The
Greek empire of Constantinople, recovered from the Crusaders,
became, it is true, such a scene of anarchy that the Othoman
conquest brought relief to the people; but in giving peace
and tranquillity to Greece, the Othoman government gradually
rendered it a desert, while the rude cultivators of the soil,
whether of Hellenic or Albanian blood, slowly annihilated all
evidence of the improvements which industry and wealth
had effected in earlier and better times. Even the relief
from the evils of war was often rather apparent than real.
The continent was generally tranquil, but the sea was always
insecure, and the repeated interruptions of commerce cut
off the inland producer from every market, and put an end
to production. The Othoman government also extended its
domination very slowly over the Greek islands; and it was
not until the power of the empire had shown signs of decline
that the supremacy of the Porte was completely established
in the Archipelago by the conquest of Candia. But my
duty as historian of the Greeks, and the space within which
I must confine my work, compel me to renounce the hope of
rendering my pages attractive by recounting the martial
deeds of the conquerors of Crete, and paying honour to the
desperate valour of the combatants in the long and bloody
wars between the Turks and the Venetians. I must leave
this theme to the historians of the Othoman empire, and of
the Christian States who opposed its progress. The Greeks
are not even entitled to boast of the courage of the tribute-
children, who left the homes of their fathers' with blooming
faces and unformed characters. The education which these
neophytes received from the Othomans gave them a new
nationality as well as a new religion. Their valour in the field,
their patience in the trenches, and their daring on the deck
of the galley, were artificial and not ancestral virtues, and
can reflect no glory on their parental race. It is not my
privilege to dwell on the gallant deeds of the Christian
chivalry that bathed every shore of Greece in blood, endeavouring to arrest the progress of Moslem conquest. The
exploits of the proud Knights of St. John, and of the prouder
nobles of Venice, who made the sieges of Rhodes, Famagosta,

and Candia rivals in fame to those of Plataea, Syracuse, and
Carthage, do not fall within the scope of my pages. In the
glories of the Latin Christians the Greeks had no share, and
with the Catholics the orthodox church had no sympathies.
In Greece, the domination of the Latins had been more
galling, if not more oppressive, than that of the Mohammedans. The prominent feature in the history of the Greek
people, during the period which elapsed from the conquest
of the Morea by Mohammed II. in 1460, to its conquest by
the Venetians in 1686, is the misery inflicted on the inhabitants of every coast accessible to the corsairs, whether
Mohammedans or Christians, who swarmed in the Levant.
The unparalleled rapacity of these pirates devastated the
maritime districts to such a degree that, even at the present
day, many depopulated plains on the coasts of the Archipelago still indicate the fear which was long felt of dwelling
near the sea.

The campaigns of Mohammed II. united all the territory
governed by orthodox princes to the Othoman empire[1]; but
even after he had completed his continental conquests, no
inconsiderable portion of the territory occupied by the Greek
race still continued subject to Catholic powers. Venice retained possession of the fortresses of Argos, Nauplia, Thermisi,
Monemvasia, Coron, and Modon, in the Peloponnesus, and
of the great islands of Corfu and Crete, to which Cyprus was
soon added. The dukes of Naxos and several signors held
various islands of the Archipelago, which they governed as
petty sovereigns. Leucadia, Cephalonia, Ithaca, and Zante
were ruled by Leonardo di Tocco, who assumed the vain title
of Despot of Arta, Duke of Leucadia, and Count of Cephalonia[2]. Genoa, after the loss of her commercial stations in
the Black Sea, continued to exercise considerable influence
in the Archipelago as sovereign of Chios, which was held
by a Genoese joint-stock company, and as protector of the
signors of Mytilene. The Knights of St. John possessed
Rhodes, Kos, and several smaller islands, as well as the
fortress of Bodroun (Halicarnassus). Cyprus was still governed

---

[1] Servia was conquered in 1458, Vallachia in 1462, Bosnia in 1463, Euboea in
1470, Caffa, from the Genoese, in 1475, and the possessions of Scanderbeg in
Albania in 1478.
[2] Buchon, *Recherches Nouvelles*, i. 322.

by the house of Lusignan, with the proud title of Kings
of Cyprus, Jerusalem, and Armenia ; but the republic of
Venice was already preparing to receive their inheritance,
while various European monarchs have the folly to assume
the empty title at the present day.   It is strange to see how
slowly common sense mounts to the heads of princes.   This
disjointed condition of the Greek nation explains the utter
absence of all national action and political feeling among the
Greeks during the three following centuries.

Mohammed II. pressed heavily on the Greek race, though
he was tolerant to Greek orthodoxy; and it would have required a high degree of security and tranquillity to enable
the people to recover from the calamities they had suffered
before and after their conquest by the Othomans.   But, for the
greater part of Greece, this period of security and improvement never came ; and at the present day, the Greek kingdom
is unable to maintain a larger population than in the fifteenth
century.   The translocations of the inhabitants of many
places by Mohammed II., mentioned in preceding volumes,
caused a great destruction of property and an immense loss
of life[1].   The same system was continued in the succeeding
conquests of the Othomans, and the inhabitants of every city
or island which Mohammed II. annexed to his dominions
during his long and active reign, were treated with as great
severity as the people of the Morea, and expatriated in considerable numbers.

The signor of Mytilene was the first of the Catholic princes
whom Mohammed II. conquered.   The Genoese family of
Gattilusio had possessed the rich and fertile island of Lesbos
for more than a century; and at this period the islands of
Lemnos, Thasos, Imbros, and Samothrace were governed by
them, and they possessed an interest in the profitable alum-
works of Phocaea, and in part of the territory of Ainos[2].
These dominions were gradually annexed to the Othoman
empire.   New Phocaea was conquered in 1456, and great
part of its Greek population reduced to slavery, so that the
place never recovered its commercial importance.   Ainos

---

[1] *See* above, vol. iii. 522 ; vol. iv. 266.

[2] Francis Gattilusio married Maria, sister of the Emperor John V. (Palaeologos), and received Lesbos as a reward for his services against Cantacuzenos
in 1355; above, vol. iii. 459. For a list of the signors of Mytilene, see Appendix II.

suffered the same fate. In the following year, Lemnos, Imbros, Samothrace, and Thasos were finally annexed to Mohammed's dominions. The best and wealthiest part of their inhabitants were removed to Constantinople, the youngest and healthiest individuals were sold as slaves, and only the poorest of the Greek peasantry remained to cultivate the soil. No person who had the means of establishing himself in the capital as a useful citizen, or the strength and beauty requisite to insure a ready sale in the slave-market, escaped deportation, unless he was fortunate enough to conceal himself in the mountains until the departure of the Othoman fleet.

In the year 1462, Mohammed put an end to the government of the signors of Lesbos. He had good reason to complain of the shelter which the excellent ports in their dominions afforded to the Catalan, Italian, and Sicilian pirates who infested the entrance of the Dardanelles[1]. These adventurers made a profitable business, not only by the capture of Turkish ships, but likewise by surprising Turks on shore, whom, if wealthy, they ransomed for money, and if poor they sold as slaves to labour at the oar in European ships. The signor of Mytilene had probably no power to suppress this piracy, even had he possessed the wish. The sultan resolved to effect it. The last signor of Mytilene was Nicholas Gattilusio. He had slain his elder brother Dominicus to gain possession of the government, yet he hardly made a show of resisting Mohammed ; and, after surrendering his capital, endeavoured to gain the favour of his conqueror by embracing Islam. Sultan Mohammed, who despised his cowardice, and knew that his conversion was produced by the hope of enjoying a life of luxurious ease, rewarded him with the bow-string, and confiscated his property. The conquest of Mytilene brought ruin on the Greek inhabitants of the island, though they had been eager and active in transferring their allegiance from the Catholics to the Mohammedans. One third were sold into slavery in order to raise money to reward the Otho-man troops ; one third were transported to Constantinople ; and the remaining third, consisting of the lowest order of the

---

[1] Compare Ducas, 333, 335. edit. Bonn ; and Chalcocondylas, 250, edit. Par. Ὁρμώμενοι δὲ ἀπὸ τῆς Λέσβου οἵ τε Ταρακοννήσιοι ἐπὶ λῃστείαν κατὰ θάλατταν τετραμμένοι. Chalcocondylas, 277, edit. Par.

townsmen and the poorest class of cultivators, were left to till the soil and collect the abundant harvests of the vineyards and olive-groves[1]. From this time the inhabitants of Mytilene have been proverbially one of the most degenerate communities among the modern Greeks. Their malice and falsehood are linked in a rhyming proverb, with the aversion generally entertained for the inhabitants of Athens and Thebes, where a large proportion of the population, consisting of Albanians, lived in a state of separation from Greek sympathies[2].

During the war between Sultan Mohammed and Venice, which lasted from 1463 to 1479, the hostile fleets ravaged many of the wealthiest parts of Greece. The galleys of the King of Naples, of the Pope, and of the Catalan cities cruised in the Archipelago under the pretence of assisting the Christians, but they plundered the property of the Greek subjects of the Porte on the coasts of Europe and Asia, whenever they found any booty undefended. In the year 1463, a Greek priest betrayed Argos to the Mohammedans; and in the war which followed, the Venetian possessions in Greece were ravaged by the Othomans, and the Greek subjects of the republic carried off into slavery in such number as to depopulate the districts round Nauplia, Modon, and Lepanto[3]. The unfortunate campaign of 1463 deprived the Venetians of all chance of conquering the Morea. Their attempt to take Corinth was unsuccessful, and they were unable to defend the fortifications they had constructed across the isthmus. The Othoman troops defeated the Venetians, and the Greeks and Albanians in the Morea, whom they had induced to take up arms, were either put to the sword or carried off as slaves[4].

While the Othoman army depopulated the Venetian possessions on the continent, the ships of the republic plundered the coasts of the sultan's dominions. The miserable inhabitants of Lemnos, Ainos, and Phocaea were robbed of all the

---

[1] Ducas (Italian translation), 512, edit. Bonn. Chalcocondylas, 280, edit. Par.
[2] Ἀθηναῖοι καὶ Θηβαῖοι
Καὶ κακοὶ Μιτυληναῖοι,
Ἄλλα λέγουν τὸ βραδὺ
Κι' ἄλλα κάμνουν τὸ ταχύ.
[3] Chalcocondylas, 294, edit. Par.
[4] Chalcocondylas, 298, edit. Par. The Albanian chief, Peter the Lame, a leader in the great revolt against the Greeks in 1454, was one of the partizans of Venice. *See* above, vol. iv. 255.

Turks had left them. Passagio, a great mercantile depôt of neutral trade, situated on the continent opposite Chios, afforded the Venetian fleet a rich booty in 1472, but the loss fell chiefly on the Genoese[1]. The Othoman galleys, manned by Jews, Greeks, and Turks, were generally far inferior to the Venetians in naval efficiency[2]. These desultory operations impoverished the Greek cities and diminished the numbers of the Greek population, but they were unable to arrest the progress of the Othomans. The great event of this war was the conquest of Euboea. In the year 1470, the well-fortified city of Negrepont was taken from the Venetians after a valiant defence. The Greek inhabitants were in great part reduced to slavery, and many villages in the island were plundered and burned[3]. This loss was poorly revenged by a Venetian fleet, which laid waste the Greek suburb of the city of Attalia, and destroyed Smyrna, a town then almost entirely inhabited by Greeks. Indeed, during this war, the orthodox Christians, whether living in the Othoman empire or the Venetian possessions, were the principal sufferers. The naval expeditions of the Venetians plundered the open towns and defenceless villages on the coast; and the Othoman armies which invaded the Venetian territory sought chiefly to carry off as many slaves as possible in order to enrich the soldiers. In the year 1478 the Othoman fleet plundered the possessions of the Knights of Rhodes, and carried off many Greek slaves from Kalymnos, Leros, and Nisyros. The peace which Sultan Mohammed concluded with Venice in 1479, relieved only a part of the Greek nation from plunder and devastation.

Almost immediately after signing that treaty, Mohammed II. extended his conquests in Greece by seizing the territories of Leonardo di Tocco. The possessions of this little sovereign originated in a grant made to one of his ancestors in 1353, by Robert II., prince of Tarentum, and titular Latin emperor of Romania, and extended over the rich district of Arta, and the provinces of Acarnania and Aetolia, as well as the islands of Leucadia, Cephalonia, and Zante. Charles di Tocco, despot of Arta, duke of Leucadia, and count of

---

[1] Cepione, *Delle cose fatte da Pietro Mocenico*, p 4. A rare work, the knowledge of which I owe to Zinkeisen, *Geschichte des Osmanischen Reiches*, ii. 403.

[2] Marino Sanuto, in Muratori, *Rerum Italicarum Scriptores*, tom. xxii p. 1170.

[3] Lonicerus, *Chronicarum Turcicarum Epitome; De Negroponti captione*, tom. i. 339, 8vo. edit.

Cephalonia, died at Joannina in 1430, and was succeeded by
his nephew, Charles II. In the following year the troops
of Sultan Murad II., under Sinan Pasha, took possession of
Joannina, and in 1449 the remainder of the continental
dominions of Charles were annexed to the Othoman empire.
Acarnania and part of Aetolia, which was then called the
country of Arta, received from the Turks the name of Karlili,
or the country of Charles. Leonardo, who succeeded his
father Charles II. in 1452, involved himself in war by neglecting to pay a stipulated tribute of five hundred ducats
annually. The islands of Leucadia, Cephalonia, and Zante
were occupied by the Othoman troops, and the duke retired
to Naples[1]. As usual, the Greek inhabitants were carried
away to re-people Constantinople, but it is said that many of
the Ionians experienced a harder fate than had fallen to the
lot of the other Greeks. They were compelled to intermarry
with negroes, in order to breed mulatto slaves for the serai[2].
The misery of the population of the Ionian Islands was
increased by the enterprises of Antonio di Tocco, the younger
brother of Leonardo, who collected a small force, and, with
the assistance of a few Catalan corsairs, succeeded in recovering Cephalonia and Zante. But as he could only maintain
his mercenaries by piracy, the injury he inflicted on commerce
induced the Venetians to expel him and his Catalans from
their conquests. Cephalonia was restored to the sultan, and
Venice was allowed to retain possession of Zante, for which
the republic engaged to pay an annual tribute of five hundred
ducats to the Porte (A.D. 1484)[3].

In the year 1480, the army of Mohammed II. besieged
Rhodes unsuccessfully, but it ravaged a great part of the
island, and carried away many Greek families into slavery.

In the year 1499, a new war broke out between the Sultan
Bayezid II. and the Venetians, which lasted to 1502. Lepanto,
Modon, Navarin, and Coron were conquered by the Othoman
armies. Modon was taken by storm in the presence of the
sultan, and all the inhabitants were slain; but Bayezid repeopled the city by compelling every town or large village in
the Morea to send five families to settle in the place. On the

[1] Buchon, *Nouvelles Recherches*, i. 307. Phrantzes, 156.
[2] Spandugnino, in Sansovino, edit. 1600, p. 171.
[3] Navagero, *Storia Veneziana*, in Muratori, *Rerum Ital. Script.*, tom. xxiii. 1189.

other hand, the Venetians took possession of Cephalonia, which they found so depopulated that they were enabled to grant lands to the Greek families who fled from Lepanto and the places conquered by the Turks in the Morea [1]. During this war the Greek population in the neighbourhood of Argos and Nauplia was entirely exterminated, and the country was repeopled by the Albanian colonists, whose descendants occupy it to the present day. Megara, which was then a populous Greek city, also received a blow from which it never recovered. The Othoman government had made it one of their principal magazines of grain and stores. The place was taken and plundered by the Venetians, who laid the greater part in ruins. The Greek inhabitants gradually decreased in number from that time, and their place was filled by poor Albanian peasants. Venetian, Catalan, and Turkish corsairs cruised in all the seas of Greece, carrying off the defenceless inhabitants to sell them as slaves; some, in their eagerness for booty, paid very little attention to inquire who was sovereign of the country, if plunder could be carried off with impunity. The Venetian government excited the activity of its mercenary troops by granting them two-thirds of all the booty they collected, and by establishing regular sales by auction of the captives brought into the camp, paying the soldiers three ducats a-head for each prisoner [2]. And as slaves have always borne a much higher value in Mohammedan than in Christian countries, it was often a principal object of the expeditions of the Othomans during the fifteenth and sixteenth centuries to obtain a large supply for their slave-markets. Those terrible incursions, which were pushed far into Styria, Carniola, and Carinthia, and into Italy, as far as the banks of the Isonzo and Tagliamento, were often made merely to gratify the troops with a rich booty in slaves, not with the intention of making any permanent conquests [3].

---

[1] Prescott, in his *History of Ferdinand and Isabella*, pt. ii. ch. x., gives a highly-coloured account of the storming of the insignificant fort of St. George in Cephalonia by Gonsalvo de Cordova, the Great Captain, and Pesaro. the Venetian admiral; and he says the arms of Bayezid *filched* one place after another from the republic (A D. 1500). Gonsalvo was one of the first great generals in Western Europe. The Othomans had already possessed several who were at least his equals in military science and strategic combinations.

[2] Chalcocondylas, 277, edit. Par. Cepione, *Cose fatte da P. Mocenigo*, 17.

[3] There is a tract on the expedition to the Isonzo in 1478, in the collection of Lonicerus, i. 339, 8vo. edit. In 1499 the Turks reached the Tagliamento,

The profits of the slave-trade must never be overlooked in examining the objects and results of Othoman expeditions, nor in estimating the causes of the misery and depopulation in Greece. Suleiman the Great, in the letter he wrote to the Grand-master of the Knights of Rhodes announcing the capture of Belgrade, boasts of the number of slaves he had made in his expedition into Hungary [1]. The number of Mohammedans retained in slavery by the Knights of Rhodes was one of the principal reasons urged by the Othomans for expelling them from the Levant [2]. Before the alliance between the Othoman empire and the King of France was formed, the Turkish corsairs extended their slave-hunting cruises even to the French coasts [3].

The dominion of the Knights of Rhodes affords an example of the different aspects under which historical facts may be viewed by different classes and nations. The nobles, the clergy, and even the people, in western Europe, willingly conceded wealth, honours, and privileges to noble blood ; and the knights of Rhodes were long admired by their contemporaries as the flower of Western chivalry, and supported as the firmest champions of Christianity, and the surest barrier of Europe against Moslem conquest. But by the Greeks generally, and particularly by their own subjects, they were felt to be proud, bigoted, and rapacious tyrants, whose yoke bore heavier on their Christian brethren, whom they pretended to defend against the Mohammedans, than the yoke of those very Mohammedans. Even Vertot, the historian and panegyrist of the Order, owns that the Turks treated their Greek subjects more mildly than the Latin knights [4]. To the Othomans they appeared as a band of lawless plunderers, who paid tribute to the sultan or plundered his subjects when it suited their interests ; while the toleration with which they treated their subjects of the smaller islands, who fitted out galleys for ravaging the Turkish coasts, made them popular with the Greek pirates [5].

destroyed one hundred towns and villages, and carried off six thousand slaves. Bembo, *Della Istoria Veneziana.*
[1] Fontanus, *De Bello Rhodio,* in Lonicerus, i. 353. *Négociations de la France dans le Levant,* i. 90.
[2] Lonicerus, i. 354–5.   [3] *Négociations de la France dans le Levant,* i. 132.
[4] Vertot, *Histoire des Chevaliers Hospitaliers de St. Jean de Jérusalem appelés depuis les Chevaliers de Rhodes, et aujourd'hui les Chévaliers de Malte,* tom. ii. 458.
[5] Vertot, ii. 459.

To us, who look back at the dominion of the Knights
through the mist of past years, dim records, and picturesque
monuments, the order of St. John of the Hospital seems
deserving of its power and fame. In an age when valour was
the best quality in men, the Knights were the bravest among
the brave. Few who read the history of the siege of Rhodes
in 1480 will fail to form an imaginary portrait of the Grand-
master, D'Aubusson, in his simple armour, with the red cross
on his breast and the red cardinal's-hat on his head [1]. Nor
will the story of the fall of Rhodes in 1522 give him a less
vivid picture of his less fortunate successor, L'Isle Adam,
whether repulsing the janissaries from the ruined walls, or
presenting himself before the great Suleiman after receiving
an honourable capitulation. The traveller who has visited
the ruins of the great hall where the Knights assembled with
L'Isle Adam for the last time, and wandered through the
long succession of uninhabited chambers where the pashas
dwelt who succeeded the grand-masters, cannot refrain from
looking towards the future after lamenting over the past. Is
the splendid island of Rhodes never again destined to nourish
an active and prosperous population?

> 'Can tyrants but by tyrants conquered be,
> And freedom find no champion?'

The splendid ruins of Rhodes have been the admiration
of the traveller in different ages. Mr. Thomas Hope records
the impressions the solitary palace of the grand-masters
and the deserted street of the Knights produced on him,
in *Anastasius*. Walter Vinisauf tells us of the profound
astonishment with which Richard Cœur-de-Lion and the
English army viewed the splendid remains of mightier works
of art before the Knights had laid the foundations of their
fortifications and their palaces. In 1191, Vinisauf saw fallen
towers and wonderful buildings of admirable architecture,
which had encumbered the ground from the time the Saracens
sold the fallen Colossus to the Jews as old bronze. He saw
ancient palaces and temples, which had subsequently been

---

[1] Pinkerton (*Essay on Medals*, ii. 110) mentions a medal of John Kendal,
who was Turcopilier of the Order of St. John at the siege of Rhodes in 1480,
as the first English medal. It is in the collection of the Duke of Devonshire,
and is engraved in the *Ducatus Leodiensis* of Thoresby. It is very large, like many
of the Italian medals of the time, and was probably executed in Italy, and not in
England. I know nothing of it but from Pinkerton.

converted into monasteries, and though recently inhabited
by crowds of monks, were then again deserted. In 1191,
everything attested the existence of an immense population
at some earlier period ; in 1853, the well-constructed fortress
and the untenanted palace, which had been built from these
earlier ruins, showed little signs of decay. They looked as
if they had been suddenly deserted, or depopulated by the
plague[1].

The Knights of St. John of Jerusalem robbed the Greek
empire of the island of Rhodes by a successful piratical
expedition in 1310, and made it the capital of an independent
state, comprising the neighbouring islands of Kos, Nisyros,
Telos or Episkopia, Chalke, Syme, Kalymnos, Leros, and
Castelorizo, as well as the fortress of Boudroun (Halicarnassus), and some smaller forts on the Asiatic continent.
The Order maintained its position as one of the institutions
and bulwarks of Catholic Europe for two hundred and twelve
years, partly by its valour, partly by its prudence, and partly
by the weakness of the Greek emperors of Constantinople
and the other sovereigns in the Levant, before the Othoman
sultans consolidated their power in Asia Minor. The sultans
regarded Rhodes as a portion of the Greek empire, and they
were only restrained from attacking it by the danger of the
enterprise. The memory of the unsuccessful siege of 1480
was at last effaced by the piracies of the Knights and the
danger of allowing the popes to possess an advanced post in
the very centre of the Othoman empire. The results produced by the urgent invitations of the popes to all Christian

---

[1] *Anastasius ; or, The Memoirs of a Greek*, i. 293, edit. of 1819 ; *Chronicles of the
Crusaders*, 179, Bohn's edit. David Chytraeus, in his *Epistola continens Hodoeporicon Navigationis ex Constantinopoli in Syriam, etc.* (in Lonicerus, *Turc. Chron.*
ii. 198) in the year 1581, gives the following short notice of Rhodes, and no
better description of its actual appearance could be conveyed in fewer words :
' Rhodum civitatem (uti mihi quidem videtur) totius Orientis pulcerrimam per-
venimus. Nam quemadmodum ab equitibus Hierosolymitanis extructa est ita
hodie videtur integra, nulla ex parte vastata. Nulli tamen Christianorum in
civitate vel habitare vel per noctem commorari absque venia licet.' I visited the
palace of the grand-masters with Mr. Newton, then Consul in Rhodes, on the
31st May, at an early hour, when the morning sun threw strong shadows on the
picturesque line of mountains, which once formed part of the continental dominions of the Rhodian republic.
    The decline of Rhodes has been rapid. In the eighteenth century it contained
eighty thousand inhabitants. During the latter part of the Greek revolution it
was governed by Mehemet Sukiur, the renegade brother of Petro Mavromichali,
bey of Maina His administration was cruel and oppressive, and the population
then fell to about twenty thousand. The population is now estimated at thirty-
five thousand.

princes and nations to take up arms against the Turks were
so trifling, that we are generally disposed to undervalue the
effect of these exhortations on contemporaries. But even the
most powerful sultans were alarmed by these papal demon-
strations; for it was long before the Mohammedans could
believe that the Christian princes paid only lip-service to
the caliph of Rome, except when their political interests
prompted them to attend to his injunctions.

The profession of the Knights, as sworn enemies of Islam,
and the piratical spirit of the age, both among Christians
and Mohammedans, made the existence of the Order a serious
interruption to the communications between Constantinople
and Syria and Egypt after their conquest by Sultan Selim I.
The exploits of the Order were the cause of repeated complaints on the part of the Turkish merchants; and even the
inhabitants of Asia Minor and Syria were exposed to incessant
plundering visits from the Greek subjects of the Knights.
Several of the smaller islands belonging to the Order were
inhabited by a population remarkable for naval skill; and
as the general system of commercial exclusion prevented
these Greeks from sending their vessels to trade in the
principal ports of the Mediterranean, they had no resource
but to carry on piracy. Their proficiency in the construction
of small vessels of war, and their activity in employing them,
were highly estimated by their sovereigns the Knights. An
open war was carried on by the Turkish and Christian
corsairs for some time before Suleiman summoned the grand-
master to surrender Rhodes. The Order held a brother of
Curtoglu, the Othoman admiral, prisoner in Rhodes, and
Curtoglu attempted to capture the grand-master, L'Isle
Adam, on his passage from France after his election. There
can be no doubt that the Sultan Suleiman was urged to the
conquest of Rhodes by every rule of sound policy[1].

The Knights made a gallant defence against the Othoman army, commanded by Suleiman the Great in person,
and L'Isle Adam obtained an honourable capitulation. The
Greek inhabitants of the dominions of the Order were

---

[1] For Suleiman's summons to the grand-master, see *Chronique du Bâtard de
Bourbon;* Vertot, ii. 636. The date, at page 622, is given erroneously, 1485 for
1522. *See,* for the complaints of piracy, *Négociations de la France dans le Levant,*
i. 90, 95; Vertot, i. 498, ii. 427, 459. For the capitulation, *Négociations,* i. 94.

exempted from the degrading tribute of furnishing children
to recruit the ranks of the janissaries. Nevertheless, the
certainty which the wealthy citizens entertained that their
lives and fortunes would be at the mercy of tyrannical and
rapacious pashas, induced a thousand Greek families to abandon Rhodes, and seek safety in the Venetian island of
Crete[1].

The Morea enjoyed a period of tranquillity after the Venetian
peace in 1502, and the interior of the peninsula was beginning
to recover some degree of prosperity, when a Spanish expedition, under Andrea Doria, again threw the country into a
state of confusion in 1532. The great Genoese admiral
took Patras and Coron; and the garrison he established in
Coron invaded the Morea, occupied Kalamata and Misithra,
and induced many Greeks to take up arms against the sultan.
But in the following year the Spaniards were expelled from
Coron, and the Greeks were treated with great severity by the
victorious Othomans[2].

A new war broke out between the sultan and Venice in the
year 1537, and the Othoman army laid siege to Corfu. The
enterprise failed; but, before abandoning the undertaking,
the Turkish troops plundered and wasted the Greek villages
in the island for eighteen days with fire and sword, burned the
churches, and carried off many thousands of the inhabitants as
slaves[3]. After this repulse, the indefatigable admiral of the
Othoman fleet, Haireddin or Barbarossa, made a series of
plundering attacks on the islands of the Archipelago still in
the possession of the Latins. Aegina, then a flourishing
island under Venetian domination, was ruined; the city was
stormed, though the garrison defended it with desperate
valour; the houses were burned to the ground, all the males
capable of bearing arms were massacred, and about six
thousand young women and children were carried off into
slavery. The island was so completely devastated that for
some years it remained deserted, nor has it to the present
time recovered from the blow it then received. A French admiral, who was sent to the Levant in consequence of the alliance

---

[1] *Négociations de la France dans le Levant*, i. 94. *Lettre de Villiers de L'Isle
Adam*, Vertot. ii. 528.
[2] *Négociations de la France dans le Levant*, i. 235 ; Hammer, v. 236.
[3] Lonicerus, ii. 155.

between France and the Othoman empire, passed Aegina shortly after the departure of the Turks, and found it without inhabitants[1]. It is probable that the first colonists who returned to cultivate the soil were Albanian peasants, whose descendants still occupy the southern part of the island, unless the present Albanian population consist of a new colony, which dates its settlement from the Turkish conquest in 1715. An immense number of Greek slaves were also carried off by the Turks from Zante, Cerigo, and the islands of the Archipelago. Nearly all the islands of the Aegean, which had fallen into the hands of Venetian signors, after the partition of the Byzantine empire in 1204, were now subjected to the sultan by Barbarossa. The Duke of Naxos was compelled to pay an annual tribute of five thousand ducats; but his submission did not save his Greek subjects from being plundered. Most of the islands of the Archipelago were conquered at the same time. Andros was taken from the family of Sommariva; Keos and Kythnos from the Gozzadini and Premarini by whom they were jointly possessed; Seriphos from the Michieli; Ios, Anaphe, and Antiparos from the Pisani; Paros from the Sangredi; Astypalaea and Amorgos from the Quirini and Grimani; and Skyros, Skiathos and Chelidromi from the Venetian republic. In the following year (1538) Skopelos, which also belonged to the Venetians, shared the same fate[2]. The coast of Crete, the most valuable possession of Venice, was plundered, and Tinos, the principal seat of the power of the republic in the Archipelago, was compelled to pay a tribute of five thousand ducats. The Othoman flag was never displayed in so dominant a position over the whole surface of the Mediterranean as at this period. Barbarossa cruised victorious in the waters of Marseilles, and threatened Venice in the Adriatic. He plundered twenty-five of the Greek islands, reduced eighty towns to ashes, and carried off thirty thousand Greeks into slavery[3].

By the treaty of peace concluded in 1540, the Venetians lost all their fortresses in the Morea; and as the Turks were

---

[1] *Journal de la croisière du Baron de Saint Blancard*, in *Négociations de la France*, i. 372.
[2] Hopf, *Urkunden und Zusätze zur Geschichte der Insel Andros*, 7.
[3] *Histoire Nouvelle des anciens Ducs et autres Souverains de l'Archipel*, 293, 350, 352; Paruta, *Historia Venetiana*, ii. 36.

now in possession of the whole peninsula, the Greeks might at
last hope to enjoy some tranquillity under the sole dominion
of the sultan. The power and influence of the Venetians
on the Greek continent seemed to be completely destroyed
by their cession of the fortresses of Monemvasia and Nauplia,
yet, after a lapse of one hundred and fifty years, they were
again enabled to conquer the Morea. The sultan also retained possession of all the islands of the Archipelago
conquered by Barbarossa.

The policy and conduct of the popes tended greatly to
nourish the suspicions of the Othoman government concerning
the fidelity of its Christian subjects. The popes considered
it their duty, and often found it for their interest, to make a
great noise in Europe, preaching crusades against the infidels;
and their endeavours to form leagues of the Christian princes,
for the purpose of attacking the Othoman empire, naturally
alarmed the sultan. Papal agents were repeatedly sent to the
East, with instructions to excite the Greeks to revolt; and
though these emissaries of Rome did little real business
beyond purchasing ancient manuscripts and engraved gems,
the apparent energy of the Court of Rome caused the Othoman government to treat the Greeks with greater severity,
and to watch all their actions with distrust [1].

The success of his attack on Rhodes induced Suleiman
to make an attempt in the year 1565 to expel the Knights
of St. John from Malta, which had been granted to them by
the King of Spain. That attack was signally defeated, and
to revenge the loss sustained by the Othoman arms the sultan
ordered his fleet to take possession of Chios in the following
year.

Chios was then held by a commercial trading company of
Genoese, called the Maona of the Giustiniani. This company
had long acknowledged the suzerainty of the sultan, and paid
tribute to the Porte. The island had been conquered from
the Greek empire in 1346 by the Genoese admiral, Simon
Vignosi, in the same piratical way that the Knights of St.
John had seized Rhodes; but the Greek inhabitants concluded
a convention with their conquerors, by which they retained all

---

[1] An Englishman will find ample proofs of the rhetorical activity of the popes
in Rymer's *Foedera.* See the letters of Leo X. to Henry VIII.

their property, rights, and local privileges [1]. The Genoese
domination in the island of Chios was so different from the
feudal government established in the other conquests of the
western Christians in Greece, that it merits particular attention.
It is the first example we find recorded in history of a
mercantile company of shareholders exercising all the duties
of a sovereign, and conducting the territorial administration
in a distant country. The origin of the company may be
considered as accidental. The public treasury of the republic
of Genoa was so exhausted in the year 1346, that the funds
for fitting out the twenty-nine galleys which composed the
fleet of Simon Vignosi were raised by private citizens, who
subscribed the money in shares. The republic engaged to
secure these citizens against all loss, and pledged a portion
of the annual revenues of the State to pay the interest on
their advances. Each subscriber paid down 400 Genoese
livres; twenty-six galleys were equipped by the commons
and three by the nobles. The expenses of each galley during
the campaign of 1346 was 7000 livres of Genoa, so that the
whole capital expended on the expedition amounted to
203,000 livres. Chios and Phocaea were both conquered.
But when Vignosi returned to Genoa, finding that the republic
was still unable to refund the expenses of the expedition, he
concluded a convention between the subscribers and the
State. The subscribers were formed into a *Maona* or joint-
stock company, and the shareholders were recognized both
as the proprietors and governors of the island of Chios, which
they were bound to administer, under the suzerainty of Genoa,
in conformity to the terms of the capitulation of the Greeks
with Vignosi for a period of twenty years. During this period
the State reserved the right of resuming the grant of the
island, on paying the capital of 203,000 livres due to the
Maona. The republic of Genoa was never able to pay off
the debt, so that the arrangements which invested the

---

[1] Sauli, *Della colonia dei Genovesi in Galata*, ii. 220; and the documents published by Pagano, *Delle imprese e dominio dei Genovesi nella Grecia*, anno 1346,
Nos. 2 and 3, pp. 261, 262. Besides these works there is a well-written history of
Chios by Dr. Vlastos, who prints a golden bull of the Emperor John V., recognizing the rights of the Maona of the Giustiniani in 1362 : Χιακὰ, ἤτοι Ἱστορία τῆς
νήσου Χίου, ὑπὸ τοῦ ἰατροῦ A. M. Βλαστοῦ, Ἑρμουπόλει (Syra), 1840, vol. ii. Cantacuzenos (681, 748) requires to be corrected by comparison with the Genoese
authorities.

Maonesi or shareholders of the company with full power to administer the revenues of Chios became permanent.

This society was afterwards called the Old Maona of Chios. Simone Vignosi revisited the island and administered the government as deputy of the Maona, while the republic sent a podestà who exercised the supreme civil and criminal jurisdiction according to the laws of Genoa. A castellano who commanded a garrison in the citadel, acted under the orders of the podestà. In this way, the government of Chios was divided between the Maona and the State. The sovereignty (*merum et mixtum imperium*) remained vested in the republic as long as the democratic constitution of Genoa remained in force[1]. The administration both civil and financial (*proprietas et utile dominium*) belonged to the Maona. The manner of collecting the revenue, that of electing the persons who conducted and controlled the administration, and that of dividing the profits among the shareholders, were regulated by conventions with the republic, and by statutes of the Maona. In the earliest constitution of the Maona, it received the right of coining money after the type of the republic of Genoa[2]. The local administration of this joint-stock company, though it almost entirely excluded the Greeks from the financial and political government of their native country, and displayed all the religious bigotry of the age, was for a long period the least oppressive government in the Levant. It was less rapacious, and it afforded better securities for the lives and properties of its Greek subjects than they had enjoyed under the emperors of the house of Palaeologos; and it was milder than the governments of the Knights of Rhodes and the republic of Venice.

The Maona derived much of its revenue from monopolies of alum and mastic. The alum mines of Phocaea yielded

---

[1] This stipulation concerning the democracy ceased in 1408.

[2] Gold coins of the Maona of Chios have been found. Hopf mentions that there is one on the model of the Venetian sequins in the Museum Correr in Venice with the name of the podestà Petrus de F(errariis); art. *Giustiniani*, in Ersch and Gruber, 332. At first the money coined at Chios bore the figure of the doge, and the inscription *Dux Januensium Conradus Rex*. See *Primo trattato fra il comune di Genova e i partecipi della Maona di Scio*, A.D. 1347; Pagano, p. 281. Coins of the Giustiniani, which I purchased at Chios, both silver and copper of different periods, have on one side *Civitas Chii*, and on the reverse *Conradus Rex*. The Emperor Conrad (A.D. 1138–1152) not having received the imperial crown at a solemn coronation, was only called *Rex Romanorum*. He first granted to Genoa the right of coining money.

immense profits, but the place was exposed to frequent attacks, and required to be vigilantly guarded against secret treachery, and valiantly defended against foreign enemies. The Maona found it advisable to farm the whole revenues of Phocaea to some powerful noble, who resided in the place and maintained a strong garrison of veteran mercenaries [1].

The mastic of Chios was farmed to a Genoese company, which after the death of Simone Vignosi farmed the whole revenues of the island from the Maona. The original shares of the Maona became soon concentrated in the hands of eight shareholders, and the intervention of the republic was rendered necessary by the violence of the disputes which arose between the Maona and the farmers in Chios. The doge Simone Boccanegra effected an arrangement in the year 1362, by which the old Maona was extinguished on receiving an idemnification for the original shares, and the company which previously farmed the revenues of Chios acquired all its rights and formed the new Maona. The greater number of the shareholders in this new company laid aside their family names and assumed the name of Giustiniani [2].

The Maona of the Giustiniani governed Chios for more than 200 years. It offers some points of resemblance to the English East India Company, which received authority to exercise territorial government in the year 1624, and which, before it ceased to exist in the year 1858, had created one of the greatest empires ever formed. The Maona of Chios like the East India Company affords ample proof that both in political prudence and military courage a society of merchants may be in no degree inferior to royal cabinets and aristocratic senates. Simone Vignosi, Pietro Recanelli,

---

[1] Phocaea consisted of two towns, old and new Phocaea. Benedetto Zaccaria at the end of the thirteenth century received 1,300,000 lire of Genoa annually from the sale of alum. He was an enthusiastic Crusader, fought in defence of Acre at the head of his own band of military followers, and expended large sums in fitting out ships to attack the Mamlouk Sultan Kalaoun. *Hopf*, art. *Giustiniani*, in Ersch and Gruber.

[2] The Giustiniani were at first the mercantile firm of the society. The title was said to have arisen from the company occupying the palace of the Giustiniani as its place of business at Genoa. The shareholders were originally 12, but a ⅔ share was added. The great shares were subdivided into many smaller parts. The celebrated Pietro Recanelli, who became possessed of two original shares. and who governed Chios for the Maona, laid aside the family name he had rendered illustrious, and is the ancestor of the existing family of Giustiniani at Genoa. He governed Smyrna for the Pope, and farmed the alum mines of Phocaea. Hopf gives a very complete history of the Maona in the article *Giustiniani* in Ersch and Gruber's *Allgemeine Encyklopädie: see* pp. 317, 341.

and Rafaele di Montaldo were men whose deeds as soldiers and whose patriotism as citizens do not suffer by a comparison with the greatest men of their time [1].

Chios became one of the principal seats of Italian commerce in the Levant after the Crusaders were driven out of Palestine, and its markets were frequented even by English merchants [2]. During the first century of the Genoese domination, the population exceeded 100,000 souls and the revenues amounted to upwards of 100,000 sequins. But the collection was made in a very expensive manner, for few but *maonesi* were employed either in the financial or civil administration of the island. There was, therefore, a constant tendency to increase the number of officials [3]. At the commencement of the sixteenth century, the surplus revenue which was divided among the *maonesi* gave only 2000 scquins to each of the original great shares. And towards the end of the Genoese domination the expenses of the Maona exceeded the revenue. The company borrowed money from the bank of St. George, and its finances fell into such disorder, that it was compelled to allow the bank to collect a considerable part of the revenues of Chios.

The original shares of the company soon became much subdivided, and most of the *maonesi* or Giustiniani settled in Chios, where they formed a distinct class of the inhabitants, enjoying many privileges and filling all the principal posts in the administration. The Giustiniani who settled in Chios preserved their Italian nationality and Genoese character by sending their children to Italy for their education [4].

[1] Bizaro, *Senatus Populique Genuensis rerum historia*, p. 131, fol., Antverpiae, 1579; Raynaldi *Ann.* 1363, No. 25; Bizaro, *De bello Veneto*, 785; Pagano, *Delle imprese e del dominio dei Genovesi nella Grecia*, 141.
[2] Ducas, 89, edit. Paris. It is said that the revenues of the customs at one time amounted to 300,000 gold ducats; Vlastos, ii. 43.
[3] Pagano (133) gives the revenue as 120,000 scudi d'oro, but he seems to follow the estimate derived from Cantacuzenos, pp. 227, 233, edit. Paris. Vlastos (ii. 43) states the revenue at a later period as 86,000 ducats.
[4] The Giustiniani of Chios produced several celebrated men. Lists are given by Jerosme Justiniani, *Description de Scios*, and Vlastos, ii. 66. Among the best known are John, to whom the Greeks ascribed the loss of Constantinople; Leonardo, bishop of Mytilene, the author of the well-known account of the taking of Constantinople by the Othomans; Michael, author of *Scio Sacra del rito latino*, Roma, 1558, and other works. The work by Jerosme Justiniani, entitled *La description et histoire de l'isle de Scios ou Chios*, with the date MDVI, which is an error for 1606 or 1616, is a small quarto of extreme rarity. The copy in my possession consists of four parts, each with its separate pagination, and these are followed by a number of documents, one dated as late as 1615. Leo Allatius was a Catholic Greek of Chios.

The burgesses formed a second class of the Latin in-habitants of Chios. This class consisted of traders, shop-keepers, artizans, Greek Catholics, retired soldiers, mariners, and serving-men. They possessed some privileges which excited the envy of the orthodox Greeks, who accused them of behaving with much insolence.

It is a melancholy task to compare the energy of the Italians, who acted a prominent part in the history of Greece during more than a century before and after the conquest of Constantinople by the Othomans, with the apathy and cowardice of the Greek population. The moral inferiority of the Hellenic race is conspicuous whenever it was brought into close contact or direct collision with the Italians. This inferiority is more striking because it was not intellectual, and it seems consequently to have originated in the defects of the education by which the hearts and affections of the Greeks were formed at an early age. The habit of obedience was strong; the sense of duty very weak. Unfortunately, the extent to which social defects and errors weaken political communities is not always apparent in the history of nations, and it is difficult to point out the precise faults of the family education, and the particular perversion of religious instruc-tion, which for three or four centuries paralyzed the energies of the Greeks, and rendered integrity, courage, and talent so rare among them, while their country was so frequently the theatre of great events.

The Greeks of Chios were secured in the possession of all the rights and privileges which they enjoyed under the Greek emperors by their capitulation with Vignosi in 1346 [1]. These privileges were confirmed by subsequent acts of the republic of Genoa, and particularly by the doge Francesco Garibaldo in 1393. The Greeks were divided into two classes, free citizens and serfs.

The archonts, who formed a kind of nobility, were allowed to retain some of the privileges which had been conferred on them by the Greek emperors, and were admitted to an active part in some details of the local administration. But they were included in the class of free citizens, which was inferior to that of the Latin burgesses. All the Greeks were obliged

---

[1] Pagano, 262.

to wear their native dress and to inhabit a separate part of the city[1]. No Greek was permitted to dwell in the citadel or in the Latin quarter; and when a Greek sold his property and emigrated from the island, he was compelled to pay one quarter of the price to the Maona of the Giustiniani.

The Greek serfs (*paroikoi* or *villani*), who formed the fourth class of the inhabitants, were little better than agricultural slaves, and were sometimes treated with so much cruelty, both by their Greek and Latin masters, that they fled from the island in great numbers[2].

One of the most important privileges possessed by the Greeks was, that no new tax could be imposed on the island without their consent. Forms were established to insure the free exercise of this privilege. The law required that the consent of the Greeks should be given with the greatest publicity, and the manner in which the business was brought before them enabled them to give their refusal without any display of opposition and with the smallest amount of personal responsibility.

Before proposing a new tax it was necessary for the podestà to obtain the consent of the Maona, the Latin burgesses, the sixty Greek archonts, and the deputies of the rural districts. A public meeting of the Greek citizens was then convoked in the church of St. Michael. When the assembly was opened, the people bowed down their heads and lifted up their hands with the usual display of Byzantine servility, while the podestà announced the nature and amount of the new tax. As soon as the Greeks heard the proposal they sat down, and some time was allowed for reflection. After this interval, all who approved of the measure submitted to the consideration of the assembly were invited to rise up. In case the majority approved (and in general there can have been little chance of dissent), the tax was immediately levied, and the consent of the people was reported to the senate of Genoa, in order that the transaction might receive a formal ratification, and a law might be passed confirming the tax.

---

[1] The *Burgus Graecorum*.

[2] A fifth class consisted of the Jews, who were confined to their *ghetto*, as at Genoa, and were compelled to wear yellow hats.

A sixth class was formed of the strangers residing at Chios, who were chiefly merchants. The Mussulmans were so numerous that they had a resident cadi, to whom, after the year 1498, the Maona was bound to pay an annual salary.

Some protection against oppression was secured to the Greeks by this arrangement. But it is the spirit of the people and not the form of the constitution which makes men free, and the tame spirit of the Chiots enabled their rulers to impose on them fiscal burdens which became at last intolerable. The emigration of the agricultural population became so considerable that the Maona was obliged to reduce the amount of taxation levied on the Greeks [1].

The ecclesiastical administration of the Catholics was far more revolting to the Greeks than the government of the Maona. The Latin bishop at first levied tithes on the orthodox Greeks, but he met with so many difficulties in collecting them that in 1480 he ceded all his territorial revenues to the Maona, and received in lieu thereof an annual payment of 400 ducats.

The orthodox Greeks elected their own bishop, who, after receiving the approval of the Maona, was confirmed by the patriarch of Constantinople. But an orthodox bishop having formed a conspiracy to murder the Giustiniani, and his plot having been discovered, he was expelled from the island and his accomplices were hanged. From that time no orthodox bishop was allowed to reside in Chios, and the affairs of the see were administered by an ecclesiastic called a *dikaios*, who was chosen by the Maona and confirmed by the patriarch. His residence was at the monastery of Nea Mone [2].

Though the Maona of the Giustiniani monopolized a part of the produce of the Greeks, and shared with the other citizens of Genoa the monopoly of the foreign trade of Chios, still agriculture flourished in the island. The price paid for the articles of export was such as insured abundant supplies. Some of these articles were peculiar to Chios, and others were produced of a better quality than could be obtained in any other place. The mastic, the terebinth, the wine, silk,

---

[1] The *Kapnikon*, or hearth-tax, amounted to 6 hyperpera for each family in the town, and from 3 to 4 in the villages, but in 1396 it was found necessary to reduce it to 2 in the rural districts. The mastic villages were exempt from this tax. A silver coin of the value of a *gros tournois* or an English groat, was called by the Latins *hyperperum*, or perper, as well as the Byzantine gold coin usually so called. Buchon, *Livre de la Conquête*, 350, 355; Vincent Belvacensis, l. xxx. c. 143; Ducange, *Glossarium med. et inf. Graecitatis*.
[2] Michael Giustiniani, *Scio Sacra;* Vlastos, ii. 31; Le Quien, *Oriens Christianus*, iii. 1061.

and fruit of this favoured island were sources of wealth to the Greek inhabitants as well as to their Latin masters.

The Maona became tributary to the Othoman sultans at an early period. In 1415 it engaged to pay Mohammed I. the sum of 4000 gold ducats annually. This payment was considered by the Genoese as the price of a treaty of commerce, which secured them liberty to trade with all the Othoman possessions in Europe and Asia. Until the year 1453 friendly relations existed between the Maona and the sultans. But in that year Mohammed II., elated with the conquest of Constantinople, began to treat all the Latins who held possessions in the Eastern empire as his vassals. He had good reason to complain of the conduct of John Giustiniani, who being a member of the Maona, which was his ally and tributary, nevertheless appeared in the ranks of his enemies and acted as general for the Greek emperor. To punish the Maona, Mohammed II. raised the annual tribute to 6000 ducats, and in consequence of some disputes which occurred, it was increased in 1457 to 10,000, and in the year 1508 it reached 12,000 [1]. By patient submission and great prudence, the Maona succeeded in preserving its commercial relations with the Othoman empire, and though it suffered from casual acts of extortion, it generally obtained effectual protection from the sultans.

The power and ambition of the Othoman sultans became at last so great, that the republic of Genoa could no longer venture to stand boldly forward as the protector of the semi-independent rulers of the island of Chios, which Suleiman the Magnificent was determined to annex to his empire. When the Genoese found that the finances of the Maona had fallen into inextricable confusion, they were unmindful of the services that the Giustiniani had rendered to Genoa, and ceased to grant them further protection. In the year 1558 the Genoese ambassador at the Porte was ordered to disavow all claim to the sovereignty of Chios on the part of the republic [2].

The Genoese had governed Chios for 220 years, when Piali Pasha annexed it to the Othoman empire in 1566. The

[1] Ducas, 177, 190, edit. Paris.
[2] *Descrizione del viaggio dell' ambasciata Genovese fatta a Suleimano nell' anno* 1558, scritta per Marcanton Marinello, in the State-archives at Turin, cited by Hopf, *Giustiniani.*

sultan had a good pretext for putting an end to the government of the Giustiniani, for the island served as a place of refuge for fugitive slaves, and of refreshment for Christian corsairs. A magistrate had been regularly appointed to protect and conceal fugitive slaves, and it was said that at one period the number that annually escaped from bondage amounted to one thousand. After the conquest of Constantinople, however, they were compelled to conciliate the Othoman government by refusing open protection to fugitive slaves, as well as by paying tribute to the sultan[1]. No notice was given to them by Sultan Suleiman when he determined to abolish the administration of the Giustiniani, whom he treated as his vassals; but as he feared they might obtain some support from the Spaniards and the Knights of Malta if they were aware of his intention, he ordered his captain-pasha to surprise the place. Piali entered the port with his galleys, landed his troops, and took possession of the capital without encountering any resistance. The principal Genoese families were seized, and sent to Constantinople as hostages, where some of their children were placed in the serai. Several suffered martyrdom because they refused to embrace the Mohammedan faith[2], and many leading Genoese were banished to Kaffa, from whence they were released at the intercession of a Giustiniani who acted as envoy of France to Sultan Selim II. in 1569.

Thus ended the domination of a mercantile company in the Levant, whose dominions extended at one time over the islands of Samos, Patmos, Ikaria, Psara, and Tenedos, and for a short time over old and new Phocaea, on the Asiatic continent. Even after the Turks had taken the place of the Giustiniani in the administration of public affairs, they continued to follow the Genoese system; and the island was long better governed than any other part of Greece. The Greeks were allowed to regulate the affairs of their own community; and though the city appeared dead, and the Genoese palaces, having fallen to the share of the Othoman conquerors, presented a dilapidated aspect, and the stillness

---

[1] Pagano, 136, from Giustiniani, *Scio Sacra*. Vlastos, vol. ii. p. 61.
[2] Eighteen children of the Giustiniani suffered martyrdom rather than renounce Christianity. Mich. Giustiniani, *La gloriosa morte dei* 18 *fanciulli Giustiniani*, Avellino, 1656.

of Turkish apathy replaced the activity of Genoese love of gain, still the villages prospered, and agriculture continued to flourish [1].

Chios could not, however, entirely escape from the desolating effects of the maritime wars that ruined the islands and coasts of Greece. An expedition of the grand-duke of Tuscany, Ferdinand I., visited the Archipelago, in the year 1595, under the pretence of a crusade against the Mohammedans, but in reality to collect plunder and slaves. This fleet made an attack on Chios, but was repulsed by the Turkish garrison of the strong citadel, built by the Giustiniani, which commanded both the town and the port. This ill-planned and worse-conducted attack caused the Othoman government to treat the Latin inhabitants of Chios with such severity that the greater part of those who escaped death and utter ruin quitted the island for ever [2].

About a century later, the Venetians, flushed with their success in conquering the Morea, sent an expedition to Chios, which conquered the island without difficulty, in 1694. But in the following year the Venetian fleet was defeated by the Othomans in a severe engagement off the Spalmadores, and the admiral, losing heart, embarked the garrison of Chios, and abandoned the island with great precipitancy. Though the Greeks had given the Othoman government proofs of their aversion to the Venetian domination by acting as spies for the Porte, they did not escape severe oppression when the Othoman power was re-established. The Catholic families, who were only sixty in number, fled with the Venetians. The Greeks were therefore compelled to satisfy the cupidity of the Turks, who had expected to enrich themselves by the sack of the city, by paying a contribution of four hundred and seventy purses (about £47,000). The payment of this sum

---

[1] Compare a letter of Palaeologos in Reusner, *Epistolae Turcicae*, ii. 142, with the *Hodoeporicon* of David Chytraeus, in Lonicerus, *Turcic. Chron.* ii. 198. The description of the island in 1581 is not inapplicable even in its present state of ruin : ' Chium quam Zio (Scio) vocant, vidimus. Chius insula a Genuensibus diu habitata, et multis superbis aedificiis et hortis amoenis ornata, atque abundantia fructuum vinique et gummi, quod mastiche dicitur, bonitate multum celebrata, hodie prae reliquis provinciis Turcicae tyrannidi subjectis (propterea quod depositis armis sponte in Turcarum devenerit potestatem), tolerabilem habet servitutem.' But in 1574 Jacob Palaeologos says that the depreciation in the value of property was so great that a palace might be purchased for 300 dollars.

[2] Hammer, *Histoire*, vii. 363 ; Dapper, *Description des Isles de l'Archipel.*, 224.

saved the island from being plundered, and it continued in a prosperous condition until the Greek revolution [1].

The year 1566 witnessed the extinction of the Catholic dukedom of Naxos. The Greek inhabitants, who were anxious to place themselves under the Othoman government, in the hope of being allowed to farm the revenues of their island, succeeded in persuading Sultan Selim II. to dethrone their duke, Jacopo IV.[2] But instead of intrusting the local administration to the Greek primates, the sultan granted the island in farm to a Portuguese Jew, Don Juan Miquez, who sent a Spanish Catholic, Francis Coronello, to govern the Greeks and collect the taxes. Miquez was a favourite of Sultan Selim, for whom he procured supplies of the choicest wines; and it was reported that on one occasion, when sharing in their liberal consumption, he was promised by his imperial protector a gift of the kingdom of Cyprus, on account of the excellency of its vintage. The proud title, which so many European monarchs now render themselves ridiculous by assuming, was then adopted with more reason by this Jewish adventurer, who publicly assumed the armorial bearings of a Christian kingdom, and began to form projects for the restoration of a Jewish monarchy, and for replacing the Greek population of Cyprus by founding Jewish colonies in the island [3].

The next great misfortune which fell on the Greek race was the conquest of the fertile island of Cyprus. In the year 1570, Selim II. sent a powerful fleet and army to take possession of the island, which belonged to the Venetians. With the candour often displayed by the Othomans in their lust of conquest, the sultan summoned the republic to surrender Cyprus, merely because he was determined to possess it at any expense of blood and treasure.

The kings of Cyprus, of the house of Lusignan, had been

---

[1] Hammer, vii. 377; Vlastos, ll. 110. When the citadel of Chios capitulated to the Venetians in 1694, six thousand Turkish inhabitants quitted the town. In 1853 I found only about nine hundred in the capital, and not two thousand in the island.

[2] When Naxos fell under the Othoman domination, the tenth of the vintage alone yielded a revenue of fifteen thousand crowns to Don Miquez. Hammer, vi. 385. After the death of Miquez and of Sommariva, A.D. 1579, the revenues of the islands of Naxos, Paros, and Andros were farmed by Suleiman Tzaoush for forty thousand dollars annually. Hammer, vii. 59.

[3] *Négociations de la France dans le Levant*, iii. 88.

compelled to pay tribute to the Mamlouk sultans of Egypt, and this tribute had been transferred to the Porte when Selim I. conquered Egypt in 1517, though the Venetians were then masters of the island. This annual tribute amounted to eight thousand ducats, and the Sultan Selim II. made its payment a pretext for claiming the sovereignty of the island. The republic had acquired possession of the kingdom of Cyprus in 1489, by an act of cession from Catherine Cornaro, a Venetian lady, widow of James II., the last monarch of the house of Lusignan, who became queen at the death of her husband. The fair face of the queen is familiar to thousands who know nothing of her political history. If, indeed, the portrait of a Catherine Cornaro by Titian, in the Manfrini Palace at Venice, be really an authentic likeness of the last queen of Cyprus, the painter's hand has conferred on the lady a fame which neither her crown, her beauty, her virtue, nor the romantic changes of her life, could give. Venice is said to have received from Cyprus an annual revenue of five hundred thousand ducats, but the queen was satisfied with an income of eight thousand ducats, and a secure residence in the town of Asolo, in the Trevisano, where she was treated with regal honours[1].

The Othoman expedition landed at Salines without encountering any opposition, for the naval power of Venice proved too weak to oppose the Othoman fleet[2]. The skill and valour of Barbarossa, Dragut, and Piali had given the Turks a naval superiority in the Mediterranean over every Christian state, and their names were as famous as those of Dandolo, Pisani, and Doria. The Greeks of Cyprus were so oppressed by the Venetian government, that they were eager for a change of masters, and not disinclined to welcome the Othomans. In the month of September 1570, Nikosia, the capital of the island, was taken after a gallant defence; and Famagosta, the only fortress which remained in the hands of the Venetians, was almost immediately invested. The siege of Famagosta is famous in Turkish and Venetian history. The attack was conducted with the extraordinary labour and indomitable

---

[1] Reinhard, *Geschichte des Königreichs Cypern*, ii. 97.

[2] Hammer says the Turks landed at Limasol (Amathus); but the fleet, it seems, really proceeded to Salines, as a more convenient port. The date given in the French translation (vi. 400) is erroneous; the landing took place on the 1st July.

courage which then distinguished the siege operations of the Othoman armies. Their trenches and their batteries were of a size and number never before witnessed by Christian troops. The defence of the Venetian garrison was long and obstinate, but the place was compelled to surrender on the 1st of August 1571.

This period marks the extreme height of Othoman pride, insolence, and power. The scenes which followed the capitulation of Famagosta stain the annals of the empire with indelible infamy. The garrison was embarked according to the stipulations in the treaty, when Bragadino, who had so bravely defended the place, waited on Mustapha Pasha to make arrangements for his own departure. Mustapha Pasha was of a mean, envious, and revengeful disposition, and he basely resolved to deprive the Venetian leaders of the honours that awaited them on their return home, and which they had well merited by their gallant conduct. Bragadino, and the officers who accompanied him to the vizier's tent, were treacherously seized. The greater part were instantly murdered, but the governor was reserved for a lingering death by the most excruciating tortures. The sufferings of the noble Venetian during ten days of agony are too horrible to be described in detail. Mustapha Pasha gave a national and religious solemnity to his own infamy, by ordering Bragadino to be publicly flayed alive on Friday, the day set apart by the Mohammedans for their public prayers to God. The Venetian bore his tortures with singular firmness, and the skin was cut from the upper half of his body before he expired [1]. Three hundred Venetians were massacred at the same time; every article of the capitulation was violated, and even the troops on shipboard were compelled to disembark, and were reduced to slavery [2]. Undoubtedly, the Turks have

---

[1] The skin of Marco Antonio Bragadino, stuffed with straw, was exposed for some years in the bagnio of Constantinople, where the Christian prisoners and slaves were confined; but twenty-five years after his death, it was purchased from the capitan-pasha by his relations, and deposited in the church of SS. John and Paul at Venice, where the monument and inscription they placed may still be seen.

[2] Hammer (vi. 416) mentions some contemporary acts of cruelty and treachery, quite as infamous, on the part of Christians; viz. the massacre of St. Bartholomew, and the desolation of Novgorod by Ivan the Terrible. The age was one of blood, and the religious murders over all Europe attest the indifference of the Christians to the feelings of humanity. The cruelty of the Venetians to the Turks was sometimes as horrible as that of the Turks to the Venetians. Hammer, vii. 193.

laid up a long arrear of hatred and vengeance on the part
of the Christians. The Greek population of Cyprus had
generally joined the Turks, in the expectation of enjoying
milder treatment under the sultan than under the republic.
They soon found themselves utterly disappointed in the
hopes which their orthodox prejudices had led them to
cherish. For about a century they were governed by pashas,
whose rapacity so depopulated and impoverished the island
that the pashalik was at last suppressed, and the fiscal
administration was committed to a mutzelim. In the year
1719, Cyprus yielded the sultan only one hundred and twenty-
five thousand ducats annually, though a century and a half
earlier, when the precious metals were of much higher value,
it yielded the Venetians five hundred thousand ducats. In
1764 the extortions of the administration caused a rebellion
of the Greeks, which, as usual, only increased their sufferings.
Since the hour of its conquest by the Turks, every succeeding
generation has witnessed the diminution of the Greek inhabitants of Cyprus and their increasing misery, so that they
are at present, in spite of the admirable situation of the
island and the richness of its soil, the most wretched portion
of the Greek nation [1].

The celebrated naval battle of Lepanto was fought shortly
after the taking of Famagosta. The political importance of
this victory has been greatly exaggerated in Christian Europe.
It has been assumed that from this defeat the decline of the
Othoman power ought to be dated. Like the victory of
Charles Martel over the Saracens at Tours, it has served
to gratify Christian vanity; and it has been declared by
ignorant historians to have been the cause of many events
with which it had no connection. Had the demoralization
of the sultan's court, and the corruption of the Othoman
central administration, not made as rapid progress as the
military and naval organization of the Christian powers, they
would probably have found no reason to boast of the results
of their victory at Lepanto. It is true that the Othoman
navy lost more than two hundred vessels in this memorable
defeat; but this loss was so rapidly repaired by the activity
of the government, and the resources of the arsenals and

---

[1] Mariti, *Voyage dans l'isle de Chypre*, 19.

A.D. 1453–1684.]

dockyards of the Othoman empire were then so great, that, in the month of June 1572, the capitan-pasha put to sea with a new fleet of two hundred and fifty galleys, boldly engaged the Venetians and their allies, who had assembled a still greater force off Cape Matapan, and arrested their further progress in a career of victory. There was no blockade of the Dardanelles. The Turks encountered the combined Christian fleets half-way between Constantinople and Venice. Well might the grand-vizier, Mohammed Sokolli, say to the Venetian bailo, Barbaro, 'In destroying our fleet you have only shorn our beard; it will grow again: but in conquering Cyprus we have cut off one of your arms.' The indecisive naval engagements which followed the victory of Lepanto taught Venice that she had little to hope by continuing the war; and the practical result of the great victory at Lepanto was, that it enabled the Venetians to purchase peace early in 1573, by paying the sultan three hundred thousand ducats, and promising the Porte an annual tribute of fifteen hundred ducats for the island of Zante. This peace has been called disgraceful to the republic; but when it is remembered that Venice was dependent for her political importance in Europe, and even for her ordinary supplies of grain, on her trade with the Levant, and when we compare the military weakness and commercial exhaustion of a single city with the immense power and resources of the extensive empire of the sultan, we must acknowledge that peace was necessary to save the republic from ruin [1].

It is interesting to observe the part which the Greeks acted in the battle of Lepanto. Their number in the hostile fleets far exceeded that of the combatants of any of the nations engaged, yet they exerted no influence on the fate of the battle, nor did their mental degradation allow them to use its result as a means of bettering their condition, for the effect of mere numbers is always insignificant where individual

[1] Hammer, vi. 435. Since the publication of Von Hammer's *History of the Othoman Empire*, new and valuable documents relating to the battle of Lepanto have been printed, particularly *Documentos sobre la armada de la liga y batalla de Lepanto sacados del archivo di Simancas*, by D. Juan Sans y Barutell, in the third volume of a collection of documents relating to the history of Spain, published by Don Martin Fernandez Navarrete at Madrid in 1843, and several letters relating to the subject in *Négociations de la France dans le Levant*, tom. iii. p. 184. See also *Historia del combate naval de Lepanto*, by Don Cayetano Rosell, Madrid, 1853, in which the principal documents of the archives of Simancas are reprinted.

virtue and national energy are wanting. The Greeks were at this time considered the best seamen in the Levant. Above twenty-five thousand were either working at the oar or acting as sailors on board the Othoman fleet, and hardly less than five thousand were serving in the Venetian squadron, where we find three galleys commanded by Greeks who had joined the papal church—Eudomeniani and Calergi of Crete, and Condocolli of Corfu. Yet these thirty thousand men, of whom many were excellent seamen, exerted no more influence over the conduct of the warriors who decided the contest, than the oars at which the greater part of the Greeks laboured. Their presence is a mere statistical fact, of no more importance in a military point of view than the number of the oars, sails, and masts in the respective ships. Nevertheless, it was in part to the naval skill of the Greeks that the Othoman government was indebted for the facility with which it replaced the fleet lost at Lepanto. Every house in Constantinople and Rhodes, as those cities were exempt from the tribute of Christian children, was compelled to furnish a recruit for the fleet, and every Greek island and seaport furnished a galley, or its contingent for equipping one; so that the losses of the Turkish navy were easily replaced. While the presence of thirty thousand Greeks in a single battle was so unimportant, the single city of Venice, whose whole population capable of bearing arms did not exceed that number, controlled the lives and fortunes of a large portion of the Greek race for many generations, and transfused Venetian feelings and prejudices into the minds of many millions of the Greek race.

The peace with Venice enabled the Turks to re-establish their naval supremacy in the Mediterranean. In the month of May 1574, the capitan-pasha, Kilidj-Ali, left Constantinople with a fleet of two hundred and ninety-eight sail, carrying an army of twenty thousand men, of which seven thousand were janissaries. The Spanish fleet was unable to oppose this force; and Tunis, which Don John of Austria had conquered, was recovered without much difficulty, though the Goletta made a gallant defence. Tunis became an Othoman dependency, and, with Algiers and Tripoli, formed an advanced guard of the empire against the Christian powers, which they tormented with their piracies until the present century. Such were the immediate results of the much-vaunted battle of Lepanto [1].

During the seventy-four years which elapsed between the battle of Lepanto and the war of Candia, the Greek nation disappears almost entirely from history. Some insignificant movements in Maina, caused by the influence of the Christian corsairs, who purchased the permission to conceal their vessels in the ports near Cape Matapan by sharing their booty with the Mainates, were the only signs of independence in Greece, and they were easily suppressed by the capitan-pasha [2]. In Crete, the Venetian colonists, who settled in the island after the suppression of the general insurrections of the Greek inhabitants during the long interval between 1211 and 1363, retained the population in complete subjection, though several partial insurrections occurred, which were generally excited by Greek nobles, who attempted to retain the taxes, levied from the cultivators of the soil, in their own hands, and not with any design to enlarge the liberties of the Greek people, and lighten the burden of the Venetian government by lessening taxation or improving the administration of justice. The terrific cruelty with which the Venetian senate suppressed the last of these insurrections, at the beginning of the sixteenth century, affords a picture of the condition of a large part of the Greek nation for several centuries. The sway of the Maona of Chios was the mildest foreign domination to which the Greeks were subjected; that of the Venetian republic was the most severe; the Othoman government was less moderate than the mercantile company, and less tyrannical than the aristocratic senate. The principles of the Venetian administration are summed up by Fra Paolo Sarpi in these words: 'If the gentlemen (nobles) of these colonies do tyrannize over the villages of their dominion, the best way is not to seem to see it, that there may be no kindness between them and their subjects; but if they offend in anything else, 'twill be well to chastise them severely, that they may not brag of any privileges more than others [3].'

Mr. Pashley has published the following account of the

---

[1] Hammer, vi. 438; *Négociations de la France dans le Levant*, iii. 504. This important event is hardly noticed in the correspondence of the French diplomatists.

[2] Hammer, viii. 205.   [3] Pashley, *Travels in Crete*, ii. 298.

proceedings of the Venetians, from a manuscript at Venice[1]:
'At the beginning of the sixteenth century, the Greeks of
Selino, Sfakia, and Rhiza, including some villages situated
almost in the plain of Khania, united together, and refused to
obey the representative of Venice. Their leaders were George
Gadhanole of Krustogherako, the Pateropuli of Sfakia, and
some other families of the Archontopuli, as they are called
(Greek primates). Gadhanole was elected Rettore of these
provinces. Duties and taxes were now paid, not to the
Venetians, but to these Greek authorities. At length the
Greek rettore suddenly presented himself at the country-
house of Francesco Molini, a Venetian noble, in the neighbourhood of Khania, and asked his daughter in marriage for
Petro, the most beautiful and bravest of all his sons, and in
whose favour the rettore declared his intention of resigning
his office on the celebration of the marriage. The alliance was
agreed on; the rettore gave his son a massive gold ring, and
the betrothal took place. The youth kissed his future bride,
and placed the ring on her finger. The wedding was to be
solemnized the next Sunday week at the Venetian's country-
house, a few miles out of Khania. Molini was merely to send
for a notary and a few friends, and Gadhanole, with his son,
was to be accompanied by a train not exceeding five hundred
men. The Greeks left the country-house of the Venetian
without suspecting treachery. On the following morning,
Molini hastened to the governor of Khania, and obtained his
promise of co-operation in exacting such signal satisfaction for
the indignity of having been compelled to promise his daughter
in marriage to a Greek, as might serve both for an example
and a warning to posterity. In order, however, to prevent
any suspicion of his good faith, Molini despatched tailors to
his country-house to prepare new dresses for the wedding, and
also sent presents of fine cloth to his son-in-law elect. During
the next few days the governor of Khania assembled about
a hundred and fifty horsemen and seventeen hundred foot-
soldiers within the city.

'On the day before the wedding, Molini returned to his
house at Alikiano, with fifty friends to be present at the
marriage. He gave orders for roasting one hundred sheep

---

[1] Pashley, *Travels in Crete*, ii. 150.

and oxen, and for making all due preparations to celebrate the nuptials with becoming splendour. The Greek rettore arrived, accompanied by about three hundred and fifty men and one hundred women, on Sunday morning, and was delighted at all he witnessed. He was received by Molini with every mark of kindness and affection. After the marriage ceremony, the day was spent in festivity and rejoicing. The Greeks ate and drank, and danced and sang. The Venetians plied their guests with wine, and the intoxication affected by them really overcame the unfortunate and too confiding Greeks. Some time after sunset, a rocket thrown up at Khania gave notice of the approach of the troops. The Greeks, overpowered by wine and sleep, were dispersed about the place. As soon as the military arrived, most of the destined victims were at once bound hand and foot, but were suffered to sleep on until sunrise. At daybreak, Molini, and the public representative of the most serene republic, hung the Greek rettore, the unfortunate bridegroom, and one of his younger brothers. Of the family of the Musuri three were shot and the rest hanged. Of the Kondi sixteen were present; eight were hung by the Venetians, and the other eight sent to the galleys in chains. The rest of the prisoners were divided into four parties, not with the intention of mitigating the penalty, for an equally merciless fate awaited them all. The Venetians hung the first division at the gate of Khania; the second at Krustogherako, which village, the birthplace of Gadhanole, was razed to the ground; the third division was hung at the castle of Apokorona; and the fourth on the mountains between Laki and Theriso, above Meskla, to which village Gadhanole had removed from Krustogherako after he became rettore.'

The Venetian senate approved of these cruelties, and sent a proveditore with authority to extirpate the seditious Greeks. Villages were burned and sacked; twelve Greek primates were hanged; pregnant women were murdered in the cruellest manner; whole families were reduced to slavery; and pardon was only granted to the proscribed on condition that they brought to Khania the head of a father, brother, cousin, or nephew who had rebelled. Such were the cruelties by which the Venetians retained possession of Crete for four centuries and a-half. Yet while they oppressed the Greeks with almost intolerable tyranny, strange to say, the internal order they

maintained allowed the country to become more populous
and flourishing than under the more apathetic and disorderly
administration of the Othomans.   Under the Venetian government, the Greek population was estimated at two hundred
thousand, and under the Othoman it never exceeded one
hundred and thirty thousand.   On the other hand, it is probable that the Mohammedan population was greater than the
Venetian, for it is said at one time to have equalled the Greek
in number[1].

A principal feature in the history of Greece, during the
sixteenth and seventeenth centuries, is the evils it endured
from the prevalence of piracy in the Levant.   A number of
Christian and Mohammedan galleys, under various flags,
carried on a species of private warfare and rapine over the
whole surface of the Mediterranean.   The coasts of Spain,
France, Italy, Corsica, Sardinia, and Sicily suffered severely
from the plundering and slave-hunting expeditions of the
corsairs from the ports of Morocco, Algiers, Tunis, and Tripoli,
but the coasts of Greece suffered still more severely from
Christian pirates, who acknowledged no allegiance to any
government.   The power and exploits of the corsairs during
this period exercised an important influence on the commercial
relations of southern Europe ; they often circumscribed the
extent and determined the channel of trade in the East, quite
as directly as the political treaties and commercial conventions
of the Christian powers with the Othoman Porte.   Not only
were the Greek inhabitants of the coasts and islands plundered, but their commerce was completely annihilated.   The
jealousy of the Othoman government rarely permitted a
Greek to fit out an armed vessel for trade ; and yet merchants
willingly paid double freight to ship their goods on board an
armed ship.   On the other hand, the protective policy and com-

---

[1] The Venetians are supposed to have found more than half a million of
Greeks in Crete.   A few examples may suffice to prove that any estimation of the
population at different periods must be very vague.   Daru publishes an account
which gives 40,000 as the number of the inhabitants of the towns, and 120,000
as that of those of the country, in 1571 ; and another which makes the population
of the island 207,798, about 1577.   *Histoire de la République de Venise*, vi. 251.
Pashley gives us a detailed account of the population some years earlier as
271,489.   *Travels in Crete*, ii. 286.   A few years after the Mohammedan conquest
it was estimated at only 80,000.   Mr. Pashley says the population was stated at
260,000 or 270,000, in 1821, nearly equally divided between the two religions.
It fell to less than 100,000 during the revolutionary war of Greece, but is said at
present (1851) to have attained 160,000, of whom 50,000 are Mussulmans.

mercial envy of the Christian powers would have exposed any armed vessel, manned with Greeks, to confiscation in almost every European port beyond Turkey and the Adriatic, unless it were sure of the immediate protection of the sultan. The Othoman fleet only put to sea in great force for some definite expedition, and rarely made a cruise to protect the trade of the sultan's subjects. The insecurity of the Greek seas became at last so great that the coasting trade was in general carried on in small boats, which escaped the pirates by creeping along the coasts and sailing by night. But when the corsairs found no vessels to plunder, they indemnified themselves by plundering the villages near the coast, and carrying off the inhabitants, whom they sold as slaves, or compelled to labour at the oar. The frequency of these expeditions at last drove the Greeks from the small towns and villages close to the sea, and compelled their inhabitants to establish their dwellings in sites of difficult access, to which it required some time to ascend from the nearest point of debarkation on the coast. The principal object sought for in the new locality was to gain time to escape from the pirates in case of their landing, so that the families and property of the inhabitants might be transported to a considerable distance in the interior, and the advance and retreat of the plunderers harassed by occupying strong positions on their line of march. Even to the present day, the continent and islands of Greece, when seen from the coast, still present the desolate aspect impressed on them by the corsairs of the sixteenth and seventeenth centuries. The records of the ravages of these Christian plunderers are traced as visibly on the shores of Greece, as the annals of the fiscal oppression of the Othoman government are stamped on the depopulated towns and abandoned villages of the interior. Many mediaeval castles, towns, and parish churches, now in ruins, overlook the sea, bearing marks of having preserved their inmates until the sixteenth century[1].

Even in the capital of the Othoman empire the Greek population lived in continual danger of their lives and property. Murad III., while playing at the djereed, fell from his horse in an apoplectic fit. The result is described by

---

[1] The author of this work, like every traveller who has cruised much in the waters of Greece, has often climbed to these now desolate sites, and speculated on the date of their decline and the cause of their total desertion.

Knolles in his quaint translation of Leunclavius: 'The sultan, falling from his horse, was taken up for dead, insomuch that the janissaries, after their wonted manner, fell to spoiling Christians and Jews, and were proceeding to further outrages, when their aga, to restrain their insolence, hanged up a janissary taken in the act of murdering a rayah[1].' Every political event was used as a pretext for plundering the Greeks; and indeed the Christian subjects of the Porte generally were treated with extraordinary severity at this period. The Mohammedans displayed an increase of bigotry, and became more tyrannical, on perceiving that the Christian states of western Europe had acquired strength to resist the progress of their conquests. Murad III. really desired to convert all the churches in his empire into mosques; and in 1595, when the news of the sack of Patras by a Spanish fleet reached Constantinople, the extermination of the Christians was discussed in the divan, but the result was confined to the publication of an order for the expulsion of all unmarried Greeks from Constantinople within three days[2].

During the period which intervened between the conquest of Cyprus and the invasion of Crete, the maritime hostilities of the Knights of Malta, who were indefatigable corsairs, constantly excited the anger of the sultan's court, while their expeditions inflicted great losses and severe sufferings on the Greek population. It would be tedious to notice the various acts of systematic devastation recorded by travellers and historians during this Augustan age of piracy. The deeds of the corsairs in the Levant, and of the Uscoques in the Adriatic, almost rivalled the exploits of the buccaneers in the West Indies[3]. A few leading examples will suffice to show how the rapacity and cruelty of the corsairs affected the position of the Greeks as Othoman subjects. The lawless conduct of the captains of ships, even in the regular service of Christian states, is proved by a memorable act of piracy, committed by a Venetian noble in command of a squadron, on some Othoman vessels during a time of peace.

---

[1] A.D. 1584. Compare Knolles, *The Turkish History*, i. 689, and Leunclavius, *Supp. Annal. Turcic.*, 381, edit. Paris.

[2] Hammer, viii. 134, 317.

[3] Hallam (*Middle Ages*, ii. 254) alludes to the plundering propensities of navigators in preceding ages. He says that one might quote almost half the instruments in Rymer in proof of the prevalence of piracy.

CRUELTY OF VENETIANS.

In the year 1584, the widow of Ramadan Pasha, late Dey of Tripoli in Barbary, embarked with her family and slaves in a vessel for Constantinople. The property she carried with her was valued at eight hundred thousand ducats, and, for security against pirates, she was attended by two armed galleys. Stress of weather drove these ships into the entrance of the Adriatic, where a Venetian squadron, under Petro Emo, was stationed to protect the trading vessels under the flag of the republic. Emo pretended to mistake the Turkish galleys for pirates. He attacked them with a superior force, and captured them after a desperate resistance. He then committed the most infamous cruelties, in order to appropriate the rich booty and compromise his crew so far as to insure their silence. Two hundred and fifty Turks who had survived the engagement were murdered. The son of Ramadan was stabbed in his mother's arms. The female slaves were ravished, cruelly mutilated, and thrown into the sea. A beautiful girl, who declared she was a Venetian, a Cornara, and a Christian, vainly implored the brother of Emo to spare her honour. She solemnly declared that she had been enslaved while a child in Cyprus, but young Emo proved deaf to her prayers. She received the same treatment as the rest, and her body was thrown into the sea. One of the Turks, however, escaped with his life, and at last found his way to Constantinople, where his story soon raised a general cry for vengeance. The Persian war, in which Murad III. was engaged, saved Venice from an immediate attack, and the republic gained time to appease the Porte by denying, explaining, apologizing, and bribing. The truth, however, could not be concealed. Emo was brought to justice and beheaded. The captured galleys were repaired and sent to Constantinople, manned by Turks delivered from slavery, in the place of those who had been slain. Four hundred Christian slaves were also delivered to the Porte, as it was said Ramadan had possessed that number at Tripoli, though it was evident no such number had been embarked in the captured ships. But of these slaves the greater number were divided among the Othoman ministers, as an additional bribe to prevent war, and only a small part was given to the widow and to the heirs of Ramadan[1].

---

[1] Leunclavius, *Supp. Annal. Turcic.*, 382, edit. Paris.

The cruelty of the Knights of Malta was not so infamous as that of the Venetians, for their warfare was open and systematic; but the losses they inflicted on the Turkish merchants and the frequent captures they made of wealthy Osmanlis on the passage between Constantinople, Syria, and Egypt, caused incessant complaints. The Porte was repeatedly urged to attack Malta, and destroy that nest of corsairs; but the memory of the losses sustained during the siege of 1565 rendered the pashas, the janissaries, and the Othoman navy averse to renew the enterprise [1].

The Knights of Malta not only carried on war with the Barbary corsairs and Othoman galleys, but they searched every corner of the land, and lurked under every cliff in the Greek islands, on the watch to capture Turkish merchant vessels. The story of many a hard-fought battle with the Barbaresques and the Othomans may be found in the annals of the Order; but very few allusions are made to their daily plunder of merchant ships, and their kidnapping exploits on the coasts of Greece, from which the Christian subjects of the sultan suffered more than the Mussulmans. Many Greeks were annually carried off to labour at the oar in Christian galleys; and the want of rowers was so great, that though they were not called slaves, they were guarded as carefully, and compelled to labour as constantly, as if they had been infidels or criminals.

The habitual proceedings of the naval forces of the Order were so near akin to piracy, that the grand-master was repeatedly involved in disputes with the Christians at peace with Turkey, by the manner in which the Knights openly violated every principle of neutrality. Even the naval forces of Venice were insufficient to protect the ships and possessions of the republic. A few examples will be sufficient to prove the general insecurity of property; for where there was danger to Venetians, there must have been certain ruin to Greeks. In the year 1575, the Knights seized a Venetian ship with a rich cargo belonging to Jewish merchants. The republic, however, insisted that the perpetual warfare which the Knights made it their vocation to wage against the Mohammedans, did not entitle them to plunder Jews under Venetian protection. The grand-master confiscated the

---

[1] Knolles, *Turkish History,* i. 710.

captured merchandise in spite of the reclamation of the Venetian senate, on the ground that the Jews were not subjects of the republic. The senate immediately seques- trated all the property of the Order in the Venetian dominions, and thus forced the grand-master in the end to make restitution to the Jews[1]. But the Knights continued to interpret their belligerent rights according to their own code; and in 1583 the Venetians seized two galleys of the Order, to compel the grand-master to restore the property of Venetian merchants taken in a Turkish merchant ship. At this time the Turkish merchants still carried on a con- siderable trade with Italy in their own ships. The extortions of the pashas and provincial governors in the Othoman empire had not yet exterminated the race of wealthy Mussulman traders, nor had the supremacy of the Christian corsairs yet excluded the Othoman flag from commercial operations[2]. We find the senate compelled to sequestrate the property of the Order as late as the year 1641, in order to force the grand-master to make restitution for acts of piracy com- mitted by the Knights[3].

Similar disputes occurred with the King of Spain and the republic of Lucca in 1638, in consequence of acts of piracy committed by French knights on Spanish and Sicilian ships, France being then at war with Spain[4].

While the corsairs of Malta were plundering the Turks and Greeks, those of the Barbary coast were equally active in capturing the Christians. Several of the European powers, however, finding that they were unable to protect their subjects by force, submitted to purchase security for their trade by paying an annual tribute to the African corsairs. Nevertheless, we find that the merchants of France, England, and Holland were frequently severe sufferers from these corsairs[5].

The conduct of Christian corsairs on the coasts of Greece increased the hatred which had long prevailed between the

[1] Vertot, iv. 110.
[2] Ranke (*History of the Popes in the Sixteenth and Seventeenth Centuries*, 97, 101, 110) alludes to the extent and importance of the Turkish trade, and the number of Turkish merchants at Ancona, in the sixteenth century. Vertot, iv. 123.
[3] Vertot, iv. 152.   [4] Ibid. 144, 148.
[5] Hammer, ix. 29, 30, 234, 281 ; Rycaut, 21.

Latins and the Greeks, in consequence of the oppression reciprocally suffered from each party when in power. In Negrepont, Mytilene, Chios, Cyprus, and many smaller islands, the Latins had long treated the orthodox Greeks as serfs, and persecuted them as heretics. At this time the Greeks revenged themselves for former cruelties by equal tyranny. The Othoman government, naturally placing more confidence in the submissive and orthodox Greeks than in the discontented and Catholic Latins, favoured the claim of the orthodox to the guardianship of the Holy Sepulchre at Jerusalem. During the sixteenth century this caused many disputes, and created a permanent irritation at the papal court. The priestly soldiers of Malta were invited by the Pope to take an active interest in the question, and the grand-master, to mark the zeal of the Order, joined his Holiness in advising the Christian powers not to spare the heretical Greeks whenever they could be made prisoners. Religious hatred was considered as good a ground of hostility as political interest, and the orthodox were consequently chained to the oar in Catholic galleys with as little compunction as Mohammedans[1]. Continual plundering expeditions against the Grecian coasts kept alive the mutual animosities. In 1620 the Knights made a most successful foray in the Morea. They took Castel Tornese, where they found an immense quantity of military stores laid up by the Othomans, which they carried off or destroyed, and retired with a rich booty in slaves[2].

The spirit of chivalry had perhaps expired in Europe before Cervantes bestowed on it an immortality of ridicule in the person of Don Quixote. But chivalry continued a thriving trade at most European courts after the spirit had fled, and an idle mimicry of chivalric mummery is still perpetuated by princes to decorate courtiers and chamberlains with stars and ribbons. In the year 1560, Cosmo de' Medici, duke of Florence and Sienna, instituted a new order of chivalry on the model of the Knights of Malta, for the express object of combating the Turks, and called them the Knights of St. Stefano[3]. The new order was marked by

---

[1] Vertot, iv. 145.   [2] Ibid. 132.
[3] Compare the different dates given by *L'Art de vérifier les Dates*, v. 295, 4to. edit.; Spondanus, anno 1562, No. 5, 39; and Napier, *Florentine History*,

the characteristics of the age. There was as much of the spirit of piracy as of the impulse of chivalry in its institutions. These knights were to seek adventures and glory in the Levant ; but they were especially instructed not to overlook plunder and profit while at sea. The pretext of the duke in establishing the Order was to supply the means of defending the coast of Tuscany against Mohammedan corsairs, and he hoped to give a new direction to the valour of the restless nobles of Italy, by mingling the love of foreign enterprise with their personal feuds and party politics. None but nobles were admitted as knights, and only those who were wealthy or distinguished in arms. The Order was endowed with considerable ecclesiastical revenues by Pius IV., and with large funds by the Duke of Florence, who reserved the office of grand-master to himself and his successors. Several families were also allowed to found hereditary commanderies in the Order by granting it large estates. The ancient city of Pisa was the seat of this new Order of St. Stefano—a noble residence for the revivors of ancient pageantry. The papal bull of confirmation by Pius IV. was dated on the 6th July 1562. Historians have carefully informed us what dress the knights wore, and they are so eloquent and so minute in their description that future times are likely to know more of the exploits of the tailors of the Order than of the deeds of the knights. Several popes conferred additional privileges on the Order, and Benedict XIV. granted them the right of audience without leaving their swords in the papal ante-chamber, a privilege which is enjoyed by other Orders and by foreign diplomatic agents at Rome, whose tongues, how-ever, rather than their swords, were the weapons which they were most likely to use in a manner offensive to his Holiness.

The Knights of St. Stefano maintained a well-appointed squadron of galleys under their own flag, which, when united with the Florentine ships of war, formed a small fleet. The Duke of Florence was quite as much the master of the one as of the other ; but the Knights of St. Stefano could commit acts of piracy without involving him in such direct responsibility

---

v. 225. *L' Art de vérifier les Dates* makes a sad mistake in the name of the pope who confirmed the order in 1562. It was Pius IV., and not Paul IV., who died in 1559.

as would have resulted from the commission of similar acts by ships under the Florentine flag. The right of private warfare had ceased, but there were still independent sovereigns in Europe who possessed neither the wealth nor the power of the Knights of St. Stefano [1].

The importance of gaining the good-will of the Greeks in the struggle between the Christian powers and the Othoman government was felt by the Florentines. Cosmo I. attempted to secure some influence in the Archipelago by establishing two Greek colonies in Tuscany, one in the island of Giglio, and another at Florence, hoping that these colonists would be able to rouse their countrymen in the Greek islands to join the sultan's enemies. Religious bigotry destroyed the duke's plans, and even rendered his political project injurious to the commerce of his subjects. The council of Florence had forbidden the free exercise of all religious opinions not in strict conformity with its decisions, so that only those Greeks who acknowledged the papal supremacy could be allowed to form a civil and religious community. The orthodox, consequently, soon discovered that they enjoyed more civil and religious liberty under the government of the sultan than was conceded to them by a Christian duke. The commercial jealousy of the people likewise aided the religious bigotry of the papal court, in preventing the Greeks from forming any national friendship with the Italians.

The plundering expeditions of the Knights of St. Stefano respected neither Greek nor Turkish property where booty could be obtained; but the Florentine government soon discovered that the piratical gains of the Order were insufficient to indemnify the State for the exclusion of its industrious citizens from all participation in the honest trade with the Othoman empire. Duke Francesco I. sought to conclude a commercial treaty with the Porte in 1577, in order to afford the Greeks an opportunity of establishing commercial houses at Leghorn under the protection of an Othoman consul. During his negotiations with the sultan, he attempted to deny all responsibility for the conduct of the Knights of St. Stefano, but the Porte insisted that he should disarm the galleys of the Order, and engage that it

---

[1] At the death of Cosmo, the united fleet of Florence and of the Order of St. Stefano consisted of sixteen galleys. Napier, *Florentine History*, v. 253.

should in future afford no assistance to the Pope and the King of Spain. The duke would not accept these conditions, and his attempt to enjoy the profits of legitimate trade in the sultan's dominions under one flag, while plundering his subjects under another, having failed, the Medici and the Knights of St. Stefano continued their piratical expeditions against the Greek islands with redoubled activity.

In the year 1594 the Florentines had a force of three thousand two hundred men serving in the Levant. The unsuccessful attack they made on Chios in the following year has been already mentioned [1]. Some years later, the united squadrons brought the richest prizes that they ever made into the port of Leghorn, consisting of the fleet from Alexandria, which was conveying the tribute of Egypt to Constantinople. Two galleons, seven galleys, seven hundred prisoners, and two millions of ducats, was announced as the official value of the booty; but much additional profit was made by ransoming wealthy prisoners [2]. At the beginning of the seventeenth century, the galleys of the Duke of Florence were accounted the best in the Mediterranean, and they carried on war both against the Turks and the Barbary corsairs with the greatest activity [3].

The spirit of private warfare, or the love of piracy, was so widely spread in Christian Europe, that we find even the English merchant-ships frequently coming into collision with the Turks wherever they met, whether in the Red Sea or the Mediterranean, and both parties appear to have generally acted in a way more likely to cause than to prevent such collisions [4].

---

[1] See p. 80, and Napier, *Florentine History,* v. 295, 365, 377.

[2] Hammer (viii. 169) places this capture in 1606 ; Napier (v. 388), in 1608.

[3] Knolles, *Turkish History,* ii. 825, 886 ; Deshayes, *Voyage de Levant,* p. 284; ' L'ignorance des ministres Turcs est si grand, qu'il y en a plusieurs qui estiment le Duc de Florence ou le Grand-Maître de Malte plus puissants que le Roi d'Espagne, parce que les deux premiers leurs font plus de mal.'

[4] See the account of Sir Henry Middleton's voyage, and the proceedings of other English ships on the coast of Arabia. For an engagement in the Mediterranean, see Hammer, ix. 234, 281 ; and Rycaut, continuation of Knolles, 21. According to Mariana, the good knight Diego de Paredes, whom the Spaniards considered a worthy rival of the Chevalier Bayard, when he lost the estates conferred on him in the kingdom of Naples by the Great Captain, Gonsalvo de Cordova, in consequence of the treaty of Blois, A.D. 1505, ' endeavoured to repair his fortunes by driving the trade of a corsair in the Levant.' Prescott, *Ferdinand and Isabella,* part ii. chap. xix.

The general feeling with which piracy was viewed by the Christian powers is exemplified by the fact that Turkish corsairs were allowed to sell the booty

Enough has been said to give the reader some idea of the various causes which combined to spread devastation over the coasts of Greece and produce a sensible diminution in the numbers of the Greek race. The poorer and more exposed districts were often entirely depopulated. At the time of the Othoman conquest, the Greeks of the small towns and thickly-peopled rural districts were accustomed to live with more of the conveniences of civilization, and to enjoy more of the necessaries, and even of the luxuries of life, than the inhabitants of other countries. When, therefore, their barns were destroyed, their wine-presses broken in pieces, their olive-groves burned down, and their silk carried off by the corsairs, they were unable to bear the privations which these losses entailed. The people first crowded into the large cities, and then gradually melted away—a process of depopulation which can now be seen going on under the influence of fiscal oppression, and of the total want of an equitable administration of justice, in almost every province of the Othoman empire. But, unfortunately for Hellenic pride, Greece itself, under a native government, appears to be making as little progress in wealth and industry as some provinces of Turkey, and many of its most favoured cities are in a worse condition than they were in the sixteenth century. Livadea, which then furnished sail-cloth for the Othoman navy, is now destitute of all industry. It grows at present little cotton, and less flax, and it suffers, perhaps, more from brigands than it ever did under the Turks[1].

Though the Venetians and Turks were at peace from 1573 to 1644, and both powers kept up a very considerable naval force for the express purpose of suppressing piracy, the Greeks never suffered more from pirates than during this period. Indeed, the fleets which were placed to protect them were often their worst oppressors. When there was a want of hands in either fleet, the Greeks were carried off from their homes to labour at the oar. The Venetians made slaves of

they had plundered from Christian vessels in the port of Civita Vecchia. Ranke observes, ' This was the issue of the labours of the chief pastor of Christendom for the protection of commerce.' *History of the Popes* (Kelly's Translation), 265.

[1] Hammer, *Staatsverfassung und Staatsverwaltung des Osmanischen Reichs*, ii. 284. Linen was supplied by Livadea, and a quantity of cotton sail-cloth by Athens, in 1608. Hammer, ii. 289. Little of either could these cities now furnish to the diminished naval force of King Otho.

A.D. 1453–1684.]

them because they were heretics, and the Othomans because they were infidels. The African corsairs set the power of the sultan at defiance, and the pirates of Dalmatia despised the authority of the republic, which could not prevent the ships of Segna from plundering even in the Adriatic. The great extent of the Othoman coasts, and the immense amount of Venetian property always afloat in commercial undertakings, held out too many inducements to corsairs to pursue their trade of pillage, for it to be an easy task to exterminate them. The corsairs of Algiers, Tunis, and Tripoli, and of Catalonia, Malta, Sicily, Genoa, Tuscany, and Dalmatia—all plundered Greece indiscriminately. The capitan-pasha only made a vain parade of the Othoman fleets, in his annual cruise to collect the tribute of the cities and islands of the Aegean Sea. The increasing venality of the Othoman governors, and the deep-seated corruption of the civil administration, rendered the permanent naval force, which the sandjak-beys of the islands were bound to maintain by their tenures, utterly inefficient[1]. The governments of Western Europe in alliance with the Porte, and the peaceable Greek subjects of the sultan, were far more alarmed at the annual parade of fifty galleys, under the capitan-pasha, than the corsairs. Kings knew the immense power which the Othoman navy could concentrate for any definite object, and the invasion of Cyprus proved that even a treaty was no sure guarantee against a sudden attack. But the corsairs were well aware of the inefficiency of the Othoman galleys, and the inexperience of their crews in naval operations, when compelled to act separately. Though the Porte could repair its losses at the battle of Lepanto with unrivalled vigour and celerity, it could never give adequate protection to the coasts of Greece.

Historians have generally adopted the opinion that the

---

[1] The beys of Rhodes, of Milos and Santorin, of Chios, Cyprus, the Morea, Lepanto, Santa Maura, Negrepont, Mytilene, Andros and Syra, Naxos and Paros, and Lemnos, were bound to furnish a number of galleys, according to the extent of their revenues; Rhodes furnishing four, Chios six, and Cyprus seven, while the Morea only furnished three. The number, however, varied at different periods. See Deshayes, *Voyage de Levant*, p. 214, before the year 1645. When Spon travelled (A.D. 1675), Naxos, Andros, Mytilene, and Samos maintained each a galley, Chios maintained two, while Mycone united with Seriphos to maintain one. Spon, i. 149. See also the number of timariot lands in several islands and districts belonging to the jurisdiction of the capitan-pasha, above, at p. 4.

Othoman navy has always been the weakest and worst organized branch of the public service in Turkey. The loss of several great battles, at various epochs, is cited as a proof of want of naval power and skill, instead of being viewed as evidence of the valour and discipline of fleets which could bravely prolong a desperate contest. The vaunting declamations of Venetian and Greek writers have even misled some historians so far, that they have described the Othoman navy as characterized by cowardice as well as incapacity. This is completely at variance with the facts recorded by history. Though the Othoman Turks were never a maritime people, they can boast of as long a period of uninterrupted naval conquests as most of the Western nations. They had no sooner conquered the Greeks on the sea-coast of Asia Minor, than they found it necessary to form a naval force to preserve their conquests, and, like the Romans, they made energy and courage supply the want of maritime experience and naval skill.

The Othoman navy was not regularly organized until after the taking of Constantinople, though Sultan Mohammed II. formed a considerable naval force to attack the Greek capital by sea. The creek in which his admiral, Suleiman Balta-oglu, constructed the Othoman ships, situated above the European castle on the Bosphorus, still commemorates the event by retaining the name of Balta Liman[1]. The first great naval enterprise which established the supremacy of the Othoman fleet in the Levant was the conquest of Negrepont, in spite of all the efforts of the Venetian navy to save it, A.D. 1475. The present chapter records the long series of conquests which followed that brilliant exploit. The glory of Haireddin (Barbarossa), who, in 1538, with only one hundred and twenty-two galleys, defeated the combined fleet of the Christian powers under the great Andrea Doria, consisting of one hundred and sixty-two galleys and many smaller vessels, far surpasses that of Don Juan of Austria, who, with a superior force, gained the well-contested battle of Lepanto. The fleet of Barbarossa was long terrible in the Italian seas, and the Turks were ready to dispute the mastery of the Grecian waters with Don Juan the year after his victory. The siege

---

[1] It is situated on the European side of the Bosphorus above the castle erected by Mohammed II.

of Malta and the battle of Lepanto reflect no disgrace on the
Othoman navy. These reverses were more than compensated
by the conquest of Cyprus, of Tunis, and of Crete. Indeed,
history offers no example of greater vigour than was displayed by the Othoman government in restoring its fleet
after every great disaster. The defeats of the Othoman navy
have been as glorious to the Othoman administration as the
victories. Nearly a century after the disastrous fight of
Lepanto, the Othoman navy sustained another great defeat.
This happened at the entrance of the Dardanelles, during the
war of Candia, in 1656, when the Venetian admiral, Mocenigo,
destroyed the fleet of Kenaan the capitan-pasha. Seventy
Turkish ships were taken or sunk; but the spirit of the
Othoman administration again rose superior to the disaster.
The activity of the government, the courage of the naval
officers, and the resources of the sultan's empire, soon repaired
the losses sustained, and this defeat, like that of Lepanto,
ultimately only increased the wonder and alarm of the Christian powers.

The battle of the Dardanelles is also remarkable for having
awakened the patriotism of a private individual, who, in
labouring to rouse the enthusiasm of his countrymen, has left
an imperishable monument of the glory of the Turkish navy.
Hadji Khalfa was a clerk in the admiralty at Constantinople,
when the great loss sustained by the fleet induced him to
write a history of the naval exploits of the Othomans, as an
incentive to every patriotic Mussulman to step forward and
repair the disaster. He had to remind his countrymen of a
long career of conquest. Hadji Khalfa died shortly after
publishing his work, before he witnessed the re-establishment
of the naval supremacy of the Othoman fleets in the Levant,
for which he was labouring; but his literary exertions may
claim some share in animating the Turkish army and navy to
bear with patience the incredible toils that render the siege of
Candia the most memorable of modern sieges, and to display
the indomitable courage that conquered the valour of Morosini and defeated the naval science of the Venetians. The
conquest of Crete was the last, the most important, and the
most glorious naval conquest of the Othomans; and Hadji
Khalfa's glory, in contributing to that conquest, is nobler and
purer than that of the warriors who are honoured for their

exploits as mere instruments of their own and their sovereign's ambition [1].

The Othomans had no love of naval enterprise, and their fleets were formed only because political necessity imposed upon them the duty of maintaining a naval force. The majority of the crews, when they gained their greatest victories, were Christian rayahs, who had no disposition to encounter danger. The Othoman officers and warriors were, consequently, obliged to watch the manœuvres of their own sailors, who sought to avoid bringing their ships to close quarters, as well as to combat their enemies. Yet, under these disadvantages, the naval policy of the Othoman government, and the obstinate courage of the Othoman officers, secured to the sultans a supremacy in the Mediterranean for three centuries [2].

The Othoman navy was organized to fight battles and to effect conquests, but the single ships of which it was composed were not fitted out in a way calculated to pursue corsairs and defend the extensive coasts of Greece. The consequence was that the Greeks were exposed to be plundered incessantly by the Knights of Malta, the Knights of St. Stephen, and the Tuscan navy, which were constantly at war with the sultan. In the year 1595 a Spanish fleet plundered the Morea, and laid Patras in ashes. Though the Greeks were the principal sufferers by this attack, the Porte was persuaded that the success of the Spaniards had been caused by collusion on the

---

[1] Hammer, *Staatsverfassung und Staatsverwaltung des Osmanischen Reichs*, ii. 347.
[2] Thevenot (*Voyage au Levant*, ii. chap. xciv.) describes the state of the Mediterranean in 1659; Spon (*Voyage d'Italie, de Dalmatie, de Grèce, et du Levant*, vol. i. 12, edit. Amst., 12mo. 1679) gives an account of the activity of the Turkish corsairs in the western part of the Mediterranean in 1674. The Dey of Algiers seized M. Vaillant, the celebrated numismatist, and other Frenchmen, to compel the King of France to restore eight Turks who were kept in slavery, though Turkey was at peace with France. When Vaillant was on his way back to France, he was again in danger of being captured by a corsair of Salé, and it was then that the numismatist swallowed twenty gold medals. The frequency of corsairs is again testified at p. 90. Mr. Vernon, who left Italy with Spon and Wheler, and whose letter from Smyrna, dated in January 1676, is the first account of Athens under the Turks by an Englishman, was also plundered of all his property, including his papers, by Greek pirates in the Archipelago. He was put on shore at Milo in a state of destitution, whence he continued his voyage in an English ship. He had been once before taken by Tunisian corsairs, and kept as a slave. After escaping these Mohammedan and Christian pirates, he was murdered on his way from Trebizond to Persia. Compare his letter in Ray's *Collection of curious Voyages and Travels*, ii. 29; Spon, *Voyage*, i. 117; and Wheler, *A Journey into Greece*, fol. 334, 358, 431, 443, 448.

part of the rayahs, and the project of a general massacre of the Christian population of the Othoman empire was seriously discussed in the divan. The treatment of the Greeks by the government of Turkey, however, proved less tyrannical than that of the Moors and Jews by the court of Spain, and the project of extermination ended, as has been already mentioned, in the sultan merely ordering all unmarried Greeks to quit Constantinople [1]. In the same year, the unsuccessful attack of the Florentines on Chios increased the sufferings of the defenceless Greeks.

In 1601 the Spaniards and their allies ravaged Maina, surprised Passava, and plundered the island of Cos [2]. In 1603 the Knights of Malta again sacked Patras, and in the following year they plundered many defenceless villages in Cos [3]. But in the year 1609 they sustained a great naval defeat from the Othomans, though they succeeded in ravaging the coast of Karamania. In the following year, a fleet, consisting of Maltese, Sicilian, and Spanish galleys, entered the port of Cos, plundered the town, and carried off a number of the inhabitants as prisoners, who, when not ransomed, were compelled to work as slaves at the oar. The Florentine squadron made an unsuccessful attempt to plunder the coast of Negrepont ; and the combined fleet failed in its attack on Albania, where the Turks, having discovered that a Greek bishop served them as a spy, flayed the unfortunate culprit alive [4]. About this time the Christians were treated with unusual severity in the Othoman empire, for the religious bigotry of the Mussulmans was roused to seek every means of revenging the tyrannical treatment which had been inflicted on the Mohammedans in Spain at their expulsion in 1609 [5]. In 1611 the galleys of Malta made an unsuccessful attempt to plunder

---

[1] Hammer. *Histoire de l'Empire Othoman*, vii. 317 ; *see* above, p. 92.
[2] Hammer, viii. 17.   [3] Vertot, iv. 128.
[4] Knolles, *Turkish History*, ii. 898, 903, 904; Hammer, viii. 170.
[5] The cruelty of the Turks to the Greeks was far surpassed by that of the Spaniards to the Moors, as the records of the Inquisition testify ; but there is a singular provision, which shows that selfishness could get the better even of Christian bigotry. When the Moors were expelled from Spain, the barons of Valentia were allowed to retain six Mohammedan families in every hundred, to teach the Catholics how to manage the sugar-manufactories erected by the industry of the Mussulmans, to make a proper distribution of the water in the canals and aqueducts of irrigation necessary to fructify the soil, and to direct the manner in which the rice was to be preserved in the granaries constructed by the Moors. Watson's *Philip III.*, i. 441.

the country round Navarin ; but they succeeded in effecting a
landing at Kenchries, sacking the town of Corinth, and securing
five hundred prisoners [1].   In 1612 the Florentine galleys
executed an enterprise which had been attempted in vain
both by the Spaniards and the Knights of Malta.   They
stormed the citadel of Cos or Lango, and carried off from
the island one thousand two hundred prisoners.   They captured many Turkish merchantmen, and ravaged the coasts of
Greece from the island of Leucadia to the island of Cyprus [2].
To replace the ships lost by the Othoman navy in 1612 and
1613 without draining the treasury, the sultan ordered the
Greeks to build and equip twenty galleys, and the Armenians
nine ; so that the more the Christian subjects of the Porte
were plundered by the Christian navies of Western Europe,
the more they were oppressed by the sultan's government [3].

Sultan Mohammed II. closed the Black Sea to every Christian power.   After capturing in succession all the towns
possessed by the Genoese in Asia Minor and the Crimea, and
destroying their commercial establishments, in the year 1475
he occupied Caffa (Theodosia) and Tana (Azof), the great
depôts of their eastern trade, and expelled them from the
Black Sea.   From this time the western Christians were
prohibited from passing out of the Bosphorus, and during
the sixteenth and seventeenth centuries no Christian flag
was allowed to navigate the Euxine.   All knowledge of
its shores was lost, its cities lay beyond the sphere of trade,

---

[1] Knolles, ii. 906 ; Vertot, iv. 129.

[2] Knolles, ii. 908, 917 ; Hammer, viii. 202.   At this time the value of slaves
was considerable, for it was the fashion in the south of Europe to have captive
Turks or Moors, and frequently Greeks, in a foreign dress, as domestics.   Sir
Francis Cottington writes from Spain in 1610, that the slaves were suspected
of committing many murders.   He adds, ' and not unlikely, for that few did here
serve themselves with other than captive Turks and Moors ; and so the multitude
of them was very great.'   Watson's *Philip III.*, ii. 385.

[3] Spon describes the ravages of the Christian corsairs in the vicinity of Athens.
In the year 1676 they plundered the village of Khasia, at the entrance of the
defile of Phyle.   ii. 75, 101, 208, 213.   Megara paid two hundred and fifty
bushels of wheat to the corsair Creveliers as an annual tribute.   ii. 220.
Wheler also gives several instances of the extent to which the corsairs carried
their devastations on the mainland.   The exploits of three famous corsairs,
Fleuri, Creveliers, and a Greek named Kapsi, are mentioned in *Histoire nouvelle
des anciens Ducs de l'Archipel*, 306, 324.   A MS. in the library of the Arsenal
at Paris, entitled ' Estat de la Marine Othomane, par de la Croix, augmenté
des divers voyages, combats, et rencontres des galères depuis l'an 1679,' No. 682,
would probably furnish some interesting information concerning the extent to
which piracy was carried at this time.   See also Rycaut, *Present State of the Greek
Church*, 337, 356.

and the countries once frequented by Genoese and Venetian merchants became as much a region of mystery as they had been before Jason made his voyage in search of the golden fleece. But the seamen of Genoa still repeated vague tales of the wealth once gained by navigating its stormy waters, and the merchants cherished traditions of the riches of Caffa and the splendour of Trebizond.

The commercial system of the Othoman government has generally allowed importation to be freely carried on at fixed duties, but it has prohibited the exportation of the necessaries of life without a special license, and it has subjected most other articles of export to restrictions and monopolies. Under this system trade soon languished. The cities on the shores of the Black Sea, which had been rich and populous until the time of their conquest by the Othomans, declined and fell into ruins. The sites of many were deserted. Cherson itself ceased to exist. The plains, which had furnished Athens with grain, were uncultivated, and thinly peopled by nomades. Extensive provinces became utterly desolate, and at last received a new race of inhabitants, composed of exiles from Poland and fugitive slaves from Russia, who formed several independent communities under the name of Cossacks. The Cossacks who inhabited the banks of the Dnieper, being orthodox Christians, waged a constant warfare with the Turks and Tartars, and, like the Russians, who had inhabited these provinces before the invasion of the Monguls, often sought plunder and slaves by making piratical expeditions with small vessels in the Black Sea.

In the year 1613 the city of Sinope was surprised by the Cossacks, whose devastations generally ruined only the Christians who were engaged in commercial enterprises on these coasts. At this time, however, the Othoman naval force was so weak, that the Cossacks succeeded in capturing two of the sultan's galleys with a considerable amount of treasure on board [1].

In 1624 the Cossacks entered the Bosphorus with a fleet of one hundred and fifty small galleys, carrying each about forty men. They plundered Buyukderé, Yenikeui, and Stenia,

---

[1] Hammer, viii. 206. The ravages of the Cossacks are mentioned by Knolles, ii. 921; and Rycaut, *History of the Turkish Empire from 1623 to 1677*, p. 4; Hammer, ix. 162, x. 342.

setting fire to the buildings in order to distract the attention of the Turks and prevent immediate pursuit, and by this manœuvre they succeeded in escaping with their booty. Next year they plundered the environs of Trebizond. In 1630 they pillaged the coasts of Thrace, landing at Kili, Meidia, Sizeboli, Varna, and Baltshik, and collecting a rich booty and many slaves. In 1639 they fought a naval battle with the Othoman fleet off the Crimea. In 1654 they plundered the European coast near Baltshik, and the Asiatic coast in the neighbourhood of Eregli ; nor did these ravages cease, until the final conquest of Crete and peace with Venice enabled the Porte to send a large division of the Othoman fleet into the Black Sea, to blockade the mouths of the rivers from which the Cossack boats issued on their plundering expeditions.

In 1614, Maina, which, from its rock-coast and precipitous mountains, was regarded as less exposed to the inroads of foreign invaders than the rest of Greece, was visited by the capitan-pasha, who took strong measures to prevent a repetition of such attacks as the Spaniards had made in 1601. The success of the invaders had been facilitated by several Greeks, both among the clergy and the laity; and to prevent the recurrence of similar acts of treason, the capitan-pasha placed garrisons in the forts, and made arrangements for the regular payment of the tribute to the Porte, which from this period was collected with great regularity. In 1619 a Florentine squadron ravaged the islands of the Archipelago ; and in 1620 the Knights of Malta plundered the coast of the Morea and captured Castel Tornese, of which they destroyed a part of the works. In addition to these external miseries, the sufferings of the Greek population were increased in 1622 by fiscal oppression, which owed its existence to a successful revolt of the sipahis, who obtained from the sultan's government the right of collecting the haratch as a security for the regular issue of their pay. This right they farmed out in districts by public auction, and as the sipahis in every province were directly interested in supporting the exactions of the collectors of the tax, this measure greatly increased the sufferings of the Christians, and accelerated the impoverishment and de-population of Greece [1].

---

[1] Hammer, viii. 205, 260, 316 ; Vertot, iv. 132 ; Spon, *Voyage*, i. 122.

The war which cost the republic of Venice the island of Crete, owed its origin to the incessant irritation caused by the Western corsairs in the Archipelago. Some strong measures adopted by the Venetians to suppress the piracies committed by Turkish and Barbary corsairs in the Adriatic, created much dissatisfaction on the part of the Othoman government, which looked chiefly to the Mohammedan corsairs as a protection against the Christian corsairs in the Levant, and considered it the duty of the Venetians to suppress the piracies of these Christians. The Porte at last resolved to seek a profitable revenge, and a pretext soon presented itself. Some quarrels in the serai induced the Kislar-aga to undertake the pilgrimage to Mecca. He sailed from Constantinople with three galleys, in which he had embarked his immense wealth. Among his slaves was the woman that had nursed the eldest son of the reigning Sultan Ibrahim, who succeeded to the throne as Mohammed IV. The Knights of Malta were duly informed of the departure of this squadron by their spies. They attacked and captured the galleys, after a desperate combat, in which the Kislar-aga and most of the Turks of rank on board were slain. Three hundred and fifty men, and thirty women, several of whom were young and beautiful, were, however, secured as slaves. Among these was the young nurse with her own child, whom the Knights of Malta pretended was a son of Sultan Ibrahim. The Maltese carried their prizes into the secluded port of Kalismene, on the southern coast of Crete, in order to refit.

When the news of this capture reached Constantinople, the personal feelings of Sultan Ibrahim were deeply wounded, and he was strongly urged to avenge the insult; but as he feared to attack Malta, he resolved to make the Venetians responsible for the shelter which the corsairs had found in Crete. The Porte pretended that Venice was a tributary state, and was bound to keep the Archipelago free from Christian corsairs, in return for the great commercial privileges it enjoyed in the Othoman empire. Preparations were made for attacking Crete, but the project was concealed from the Venetian senate, under the pretence of directing the expedition against Malta. The Venetians, however, had good reason for concluding that their possessions offered a more inviting lure to the ambition of the Othomans than the fortress of Malta, and that Crete would be invaded in the same treacherous manner as Cyprus; but the republic resolved to make every sacrifice to avoid war. Though the sultan remained at peace with the republic, several circumstances occurred which convinced the senate that hostilities could not be avoided. A Venetian ship, laden with stores for Candia, was attacked by some Turkish corsairs. One of the Turkish ships was sunk, but the others which escaped spread the report as far as Constantinople, that they had been assailed by the Venetians[1]. Yet, as the sultan still refrained from declaring war, the republic hoped that its explanations, both with regard to the impossibility of preventing the entrance of the Maltese into the desert port in Crete, and the proofs that the transport had only acted in self-defence, were satisfactory to the Porte. The senate flattered itself that the storm preparing at Constantinople would really burst on Malta.

The Othoman fleet sailed from Constantinople attended by numerous transports, stopped at Chios and Karystos where it received considerable reinforcements, and after embarking additional troops at the port of Thermisi, in Argolis, the whole expedition again dropped anchor in the port of Navarin. It was not until it sailed from that port that the real object of attack was announced to the captains of the

---

[1] The Othoman government was never more insolent to the Christians than at this time. Rycaut (59) mentions an anecdote which proves that the oppressive conduct of the government to Christian traders at Constantinople rivalled the rapacity of the corsairs at sea. In 1649, thirteen English ships were forced to transport troops and ammunition to Crete (p. 83). In 1662, eleven Englishmen were taken by the Turks and reduced to slavery. They were part of the crew of the 'Ann,' an English frigate, whose captain landed sixty men to cut wood in the Morea. The ambassador, who could not reclaim them, as they were taken plundering and burning the forests, ransomed them for one thousand four hundred dollars (p. 129). Justice seemed to have been as little respected by the Christians as by the Turks, in the East, at this time, though on one occasion the mufti observed that the English always persisted in what they said, even at the peril of their lives; which he considered a proof of their obstinacy, and of the rudeness of their nature, not of their love of truth and justice. Hammer, x. 268. Though the king of France affected to be the staunchest friend of the sultan in Christendom, and his representative at Constantinople claimed to be treated with peculiar honours, the French now fared no better than others. In 1658, M. de la Haye, the French ambassador, sent his son to confer with the grand-vizier Mohammed Kueprili, who was then at Adrianople. The grand-vizier, offended at the behaviour of the envoy, ordered his servants to administer the bastinado to young De la Haye, which was done with great severity. The ambassador himself was subsequently imprisoned, and Louis XIV. was forced to digest the insult. Hammer, xi. 45.

ships. The announcement was received with enthusiasm, for
the disastrous siege of Malta in 1565 made the bravest Turks
fearful of attacking that fortress. In the month of June
1645, the Othoman army landed before Khania, which capitulated on the 17th of August. This treacherous commencement of the war was considered by all Christian powers as
authorizing them to dispense with all the formalities of international law in lending assistance to the Venetians. The
war of Candia lasted nearly twenty-five years, and during
this long and celebrated struggle the Venetians generally
maintained a superiority at sea; yet they were unable to
prevent the Othoman navy from throwing in supplies of
fresh troops and stores, so that the Othoman army was
enabled to command the whole island, and to keep Candia,
and the other fortresses of which the Venetians retained possession, either blockaded or besieged. The Greeks generally
favoured the Turks, who encouraged them to cultivate their
lands by purchasing the produce at a liberal price, for the
use of the army. Indeed, the communications of the invading
army with the Othoman empire were often interrupted for
many months, and without the supplies it derived from the
Greek cultivators, it would have been impossible to have
maintained a footing in Crete. The fact that the Othoman
troops found the means of persisting in the undertaking until
success at last rewarded their perseverance, is of itself a strong
testimony in favour of the excellent discipline of the Othoman
armies in the field. The Venetians in vain endeavoured to
compel the Turks to abandon the siege of Candia, by landing
troops on different parts of the island and destroying the
harvests of the Greek inhabitants. No important result was
produced by the partial devastation of small districts by
bodies of men who dared not venture to remain long on
shore, or to march far from their ships. The spirit of pillage
displayed both by the officers and men, generally rendered
the enterprises of the Venetians ineffectual as military operations[1]. In the meantime the squadrons of the republic often
ravaged the coasts of the Othoman empire, and on one occasion they carried off about five thousand slaves from the
coast of the Morea, between Patras and Coron[2]. In the year

---

[1] Daru, *Histoire de Venise*, iv. 603; Hammer, xi. 103.
[2] It was on hearing of these ravages that sultan Ibrahim is said to have pro-

1656, after Mocenigo's great victory at the Dardanelles, the Venetians took possession of the islands of Tenedos and Lemnos, but they were driven from these conquests by the Othoman fleet in the following year.

At the end of the year 1666, the grand-vizier, Achmet Kueprili, one of the greatest ministers of the Othoman empire, assumed the command of the besieging army. The whole naval force of Venice, and numerous bands of French and Italian volunteers, attempted to force the grand-vizier to raise the siege; but the skill of the Italian engineers, the valour of the French nobles, and the determined perseverance of Morosini, were vain against the strict discipline and steady valour of the Othoman troops. The works of the besiegers were pushed forward by the labours of a numerous body of Greek pioneers, and the fire of the powerful batteries at last rendered the place untenable. At this crisis Morosini proved himself a daring statesman and a sincere patriot. When he found that he must surrender the city, he resolved to make his capitulation the means of purchasing peace for the re-public. The step was a bold one, for though the senate was convinced of the necessity of concluding a treaty as soon as possible, the extreme jealousy of the Venetian govern-ment made it dangerous for Morosini to act without express authority. Morosini, however, seeing the peril to which his country would be exposed, if the favourable moment which now presented itself was lost, assumed all the responsibility of the act, and signed the treaty. Its conditions were ratified by the senate, but the patriotic general was accused of high treason on his return to Venice. He was honourably acquitted, but remained for many years unemployed. On the 27th September 1669, Achmet Kueprili received the keys of Candia, and the republic of Venice resigned all right to the island of Crete, but retained possession of the three insular fortresses of Karabusa, Suda, and Spinalonga, with their valuable ports. No fortress is said to have cost so much blood and treasure, both to the besiegers and the defenders, as Candia; yet the Greeks, in whose territory it was situated, and who could

---

posed exterminating the Christians (*see* above, p. 30); but his rage was probably chiefly directed against the Catholics in Turkey, as friends and spies of the Venetians, not against his own orthodox subjects, who at this period displayed a decided preference for the Othoman domination. Hammer, x. 111.

have furnished an army from the inhabitants of Crete sufficiently numerous to have decided the issue of the contest,
were the people who took least part in this memorable war.
So utterly destitute of all national feeling was the Hellenic
race at this period[1].

The position of Maina has given that district a degree of
importance in the modern history of Greece incommensurate
with the numbers of the inhabitants, and with the influence
it has exercised on the Greek nation. Pedants have termed
the Mainates descendants of the ancient Spartans, though the
Spartan race was extinct before the Roman conquest; and
history points clearly to the alternative, that they must be
either descended from the Helots, who became freemen after
the extinction of the Spartans, or from the Perioikoi, who
disappear as a separate class in the great body of Roman
provincials. To an older genealogy they can have no pretensions. The population of the twenty-four Laconian towns,
which received the confirmation of their municipal charters
from Augustus as Eleuthero-Lacones, consisted of burghers,
who, as a privileged caste, probably became extinct when the
towns they inhabited became depopulated. We learn from
Pausanias, that about a century and a half after these towns
received their charters, six had already ceased to exist; of
the eighteen whose names he records, only eight are situated
within the limits of Maina[2].

It is said that Maina never submitted to a foreign conqueror.
Though the assertion is repeated by many writers of authority,
this also is a vulgar error. It might be said with greater
truth that order and justice never reigned in Maina. Foreign
force has more than once established the supremacy of
strangers since the extinction of the Roman domination, yet
it is impossible not to feel some admiration for a small population which shows itself always ready to make some sacrifices
to defend its independence against foreigners. Our sympathy
leads us to overlook the evils of a state of anarchy which makes
every man a warrior, and we fondly admit, on the scantiest

---

[1] During the war of Candia, several of the islands of the Archipelago were
compelled to pay their taxes twice over; for as the Venetians generally commanded the sea, they levied payment by force, while policy induced the inhabitants
to remit the usual amount of tribute to the Porte. *Relation de l'Isle de Sant-Erini,*
par le Père Richard, 29, 376.   [2] Pausanias, iii. 21. 6.

proof, that a patriotic cause which we approve has always met with the success it merited. A disposition to eulogize every armed resistance to power has also caused the misapplication of a good deal of rhetoric by continental writers, who have made Maina the medium for parading a love of liberty abroad which shunned exhaling itself in domestic patriotism. The fact is, that Maina has submitted to the domination of the Romans, the Byzantine emperors, the Sclavonians, the Franks, the Venetians, and the Othoman sultans, but it has never been a servile, and rarely an obedient province.

The geographical configuration of the mountain range, which forms the great promontory called Maina, renders it of difficult access by land as well as by sea, and it has successfully repulsed many invaders, and obtained favourable treatment from every conqueror. Its population, being dependent for many of the necessaries of life on foreign commerce, is easily compelled to submit to reasonable terms of capitulation when attacked by an enemy powerful enough to occupy its ports and blockade its coasts, and prudent enough not to attempt any expedition into the interior of the country; as was seen by the ease with which the capitan-pasha compelled it to pay the haratch in 1614.

Another prevalent error concerning Maina is, that the whole district consists of a poor and arid territory. This is very far from being the case with its two northern divisions. In the year 1843 Maina was more densely peopled and more productive than Attica, excluding Athens from the calculation, as being the capital of the Greek kingdom, and the seat of a centralized system of administration. Maina is divided by nature into three divisions, western, eastern, and southern. The district lying to the west of the great ridge of Taygetus overlooks the plain of Messenia, and possesses two ports, from which its commercial business is carried on, Armyros and Vitylos[1]. It exports a considerable quantity of silk, oil, valonia, and red dye, and imports grain and iron. The wealth of this district in the thirteenth century is mentioned by Pachymeres, and is recorded in a poem written towards the end of the eighteenth[2].

---

[1] The produce of Western or Ἔξω Μάνη is thus described: Μετάξι, λάδι περισσὸν, καὶ πρινοκόκκο κάμνει.

[2] Pachymeres, i. 52. I have quoted the passage in vol. iv. p. 199. The poem

The eastern district, of which Marathonisi is the principal
port, is nearly as populous and as productive as the western.
Its exports consist of valonia and silk ; but, formerly, it exported a considerable quantity of cotton [1]. The southern district, on the contrary, is a promontory of barren rocks, termi-
nating in Cape Matapan. It commences at Tzimova, and is
called by the northern Mainates, as well as by the other Greeks,
on account of the manners of its inhabitants, Kakavoulia,
the land of bad designs. The furious winds which generally
prevail arrest vegetation ; yet, wherever there is a ravine with
a little soil, it is laboriously cultivated by the women, and the
population is considerable. Wheaten bread is rarely seen,
and the common food is a black cake made of lupins. The
poem already mentioned sarcastically notices its products,
as consisting of quails and the fruit of the cactus. Beans
and barley are luxuries [2]. Its inhabitants have been for ages
more celebrated for their piracies than for their independence.
The Byzantine emperors and the western Crusaders appear
to have found that the only way to restrain the piracy of the
southern Mainates was to destroy all the towns on the coast.
Of these towns, and of the cisterns which supplied them
with water, considerable remains still exist. After the destruction of their towns, the people became even more dependent on piracy for their subsistence than they had been
previously. Their poverty, their strange usages, their patience
under privations, their thefts, their bloody feuds, and the
daring courage displayed in their acts of piracy, rendered the
Kakavouliots the wonder and the terror of the other Greeks.
The vices of their character and the peculiarities of their
country were thus attributed to all the Mainates [3].

was found by Colonel Leake, and some part of it, with a translation of the
remainder, is published by him in his *Travels in the Morea*, vol. i. p. 332. The
whole poem is printed in *Das Griechische Volk*, by Maurer, vol. iii. p. 1. He is
wrong, however, in supposing that the date is the time of Tzanet Koutouphari,
who was named Bey of Maina by Hassan Ghazi. The Tzanet of the poem was
Gligoraki, who held the office of Bey for ten years, from 1785 to 1795, when
he was deposed for favouring French influence.

[1] The produce of Eastern or Κάτω Μάνη is thus described : Ὁποῦ βαμβάκι περισσὸν καὶ βαλανίδι κάμνει. Μάνη is the name given by the modern Greeks to the
district, corrupted from that of Μάϊνα, the chief town during the Byzantine empire.

[2] Ὀρτύκια, φραγκόσυκα ἡ πρώτη τοὺς ἐντράδα,
Καρπὸν κουκία μοναχὰ καὶ ξεροκρίθι κάμνει.

[3] Αὐτοὶ τὴν Μάνην τὴν λοιπὴν τὴν κακονοματίζουν,
Καὶ ὁποῦ πάγουν τ' ὄνομα αὐτῆς τὸ μαγαρίζουν.

The celebrity of Maina, and the independence it had assumed during the war of Candia, which secured to it the constant protection of the Venetian fleet, induced Achmet Kueprili to take measures for its complete subjection. He knew that as long as the pirates of Maina remained unpunished, and the ports of Maina afforded shelter to Venetian and Maltese cruisers, the commerce of Crete would be insecure and the conquest imperfect. Accordingly, in the year 1670, while Achmet was reposing at Chios, after his victory, he sent Kuesy Ali Pasha with a strong naval and military force to re-establish the sultan's supremacy in Maina. The piratical vessels of Porto Quaglio and of Tzimova were pursued into their places of refuge, and captured or burned; but the Othoman force made no attempt to attack the Kakavouliots in their fastnesses. On the other hand, the inhabitants of the northern part of Maina, being dependent on foreign commerce, were easily compelled to submit. Ali Pasha occupied the ports of Armyros, Vitylos, and Marathonisi with his fleet, and landed troops, who succeeded in occupying the fortresses of Zarnata, Kielapha, and Passava. By this means he obtained complete command over the communications of the Mainates with the sea. The forts were repaired, armed with artillery, and strongly garrisoned. No expedition of Turkish troops was attempted into the interior, but Ali executed the orders of Achmet Kueprili with ability as well as energy; he formed alliances with several of the leading chieftains who were engaged in feuds with their neighbours, and by supplying them with arms and ammunition, and refusing to employ Mussulman troops in their broils, he rendered himself arbiter of their disputes. He then showed them that it was in his power to ruin and even to starve them, unless they consented to submit to his orders and pay haratch to the sultan. The amount which they agreed to pay was only fifteen purses, at that time rather more than £1500 sterling; but whether haratch tickets were distributed by the chieftains among the rural population, either in 1614 or at this time, seems not to be accurately known. By some it is asserted to have been the case; by others it is denied. The regular custom-duties were exacted on the exports of Maina by the Turkish authorities at Armyros, Zarnata, Vitylos, Kielapha, Marathonisi, and Passava, but they were generally farmed to

Mainate chieftains ; while, to repress permanently the piracies on the coast, Othoman galleys were stationed at Tzimova and Porto Quaglio. By these measures Achmet Kueprili gave a degree of security to the commerce of the Levant which it had not enjoyed for many generations, and his fame as a states- man in Christendom soon rivalled the military glory he had gained as the conqueror of Candia. The Othoman garrisons diminished the influence of the chieftains, and deprived many of those who had long lived by feuds and piracy of their means of livelihood ; but, at the same time, property was not rendered more secure, nor industry more profitable. The Mainates, consequently, became eager to quit their country, and as soon as it was known that they would meet a good reception from the Neapolitan viceroys, a considerable emi- gration took place to Apulia [1]. About the same time another colony of Mainates emigrated to Corsica [2].

---

[1] Spon, i. 123 ; *Sendschreiben aus dem Lager vor Modon vom* 19/29 *Julii*, 1686, p. 10 ; a small German tract, printed in 1686, written by a volunteer in the Saxon contingent of the Venetian army. [It was probably at this time that the Greek ballad called ʽΗ Ῥωμαιοποῦλα, on the subject of a Greek girl refusing the suit of a Turkish lover, notwithstanding her mother's solicitations, made its way into southern Italy. It is found in Comparetti's *Saggi dei Dialetti Greci dell' Italia meridionale* (No. 36, p. 38), and is a favourite subject in Greece at the present day. Compare the corresponding ballads in Passow's *Popularia Carmina Graeciae recen- tioris*, Nos. 574, 574 a, and 587. *See* also vol. i. *Greece under the Romans*, p. 401 *note*. Spon, whose evidence is referred to above, was in Greece shortly after this emigration took place. ED.]

[2] It was on the 3rd October, 1673, that an emigration of seven hundred and fifty persons took place from Vitylos. These families, after passing the winter at Genoa, were settled by the Senate on lands granted to them by the Republic at Paomia in Corsica. The greater part of these colonists are said to have been expelled from the island on account of their attachment to Genoa, in the year 1730, when the Corsicans rebelled, but a few families remained at Ajaccio when France took possession of Corsica. Villemain, *Essai historique sur l'état des Grecs*, 123. [In 1731 the Greeks were expelled from Paomia, but not from the island ; they remained at Ajaccio until Corsica passed into the hands of France, and in 1774 they were placed at Cargese, on a headland on the west coast, about a day's journey north of Ajaccio, near the position where Paomia stood. At that place they have remained until the present time, except during the period from 1790 to 1814, when their neighbours, taking the opportunity of the French revolution, again drove them out ; and, when they returned, a part of the colony preferred to remain behind in Ajaccio. I visited Cargese in 187?, and found the com- munity to consist of about 400 persons. The Greek that is spoken there is almost identical with the Romaic of the Greek islands ; but it will soon be extinct, for the older people speak Corsican with equal fluency, and the younger generation are for the most part unacquainted with it : they find it more profitable to ignore their nationality. They are Roman Catholics, it having been stipulated from the first that they should submit to the Pope ; but they are allowed to observe the Greek rite, and still use the old service-books which they brought with them from Maina, and the priests wear the dress of the Greek Church. A short notice of the colony will be found in the *Journal of Philology* for 1876 (vol. vi. p. 196), prefixed to a collection of their ballads, which were obtained for me from the mouth of the people. Most of these must have come down from the time of their migration, for

A considerable decrease took place in the numbers of the Greek race during the seventeenth century, and a still greater decline is observable in the material wealth and moral condition of the people.   Communications by sea and land became more difficult for the Greeks, who were reduced to live in a more secluded, poorer, and ruder manner.   In the mean time, the numbers of the Turkish landed proprietors and militia increased, and janissaries were permanently formed into corporations in the principal towns.   Thus, the relative importance of the Greek to the Turkish population was diminished on the continent, and in the islands misery and the ravages of the corsairs thinned the numbers of the inhabitants.   It was during this century that many fresh colonies of Albanians took possession of the Hellenic soil[1].   The Greeks were never so much depressed and despised, and never was the number of renegades so considerable among the middle and lower orders of society.   Immediately after the conquest of the Greek empire, the higher orders had shown much greater readiness to forsake their religion than the mass of the nation.   We find several pashas of the name of Palaeologos among the renegades, and the learned George Amiroutzes of Trebizond abandoned the orthodox faith in his declining years, not to mention innumerable examples of less eminent persons.   The Greeks at that time were not exposed to any very serious sufferings on account of their religion, and they suffered less fiscal oppression from the sultans than they had previously suffered from their native emperors.   Until the end of the sixteenth century the Othoman government was remarkable for the religious toleration it displayed.   The Jews, when expelled from Spain, were charitably received in Turkey.   The orthodox, who were denied the exercise of their religious forms in Italy, and the heretics who were driven into exile by the tyranny of the

they correspond to some of those that are now sung in Greece.   The only occasion on which we have evidence of communication between the colony and the fatherland, was when two persons of the name of Stephanopulos were sent on a political mission by Buonaparte to Greece.   ED.]

[1] The majority of the peasantry of the island of Ios were of the Albanian race in the early part of the seventeenth century. If any of their descendants remain at present, they have forgotten their language, and laid aside their peculiar customs.   The present inhabitants appear to be entirely Greek.   *Relation de l'Isle de Sant-Erini*, par le Père Richard, 337.   The Albanians were settled in Ios by Mark Crispo, brother of John II., Duke of Naxos.   *Histoire nouvelle des anciens Ducs de l'Archipel*, 214; see vol. iv. *Mediaeval Greece*, p. 302.

Inquisition, found that toleration in the Othoman dominions which was denied in every Christian land. The religious bigotry of the Mussulmans was inflamed into a spirit of persecution by the injustice and intolerance of the Christians —by the expulsion of their co-religionaries from Spain, and by the refusal of every Christian power with whom they held intercourse to allow the public exercise of the Moham- medan worship and the erection of mosques in Christian cities. Still, it was not from direct oppression alone that the number of the Greek renegades was increased towards the middle of the seventeenth century. Those who quitted the orthodox faith were generally led to take that step by a feeling of despair at their despised position in society, and by a desire to bear arms and mix in active life. The spirit of the age was military, and violence was one of its characteristics. The Greeks could only defend their families against the insolence of the Turks and the rapacity of the Frank corsairs by changing their religion; when galled by acts of injustice, and eager for revenge, they often flew to the most violent and most effectual remedy their imagination could suggest, and that was to embrace Mohammedanism.

David Chytraeus, who witnessed the public rejoicings at the circumcision of Mohammed, the son of Murad III. (A.D. 1582), tells us that he then witnessed the miserable spectacle of a great number of Greeks embracing the Mohammedan faith. On this occasion about one hundred Christians, Greeks, Albanians, and Bulgarians daily abjured the Christian religion during the whole period of the celebration, which lasted forty days[1]. Cases of apostasy are even found among the highest dignitaries of the orthodox church, and in 1661 an ex-metro- politan of Rhodes had the honour of being the first Mussul- man who was condemned to death by a fetva of the mufti[2]. The preponderant influence of the tribute-children and of renegades in the administration of the Othoman empire, and the great inducement held out to apostasy, is proved by the fact, that the greater number of the grand-viziers before the middle of the seventeenth century were either renegades or the children of Christians—Greeks, Albanians,

---

[1] Compare Chytraeus, *Hodoeporicon*, in Lonicerus, ii. 202, 8vo.; and Hammer, vii. 151.
[2] Hammer, xi. 117.

and Sclavonians. Of the forty-eight grand-viziers who succeeded to the office after the conquest of Constantinople,
twelve only were native Turks[1]. A large portion of the
Greek population in Euboea and Crete embraced the Mohammedan religion, and about the end of the seventeenth century
it is supposed that at least a million of the Mussulmans
in Europe were descended from Christian parents who had
abjured their religion[2].

---

[1] Hammer, viii. 421.

[2] Pococke (*A description of the East and some other countries,* vol. ii. part 1.
p. 268) mentions the apostasy of the Christians in Crete. [Some of the Cretans
must have been Mohammedans only in name, for there are still concealed
Christians among them, though the number of these has declined of late years.
These baptize their children secretly, and observe other Christian rites in private.
The greater number are now to be found on the northern slopes of Mount Ida.
Ed.]

CHAPTER III.

THE change produced by the submission of Greece to
the Turks was effected with unexampled rapidity, for a single
generation extinguished all the boasted intelligence of the
Hellenic race, and effaced every sentiment of patriotism
and moral dignity in the higher orders of society. The
people resigned themselves to passive slavery, but the nobles
and dignified clergy became active as well as servile syco-
phants. The sack of Constantinople, and the depopulation
of Trebizond, destroyed the power of the aristocracy, and
drove the learned into exile. This, though a calamity to
the courtiers and pedants, who consumed a large portion of

the fiscal burdens imposed on the people, was in some degree
a national benefit, since it swept away a class of men who
had formed an insuperable barrier to the moral improvement
of a degraded nation, and to the political reform of a corrupt
administration. The destruction of the higher classes relieved the people from the trammels of innumerable privileges
and monopolies.

The first effect of the extinction of the Byzantine aristocracy and the flight of the literary men was to constitute
the provincial landowners and the peasant cultivators of the
soil the real representatives of the Greek nation. The agricultural classes formed at this period the majority of the
Greeks, and, though ignorant and bigoted, they were far
superior to the aristocracy in usefulness and honesty. The
inhabitants of each rural district, and often of each valley
in the mountains, lived in a state of isolation, connected with
the world beyond its limits only by the payment of taxes
to the sultan's government, and of ecclesiastical dues to the
orthodox church. They were profoundly ignorant of all the
political events which were passing beyond their own horizon.
Their religion alone awakened some general ideas in their
minds, but the priesthood, to whom they owed these ideas,
possessed only such elements of knowledge as were accordant
with a corrupt ecclesiastical system. The intellectual cultivation of the Greeks was consequently restricted for nearly
two centuries to a very slight acquaintance with the national
literature, from which they imbibed little more than a vague
persuasion of their own superiority over the rest of mankind,
as being Romans and Christians—the true representatives of
the ancient conquerors of the world, and the only followers
of the pure orthodox faith[1]. This ignorance of the world

---

[1] Ῥωμαῖοι καὶ Χριστιανοί. Until the revival of learning among the Greeks,
towards the end of the last century, when they caught the enthusiasm for
liberty awakened by the success of the American Revolution, they had been
proud of the name of Romans. The appellation Hellenes was given only to
the pagans of ancient Greece. Even at present, although the Greeks have
imbibed their political civilization from the French school of the Revolution,
they still arrogate exclusive orthodoxy to their Church, and the people restrict
the appellation of Christians solely to the Eastern Church. Before the commencement of the present century, no modern Greek would have boasted of
any ancestral connection with the pagan Hellenes, any more than he would
yet think of pretending to a Pelasgic, Dorian, Ionian, or Achaian pedigree.
The Greeks now overlook the fact, that where there have been no genealogies
there can be no purity of blood. Of all people it might be thought that the
Greeks would be the least disposed to talk much of their ancestors, as they

at large restricted the feelings of the Greeks to a few local and hereditary prejudices. Their thoughts were divided between the strict observance of ecclesiastical formalities and the eager pursuit of their individual interests. Superstition and bigotry became the most prominent national characteristics during the following centuries.

As soon as the great translocations of the inhabitants of various parts of Greece, effected by order of Mohammed II., had been completed, and the Othoman administration regularly established, the condition of the rural population was found to be much more tolerable under the government of the sultan than it had been under the Greek emperor. The agricultural classes were harassed by fewer exactions of forced labour, extraordinary contributions were rarely levied, and the mere fiscal burdens proved trifling when compared with the endless feudal obligations of the Frank, or the countless extortions of the Byzantine sovereignty. The material advantages enjoyed by the bulk of the Greek population at the commencement of the Othoman domination quickly reconciled the people to their Mussulman masters, and even the tithe of their male children was not considered too high a price for this increased security. A single child of each family was sent out into the darkness of Mohammedanism, as a scape-offering to preserve the flesh-pots of a Christian generation. The tameness and silence with which the Greek rural population submitted to this cruel exaction for two

---

must ascend through immediate progenitors who have been slaves and syco-phants for two thousand years, before they reach the last rays of liberty. Verily, the blood of Aristides, if it still flow in living veins, has flowed through polluted channels. Tacitus (*Ann*. ii. 55) tells us that the race of the old Athenian citizens was extinct in his day, and that Athens was then, as it is at present, peopled by an assemblage of men of different races. The native Athenians are only one-third of the whole population, and of these native Athenians more than one-third are of the Albanian race. who still use their own language in the streets of the capital of the Greek kingdom. [It is not quite accurate to say that at present ' the people restrict the appellation of Christians solely to the Eastern Church.' What is taught to the people in their catechisms is, that the universal Church is the aggregate of all the bodies of Christians which are found throughout the world, but that the Orthodox Church is in a higher and more guaranteed position. The further question of the value of the national pedigree of the modern Greeks is exposed to the same difficulties in discussion as the correspond-ing one of family pedigree. But in both the most important element is probably that of honourable associations in past times, with the obligations they involve ; and in the case of families it is usual for the sake of these to ignore many blots in the intermediate annals. The danger, both to individuals and nations, which no doubt Mr. Finlay felt strongly, is that of trading on the virtues of ancestors, instead of imitating them. ED.]

centuries, is the strongest proof of the demoralization of the Hellenic race.

The conquest of Greece by the Turks diminished the extent of country peopled by the Greeks. Large bodies of the population were removed to Constantinople and other cities of the sultan's dominions, to replace the ravages of war. The losses arising from these forced emigrations would, in all probability, have been soon replaced by the natural increase of the surviving Greek peasantry, had the state of the country allowed the cultivators of the soil to improve their condition. But this was the case only to a limited extent. The introduction of the feudal or timariot system created a Turkish military aristocracy in the rich agricultural districts in Greece; and no condition of society has proved more adverse to the increase of population, or to an amelioration of the condition of the people, than that in which a hereditary militia of proprietors has formed the predominant class. On the other hand, the Greek landowners, who had been in easy circumstances before the conquest, were no longer able to obtain slaves for the cultivation of their estates, nor to retain their former serfs by force, and they consequently soon descended to the rank of peasant proprietors, and were compelled to till their lands by their own labour. Their rights of pasturage, their property in fruit-bearing trees of the forest like the valonia oak, and in wild dye-woods, their profits from limekilns and charcoal, were all confiscated as invasions of the fisc, or transferred to Turkish feudatories, who received grants of estates in their vicinity. The extermination of the Byzantine aristocracy was no loss to the nation, for never did a more unprincipled set of men exist, as we find them portrayed in the life-like sketch which Cantacuzenos gives us of the archonts of the Morea, unless, indeed, they be compared with the official aristocracy created by the Othoman administration, and called Phanariots, from the filthy quarter of the Phanar in Constantinople where they dwelt and carried on their intrigues.

Even the peasant proprietors in many districts did not long enjoy the relief from oppression which cheered them during the early period of the Othoman domination. The devastations of war, the incursions of corsairs, the exactions of the Othoman officials, and the diminution of consumption, caused by the increased difficulties of transport, entailed the destruction of olive-groves, orchards, and vineyards. The Mussulman drank no wine, but he loved to sit by a public fountain under a broad platane tree. A portion of the water which the Greeks had reserved for their gardens was turned into the court of the mosque, and wasted on the roadside in numerous fountains. A little care, and a trifling expenditure, would have enabled the spring to supply both the gardens and the fountains; but few things have succeeded that required the smallest degree of constant care on the part of the Turks, and nothing has yet prospered that demanded unity of purpose between Othomans and Greeks.

The Othoman conquest effected a considerable change in the extent of country occupied by the Greek race, and in which the Greek language was predominant. Several extensive tracts in Thrace, Macedonia, and Thessaly were occupied by pastoral tribes from Asia Minor, called Yuruks, and whole districts were granted as military fiefs to Seljouk Turks, who had taken service under the early Othoman sultans, and received the name of Koniarides or Iconians[1]. These two classes are the only considerable portions of the Mussulman population in European Turkey which are not descended from Christian renegades or from tribute-children. The place that had been previously occupied by the Greeks, as the principal element of the urban population in Bulgaria, Thrace, and Macedonia, was filled by the Othoman Turks. Even within the limits of Greece and the Peloponnesus the Greek rural population abandoned extensive districts to the Albanian race, which extended its settlements, and became the sole inhabitants of many sites celebrated in ancient history. The Greek language was banished from its classic haunts, and the very names of Olympia, Delphi, and Nemea were forgotten in those spots which had once been the lungs of

---

[1] Leake, *Travels in Northern Greece*, iii. 174. But it is probable that the settlements of the Koniarides in Thessaly commenced as early as the time of the emperor Cantacuzenos. [In Urquhart's *Spirit of the East* (vol. i. pp. 334 foll.) there is an interesting account of the first settlement of the Koniarates in Thessaly, taken down from the mouth of the Kaimakam of Tournovo, a descendant of the original Turkish founder, a memoir of whose life is contained in an Arabic manuscript in the library of the town. According to this, Turakhan Bey, in the time of Murad II., when he had established himself in the country, but found his force of Turks too small to enable him to hold it, sent emissaries to Iconium, and induced five or six thousand families to emigrate from thence to Thessaly, where he gave them lands on the north of the plain. ED.]

Hellenic life. Albanian peasants cultivated the fields of Marathon and Plataea, drove their ploughshares over the roomy streets of the Homeric Mycenae, and fed their flocks on Helicon and Parnassus. The whole of Boeotia, Attica, Megaris, Corinthia, and Argolis, a considerable part of Laconia, several districts in Messenia, and a portion of Arcadia, Elis, and Achaia, were colonized by Albanians, whose descendants preserve their peculiar language and manners, their simple social habits, and their rude system of agriculture, to the present day[1]. In these districts the Turks dwelt as a territorial aristocracy, while the Greeks only survived in the towns as artizans and shopkeepers. The colonization of so large a portion of the eastern shores of Greece by an alien race, in an inferior grade of civilization, tended to diminish the influence of the Greek race in the sixteenth and seventeenth centuries, just as the earlier colonization of the country by the Sclavonians had produced a similar effect in the sixth and seventh centuries.

The energetic government of Mohammed II. revived the commerce of his Greek subjects. The concessions which the Italian republics had extorted from the weakness of the Greek emperors, were abolished; and the Othoman domination restored to the Greeks a share in the commerce of the Levant. Unfortunately the fiscal corruption of the sultan's government soon favoured the commerce of foreigners more than that of natives. Political advantages and large presents obtained relaxations of duties for the subjects of foreign states, which individual native merchants could not purchase. The foreign commerce of the Levant was again transferred to the western nations, while the coasting trade was destroyed by pirates. The Venetians and Genoese succeeded in securing to themselves commercial monopolies in the Othoman empire, and in rendering the reciprocity of trade, which they granted to the subjects of the sultan, an empty privilege[2]. The

---

[1] The words of Byron—
'Their place of birth alone is mute
To sounds which echo farther west
Than their sires' islands of the blest,'—
are literally true. I have visited hundreds of villages in Greece, and there are some at this moment in Attica, in spite of kingdom, constitution, and university, in which many of the women and children under ten years of age understand very few words of Greek.

[2] Even the republic of Ragusa complained to the sultan, as its protector, of the

authority of the Othoman government, nevertheless, enabled the Greeks to raise their commerce from the depressed condition into which it had fallen under the Greek emperors, and the material interests of the boatmen and petty merchants of Greece were greatly benefited by the conquest, though their advantages were not so apparent as those of the cultivators of the soil and of the regular clergy. Sultan Mohammed II. brought so great an alleviation of the sufferings of the people, by putting an end to the domestic feuds of the nobles, the civil wars of the despots, and the fiscal oppression of the emperors, that we must not wonder that he was regarded as a benefactor by the majority of the Greeks, in spite of the declamations of orators and historians. These benefits explain the tame submission of the Greeks to the dominion of the sultans, for the extermination of the Byzantine aristocracy caused an immediate improvement in the material condition of the lowest order of society engaged in agricultural pursuits, and removed the most obvious motive for resistance to foreign conquest. Unfortunately, the causes which enabled the people to better their condition physically, produced a moral and social debasement of the whole Hellenic race. The diminished population lived with little labour in plenteous ease. Olives, oil, fruit, wine, and silk were abundant. The plains were so easily cultivated as to furnish large supplies of wheat, of which a part was annually exported. Venice was dependent on the Othoman empire for the greater part of the grain it consumed during the fifteenth and sixteenth centuries; and the liberty of exporting wheat to France from Cyprus, the Morea, Negrepont, and Albania, was a favour which the diplomatic agents of the King of France often solicited from the Porte [1].

---

strictness of the Venetian protective system in 1484, which threatened to put an end to the trade of Ragusa. The Venetians declared the existence of their state depended on the maintenance of their prohibitive system. Navagiero, *Storia Italiana*, in Muratori, *Script. Rer. Ital.* xxiii. 1191. See some of the orders of the senate on this subject in Marin, *Storia civile e politica del commercio de' Veneziani*, vii. 326, 347.

[1] Guicciardini, *Istoria d'Italia*, lib. vi. p. 320. Wine, oil, soap, cheese, salt, morocco leather, dyeing materials, fruit, flax, cotton, silk, and valonia, were imported into Italy, as well as grain; Marin, *Storia del commercio de' Veneziani*, vii. 188, 203: wheat into France; *Négociations dans le Levant*, iii. 902. Cattle and grain were exported from the Morea and Roumelia to Sicily and Marseilles, at the end of the seventeenth century. Spon, *Voyage d'Italie, de Dalmatie, de Grèce et du Levant*, ii. 5, 7, 19. Currants were imported into England in large quantities at the beginning of the seventeenth century. English ships visited both Zante and

The Greeks failed to secure to themselves any permanent advantages from the various favourable circumstances in which they were placed by the revival of their commerce and the increased demand for the produce of their soil. As had been the case for centuries, their national character was in disaccord with their position. Partly from the jealous and envious disposition that prevents their uniting together for a common object or acting in concord for any length of time, and partly from the suspicion with which any popular action was regarded by the clergy, the Phanariots, and the Othoman government, the Greeks could neither form great mercantile associations, permanent and influential banking companies, nor well-organized rural municipalities. To carry on a secure and profitable commerce by sea, it was necessary to possess well-armed vessels, but it was only by singular favour and constant bribes that a Greek vessel could obtain a license to carry arms ; and even when armed there was some danger that any vessel under the Turkish flag would be treated as a pirate, in consequence of the jealousy of rival merchants in every port of the Mediterranean.

The long contests between the Greek clergy and the court of Rome, which prevailed from the recognition of the papal supremacy by Michael VIII. (Palaeologos), were only terminated by the death of the last Constantine, who died in communion with the Pope. The religious bigotry of the orthodox clergy, which reached the highest pitch of frenzy during the last years of the Greek empire, was calmed by the calamities which attended the sack of Constantinople,— for the orthodox viewed this great catastrophe as a divine judgment on the imperial heretic. The Greek priesthood, in the long struggle it carried on with the imperial government and the papal power, had succeeded in persuading the people that orthodoxy in doctrine, and the strict observance of ecclesiastical forms, were the true symbols of Greek nationality. The Greeks warmly espoused these opinions, and loudly expressed their thoughts with all their usual volubility and confidence. The orthodox enthusiasm was undoubtedly both national and sincere, yet never did such a loud and general

Cephalonia; and at the latter island they paid export duties to the republic of Venice for currants alone, to the amount of forty thousand scudi annually. Deshayes, *Voyage de Levant*, pp. 452, 468.

expression of public opinion produce so little moral effect. History has transmitted the name of no orthodox hero to posterity, who was honoured with the respect and blessings even of the Greeks themselves. The real heroes of Eastern nationality at the time of the conquest of Greece were the Catholic emperor Constantine and the Albanian prince Scanderbeg, and both were members of the papal, not of the orthodox church.

Mohammedan princes have generally been more tolerant to their unbelieving subjects than Christian rulers, the commands of the Koran having been more implicitly obeyed than the precepts of the Gospel. Mohammed II. granted the fullest toleration to the Greeks which the Koran allows to unbelievers, and motives of policy induced him to add some particular favours to the general toleration he conceded to all his Christian subjects. With that consummate prudence which he displayed on all great occasions during his unfeeling and violent career, he made the bigoted feelings of the orthodox instruments for the furtherance of his objects. He not only tolerated the political and social influence of the Greek clergy, but even added to it. In displaying this spirit of toleration, however, his object was not to favour the Christians ; it was to render the orthodox clergy a useful instrument of police for securing the tranquillity of his recent conquests and riveting the fetters with which he bound the people. It depended on Mohammed II., after the taking of Constantinople, to render the Greeks an expatriated race like the Jews, for their military weakness, political incompetency, and moral degradation had rendered them powerless to resist their conquerors. Four rival nations, each equal to the Greeks in number, were competing for his favour, and could have filled up any void created by forcible translocations of the Hellenic race. Had Mohammed II. treated Greece as Ferdinand and Isabella treated Granada, Turks, Sclavonians, Vallachians, and Albanians would have instantly occupied the country. But the conqueror chose a wiser course. He felt the fullest confidence that he could direct the minds of the Greeks, and master their intellects, as easily as he had conquered their persons, and without fear he gave them a new centre of nationality by restoring the orthodox patriarchate of Constantinople. He united all the dissevered members of the orthodox church under a central authority, over which he exercised a direct control as its real head. The boon thus voluntarily conferred on the Greek nation enlisted the prejudices and bigotry of the people in the cause of his government. He was accepted as the temporal head of the orthodox church, because he was regarded as its protector against Catholicism. By this insidious gift the sultan purchased the subservience of the Greeks, and for the two succeeding centuries his successors were the acknowledged defenders of the orthodox against the pretensions of the popes.

It must be owned that the contrast between Mussulman toleration and papal intolerance was too glaring not to extort some sentiments of gratitude towards the sultan, even from the hard character and utter selfishness of the Greek people. While the pope and the Christian princes in Western Europe were fierce in their persecution of heresy, and eager to extend the cruelties of the inquisition, the sultans of Turkey and Egypt were mild in their treatment of unbelievers, and tolerant in the exercise of their undoubted authority as absolute sovereigns. Not only was the Christian treated with more humanity in Mussulman countries than Mohammedans were treated in Christian lands, even the orthodox Greek met with more toleration from Mussulmans than from Catholics; and the knowledge of this difference formed one strong reason for the preference with which the Greeks clung to the government of the Othoman sultans in their wars with the Christian powers for more than two centuries.

Of one sad fact history leaves no doubt: the fabric of Greek society, private as well as public, was utterly corrupt. Vice was more universal among the Greeks than among the Turks. The venality of Greek officials, and the cowardice of Greek armies, had allowed the Othoman tribe to found an empire by conquests from the Greeks. The ease and rapidity with which the Greek nation was subdued, and the tameness with which the people bore the yoke imposed on them, prove that the moral degradation of the masses contributed as much to the national calamities as the worthlessness of the aristocracy and the clergy, or as the corruption of the imperial government. The moral inferiority of the Greek race at this period is forcibly intruded on the attention of the reader of

Othoman history. The orthodox Mussulman was remarkable for his strict observance of the moral obligations of the Mohammedan law: but the orthodox Christian neglected the great moral precepts of his religion, and was only attentive to the distinctive ceremonies and peculiar formalities of his own church. A strong sense of duty directed and controlled the conduct of the Mussulman in the everyday actions of life; while among the Greeks a sense of duty seems to have failed entirely, and there appears to have been an utter want of those deep mental convictions necessary to produce moral rectitude. Yet, among the Othomans, we find that the strict observance of all the outward formalities of their law was united with a profound devotion to its moral and religious ordinances. This remarkable circumstance must have originated in the wise system of education which enabled the Othoman Turk to emerge as a superior being from the corrupted populations of the Seljouk and Greek empires. Among the Greeks the regular performance of church ceremonies, and the fulfilment of some vain penance, became an apology for neglecting the weightiest obligations of Christ's moral law. In the fifteenth and sixteenth centuries, Islam breathed faith into the hearts of its votaries, while orthodoxy deadened the moral feelings of the soul, by using idolatrous forms as a substitute for faith. This spiritual elevation of Mohammedans long continued to form a marked contrast with the degraded moral condition of the orthodox Christians. No period of Greek history offers us so sad an example of the perversity with which man can stray from the guidance of truth, and set up the ordinances of man's imagination above the laws of God.

The nature of Mohammedanism gives it a political advantage over Christianity, which must not be overlooked in examining the relations between the Othomans and the Greeks. The outward forms of Islam are an inherent portion of its doctrines; they are tests of religion, not of orthodoxy; and the public manner in which they are hourly exhibited unite all Mussulmans together as one people, while by these very forms a strong line of separation is drawn between them and the rest of mankind. Thus all Mohammedans living in constant intercourse with Christians feel and act as if they composed one nation. The Arab, the Mongol, and the

K 2

Turk find that their common religion effaces their national differences.

Christianity presents another aspect. The religious divisions of Christians form as strong contrasts as their national distinctions. The Catholic and orthodox Greeks are as completely separated as the Greeks and Armenians. The Orthodox and the Catholics, the Armenians, the Nestorians, and the Jacobites, are as much separated by the articles of their faith as by the diversity of their nations. Those beyond the pale of Christianity could hardly believe that Christianity was really one religion, so marked were the distinctions among Christians, and so violent the animosity which the rival churches entertained to one another. In the individual, the contrast was as great as in the mass. The Mohammedan generally obeyed the commands of his prophet to the letter; while the Christian assumed the wildest license in interpreting the word of God. The pope taught publicly that the doctrines of Christ were not of universal application, and assumed the power of authorizing Christian princes to violate the promises they made to infidels even after they had sworn on the Gospel that they would keep their word[1]. This moral laxity among Christians, and want of an all-pervading religious faith, was the principal cause of the apostasies so prevalent in the fifteenth and sixteenth centuries. The Ottoman army and administration were filled with Christian renegades, while hardly an example could be found of a Mohammedan forsaking his religion.

The fermenting leaven of self-destruction, which exists in all corporate bodies placed beyond the direct control of public opinion, had so corrupted the Greek clergy in the fifteenth century, that the cause of Christianity suffered by the conduct of its priesthood. Religion was the predominant feature of society; but the religion of the Greeks was far removed from the purity of the apostolic precepts, and from the mild doctrines of Christianity. The characteristics of

---

[1] Two examples were notorious in the East. Pope Eugenius IV. excited Ladislas, king of Hungary, to break his treaty with Sultan Murad II.; an act of faithlessness which caused his defeat and death at Varna, A.D. 1444. Pope Pius II., on the same pretext, that an oath to the enemies of the Christian religion was not binding, persuaded Scanderbeg to violate the treaty he had just concluded with Mohammed II. in 1461. Pray, *Ann. Hung.* ii. part 3, 17; Bonfinius, *Res Hungaricae*, dec. iii. lib. 6; Raynaldi, *Ann. Eccles.* ix. 430, edit. Mansi; Barletius, *Vita Scanderbegi*, 198.

Byzantine religion were austerity and superstition, two qualities impressed on it by monastic influence. The dignified
clergy, who had long exercised considerable authority in
civil affairs, could only be chosen from among the monks.
This prerogative extended the authority of monachism, by
making the monastery a surer path to wealth and power
than to heaven. Men of rank sent their children into the
monastery as a means of securing them a high social position.
History affords innumerable examples of the facility with
which single classes of society can falsify the opinions of a
nation,—so that there is nothing surprising in the power
and corruption of monachism in Greece. Ambition introduced the spirit of intrigue among the monks, and a wish
to conceal the vices of the clergy spread religious hypocrisy
through the whole frame of Greek society, and silenced many
of the truths which speak most plainly to the human under-
standing. Under monastic influence, it became the highest
virtue in a Greek to repudiate many of his duties to his
country and his fellow-creatures, in order to secure a reputation of sanctity as a monk. Some rose to power as
courtiers, others as demagogues. The most worthless monk
was allowed privileges denied to the best citizen. The pre-
vailing hypocrisy, it is true, could not conceal the truth from
all. The common sense of the people ventured at times to
question the pretension that the monk was always a better
man on account of his monastic garb; but it was nevertheless
generally believed that the profession of monachism was a
valid reason for exemption from punishment in this world,
and a sure mitigation of divine wrath in the world to
come. The homage rendered to the monastic order was
consequently very great, and the monastery became a retreat for the intriguing politician as well as for the pious
enthusiast.

The fermentation of monastic society in the East had
passed into a principle of corruption before the fifteenth century. The Greek Church declined with the Byzantine Empire.
No examples were any longer to be found of that zealous
abnegation of humanity which elevated men for life on the
tops of columns, or perched them in the branches of trees.
Even the active charity which reflects some rays of glory on
the darkest periods of Byzantine history, was almost extinct.

The Stylites and Dendrites of earlier times; the hospitals of
Constantinople, and the names of the saints who have been
admitted into the Greek calendar for deeds of true Christian
charity, form part of the social records of mankind in the
East. But in the fifteenth century the moral weakness of the
Greek race rendered it incapable of emulating the stern sufferings, or of feeling the tender sympathies, of early Byzantine
society. Ecclesiastical learning declined, hypocrisy increased,
and bigotry became aggressive. The monasteries no longer
supported hospitals and poor-houses, nor did the monks any
longer study as physicians, and serve as attendants on the
sick. Those who could not advance in the career of ecclesiastical preferment, turned their attention to money-making.
They frequented the public marts as dealers in pictures,
ancient and modern, profane and sacred; but as picture-
dealing alone was not sufficient to enrich them, many became
cattle-dealers and wool-merchants. Those who restricted
their attention to cultivating and extending the religious
influence of their order, dealt only in sacred images—the
gilded pictures which had been the abomination of the Icono-
clasts—and excited the people to purchase them at an
exorbitant price, by forged visions and pretended miracles.
Eustathios, Archbishop of Thessalonica in the twelfth century,
a man of virtue and a scholar, whose commentaries on Homer
and Dionysius Periegetes are still studied by the learned,
declares, that in his time the monks neglected the study of
Greek literature, and had begun to sell the ancient manuscripts in the libraries of the monasteries[1]. The ignorance
and vices of the monks were long the subject of general
animadversion; but in this matter, as in many others, Greek
society proved incompetent to reform its own abuses. The
destructive energy of a foreign conqueror was necessary to
sweep away abuses and open a field for improvement[2].

Many of the social vices of the Greeks under the domination
of the Othomans must be traced back to the corrupt monastic
influence predominant in the thirteenth and fourteenth centuries. The monks taught the people that vice might be

---

[1] Eustathii *Opuscula*, edit. Tafel, *De emendanda vita monachica*, 229, 230, 249.

[2] Nicetas (*Isaac et Alex.* p. 358, edit. Paris) passes a severe censure on 'the
accursed monks' about the person of the Emperor Isaac. Mazaris alludes to the
licentiousness of the nuns and the hypocrisy of the monks. Boissonade, *Anecdota
Graeca*, iii. 128, 129.

atoned for by prostrations and fasting. Intolerance became a national characteristic. The hatred of foreigners, which Strabo cites as a mark of utter barbarism, grew to be the prominent feature of Greek nationality [1].

The complete separation effected by monachism in the social standing of the regular and secular clergy—between the bishop and the parish priest—exercised a corrupting influence on the whole clergy. The monks and the dignified clergy became intriguers at Turkish divans, flatterers of Othoman officials, and systematic spies on the conduct of the parish priests and on the patriotic sentiments of the laity. They served for three centuries as the most efficient agents of the Othoman government, in repressing any aspirations for independence among the Greeks.

The only administrative authority which was not entirely annihilated by the Othoman conquest, was that of the church. The modern Greeks boast that their church, having survived the loss of their independence, was the means of preserving their nationality during three centuries of servitude. This may be regarded as true only to a very limited extent. The Greek clergy, doubtless, by becoming the agents of the sultan's government, secured a legal position in the Othoman empire to the Greeks, as the representative people among the orthodox Christians; but the primary cause of the persevering endurance of the Hellenic race was in its own obstinate nationality, not in the ecclesiastical organization which was capable of being converted into an instrument of Othoman oppression. The virtues which the rural population practised, and not the power which the church prostituted to the service of a Mohammedan government, preserved the nation. The church of Constantinople was always more orthodox than it was Greek.

The church of Constantinople received from Mohammed II. an organization which rendered it subservient to his will; and the Greek clergy were the active agents in their own degradation. In judging the relations between the conquered and the conquerors, we must not allow our detestation of tyranny to

---

[1] Strabo, lib. xviii. p. 802. The Greeks were never hospitable to aliens in race and language. In the Middle Ages they were regarded as extremely inhospitable. Luitprand, *Legatio ad Nicephorum Phocam*, p. 371, edit. Bonn; 'In omni Graecia (veritatem dico, non mentior) non reperi hospitales episcopos.' See also Saewulf's *Travels*; Bohn, *Early Travels in Palestine*, 34; 'The Greeks are not hospitable.'

nourish in our minds a feeling of sympathy with the servility of parasites. No class of men can long remain undeserving of the social position it occupies ; even the misfortunes of nations are generally the direct consequence of their own vices, social or political.

One great temporal characteristic of Christianity is, that it connected mankind by higher and more universal ties than those of nationality. It teaches men that religion ought to bind them together by ties which no political prejudices ought to have strength to sever, and thus reveals how the progress of human civilization is practically connected with the observance of the divine precepts of Christ. The Greeks have never admitted this truth into their minds. On the contrary, they have laboured strenuously to corrupt Christianity by the infusion of a national spirit. Their church is a great effort to make Christianity a Greek institution ; and when the pure principles of religion were found to be at variance with ecclesiastical restrictions, the Greeks made ecclesiastical orthodoxy, not Christian piety, the essence of their national church. They resuscitated the spirit of Paganism under a new form. At a very early period the Greeks placed the Gospel in a subordinate position to the councils of the church, by making them legislative assemblies of Christianity, instead of being administrative councils for maintaining national churches in strict conformity with the precepts of Christ's Gospel.

Mohammed II. understood perfectly the character of his subjects. He spoke their language, and knew their thoughts. After the conquest of Constantinople, he availed himself of the hoary bigotry and infantine vanity of Hellenic dotage to use the Greek Church as a means of enslaving the nation. The orthodox clergy had separated themselves from the imperial government before the taking of Constantinople, and Mohammed II. availed himself of the hostile feeling with which they regarded the last unfortunate emperor, to attach them to his government. The last patriarch of the Greek empire retired to Rome in the year 1451, where he died eight years later[1]. The sultan found the Greek Church in such a state of disorganization from the flight of the patriarch and

---

[1] Phrantzes, 217, edit. Bonn; Crusius, *Turco-Graecia*, 5 ; Cuper, *De Patriarchis Constant.* 191.

its disputes with the Emperor Constantine, as to admit of his reconstituting its hierarchy, according to his own political views. The orthodox party was restored to power, and George Scholarios, who assumed the monastic name of Gennadios, was selected by the sultan to fill the office of patriarch, and act as minister of ecclesiastical affairs for the Sublime Porte. Gennadios was respected by his countrymen for his learning and morality; but his public conduct testifies that he had more than an ordinary share of the narrow-minded bigotry which perverted the judgment of his contemporaries.

When the unfortunate Emperor Constantine XI. confirmed the union of the Greek and Latin Churches in the year 1452, Gennadios exerted all his influence to prevent the orthodox from assisting the schismatic emperor in the defence of Constantinople. His bigotry so completely extinguished his patriotic feelings that he predicted the destruction of the Greek empire as a punishment which Heaven would inflict on the people, to mark God's reprobation of Constantine's fall from orthodoxy. Sultan Mohammed, who spoke Greek fluently, and who was perfectly acquainted with the influence the different parties in the church possessed over the people, treated the most popular of the clergy with marked favour[1]. He saw the advantages that would result from using them as his agents in reconciling the laity to the Othoman domination. With that profound political skill which enabled him to use his opponents as the instruments of his ends, he selected the bigoted Gennadios as the new orthodox patriarch, and made use of him as an instrument to obtain for himself, though a Mohammedan prince, the ancient personal position of the Byzantine sovereigns as protector of the orthodox church and master of the Greek hierarchy. His policy was completely successful. The sultans never involved themselves in ecclesiastical disputes. The contempt which the Mussulmans then entertained for all Christians saved them from this folly; to them the Orthodox and the Catholic were equally distant from the light of truth. Theological differences and church government only interested them as questions of public order and

---

[1] Phrantzes, 93, 95. The *History of the Patriarchs of Constantinople* says—
Ἥξευρε τὰ Ῥωμαϊκὰ καλλὰ καὶ λεπτότατα, καὶ τὰς τάξεις τῶν Ῥωμαίων—ἀγάπησε δὲ πολλὰ τὸ γένος τῶν Χριστιανῶν καὶ ἔβλεπε καλῶς. *Turco-Graecia*, 107, 120, edit. Crusii.

police, and personal preferences were only determined by pecuniary payments. Hence the Greek Church was for a long period left at liberty to arrange its own internal affairs ; its vices and its virtues were the spontaneous efforts of its own members ; its religious action was rarely interfered with, and it must bear the blame if morality and faith did not prosper within its bosom.

It is generally said that, in virtue of the privileges conceded by Mohammed II. to the Greek Church, the Patriarch of Constantinople is elected by an assembly composed of Greek bishops who happen to be officially resident at the seat of the patriarchate, joined to a certain number of the neighbouring clergy, under the presidency of the metropolitan of Heraclea[1]. But the truth is, that the Patriarch of Constantinople is appointed by the sultan pretty much in the same way as the archbishop of Canterbury is appointed by the sovereign of England. Mohammed II., after naming Gennadios patriarch, wished him to be instituted in his ecclesiastical dignity according to the ancient ceremonial of the church, in order to prevent the election producing new dissensions. The great object of the sultan was to re-establish the patriarchate in such a manner as to give it the greatest influence over the minds of the whole body of the orthodox clergy and laity. The patriarch Gennadios, and the bishops who survived the taking of Constantinople, were supported by the Othoman government in their exertions to restore the whole fabric of the Eastern Church, in outward form as well as in religious doctrine, to its condition before the Council of Florence in 1439. The synods and councils of the Greek Church, since the taking of Constantinople, have been tolerated by the Sublime Porte only so far as they facilitated administrative measures, without conferring any independent influence on the Greek clergy. The rescript of the sultan has always been necessary to authorize a bishop to exercise his ecclesiastical functions in the see to which he has been elected[2]. The Mohammedan sovereign, as master of the orthodox church, retained in his own hands the unlimited power of

---

[1] Le Quien, *Oriens Christianus*, i. 146.
[2] Waddington (*Greek Church*, 54) says the words of the barat of the sultan were, 'I command you to go and reside as bishop at (Athens) according to the ancient custom, and to the vain ceremonies of the inhabitants.'

deposing both patriarchs and bishops. The absolute power of condemning every Greek ecclesiastic, whether patriarch, monk, or parish priest, to exile or death, was a prerogative of the sultan which was never doubted.

Mohammed II., nevertheless, invested the patriarch with privileges which gave him great civil as well as ecclesiastical power over his countrymen. He was authorized by the usages of the church to summon synods and decide ecclesiastical differences; and by the concessions of the sultan to hold courts of law for the decision of civil cases, with permission to enforce his sentences by decrees of excommunication, a punishment which few Greeks had courage to encounter. A virtuous and patriotic clergy might have rendered these privileges a source of national improvement, an incitement to good conduct, and an encouragement to true religion, for Mohammed and his successors would willingly have employed Christians, on whose morality they could depend, as a counterpoise to the military power of the Seljouk feudatories and the independent authority of the Ulema.

The demoralization of the clergy and laity was so great at the time of the Othoman conquest, that it would have required some time, and patient perseverance on the part of virtuous and able patriarchs, to render honesty an influential element in orthodox society. Gennadios had not even the purity of character necessary to stem the current of evil, and despairing of his own success in any project for the benefit of the church, he resigned the patriarchate towards the end of the year 1458, and retired to the monastery of St. John the Precursor, on Mount Menikion, near Serres. Gennadios, and the three patriarchs who followed him in succession, entered on their office without making any present or paying any tribute or purchase-money to the Porte; but their government of the church was disturbed by internal dissensions and intrigues among the clergy and laity. The third patriarch, Joasaph, a man of tranquil disposition, was driven frantic by the incessant quarrels around him, in which he could not avoid taking some part. Despair and disgust at last so far overpowered his reason, that he attempted to put an end to his life by throwing himself into a well. He was fortunately taken out alive, and the Greeks were spared the scandal of hearing that their patriarch had voluntarily plunged into the pains of hell to escape the torment of ruling the orthodox church on earth [1].

After the conquest of Trebizond, the Greek clergy and nobles formed themselves into two great parties, the Constantinopolitans and the Trapezuntines, who contended for supremacy at the patriarchate as the green and blue factions had striven in the hippodrome of the Byzantine empire. The exiles of Trebizond spared no efforts to place a member of their party at the head of the orthodox church. They knew that much valuable patronage in the church would be placed at their disposal, and, spurred on by interest, they allowed neither a sense of justice nor a feeling of patriotism to arrest their intrigues. To gratify their ambition, they suggested to the sultan a new source of revenue, drawn from the demoralization of the clergy and the degradation of their nation. The fourth patriarch who was appointed without simony was Markos, a Constantinopolitan. The dissensions which had driven Joasaph frantic increased under Markos, and the Trapezuntine party brought forward various charges against him. At last they supported their petition for his deposition by offering to pay into the sultan's treasury a thousand ducats on the election of their own candidate. Mohammed II. is said by a Greek historian to have smiled at the intensity of the envy displayed by the Greeks, which rendered their customs, their laws, and even their religion, powerless to restrain their intrigues [2]. He accepted the purchase-money, and allowed the Greeks to introduce that black stain of simony into their hierarchy which soon spread over their whole ecclesiastical establishment. From this time simony, which is the worst of ecclesiastical heresies, became a part of the constitution of the orthodox church [3].

Simeon of Trebizond, who gained the patriarchal throne by this act of simony, lost it by female influence. The ladies

---

[1] *Historia Patriarchica*, in Crusius, *Turco-Graecia*, 121.

[2] Ibid. 125.

[3] It appears that this heresy prevails in King Otho's administration. I find a letter in the Greek newspaper *Athena*, No. 2332, 28th October, 1855, from the Bishop of Andros and Keos, Metrophanes, in which that prelate declares that common report attributed the recent election of some ignorant (ἀναλφαβήτους τινάς) bishops to simony, and that a senator, whom he names, offered to procure his own election at the same time for the sum of one thousand dollars—a price he subsequently reduced to five hundred. When the worthy Metrophanes refused, the Greek senator exclaimed, ' You know nothing of the world; you will never be a bishop unless you pay.'

of the sultan's harem began already to traffic in promotions. But it would answer no good purpose to pursue the history of these corruptions into greater detail. The bribe paid to the Porte was increased at each election, and when it became evident to all that the patriarchate could be obtained by money, an additional impulse was given to the spirit of intrigue and calumny, which has always been too active in Greek society. The vainglory of the Greeks, as much as their ecclesiastical extortions, roused the ambition of the Servians, who succeeded in placing a Servian monk, named Raphael, on the patriarchal throne of Constantinople as eighth in succession under Othoman domination. His nomination was purchased by an engagement to render the church liable to an annual tribute of two thousand ducats.

The account the Greeks give of the Patriarch Raphael presents their church in a very contemptible light. They say that he was a confirmed drunkard, and frequently appeared at the most solemn services of religion in such a condition as to be unable to stand without support. He was also so ignorant of the Greek language as to be compelled to use an interpreter in his communications with the Greek clergy who had elected him. His love of wine was a just ground for his deposition; his ignorance of Greek ought to have prevented his election[1].

Maximos, who succeeded Raphael, had a slit nose. His face had been thus disfigured for defending the cause of Markos against the Trapezuntine party. Mohammed II. died during the patriarchate of Maximos, A.D. 1481. The tenth patriarch was Niphon, metropolitan of Thessalonica, whose father was an Albanian primate of the Morea, but whose mother was a Greek. He was highly esteemed by his contemporaries for his eloquence, but his moral conduct was not irreproachable, as appears from an anecdote which proves that he was guilty of perjury. Simeon of Trebizond died without leaving any heir to his wealth, which was very great. Niphon suborned false witnesses, in order to appropriate the fortune of Simeon to the use of the patriarchate. The perjury was discovered by the Turks, and Niphon was deposed[2].

---

[1] *Historia Patriarchica,* 129, 130.
[2] The Church of the Holy Apostles at Thessalonica, near the Vardar gate, which retains its name though it has been converted into a mosque, appears, from

The misconduct of the clergy degraded the position of the church, and stimulated the avarice of the Turks by augmenting the offers of purchase-money for ecclesiastical offices. In this public prostitution of religion, the clergy endeavoured to persuade the people that patriotic feeling, more than personal interest, was the principal motive of their intrigues and crimes, and the bigotry of the people prevented their scrutinizing very severely any conduct likely to prove advantageous to the church.

The credulity of the Greeks enabled the clergy to increase their popularity by circulating strange falsehoods among the people. We find a curious instance of the ignorance and credulity of the people, and of their readiness to confound right and wrong for the glory of their church, recorded in the history of the patriarchs. Though a fable, it deserves notice as a reflection of the national mind.

During the reign of Sultan Suleiman the Lawgiver, while Loufti Pasha, the historian, was grand-vizier (A.D. 1539–1541), the attention of the divan was called to the circumstance that it was the duty of the sultan, as caliph of Islam, to destroy all the places of worship possessed by infidels in every town taken by storm[1]. As Constantinople had been so conquered by Mohammed II., it was consequently the duty of Suleiman to shut up all the Greek churches in the city, or to convert them into mosques. A fetva to this effect was delivered by the mufti, and the sultan issued an ordinance to carry it into effect. The Patriarch Jeremiah was smitten with terror on hearing the news. He immediately mounted his mule and hastened to Loufti Pasha, who had always treated him with kindness. The grand-vizier and the patriarch held a secret conference, and concerted a scheme for evading the execution of the sultan's orders.

A meeting of the divan was held shortly after, for the purpose of communicating the ordinance to the patriarch and

the inscription over the door and the monograms on the columns of the portico, to have been constructed by a patriarch of Constantinople named Niphon. Bayezid II. expressed great anger at seeing a church which Joachim, the successor of Niphon II., covered with new tiles. *Historia Patriarchica*, 128. This church must therefore date from the patriarchate of Niphon I., A.D. 1313.

[1] *Historia Patriarchica*, 156. This story cannot be reconciled with chronology. The grand-vizier is called Toulphi, and the date given is 1537. It is to be hoped that the report of Loufti having beaten his wife, who was the sultan's sister, current some years after at Constantinople, was not truer than this story. See *Négociations de la France dans le Levant*, i. 496.

the Greek priests. Jeremiah appeared before the ministers of the Porte, and stated with confidence that Constantinople did not fall within the provisions of the ordinance, not having been taken by storm by the Mussulmans. He declared that a capitulation had been concluded between the Emperor Constantine and Sultan Mohammed before the gates were opened. Well might the members of the divan wonder, cast up their eyes to heaven, and caress their beards at this strange information ; but as they had all received large presents from the patriarch before the meeting, they waited in silence to see what turn matters would take. The grand-vizier declared that, as the business now assumed a new character, it would be better to discuss it in a grand divan on the following day.

The report that all the Christian churches in Constantinople were to be destroyed excited general interest, and, long before the meeting of the divan, crowds of Turks, Greeks, Armenians, Catholics, and Jews were assembled to hear the result [1]. The whole open space from the gate of the Seraï to the court of St. Sophia's was filled with people. The patriarch waited long without before he was summoned to enter the divan. When he was at last admitted, he made his prostrations to the viziers with becoming reverence, and then stood erect to speak boldly for his Church. The archonts of the Greek nation crowded behind him. All admired the dignity of his aspect. His white beard descended on his breast, and the sweat fell in large drops from his forehead, for the Greek historian, with national exaggeration and irreverence, suggests that he emulated the passion of Christ, of whose orthodox church he was the representative on earth. A long pause intervened, according to the supercilious and grave etiquette of the Othomans. The grand-vizier at length spoke, ' Patriarch of the Greeks, the sultan has issued an ordinance to enforce the execution of our law which prohibits the existence of any place of public worship for infidels in the walled cities we have conquered with the sword. This city was taken by storm by the Great Sultan Mohammed II., therefore let your

---

[1] Suleiman the Magnificent does not appear to have been tolerant in his disposition, for in his letter to Francis I., A.D. 1528, he boasts that the Christians who live under his protection are allowed to repair *the doors and windows* of their places of worship. *Négociations de la France,* i. 131.

priests remove all their property from the churches they now occupy and deliver up the keys to our officers.' To this summons the patriarch replied in a distinct voice, 'O grand-vizier, I cannot answer for what happened in other cities of the sultan's empire, but with regard to this city of Constanti-nople, I can solemnly affirm that the Emperor Constantine, with the nobles and people, surrendered it voluntarily to Sultan Mohammed.' The grand-vizier cautioned the patri-arch against asserting anything which he could not prove by the testimony of witnesses, and asked if he was prepared to prove his assertion by the evidence of Mussulmans. The patriarch replied in the affirmative, and the affair was adjourned for twenty days.

The Greeks were greatly alarmed, and men of every rank offered to furnish the patriarch with large sums of money, in order to enable him to bribe the members of the divan to save their churches, but the patriarch had already concerted his plan. He sent an agent to Adrianople to find two aged Mussulmans, who, as was doubtless well known to the grand-vizier, were willing to testify to anything the patriarch might desire, on being well paid. The witnesses were found and conducted to Constantinople, where the patriarch welcomed them on their arrival, embraced them, and took care that they should be well lodged, clothed, and fed. After they had rested from the fatigues of their journey, they were conducted to the grand-vizier, who spoke kindly to them, and assured them that they might give evidence in favour of the patriarch of the Greeks without fear.

The day appointed for the final determination of the cause having arrived, the patriarch presented himself before the divan. The grand-vizier inquired if he was now prepared to adduce the testimony of Mussulman witnesses. Two aged Turks were then led into the divan. Their beards were white as the purest snow, red circles surrounded their eyes, in which the tears gathered incessantly; their hands and their feet moved tremulously. The viziers were amazed, for no one remembered to have seen men so advanced in years. They stood together before the assembly like two brothers whom death had forgotten.

In reply to the questions of the grand-vizier, they told their names, and said that eighty-four years had elapsed since the conquest of Constantinople. Both declared that they were then eighteen years old, and that they had now attained the age of one hundred and two. They narrated the conquest of Constantinople in the following manner :—

After the siege had been formed by land and sea, and breaches were made in the city walls, the Emperor of the Greeks, seeing that there was no possibility of resisting the assault, sent a deputation to the great sultan to ask for terms of capitulation. The sultan granted him the following conditions, a copy of which he signed, and read aloud to the army :—

'I, Sultan Mohammed, pardon the Emperor Constantine and his nobles. I grant their petition that they may live in peace under my protection, and retain their slaves and property. I declare that the people of the city of Constantinople shall be free from illegal exactions, and that their children shall not be taken to be enrolled among my janissaries. The present charter shall be binding on me and my successors for ever [1].' The deputation delivered this charter to the emperor, who came out of the city and presented the keys to the sultan, who, on receiving them, kissed Constantine, and made him sit down on his right hand. For three days the two princes rejoiced together. The emperor then conducted the sultan into the city of Constantinople, and resigned his empire.

The members of the divan, after listening to this account of the conquest from the old men who were present, drew up a report, and Sultan Suleiman, on reading this report, ordered that the Christians should retain possession of their churches, and that no man should molest their patriarch or their priests. Such is the modern myth by which Romaic vanity glorified its own talents, and satirized the ignorance and corruption of the Turks.

---

[1] This may be admitted as a proof that the tribute of Christian children had not been regularly enforced in Constantinople. The anxiety of Mohammed II. to repeople his new capital was doubtless the real cause of the exemption. At a later period the Christian families were compelled to furnish a rower for the imperial fleet from each house. The story of the Patriarch Jeremiah seems to have originated in a threat of Sultan Suleiman, that he would destroy all the Christian churches in his dominions, as a reprisal for the ravages committed by the Spanish garrison of Coron in 1533. See the report of Hieronymus, the ambassador of Ferdinand, king of the Romans. Gevay, *Urkunden und Actenstücke zur Geschichte der Verhältnisse zwischen Oestreich, Ungarn und der Pforte im 16ten und 17ten Jahrhunderte*, p. 5.

The great Suleiman, called by Christians the Magnificent, and by the Othomans the Legislator, is represented as an ignorant barbarian, and his learned grand-vizier, Loufti, the historian of the Othoman empire, as a corrupted tool of a Greek patriarch. But the strangest feature of the fable is, the candid simplicity with which the falsehoods and frauds of the patriarch are held up to the admiration of Christians. The fruits of simony in the church are displayed in the moral obtuseness of the people. The ignorance of the inventor of the tale is perhaps less astonishing, for even the wealthiest Greeks at this time penetrated with difficulty into Othoman society. The ecclesiastical historian was ignorant of the name of the person who had been grand-vizier eighty-four years after the taking of Constantinople; it is not wonderful, therefore, that he had never heard of the learning of Loufti Pasha. He probably knew that Loufti was an Albanian by birth, and the Albanians were proverbially an unlettered race; he could not, therefore, suspect that Loufti had employed the years he lived as an exile at Demotika in writing a history of the Othoman empire, which is still preserved[1]. A comparison of the flourishing state of Turkish literature with the degraded state of knowledge among the Greeks during the three centuries which followed the Othoman conquest, offers a singular anomaly when contrasted with the constant assumption of mental superiority on the part of the ignorant Greeks over their more accomplished masters. The estimation in which Turkish literature was held in Western Europe was not very different from its appreciation by the Greeks, until Von Hammer, in his History of the Othoman Empire, furnished us with accurate information concerning the many learned men who flourished at Constantinople. From him Christian Europe heard, for the first time, that several distinguished statesmen had employed some portion of their time amidst the toils of an active and glorious public life, in the cultivation of literature and in the labours of historical composition; and that the literary productions of several sultans are still known, even to the present degenerate race of Othomans. For several generations after the conquest of Constantinople, the Othoman Turks were really entitled

---

[1] Hammer, *Histoire*, v. 304, 533.

to take as high rank in literature as in politics and war. But the Greeks have always viewed the history of other races through a mist of prejudices, which has distorted the objects they contemplated.

The Greek clergy, and those who believe that the nation owes its preservation to the church, have boasted that the priesthood persuaded the people to repudiate the judicial administration of the Othoman government, and to refer their differences to the decision of their patriarchs and bishops. This, however, is hardly a correct view of Greek society. Under the Othoman domination, the great mass of the Greek nation was engaged in agricultural pursuits, and lived scattered in small villages, removed from immediate contact with Turkish courts of law. Fortunately for them, the communal system, by which they elected their village magistrates or head men, was not disturbed by the Othoman conquest; on the contrary, the Turks allowed these village chiefs more liberty of action than they had enjoyed under the centralizing and aristocratic spirit of the Greek empire. The head men of the village, aided by the parish priest, decided all ordinary judicial cases relating to rights of possession, in a court held before the church, and in this court the most respected among the inhabitants formed a kind of jury. The cases which required a reference to another tribunal were usually those relating to questions of succession, which, by the privileges granted to the Greek Church, were placed under the jurisdiction of the bishop. The usages of the people had more to do with the repudiation of Othoman courts of law than either the conduct or the example of the clergy. The bishop was too distant, and too decidedly an instrument of the Othoman government, to secure the implicit confidence of the people where religion was not directly concerned, while, on the other hand, the general ignorance of the secular clergy prevented their acquiring any judicial authority even as arbiters. The fact, however, is incontestable, that the Greeks displayed a steady determination to avoid, as much as lay in their power, every reference to Turkish tribunals. This determination arose, in part, from the defective administration of justice established in the Othoman empire, and the notorious corruption of the judges. Indeed, the Mussulmans themselves entertained the greatest aversion to seek redress from their own tribunals, and the dislike manifested by the Turkish population to litigation, often spoken of as a national virtue, was nothing more than a dread of being plundered by their judges. This corruption of the Turkish tribunals being generally acknowledged, it was regarded as one of the worst crimes of which a Greek could be guilty, to appeal to a Mohammedan judge if a Christian bishop could be made arbitrator of his difference. The bishops, however, never assumed more judicial authority than had been conceded to them by Mohammed II. Their gains, as instruments of the sultan's power, induced them to recognize the power of the sword in civil and criminal justice, and, to justify their obedience, and even servility, they cited our Saviour's words, 'My kingdom is not of this world.'

We have seen with what eagerness the Greek clergy recognized the sultan as the judge of their patriarch's fitness for his sacred office. They displayed the same readiness to appeal to the Turkish law tribunals, when by so doing they could increase their ecclesiastical revenues. The conduct of the Patriarch Jeremiah affords a memorable example. The Archbishop of Achrida claimed the bishopric of Berrhoea, as one of the sees dependent on his jurisdiction as Patriarch of Bulgaria; but the Patriarch of Constantinople considered this bishop as a suffragan of the metropolitan of Thessalonica, and within the patriarchate of Constantinople. To decide the question, Jeremiah applied to the mufti for a fetva, declaring that after a lapse of one hundred years' uninterrupted possession, it was unlawful to revive a claim to property. With this fetva the patriarch presented himself before the divan; and having proved that the church of Constantinople, and not that of Bulgaria, had exercised jurisdiction in the bishopric of Berrhoea for more than a century, his rights were fully recognized. The production of the fetva had, however, been supported by a considerable bribe, according to the established procedure of Turkish justice, and Jeremiah burdened the church with an annual tribute of four thousand one hundred ducats [1]. Under the Patriarch Dionysius, who succeeded Jeremiah, the election present, or bakshish, to the Porte was increased to three

---

[1] *Historia Patriarchica*, 164.

thousand ducats. The contemporary ecclesiastical history of the Greeks is filled with complaints of the simoniacal practices of the clergy, and the Turks displayed their increased contempt for the Greek priesthood by ordering them to take down the cross which had until this time crowned the dome of the belfry at the patriarchate[1].

The traffic in ecclesiastical preferment went on increasing. The patriarchs, having purchased their own place, disposed of the vacant bishoprics in the orthodox church to the highest bidder; they added to the dues they exacted from their clergy, and augmented the debts of the church. To such a degree had these corruptions proceeded, that in the interval between 1670 and 1678, the Patriarch of Constantinople was changed six times, and the purchase-money of a new candidate was raised to the sum of twenty-five thousand dollars. The annual tribute had then reached six thousand ducats, and the debts of the patriarchate amounted to three hundred and fifty thousand dollars, two dollars being nearly equal to one ducat[2].

Mutual distrust was a feature in the character of the higher clergy at Constantinople, and if it did not originate, it perpetuated and enforced, one measure which was adopted by the members of the synod, to guard against treachery on the part of any single individual of the body. The patriarchal seal was divided into four parts, the custody of which was intrusted to four metropolitans, but these four parts could only be used when united by a key of which the patriarch retained possession, and he consequently alone possessed the power of affixing it to a public document[3]. By this contrivance no patriarchal writing could be legalized without the concurrence of the four prelates. Want of confidence was shown in every rank of Greek society, at least among the urban population. The common people declared that they considered it a blessing to give hospitality to a

---

[1] *Historia Patriarchica*, 167, 168.

[2] Compare Rycaut, *Present State of the Greek Church*, 98, 107; and De la Croix, *État présent des nations et églises Grècque, Arménienne, et Maronite en Turquie*, 109.

[3] Thiersch, *De l'état actuel de la Grèce*, ii. 181. The clergyman and church-wardens in many parts of England have each their separate keys to the parish chest, which are all needed to open it. In this case, combined responsibility is the object sought. Each of the four archonts of Psara had in his custody a quarter of the public seal. Gordon, *Greek Revolution*, i. 168.

parish priest, but that it was a curse to be obliged to receive a monk into their houses. The secular priests in Greece must always be married before they enter on their parochial functions; the monks, who wandered about the country, or who dwelt in the cities, were often men of doubtful character, or men deeply engaged in political and ecclesiastical intrigues, either for themselves or as agents for others.

From what has been said, it is evident that, both as a political and ecclesiastical institution, the Greek Church offered a feeble resistance to the Othoman government. It had been unsuccessful in opposing the progress of Mohammedanism with the Arabs in the seventh and eighth centuries, and with the Seljouk Turks in the eleventh and twelfth, and it proved very ineffectual as a barrier to its progress under the Othomans in the fifteenth and sixteenth centuries.

The weakness of the Greek Church arose in part from the defective constitution of Greek society. The governing class in the ecclesiastical establishment was selected from the aristocratic element, and no more selfish and degraded class of men has ever held power than the archonts of modern Greece and the Phanariots of Constantinople. Under the Greek emperors and the Othoman sultans we find them equally ready to sacrifice the interests of their nation and the good of posterity to the gratification of their own avarice and ambition. The Greek hierarchy only shared the character of the class from which it was selected.

The division of the orthodox clergy into regular and secular increased the worldly-minded tendencies of the priesthood. It rendered the regular clergy avaricious and intriguing; it reduced the secular clergy to so low a rank in society that they were generally obliged to gain money by manual labour. The bishops possessed considerable revenues, and a jurisdiction in civil affairs; the monasteries possessed large landed estates; and the whole patronage of the establishment was vested in the hands of the patriarch and the bishops, who were selected from the monastic class. The monasteries served as places of retreat and shelter for the members of the aristocracy who sought to escape Turkish oppression, or who aspired at ecclesiastical promotion. The wealth of the monasteries rendered the lives of these noble monks easy, and they devoted their leisure to political intrigues, to which the quasi-elective forms and open simony of ecclesiastical nominations opened an extensive field. The result was, that though for three centuries the Greek monks were placed in not unfavourable circumstances for the cultivation of Hellenic literature and Christian theology, they forsook these studies entirely, and were more active as Othoman agents than as Greek priests.

The prudent policy of the Othomans to a certain extent conciliated the feelings of the orthodox. They treated the higher clergy with far more respect than was shown to them by the Latins. The sultan conceded some marks of honour, and considerable power and wealth, to the higher Greek clergy; while, on the contrary, the Venetians and Genoese, in their possessions in Greece, excluded the Greek clergy both from honour and power. The consequence was, that the bigotry of the people was inflamed by the galled feelings of the higher clergy: hatred to the Latins was inculcated as the first of orthodox virtues.

This spirit of bigotry drew a strong line of separation between the Eastern and Western Christians, and tended greatly to impede the progress of political civilization among the orthodox. Yet so servile was the priesthood in pursuing its personal advantages, that many members of the Greek Church were found who pretended to countenance both Catholic and Protestant interpretations of the doctrines of the church, when the influence of the French, the Dutch, or the English ambassador at Constantinople appeared most likely to advance their intrigues. Most of the disputes in the Greek Church, which during the seventeenth century induced the Catholics and the Protestants in turn to hope for the establishment of a close union with the orthodox, must be attributed to political interest, not to conformity of doctrine. Cyril Lucar doubtless held some theological opinions tending to Calvinism, and Cyril of Bcrrhoea, his successor, inclined to admissions that savoured of Catholicism; but public opinion, both among the clergy and the people of Greece, remained unshaken in its devotion to the national and orthodox church, and bigoted in its hostility to every other. The historian of the Greek Church cannot, therefore, appeal to the contests among the Greek ecclesiastics in the seventeenth century with any confidence, as indicating a wish in either party to modify the theological doctrines, or reform the simoniacal practices, of their church [1].

The obligations which the modern Greeks really owe to their church, as an instrument in the preservation of the national existence during the fifteenth and sixteenth centuries, have been greatly magnified by the wish of the people to invest the only prominent national institution they possessed with all imaginary power and virtue. We have seen how little the regular clergy did to resist Othoman supremacy and the moral power of Mohammedanism. Still there can be no doubt that the secular clergy supplied some of the moral strength which enabled the Greeks so successfully to resist the Othoman power. It is true the parish priests were a class of men destitute of learning, and possessing no great personal authority; but as the agricultural classes in the villages formed the heart of the nation, the parish priests had an influence on the fate of Greece quite incommensurate with their social rank. The reverence of the peasantry for their church was increased by the feeling that their own misfortunes were shared by the secular clergy. They believed that every doctrine of their church was of divine institution, and they adhered to all its ceremonies and fasts as affording visible symbols of their faith. As with the Mohammedans, forms became the strongest bond of religion. In the mean time, the secular clergy, without seeking the mighty charge, and without being suited worthily to fulfil the mission, became by the nature of things the real representatives of the national Church, and the national ministers of religion. To their conduct we must surely attribute the confidence which the agricultural population retained in the promises of the Gospel, and their firm persistence in a persecuted faith. The grace of God operated by their means to preserve Christianity under the domination of the Othomans.

The situation of the secular clergy in large towns was neither so respectable nor so influential as in the agricultural districts. They were generally as ignorant as the village priests, and were too often men of much less virtue. Indeed, we find that the ignorance and low condition of the secular

---

[1] For an account of these contests from the English point of view, see Waddington, *Condition of the Greek Church*, 78, &c. For a dispassionate summary of facts, Kimmel, *Monumenta Fidei Eccl. Orthod.*, proleg. 4, &c.

clergy in the towns of the Othoman empire, which excited the contempt of travellers, was too generally taken as the indication of their rank and position in the rural districts. But in the agricultural villages they were the equals of the leading men among the laity, while in the towns they were the equals and companions of the lower orders. In the agricultural districts they escaped the influence of that corruption which demoralized the higher clergy; but in the towns they displayed the vices of their own low grade of society, which were more disgusting to others, and more generally offensive, than the polished wickedness of their superiors. Spon tells us that three instances of apostasy occurred among the secular clergy of Corinth in the year 1675[1]. All general descriptions of society must be liable to many exceptions, and never were anomalies more numerous than in Greece. There was probably no town in which some virtuous members of the secular clergy did not reside, and there were doubtless many rural districts in which the name of a virtuous bishop was respected. Many a city had its respected archont; and many a province had its much-feared brigand and its loathed apostate.

The parochial clergy of Greece lived and died in the same social circle in which they were born and bred. Their education in the country was the same as that of the better class of the village proprietors around them, of whom they were the companions and spiritual guides. As a body, they were taught by their position to feel the necessity of securing the respect of their parishioners, and on the whole they succeeded. Their ignorance and rusticity, not their immorality and avarice, are made the themes of reproach by travellers, who echoed the opinions of the inhabitants of towns and of the higher orders of the clergy. The parochial clergy could form no ambitious projects which required them to flatter Othoman officials, and hence they held little intercourse with the Turks; while the most active members of the monastic order were eager to cultivate Mussulman society, and to study the Turkish language, as a means for advancing

---

[1] Spon, ii. 231. Apostasy, however, was as common among the monks as among the secular clergy. A curious example of the spirit of toleration and respect for public decency among the Turks is mentioned in a Venetian report, dated 1679. A renegade monk, or kalogeros, was beheaded for cursing the religion of Christ in the divan. Hammer, xii. 45.

their preferment in the church. Not unnaturally, therefore, we find the secular clergy as superior to the regular in patriotism as they were inferior in learning; and this superiority gave them no inconsiderable moral influence in defending the orthodox church against the attacks of Mohammedanism. Their simple lives, and the purity of their moral conduct, united them in harmony with the laity, in whose fortunes they were directly interested, and in whose feelings they participated. In the lowliness of their social position they emulated the worldly rank of their divine Master; and the history of the Greek people attests that their humble efforts strengthened the great body of the people to persist in their devotion to the Christian faith unto the end [1].

But, after all, the national existence of the Greek race depended ultimately on the character and fortitude of the people themselves, which could only be partially strengthened by the influence of the clergy. Interest or ambition may be powerful enough to induce a single class of men, a church, a nobility, a corporation, or a privileged body, to assume an artificial character, but a whole people cannot conceal its national vices, nor imitate virtues which it does not possess. No nation can boast of greater firmness of purpose, or stricter devotion to its church, than the Greek. Yet Greek society was divided into so many branches, living under the influence of such different social circumstances, that during the fifteenth, sixteenth, and seventeenth centuries it offers a great variety of aspects. Orthodox Greeks differed from Catholic Greeks; the subjects of the sultan were unlike the subjects of the Venetian republic; there was a marked contrast between the urban and rural population, and between the regular and secular clergy, even in the different provinces of the Othoman empire. In no other race of men did so little sympathy exist between the different portions of the nation as among the various orders of the Greeks at this period, yet none more vigorously repudiated all foreign influence.

The nation was divided into two great divisions, whose character is more distinct, and whose separation is much more complete in the East, than among the Germanic and Anglo-Saxon races; namely, the urban population, and the culti-

---

[1] The parochial clergy in the Greek Church must marry a virgin before ordination, but cannot marry a second time.

vators of the soil. These two classes have perpetuated their existence for ages in different stages of civilization, and their increase and decrease have been determined by different political circumstances and social laws. The cultivators of the soil formed, as I have said before, the great majority, and, in fact, really constituted the Greek nation during the period embraced in this chapter. Among the rural population alone some sentiments of manly vigour and true patriotism still survived. The citizens had adopted the philanthropic selfishness of the archonts, regular clergy, and Jewish colonists, with whom they lived, and with whom they struggled for preferment in the Othoman service. The agricultural population, therefore, the despised and ignorant peasantry, were the only class to which the patriot could look forward as likely at any future period to afford materials for recovering the national independence. The extinction of this class, which was often a possible contingency, would have reduced the Greeks in Constantinople, Athens, and Sparta to the same condition as the Jews in Palestine and the Copts in Cairo.

The urban population was again subdivided into two sections, which had almost as few feelings and interests in common as if they had belonged to different nations. These were the aristocracy, which grew up as officials and servants of the Othoman government, and the industrious classes, whether merchants, shopkeepers, artizans, or day-labourers. But this latter class, having no organ among the clergy, and being unable to give expression to its feelings, was compelled to accept the leading of the official aristocracy and the dignified clergy, and to treat its worst oppressors as national leaders. Thus we see that the monastic and parochial clergy, the officials in the Turkish service, the industrious classes in the towns, and the agricultural population, formed five distinct bodies in the Greek nation, acting under the guidance of different, and often of adverse, circumstances and interests. These heterogeneous elements prevented the Greeks from coalescing into one body and offering an united national resistance to the Othoman domination. Socially, as well as geographically, the Hellenic race did not form one compact body.

A correct estimate of the condition of the people can only

be obtained by observing how the individuals in each class passed through life; how far they were enabled to better their fortunes; or how they sank gradually in the social scale under the weight of Othoman oppression. The authority and importance of the higher clergy, and the restricted sphere of action of the parish priests, have been already noticed. The patriarch and the bishops purchased their dignities, and repaid themselves by selling ecclesiastical rank and privileges; the priests purchased holy orders, and sold licenses to marry. The laity paid for marriages, divorces, baptisms, pardons, and dispensations of many kinds, to their bishops. The extent to which patriarchs and bishops interfered in family disputes and questions of property is proved by contemporary documents[1].

The trade of the Greeks had been ruined by the fiscal oppressions of the Greek emperors; and, before the conquest of Constantinople, the commerce of Greece had been transferred to the Italian states. Under the firm government of Mohammed II. a wider sphere was opened for the commercial activity of his Greek subjects. They not only received protection within the extensive bounds of the Othoman empire, but foreign states were compelled to admit them into ports under the sultan's flag, from which they had been excluded in the time of the Greek emperors. During the early part of the sixteenth century the port of Ancona was crowded with vessels under the Othoman flag, loading and unloading their cargoes; and the exchange was filled with Greek and Turkish merchants, some of whose houses were said, by their rivals the Venetians, to do business to the amount of 500,000 ducats annually. In the year 1549, about two hundred Greek families were settled as traders in Ancona, where they were allowed to have their own church[2]. Barcelona also carried on a considerable trade in the produce of the Levant with Ragusa, Rhodes, and Cairo. The long wars of Spain with the Othoman empire prevented all direct trade, but it was the fiscal measures of Philip II., and not the extension of Spanish commerce with America, which at last ruined the trade of Catalonia with the Levant. Greek merchants travelled to

---

[1] Several letters in the *Turco-Graecia* of Crusius.
[2] Ranke, *History of the Popes*, 97 (Kelly's translation), who quotes Saracini, *Notizie storiche della città d'Ancona*, Roma, 1675, p. 362.

Azof, Moscow, and Antwerp, where their gains were very great. They wore the dress and assumed the manners of Turks; for they found that in western Europe they were more respected in the character of Othoman subjects than as schismatic Greeks. The middle classes in the towns were also at this period superior in industry to the same classes in many parts of western Europe. Various manufactured articles were for two centuries generally imported from the sultan's dominions into other countries, particularly camlets, a strong stuff composed of silk and mohair called grogram, rich brocaded silks, embroidered scarfs, Turkey carpets, leather, and yarn; besides Angora wool, cotton wool, and raw silk, flax, and hemp, in addition to the usual produce exported from the Levant, southern Italy, and Sicily, at the present day. Before the middle of the seventeenth century the people of Manchester had already turned their attention to the cotton manufacture, and the material they used was purchased in London from the merchants who imported it from Cyprus and other parts of Turkey [1]. Livadea and Athens, as has been already mentioned, supplied sailcloth for the Othoman navy. English ships already visited the Morea and Mesolonghi to load currants, and often brought back rich scarfs, sashes of variegated silk and gold tissue, and Turkey leather of the brightest dyes, which were manufactured in different towns in Greece, particularly at Patras, Gastouni, and Lepanto [2].

Soon after the taking of Constantinople, the ancient aristocracy of Greece was exterminated. The young children were forcibly torn from their parents and educated as Mohammedans; many adults voluntarily embraced Islam. Mohammed II. systematically put to death all men whom he supposed possessed sufficient power or influence to disturb his government. Manuel, the last male scion of the imperial family of Palaeologos, embraced Mohammedanism. But the protection which the sultan granted to the lower classes, soon enabled a number of individual Greeks to acquire wealth by commerce as well as by acting in the capacity of agents for provincial pashas, and of farmers of the revenue. Several of these men

---

[1] *The Merchants' Map of Commerce*, by Lewes Roberts, fol., London, 1638, quoted in Craik, *History of British Commerce*, ii. 49.

[2] *See* above, p. 127, *note.*

claimed a descent from females of the great Byzantine families, and, according to a common practice among the Greeks, assumed any surname they pleased. One of the best known of this class is Michael Cantacuzenos, who was famous for his wealth and pride in the latter half of the sixteenth century. His rapacity is celebrated in Greek history, and his magnificence and misfortunes in modern Greek poetry[1].

Michael Cantacuzenos had accumulated great wealth by successful mercantile speculations. To increase his riches and gratify his ambition he became a farmer of the revenue, and, as such, he was remarkable for his rapacity, and the inexorable severity with which he collected the taxes due by the Christians. His corruption and exactions obtained for him the execration of the Greek people, and the name of Sheitanoglu, or Devil's Child. His influence with Mohammed Sokolli, the celebrated grand-vizier of Selim II. and Murad III., enabled him to mix in every political intrigue by which he could gain money. He carried on some of his projects with the concurrence of the Patriarch Metrophanes, but having afterwards quarrelled with the patriarch, he accused Metrophanes of revealing state secrets to the ambassadors of the Emperor of Germany, Busbeck and Wys, who had purchased many valuable ancient manuscripts from the clergy. Metrophanes was deposed, and he then demanded from Cantacuzenos the repayment of 16,000 ducats which he had paid as a bribe to purchase that archont's support. As the grand-vizier Mohammed Sokolli, and the viziers Pialé and Achmet, shared in the extortions of Cantacuzenos, the patriarch could obtain no redress. The wealth of Cantacuzenos was so enormous, that he was able to build and present to the sultan several galleys after the battle of Lepanto.

Cantacuzenos, like every Greek, had a mortal enemy among his own countrymen; the name of this rival was Palaeologos; and these two Turkish tax-gatherers revived the feuds of the houses whose names they had assumed. Cantacuzenos amassed his wealth with the rapacity which has been the standing reproach of Greek officials in the Othoman empire.

---

[1] Letter of Zygomalas, in Crusius, *Turco-Graecia*, 91. Ranke and Hammer consider the song on the death of Kyritsos Michaele, in Fauriel, *Chants Populaires de la Grèce Moderne*, i. 212, as written on the death of Michael Cantacuzenos. It is a rude and simple composition, without even plaintive grace.

A.D. 1453–1676.]

But he lavished it with an ostentation of aristocratic pride which increased the envy of his rivals. When he rode through the streets of Constantinople on his mule, he was preceded by six running footmen, and followed by a train of slaves. When the influence of Mohammed Sokolli declined, it was easy for the intrigues of Palaeologos to inspire Sultan Murad III. with a desire to appropriate the wealth of Cantacuzenos—wealth extorted from the sultan's subjects, and therefore considered by the sultan as of right belonging to the imperial treasury. A political accusation was soon found, and Cantacuzenos was ordered to be strangled for intriguing in Moldavia. On the 3d of March 1578 he was hung in the gateway of a splendid palace at Anchialos, on the construction of which he had expended twenty thousand ducats [1].

At this period the wealth of the Greek merchants, bankers, and farmers of the revenue, and the luxury and lavish expenditure of their wives and daughters, excited the wonder of European ambassadors and noble travellers who visited the East.

During the seventeenth century there was a constant destruction of the capital, employed in preceding ages on works of public utility and private advantage, over the whole surface of the Othoman empire. The neglect of the Porte, the extortions of pashas and primates, the ravages of corsairs, and the plundering of brigands, compelled the Greek landowner with each successive generation to sink lower in the social scale. Accordingly, during this period the Greek race disappeared from several districts, and abandoned the cultivation of the soil exclusively to Albanian peasants of a hardier frame and ruder habits of life. Into such a state of disorder had the Turkish administration fallen, that when Sultan Mohammed IV. led his army to Belgrade in 1683, before sending his grand-vizier to besiege Vienna, it was regarded as a favour by the inhabitants of the villages on his line of march through Thrace, to be allowed to burn their houses, and conceal themselves and their property in the mountains, in order to escape the exactions of the feudal militia of Asia, who were now little better than brigands [2].

The arrival of the Spanish Jews in the Othoman empire at

---

[1] Hammer, vii. 60 ; Crusius, *Turco-Graecia*, 43, 211, 224, 274, 497.
[2] Hammer, xii. 81.

a period of great political depression in the whole Christian population, was particularly injurious to the Greeks. The Jews expelled from Granada settled in the towns of Turkey about the time that a large number of Turkish military colonists settled in Europe; and the sudden increase of the Mussulman warriors and landlords required a corresponding addition to the class of artizans and traders. The Greek population of the towns had suffered so severely in the fifteenth century from famines and plagues, as well as from the incessant slave-forays of the Seljouk and Othoman Turks, that Mohammed II. was often compelled to have recourse to the rural population of Greece to repeople the towns he conquered. When subsequent conquests enriched the Othomans, and augmented the demand for all articles of luxury, the demand, suddenly created by a rapid career of conquest, was as suddenly supplied by the bigotry of Ferdinand and Isabella of Spain, who drove the Jews and Moors of their dominions into exile. In the latter part of the fifteenth century, Jewish colonists settled in great numbers in most of the large commercial cities of Turkey, where they immediately occupied various branches of industry formerly exclusively exercised by Greek artizans. Their arrival filled a void in society, and their superior dexterity in many branches of industry enabled them to resist successfully the rivalry of the Greek emigrants, who quitted the country to seek their fortunes in the commercial cities. For more than a century after the arrival of the Jews in the Othoman empire, they occupied a high social position. They were the principal physicians as well as merchants and bankers of the Turks. Throughout the greater part of the empire the best medical practitioners were Jews. They were the first to open regular shops in the streets of towns throughout the East for the sale of articles of common use, distinct from the magazines and workshops of the fabricant[1].

Before the end of the fifteenth century, from 30,000 to 40,000 Jews were settled at Constantinople, from 15,000 to 20,000 at Thessalonica, and great numbers at every seaport in Turkey. They were eager to display their gratitude to the Othomans, and the inhuman cruelties they had suffered from

---

[1] Belon, *Observations de plusieurs singularités en Grèce, Asie,* &c. p. 182, edit. 1555; Prescott, *Ferdinand and Isabella,* 263.

the Inquisition made them irreconcilable enemies of the Christians. It was natural, therefore, for them to employ all the influence they gained in the Othoman empire, by their services and industry, to inspire the Mussulmans with their own hatred to Christianity; and when the Mohammedans in Spain were persecuted and driven into exile, their efforts were attended with signal success. Thus the punishment of the bigotry and injustice of the Catholic Christians in Spain fell with greatest severity on the orthodox Christians in the Turkish dominions.

There was always a marked contrast in the character and conduct of the Turkish and Greek population, even when living in the same towns, moving in the same rank of life, and speaking, as was the case in some places both in Asia and Europe, the same language. The Turks, though they were more courageous, cruel, and bloodthirsty than the Greeks when roused to war, were in general far more orderly in conduct, and more obedient to established social laws. The Greeks, though servile and submissive when in the presence of power, were turbulent and insolent whenever there seemed a chance of their misconduct escaping punishment. With such a disposition, fear alone could secure order ; and it is surprising how well the Othoman government preserved tranquillity in its extensive dominions, and established a greater degree of security for property among the middle classes, than generally prevailed in European states during the fifteenth and sixteenth centuries. This end was obtained by a regular police, and by the prompt execution of a rude species of justice in cases of flagrant abuses and crimes. In the populous cities of the Othoman empire, and particularly in Constantinople, which contained more inhabitants than any three Christian capitals, the order which reigned in the midst of great social corruption, caused by extreme wealth, the conflux of many different nations, and the bigotry of several hostile religions, excited the wonder and admiration of every observant stranger. Perfect self-reliance, imperturbable equanimity, superiority to the vicissitudes of fortune, and a calm temper, compensated among the Othomans for laws which were notoriously defective and tribunals which were infamously venal [1]. Knolles says, 'you seldom see a murder or a theft

[1] 'Et mirum est inter barbaros in tanta tantae urbis colluvie nullas caedes

committed by any Turk[1].' European gentlemen accustomed
to the barbarous custom of wearing swords on all occasions,
were surprised to see Turks of the highest rank, distinguished
for their valour and military exploits, walking about, even in
provincial towns, unarmed, secure in the power of public
order and the protection of the executive authority in the
State[2].

The darkest night of ignorance covered Greece in the
sixteenth and seventeenth centuries, and it was then almost
as much forgotten in Christendom as it was neglected by the
Othoman government. The Greeks had their whole attention absorbed by the evils of the passing hour; they were
forced to think day and night how they could best save their
children from the collectors of the living tribute which recruited the ranks of the janissaries; their own persons from
being enslaved by the pirates who never quitted their coasts;
and their means of subsistence from being consumed by the
exactions of pashas, and Othoman officials who appeared to
be in perpetual motion in the sultan's dominions. Ancestral
records were forgotten, and no hope urged them to look
forward to an earthly future. A few orthodox prejudices
and local superstitions became the whole mental patrimony
of the Hellenic race. Poverty, depopulation, and insecurity
of property, seemed to threaten the Greeks with utter ruin.

At this crisis of the national fate, the sultan's government
lightened the sufferings of the Greeks by ceasing to enforce
its worst act of oppression. The tribute of Christian children
fell into desuetude in consequence of the decline in the
numbers of the Christian population engaged in agriculture,
which began to be felt as an evil by the Porte. A considerable portion of the Greek population in Asia Minor, and
of the Sclavonian and Albanian population in Europe, embraced Mohammedanism to escape this tribute. The example
began to be followed by the Greeks in Europe, and a con-

---

audiri, vim injustam non ferri, jus cuivis dici. Ideo Constantinopolin Sultanus
refugium totius orbis scribit : quod omnes miseri ibi tutissime lateant ; quodque
omnibus (tam infimis quam summis, tam Christianis quam infidelibus) justitia
administretur.' Crusius, *Turco-Graecia*, 487.

[1] Knolles (*Turkish History*) adds, 'if any foul act be committed, it is most
commonly done by Grecians;' but Spon (i. 244) with more discrimination,
observes, that the Arabs in Asia, and the Albanians in Europe, were the chief
brigands.

[2] Spon, i. 161.

siderable number of the Cretans apostatized soon after the conquest of their island. The sultan found no difficulty in recruiting his armies from the increased Mussulman population of his empire[1]. The corps of janissaries ceased to admit tribute-children into its ranks. The permission which its members had received as early as the year 1578 of enrolling their children as recruits in the corps, ultimately transformed the finest body of regular troops in the world into a hereditary local militia of citizens. About the time this change was going on, the numerous renegades who were constantly entering the sultan's service filled the Othoman armies with good soldiers, and saved the government the expense of rearing and disciplining tribute-children.

About the same time the fiscal oppression of the Porte fell so heavy on the landed proprietors and peasants, that the tribute of the healthiest children became an insupportable burden. The peasant sought refuge in the towns; the Turkish aga found his estate depopulated and uncultivated, and the timariot could no longer take the field with the armies of the sultan, attended by well-armed followers, as his father had done. The agricultural population of the Othoman empire, Mussulman and Christian, consequently united in opposing the collection of the tribute, and the Porte, feeling no urgent necessity to enforce its collection, gradually ceased to exact it.

For two centuries the Greek population had been diminishing in number, and the Turkish had been rapidly increasing. This change in their relative numbers was the principal cause of the abolition of this singular institution, which long formed the chief support of the sultan's personal authority and the basis of the military superiority of the Othoman empire. It fell into disuse about the middle of the seventeenth century, not long after the conquest of Crete. The last recorded example of its exaction was in the last year of the administration of the grand-vizier Achmet Kueprili, A. D. 1676[2].

---

[1] For the extent of the conversions to Mohammedanism among the Christians and Jews, see Rycaut, *Present State of the Greek Church*, 22; and Milman, *History of the Jews*, in *The Family Library*, iii. 394. Rycaut perceived that this increase of the Mussulman population acted as one of the causes of the abolition of the tribute.

[2] Hammer, xi. 444. The French translator Hellert would lead us to infer, by a passage at p. 389, that the tribute was abolished in 1672, but at 397 we find that a levy of two thousand children was made in 1674. The levy in 1676 was of

Thus the Greeks were relieved from the severest act of tyranny under which any nation had ever groaned for so long a time, by the force of circumstances and by the neglect of their masters, without a struggle on their part to rend their chains. History furnishes no example of a nation falling from so high a state of civilization, and perpetuating its existence in such degradation. As long as the Greeks furnished a tithe of their children to augment the strength of their oppressors, their condition was one of hopeless misery. That burden removed, the nation soon began to feel the possibility of improving its condition, and to look forward with hope into the future.

three thousand children. Hammer nevertheless mentions another levy of one thousand Christian children in the reign of Achmet III. (A.D. 1703) which he calls the last attempt to enforce this species of tribute, already fallen into disuse for more than half a century; vol. xiii. 136, 373. Rycaut (*Present State of the Greek Church*, p. 22) writing in 1678, speaks of this tribute as having long fallen into disuse.

CHAPTER IV.

VENETIAN DOMINATION IN GREECE. A. D. 1684–1718.

Behaviour of the Othoman government to the representatives of the Christian
powers at the Sublime Porte.—Venetian Republic declares war with the
Porte.—Morosini Captain-General of the republic.—Campaign in Greece,
1684.—German mercenaries in the service of Venice.—Campaign of 1685,—
of 1686,—of 1687.—Siege of Athens and destruction of the Parthenon.—
Campaign of 1688.—Siege of Negrepont.—Venetian deserters.—Peace of
Carlovitz.—Venetian administration in the Morea.—Population, revenues,
and commerce.—Civil government and condition of the people.—Mainates.—
State of property and administration of justice.—Ecclesiastical administration.
—Catholic clergy.—Relations of the Porte with the European Powers when
war was renewed with Venice in 1715.—Conquest of the Morea by the
Grand-vizier Ali Cumurgi.—Following events of the war.—Peace of Passa-
rovitz.

THE ambassadors of the Christian powers were never
treated with greater contempt at the Sublime Porte than
after the conquest of Candia. The sultan's government complained, and not without reason, that no treaty of peace with
a Christian monarch afforded any guarantee for its faithful
observance. While the ambassador of France boasted that
his sovereign had always been the firmest ally of the sultan,
French corsairs levied ransom-money from the towns in
Greece, and made slaves of the Mohammedan subjects of
the sultan[1]. Frenchmen, too, as Knights of Malta, were
active in carrying on an incessant warfare against the Othoman flag over the whole surface of the Mediterranean.
Matters were not very different with the other Christian
powers; nor was peace better observed by land than by sea.
On the frontiers of Poland, Hungary, and Dalmatia, bands
of organized troops called Cossacks, Haiduks, and Morlachs,

---

[1] Petis de la Croix, *État général de l'Empire Othoman*, ii. 270 ; *Histoire des
anciens Ducs de l'Archipel*, 314.

made frequent forays into the Othoman territory. In vain the sultan's ministers required the emperor of Germany, the King of Poland, and the republic of Venice to put a stop to these invasions; their complaints became the subject of interminable discussions, in which the Christian governments displayed their weakness and bad faith by attempting to repudiate all responsibility for these acts of hostility, on the ground that they were committed by bands of lawless brigands; or else they excused them by asserting that the acts of brigandage committed by the Christians were in revenge for similar deeds of Othoman subjects. If the assertion was true, it appears that the Porte paid more attention to the sufferings of the plundered Mussulmans than the Christian governments paid to the calamities of their subjects. Indeed, the feelings of the Othomans were so much excited by the incessant hostilities to which they were exposed, that the sultan was compelled to demand explanations from all his Christian neighbours. The Othoman ministers assumed a menacing tone in their intercourse with Christian ambassadors; and then they very soon discovered that the diplomatic agents of their most formidable enemies were disposed to submit to a great deal of insolence rather than involve their country in war.

The tyrannical government of the house of Austria had caused such widespread discontent in Hungary, by its fiscal exactions and bigoted treatment of the Protestants, that there was some danger of hostilities in that country ending in the total loss of the kingdom. More than one-half of Hungary was already annexed to the Othoman empire; and it seemed not improbable that the inhabitants of the remainder might prefer Turkish toleration to German tyranny.

The republic of Venice was so intent on preserving its commercial relations with the Levant, as a means of recruiting its finances after the great expenditure caused by the war of Candia, that it bore many insults on the part of the Porte with patience, and rarely uttered a complaint, except when some act of the sultan's officers seemed likely to circumscribe the trade and diminish the gains of its subjects.

The deportment of the other Christian powers at Constantinople did not increase the consideration in which they were held. The ambassadors of France made several displays

of petulance and presumption, which the Othomans repressed
with insolence and scorn.   Many scandalous scenes occurred.
The son of M. de la Haye, the French ambassador, was
bastinadoed by the Turks, and his father imprisoned.   Louis
XIV. sent M. Blondel as envoy-extraordinary to demand
satisfaction for the insult; but this envoy could not gain
admittance to Sultan Mohammed IV., and returned to France
without delivering his sovereign's letter.   Some time after,
the younger de la Haye, who had received the bastinado,
became himself ambassador, and conducted himself in such
a manner at his first meeting with the grand-vizier, that
he was pushed off the stool on which he was seated, and
beaten by the grand-vizier's attendants[1].   The marquis of
Nointel, who was sent to Constantinople in 1670 to repair
the imprudences of his predecessors, distinguished himself
rather by ostentation and petulance than by prudent and
dignified conduct[2].   He had far more violent disputes with
the grand-vizier Kara Mustapha concerning the position of
his seat in the audience-chamber, than concerning the trade
of French subjects or the political interests of France.   The
lavish expenditure by which he sought to maintain his pretensions involved him in debt, and made him descend to
several very mean expedients in order to obtain money.
He borrowed large sums from Constantinopolitan Jews, and
when his credit was exhausted, he compelled the French
merchants of Pera, by an unwarranted exercise of his authority,
to supply him with funds.   These proceedings formed a
shameful contrast with his public displays, and did not tend
to increase the respect of the Turks for the agents of the
great monarchs of Christendom[3].

    The eagerness with which the ambassadors of the Christian
powers intrigued and bribed, in order to overreach one another at the Porte, the importance they attached to sitting
in an arm-chair in public, and the tricks they made use of
to obtain exclusive privileges, led the Turks to conclude
that the Christian character was a very despicable compound
of childish folly and extreme selfishness[4].   The Othoman

---

[1] Hammer, *Histoire de l'Empire Othoman*, xi. 45, 229.
[2] Hammer, xi. 341.   Compare a letter of Nointel, in Laborde's *Athènes aux XV., XVI., et XVII. Siècles*, i. 137.
[3] Laborde, *Athènes aux XV., XVI., et XVII. Siècles*, i. 140.
[4] Nointel endeavoured to insert an article in the treaty with France, by which

ministers, acting on this persuasion, treated the representatives of the Christian powers at Constantinople with contempt, and made the commerce of Christian nations the object of frequent exactions.

These circumstances were operating to produce a collision between the sultan and his Christian neighbours when Achmet Kueprili, who had been grand-vizier for fifteen years, died, at the early age of forty-one, A.D. 1676, leaving the Othoman empire at the greatest extent it attained[1]. Achmet was as remarkable for his honourable conduct as for his great talents. He was a lover of justice, and a hater of presents, which he knew were one of the great sources of corruption in Turkey. Kara Mustapha succeeded this great man as grand-vizier. He was distinguished by his excessive cupidity and insolence, as Achmet had been by his extraordinary disinterestedness and prudence. The rapid degradation of the Othoman character, and the decline of the empire, date from his accession to office. The negotiations of the Porte with foreign governments were employed by Kara Mustapha as a means of gratifying his avarice and extorting money. His presumption was as unbounded as his avarice was sordid. At the first audience he gave to the French ambassador, one of those scandalous scenes happened which we have seen reacted with a more tragical afterpiece by a Russian prince. M. de Nointel was offended at the position of his seat at an audience, and when he insisted on having his seat placed on the same level as the sofa of the grand-vizier, he was turned out of the room by his shoulders, the tshaous shouting as he pushed him along, ' March off, infidel[2]!'

A few examples of the exactions of Kara Mustapha give a faithful portrait of the state of the Othoman administration. The republic of Ragusa was under the protection of the sultan, and paid an annual tribute to the Porte. The city had been almost entirely destroyed by an earthquake in 1666, and envoys were sent to Constantinople to represent the impoverished state of the republic, and solicit a remission of

---

the Porte engaged not to admit vessels of several of the European powers to trade in the Othoman empire, unless under the French flag. Hammer, xi. 344.

[1] He added Candia, Neuhausel in Hungary, and Kaminiec in Poland, to the empire.

[2] ' Haïdé kalk ghiaour.' Hammer, xii. 8. Prince Mentschikoff is said to have wounded the pride of the Porte by wearing an old coat at an audience, and some persons attribute the Crimean war to pride as much as to policy.

the tribute. To this petition Kara Mustapha replied by immediately demanding payment of a sum of three hundred purses, or one hundred and fifty thousand dollars, on account of the additional amount of customs which Othoman subjects had paid in the port of Ragusa during the war of Candia, when they were excluded from trading in the other ports of the Adriatic. The envoys were thrown into prison, and threatened with torture ; but, after a year's imprisonment, the matter was compounded by the republic paying one hundred and twenty purses or sixty thousand dollars [1].

The Dutch ambassador Collier was compelled to pay a large sum to prevent the trade of Holland from being interrupted [2].

The Venetian bailo, Cuirana, having smuggled some valuable merchandise into his residence in order to defraud the Porte of the legal duty, was obliged to compound for his misconduct by paying the grand-vizier thirty thousand dollars [3]. On the arrival of a new bailo, Morosini, new disputes occurred, in consequence of some Christian slaves making their escape on board the Venetian galleys in the port. These disputes were again arranged by paying the sum of fifty thousand dollars, which was distributed among the grand-vizier and the principal agents of his party. Again, when the news reached Constantinople that a number of Turks had been slain in a foray on the Dalmatian frontier, the bailo of Venice was imprisoned in the Seven Towers, and not released until the republic paid the sum of two hundred thousand dollars as indemnity [4].

The Genoese resident, Spinola, was accused of circulating forged coin, and he was compelled to pay the Porte five thousand dollars before he could obtain the permission to embark for Genoa. On a previous occasion he had paid a

---

[1] Rycaut, *History*, iii. 4 ; Hammer, xii. 38.

[2] Fifty purses to the grand-vizier, ten to his kihaya, three to the reis effendi, and eight to the aga of the custom-house ; not six thousand purses for an audience, as the French translation of Hammer says. Compare Rycaut, iii. 12, with Hammer, xii. 40.

[3] Even the Greek government has been compelled to send circulars to the foreign ministers at King Otho's court, complaining of the frauds committed by diplomatic agents ; and frauds on the part of the royal household have been detected. Such are the results of diplomatic and court privileges where honour is the only guarantee for honesty.

[4] Rycaut, iii. 10 ; Hammer, xii. 38.

large sum as a bribe, because he established a manufactory of brandy, and a cellar for the sale of wine, in his residence[1].

The position of the French ambassador's seat, at his audience with the grand-vizier, was frequently a question of State between the court of France and the Sublime Porte. Kara Mustapha persisted in denying to M. de Guilleragues the privilege of sitting on the soffra. The French submitted to this indignity, but even by their obsequiousness they could not escape the exactions of the Othoman government. Eight ships, belonging to the corsairs of Tripoli in Africa, having been pursued by a French squadron under Admiral Duquesne, sought refuge in the port of Scio, where they were fired on by the French, whose shot did considerable damage to the town, and killed several Mussulmans. The grand-vizier, who availed himself of every opportunity to fill his coffers, demanded an indemnity of three hundred and fifty thousand crowns from the French ambassador for this wanton act of hostility, and threatened to send him to the Seven Towers. After a few days' detention, M. de Guilleragues signed an agreement to pay a present to the Porte, and was released. A good deal of bargaining was required to fix the amount of the present, and the manner in which it was to be presented to the Porte. At length the secretary of embassy and the dragoman presented themselves with articles valued at sixty thousand dollars; a curtain was suddenly drawn up, and the representatives of France found themselves in the presence of the sultan, who was seated on an elevated throne. The imperial usher then proclaimed, 'Behold the agents sent by the King of France to make satisfaction for the misconduct of his ships at Scio,' and the different articles were mentioned, with the value attached to each[2].

The English ambassador was exposed to even severer pecuniary exactions than the French. The Turkey Company was accused of having imported an immense quantity of Venetian lion-dollars, of base alloy, into Aleppo. Though the accusation appears to have been false, the Turkey merchants preferred paying the grand-vizier a bribe of seventeen thousand dollars rather than engage in a contest which must

[1] Rycaut, iii. 11; Hammer, xii. 18.
[2] Rycaut (iii. 8) says they were valued at ten times their real cost; compare Hammer, xii. 54.

have entailed great loss, and, from the notorious venality of the Othoman administration, no decision would have established their innocence, unless their commercial character in their general dealings had refuted the accusation.

Another device of Kara Mustapha to extort money from the English was singularly mean, but completely successful, on account of that very meanness which none could have suspected. Sir John Finch, the ambassador, was requested to send the capitulations, as the treaties between England and the sultan are called, to be examined at the Porte. He complied, and was then informed that a new treaty was necessary, which always required a number of presents. The ambassador protested that he was satisfied with the existing capitulations, and asked for their restoration in vain. Kara Mustapha ordered every obstruction to be thrown in the way of English trade, and the losses to which the merchants were exposed were so great that, to avoid further exactions, they furnished the ambassador with twenty-five thousand dollars to bribe the grand-vizier to restore the capitulations. A new ambassador, Lord Chandos, was specially instructed to complain of this exaction, and, to avoid exposure, Kara Mustapha deemed it prudent to restore the money; but other grounds were discovered for compelling the English merchants to leave the greater part of the sum in his hands[1].

The avarice and injustice of Kara Mustapha were so notorious that Suleiman, who was afterwards himself grand-vizier, said during his predecessor's vizirate, 'In this man's time the true believers cannot expect better usage than the infidels[2].'

The tameness with which the European powers submitted to the insolence and extortions of the grand-vizier increased his pride. When their subjects complained, he replied, 'Do you not breathe the sultan's air, and will you pay nothing for the privilege?' At length he made the affairs of Hungary a pretext for commencing war with Austria. His presumption led him to believe that he would find no difficulty in adding Vienna to the sultan's dominions, and, with all his incapacity, he would probably have succeeded, from the greater incapacity of the German emperor, had the house of Austria not been

---

[1] Rycaut, iii. 8.
[2] Suleiman Pasha perished when Sultan Mohammed IV. was dethroned.

saved by the Poles. The first campaign was signalized by
the memorable siege of Vienna, the victory of John Sobieski,
and the death of Kara Mustapha, who was strangled as a
punishment for his bad success, A. D. 1683.

When the republic of Venice saw that the army of the
grand-vizier had been completely destroyed by the disastrous
campaign of 1683, the senate considered that an immediate
war with the sultan would be the best policy. The sacrifices
Venice had made to preserve peace, both of money and
dignity, were always met by fresh displays of insolence and
new exactions on the part of the Othoman government, so
that sooner or later the republic felt that it would be compelled to make a stand and defend itself by arms. It seemed,
therefore, more prudent to seize the present moment for
weakening the resources of its enemy, by attacking him in
the south while all his best troops were employed on his
northern frontier, than to wait supinely until he found leisure
to choose his own time for commencing hostilities with Venice,
as he had done with Austria. The Pope joined the Emperor
of Germany and the King of Poland, in urging the republic
to form an alliance for prosecuting the war against the
Mohammedans in concert. Many allusions were made to the
glorious victory of Lepanto—allusions which must have suggested to Venetian statesmen the trifling results of that great
battle, and convinced them that in the war they were about
to undertake, their only hope of success ought to be placed
in their own resources. An offensive and defensive treaty
was concluded between the republic, the Emperor of Germany,
and the King of Poland, under the guarantee of Pope Innocent
XI.[1] In the month of July 1684, Capello, the Venetian
resident at Constantinople, presented himself at the Porte,
and communicated the declaration of war to the kaimakam,
the grand-vizier being at Adrianople with the sultan. As
soon as he had executed his commission, he disguised himself
as a sailor, and escaped on board a French ship.

The war which now commenced was the most successful
the republic ever carried on against the Othoman empire,
yet it affords signal evidence that both the machine of
government and the energy of the people had suffered greater

---

[1] Rycaut (iii. 136) gives the articles of the treaty.

deterioration among the Venetians than even among the Othomans. The glory acquired by Venice, and the conquests she gained, must be ascribed entirely to one great man, whose influence remedied the defects in the administration, and whose character supplied its wants. Francesco Morosini, who had been elevated to the dignity of Knight and Procurator of Saint Mark for his valour in the war of Candia, was subsequently accused of having betrayed his country's interests when he concluded the peace which surrendered to the sultan an untenable fortress. He was honourably acquitted, but during fifteen years of peace his former services were depreciated, and he lived retired as one of the common herd of princely nobles in Venice. When, however, it was again necessary to meet the Othomans in battle, all men remembered the bloody contests of the former war and the indomitable courage of Morosini. The dignified behaviour of the patriotic general at last received its reward, and Francesco Morosini, now sixty-six years of age, was intrusted with the chief command of the forces of the republic as captain-general.

Morosini occupies so conspicuous a place in the history of Greece as well as Venice, that his private character deserves to be noticed in order that his public career may be better understood. Though he was wealthy and noble, he had passed the best years of his youth and manhood at sea. From his twentieth to his forty-third year he had been constantly engaged in active service on board the Venetian fleet, where he had gained great honour by his enterprise and daring. His mind was firm and equable; his perseverance was not inferior to his courage, yet he was neither rash nor obstinate; his constitution was vigorous and healthy; his personal appearance was dignified and his countenance cheerful; his manner bold, and somewhat haughty; his language frank and rough, or grave and courteous, according to the rank of his associates; his naval and military skill of a high order, and improved by long experience in the Othoman wars. His career proves that he possessed considerable knowledge of administrative and warlike science, but his campaigns seem also to indicate that he was not endowed with high strategical prescience. The military and naval operations under his direction were not sufficiently combined, nor were his campaigns marked by that unity of purpose which attains a definite

object by regular progress. We must, however, always bear
in mind that the armies he commanded were comparatively
small, that his power over the best part of his land forces was
limited by conventions, that he could not act without con-
sulting a council of war, and that his plans were controlled
by a jealous senate. It need not, therefore, excite our
wonder if his mind turned habitually from the contemplation
of enlarged views to the attainment of immediate advantages. The impatience of successful results is one of the
evils of controlling distant military operations by numerous
assemblies, whether aristocratical or democratical. Party
objections and ignorant criticism have so much scope for
their activity, that generals under such control must secure
every trifling success, even though the insignificant victory
entails the sacrifice of some greater results, which steady
perseverance, patient progress, and long delay could alone
have gained.

The naval forces of Venice, at the commencement of the
war, consisted of a well-appointed fleet of ten galleasses,
thirty ships of the line, and thirty galleys, besides a number
of smaller vessels. The army, on the other hand, was in a
neglected condition ; the regular troops amounted to only
eight thousand, and they were by no means in good order
or well disciplined. The provincial militia, though numerous, and generally well armed, could hardly be made
available for foreign service. The revenues of the republic
did not greatly exceed two millions of sequins. With these
limited resources Venice engaged in a contest with the
Othoman empire.

It was of the greatest importance to Venice to follow
up the declaration of war by some great success, before
the Othoman government had time to reinforce its garrisons
in Dalmatia and Greece. In both these countries military
operations were carried on with activity, but those which
relate to Greece alone require to be noticed in this work.
It was by conquests in Greece that the Venetians expected
to acquire such an increase of revenue as would indemnify
the republic for the expenditure of the war. This consideration, and not the ambition of becoming the conqueror
of Sparta and Athens, induced Morosini to recommend
Greece as the chief field of military operations. He opened

the campaign of 1684 by laying siege to Santa Maura. The attack was pushed with vigour, and the place surrendered in sixteen days (6th August). This conquest was of primary importance for the prosecution of hostilities against the Morea, and for the security of Venetian commerce, Santa Maura being one of the principal places of refuge for the Barbary corsairs who infested the entrance of the Adriatic. As Prevesa might have performed the same office, Morosini followed up his first success by besieging that place, which fell into his hands on the 29th of September. A plundering expedition into Acarnania, the destruction of five Turkish villages, and the capture of a few slaves, occupied the fleet and army during the interval between the capture of Santa Maura and the attack on Prevesa[1]. At this early period of the war, disease began to make great havoc in the ranks of the Venetians, and it seems to have increased in intensity in every succeeding campaign. Count Strasoldo, the general of the land forces, was one of its victims.

In order to prosecute hostilities with vigour, the senate found that it was necessary to augment the army by the addition of foreign troops already organized in battalions and experienced in military duties. The Pope, the Grand-duke of Tuscany, and the Order of Malta had promised to send some veteran auxiliaries, but the chief dependence of the republic could only be on its own troops. Veteran mercenaries were sought in Germany. The alliance with the Emperor enabled the Venetian government to conclude military conventions with several of the German princes, who were in the habit of hiring their troops to foreign states. Many of the German princes had taken up the trade formerly exercised by the Italian condottieri, in order to maintain larger military establishments than the revenues of their dominions could have otherwise supported, and give themselves thereby additional political importance. The war in Candia had proved that the brilliant military services of the noble volunteers of France, in spite of all the noise made about them, were of little real value in a long campaign. The professional soldiers of Germany proved

---

[1] Coronelli, *Description Géographique et Historique de la Morée reconquise par les Vénétiens;* fol. Paris, 1687 ; pp. 67-70.

more efficient troops, and during the present war they
displayed not only steady courage on the field of battle,
but also great patience in the camp when disease was destroying their strength and thinning their ranks. Conventions for the supply of entire regiments, completely equipped
and disciplined under the command of experienced officers,
were concluded with the princes of Brunswick and Saxony,
each of whom bound himself to furnish the republic with
two thousand four hundred men [1]. The treaty with the
Duke of Brunswick, afterwards Elector of Hanover, was
concluded in December 1684, and the Hanoverian troops,
after marching through Germany in winter, reached Venice
in April, and joined Morosini at Dragomestre in June 1685 [2].
Their number, including officers and camp-followers, amounted
to 2542 men. Though valuable troops, they were not easy
to rule, complaining constantly of the treatment they received
from the Venetian government and the captain-general, and
quarrelling frequently among themselves [3].

The great object of Morosini was to conquer the Morea.
He considered that it would be as easily conquered, and
more easily defended, than Candia, as it lay nearer the
resources of Venice. Some of the chiefs of Maina had
promised to join the Venetians and rouse the rest of the
Greek population to arms, if Morosini would appear in Greece
with a formidable force. These chiefs induced Morosini to
hope that he should be able to take possession of Misithra
and Leondari without difficulty, and, by commanding the
centre of the Morea, interrupt the communications of the
Turks with the sea-coast. The maritime fortresses could
then have offered very little resistance to the Venetians, who
already commanded the sea. The Mainate chiefs boasted
of what they had no means of performing. The grand-vizier

---

[1] Gratiani *Historiarum Venetarum libri xxiv.*, vol. ii. 321 ; Locatelli, *Historia
della Veneta Guerra in Levante contro l'Impero Ottomano*, i. 112. Alessandro
Locatelli was secretary to Morosini from June 1684 until he returned to Venice
in 1689. His work was printed at Cologne, after his death, in two volumes, folio,
1705.

[2] Schwenke (*Geschichte der Hannoverischen Truppen in Griechenland*, 1685–1689,
p. 182) gives the treaty with Ernest Augustus, Duke of Brunswick, father of
George I. of England.

[3] Schwenke, 42, 126, 155, 170. On one occasion they complained that they
were unfairly treated in the division of the spoil, because they received no black
slaves, like the Venetian captains. Pfister, *Zwei Feldzüge aus dem Kriege von
Morea in den Jahren 1687 und 1688*; Kassel, 1845, p. 122, *note* 3.

Achmet Kueprili had reduced Maina to a state of complete subjection, and the Othoman garrisons in the three fortresses of Zarnata, Kielapha, and Passava, had so completely established the authority of the sultan in the country, that the mountaineers were too much intimidated to think of taking up arms[1]. Ismael Pasha had also taken precautions to preserve tranquillity by marching additional troops into Maina, and compelling the principal families to give hostages for their good conduct. When Morosini arrived at Sapienza he met a deputation of Mainates, who besought him not to approach their coast, as they were entirely at the mercy of the Turks, and the people would not venture to take up arms until they saw the Venetians in possession of some important fortress in their vicinity, where the republic would be able to maintain a powerful garrison and fleet to protect the movements of their friends. Morosini, who had with him about eight thousand troops, immediately commenced the siege of Coron[2]. The pasha of the Morea hastened to its relief with a considerable force, but was defeated. Coron was taken, after a vigorous defence, on the 11th August, and though arrangements were made for its capitulation, a suspicion of treachery caused its defenders to be massacred[3].

As soon as Morosini had repaired the fortifications of Coron, and put the place in a condition to repel any attack of the Turks, he crossed over the gulf to Maina. His object was to encourage the Mainates to take up arms and to gain possession of Kalamata, before which the capitan-pasha had formed an intrenched camp with an army of six thousand infantry and two thousand spahis. Morosini was well acquainted with the country, for twenty-six years before he had taken and destroyed Kalamata, carrying off the cannon from the castle, and the able-bodied men, whom he condemned to work at the oar in his galleys, after he had burned all the houses in the town[4]. He now summoned

---

[1] Hammer, xi. 337, 374; Locatelli, i. 101, 128.
[2] The Venetian army consisted of Venetians, Sclavonians, and Hanoverians; the auxiliaries of Maltese, Florentine, and Papal troops.

Venetians	.	.	3000	Maltese	.	.	1000
Sclavonians	.	.	1000	Florentines	.	.	300
Hanoverians	.	.	2400	Papal troops	.	.	400
			6400				1700

[3] Schwenke, 41.   [4] Gratiani F. *Mauroceni gesta*, 71.

the place to surrender, under the penalty of being treated like Coron if it resisted. The capitan-pasha rejected the summons with disdain. In the mean time the Venetians rendered themselves masters of Zarnata, which was only five miles distant from Chitries, where the fleet lay at anchor. The Othoman governor of Zarnata had referred to the capitan-pasha for orders, but Morosini intercepted these orders, and opened negotiations with the garrison, to whom he offered such favourable terms, that he persuaded the aga to surrender the place on the 10th September. Six hundred Turks, with their arms and baggage, were landed near Kalamata, but the aga retired to Venice, where his treachery or cowardice was rewarded with a pension. The Venetian army, increased by the arrival of three thousand three hundred Saxons, was now placed under the command of General Degenfeld, and ordered to attack the capitan-pasha. A council of war was held, and its members agreed with Degenfeld in thinking that the position of the Turkish camp was too strong to be assailed. When, however, it was proposed to sign a written declaration to this effect, in order to transmit it to the captain-general Morosini, the Hanoverian prince, Maximilian William, declared that Morosini having given express orders to attack the Turks, in his opinion the best thing they could do would be to obey them without losing time [1]. This observation of the young prince changed the resolution of Degenfeld, who appears to have intended to set up his own authority as a control on that of the captain-general, either from personal jealousy, or a desire to prolong the war; for he was a man of courage, and when he resolved to advance, he conducted the operations of the army with promptitude. The Turks were completely defeated, and both their camp and the town of Kalamata taken. The castle of Kalamata, being found incapable of defence, was again destroyed, as it had been in 1659, but the inhabitants on this occasion remained in possession of their property under Venetian protection. The Othoman

---

[1] Schwenke, 47. The prince was the third son of the Duke of Brunswick. He was then nineteen years old. He was a giddy youth, and got into disgrace at his father's court by ridiculing the rouged figure of the Countess of Platen, his father's mistress. He made the whole circle of envious beauties partake in his amusement, by squirting pea water, instead of rose water, in their faces, which left sad traces of artificial adorning on the painted visage of the countess.

A.D. 1684-1718.]

garrisons in the forts of Kielapha, near the harbour of Vitylo, and of Passava, near Marathonisi, now capitulated, and evacuated Maina. Kielapha contained fifty-eight pieces of artillery, including some small guns mounted on the curtains. Passava was destroyed as of no use to the Venetians, who kept possession of Marathonisi ; but they placed garrisons in Zarnata and Kielapha, in order to watch the Mainates, and to secure the command of the ports of Armyro and Vitylo, from which the greater part of the produce of the Zygos was exported. The Venetians placed as little reliance in the unsteady disposition of the Mainate chiefs as the Turks, and employed nearly the same means for preserving their ascendancy in the country. The army of the republic was put into winter-quarters at Zante, Santa Maura, and Corfu, in the month of October, but disease continued to thin the ranks of the Germans [1].

The campaign of 1686 was opened by the Othomans in the month of April. They penetrated into Maina and besieged Kielapha, but were compelled to abandon the enterprise on the approach of a Venetian fleet under Venieri. The republic had now secured the services of an able general to direct the operations of its army in Greece. Otho Koenigsmark, field-marshal in the Swedish service, was appointed commander-in-chief of the land forces under the orders of the captain-general [2]. The Hanoverian troops had been increased to upwards of three thousand men, but the whole army did not exceed eleven thousand, and it was assembled so slowly that the campaign did not commence until June. Old Navarin (Pylos) was besieged, and being dependent for its supply of water on an aqueduct, immediately capitulated. The garrison consisted chiefly of negroes, who were conveyed to Alexandria. New Navarin, which had been constructed by the Othoman government in 1572, the

---

[1] The Hanoverians passed the winter at Zante, and they had some reason to complain of neglect on the part of the Venetian government. They had great difficulty in procuring firewood to cook their victuals ; the barrels of rice were sometimes half-filled with spoiled macaroni, and everything rose in price on their arrival. From April, 1685, to January, 1686, they lost 256 in battle, and 736 died in hospital. Schwenke, 57.

[2] This Count Otho Koenigsmark was the uncle of Philip, the lover of Sophia Dorothea, the wife of George I.; and his sister, Maria Aurora, was the mistress of Frederick Augustus I., Elector of Saxony and King of Poland, and mother of Marshal de Saxe.

year after the battle of Lepanto, to defend the entrance of
the magnificent harbour, in which the largest fleet may ride
at anchor, was next attacked. The seraskier of the Morea
attempted in vain to relieve it, and Sefer Pasha was compelled
to sign a capitulation, binding himself to surrender the place
in four days. The explosion of a powder magazine on the
night he signed this capitulation, by which he and many
of the principal Turks perished, induced the survivors immediately to admit the Venetians into the fortress[1]. Three
thousand souls, of whom one thousand five hundred were
soldiers, were conveyed to Tripoli. The army then besieged
Modon, encamping among the luxuriant gardens in its
vicinity. The place was well fortified, provided with ample
supplies of provisions and ammunition, with an excellent
artillery of one hundred guns, and defended by a garrison
of one thousand men ; but it capitulated, after a feeble
defence, on the 10th of July, and the inhabitants, four
thousand in number, were transported to the regency of
Tripoli. Considerable booty was found in Modon, but
Morosini was accused of allowing the Italians to purchase
the property of the emigrants at their own terms. Of four
hundred black slaves taken in the town, the Hanoverians
complained that they only received seven men and three
women for their share, and they said that all their
booty consisted of some copper, which was sold for forty
sequins.

The Hanoverians were at this time much dissatisfied with
the Venetian service, in which they gained less plunder than
they expected ; and Morosini was extremely unpopular
among them. His courage was admired, for they recounted
that on one occasion, when it was expected that Modon
was about to surrender, the captain-general visited the
advanced battery with a train of magnificently-dressed
Venetian nobles. The Turks, however, suddenly broke off
the negotiations, and opened their fire on this battery :
the consequence was, that all the fine-dressed nobles ran

---

[1] It was supposed that Sefer Pasha blew up the magazine, where he had invited
many of the principal Turks to assemble, in order to revenge himself on them for
having compelled him to capitulate. This report, however, is not mentioned in
the letter of a Saxon volunteer, entitled *Gründlicher und genauer Bericht aller
merkwürdigen Sachen welche bei Belager und Eroberung der Vestungen in Morea,
Navarino, und Modon täglich vorgelaufen;* gedruckt im Jahr 1686.

to hide themselves under cover, leaving Morosini standing alone. Complaints were made of his severity, and the Germans declared that they would not remain in the Venetian service unless the article of the convention, which placed the administration of justice and the power of punishment in the hands of an officer named by their duke, was strictly observed. Morosini, they asserted, sometimes ordered the highest Venetian officers to be put in irons and flogged, without the sentence of a court-martial [1]. If this be true, there can be no doubt that the captain-general found it necessary to employ these strong measures to put an end to fraud and peculation. The complaints of the Germans were not always reasonable. The officers were discontented at the frequent change of place in this campaign, which compelled them to sell the horses and camp-equipage they had picked up at an inadequate price, as they were not allowed space to transport it on board the Venetian ships. The red uniform of the Hanoverians, though it was greatly feared by the enemy in battle, was too conspicuous to allow the soldiers to make much booty, and, to their great regret, prevented them from catching buffaloes, which were numerous in the Morea [2].

Nauplia was the next object of attack. On the 30th July, Count Koenigsmark landed at Port Tolon. The rock Palamedi, being then without fortifications, was immediately occupied by the Venetians. But though the town was commanded by this position, it was so strongly fortified, that it was found impossible to make any progress with the siege until the seraskier, who had posted himself at Argos with four thousand cavalry and three thousand infantry, was driven from the vicinity of the place. This was effected after a sharp engagement, in which, from want of horses, the Hanoverian artillery-officers employed Greeks to drag their guns [3]. The Turkish cavalry was well mounted, bold, and active, and covered the retreat to Corinth. The batteries on the Palamedi soon set the houses of the town on fire, but the place continued to make a brave defence, as the seraskier was expected

---

[1] Schwenke, 88.　　　　　　　　　　　　　[2] Ibid., 105.
[3] Lieut. Heerman says, 'Als ich jüngst mit den Stücken avanciren sollte, habe ich mich erst nach meinen menschlichen Pferden, den Griechen, umsehen und sie zusammen suchen müssen.' Schwenke, 104.

to return with fresh reinforcements. The Venetian army, which was encamped in the low ground between Tiryns and Nauplia, suffered from an autumnal fever called the plague. The Hanoverians could only muster one thousand five hundred and fifty men under arms, and they had one thousand two hundred sick and wounded. The seraskier now thought that the time had arrived for assailing the Venetian army with every prospect of success. He advanced from Corinth, and made a desperate attack on their camp on the 29th of August, which was not repulsed until Morosini landed a body of two thousand men from the fleet, who opened their fire on the flank of the Turks. Koenigsmark distinguished himself by his skill and courage in this battle, which ended in the total defeat of the Othoman army. Nauplia, being now deprived of all hope of relief, capitulated on the 3rd of September, and seven thousand persons, including one thousand two hundred men of the garrison, were landed at Tenedos. The Sclavonians in the Venetian service distinguished themselves greatly before Nauplia. Disease continued to make destructive ravages among the Germans. Their complaints were loud, and their disputes with Morosini unusually violent, when he wished to put them into winter-quarters at Nauplia. Morosini had some reason to complain, for the German officers quarrelled among themselves, intrigued against one another, and increased the service of the soldiers by carrying an excessive number of private servants on the regimental muster-rolls[1].

The campaign of 1687 is memorable in the history of Europe for the destruction of the Parthenon of Athens, the most wonderful combination of architecture and sculpture, and perhaps the most perfect work of art, which has yet been executed. Germany again sent new troops to reinforce the army of the republic. The Saxons returned home at the end of the last campaign; but conventions having been concluded with the Landgraf of Hesse and the Duke of Würtemberg, the strength of the German contingent was not diminished[2]. The Hanoverian battalions received an addition of one thousand two hundred men, but these new recruits were not veteran soldiers like those who had arrived in the

[1] Schwenke, 120, 126.   [2] Pfister, *Zwei Feldzüge aus dem Kriege von Morea.*

preceding years. All Germany was at this time filled with recruiting parties for the Austrian armies in Hungary, and in anticipation of war with Louis XIV. The officers of Brunswick had even accepted French deserters into the ranks, in order to complete their companies. On the march to Venice forty of these French recruits again deserted in one day, carrying with them the arms with which they had been supplied, and before reaching Venice the loss from desertion exceeded two hundred men.

The Turks had prepared for resisting the further progress of the Venetians by forming a camp near Patras, in which ten thousand men were strongly intrenched under the command of Mehemet Pasha. The delay which took place in the arrival of the troops from Germany, and the fear of placing the army in too close communication with the fleet, in which the plague had appeared, prevented the captain-general from opening the campaign before the end of July. The troops were landed to the west of Patras, and the fleet passed through the Dardanelles of Lepanto during the night of the 22nd July. Koenigsmark found that it was necessary to drive the Turkish army from its camp before commencing the siege of Patras. The position of Mehemet Pasha was strong and well chosen, but by marching round it, he succeeded in attacking its weakest point, and in storming it, after a well-contested battle. Patras, the two castles commanding the entrance of the gulf of Corinth, and the town of Lepanto, were immediately evacuated by the Turks with the greatest precipitation.

These successes excited great enthusiasm at Venice, where the delay in opening the campaign had caused some anxiety. Morosini, who had been raised to the rank of hereditary knight after the taking of Nauplia, now received the title of 'the Peloponnesian.' His portrait was placed in the hall of the Great Council, an honour never granted before to any Venetian during his lifetime[1]. Koenigsmark, who was supposed to want money more than mere titles, was presented

---

[1] Morosini was authorized to transmit his hereditary knighthood to his nephew, as he had no son. The only families who possessed this honour were those of Contarini and Quirini. Daru, iv. 645. In England the title of baronet has become a mere handle to men's names, being usually conferred by ministerial favour on rich landlords who can give political support to men in office who have the disposal of court favour.

with six thousand ducats in a gold basin. The prince of
Hanover received a jewelled sword valued at four thousand
ducats, and other officers were rewarded with gold-hilted
swords or gold chains. The liberality of the republic was
more than royal. Koenigsmark's pay was raised to twenty-
four thousand ducats annually.

Castel Tornese, Salona, and Corinth were abandoned by
the Turks, who fled in confusion to Thebes and Negrepont.
Those in the Morea who could not escape out of the peninsula, retired to Misithra and Monemvasia, the only cities of
which they retained possession. The retreat of the Turks
was marked by the same acts of barbarity, both on their part
and on that of the Greeks, which have been renewed on a
greater scale in our own times. The Turks destroyed all
the Greek villages on their line of march, and carried off many
Christians as slaves. They frequently massacred even their
own Christian slaves, when unable to take them away. The
Greeks, on the other hand, waylaid and murdered every
Mohammedan, man, woman, or child, whom they could surprise or capture.

The Venetians occupied Corinth on the 7th August, where
they were joined by one thousand Hessians. On the 12th of
August the captain-general commenced fortifying the isthmus,
carrying his works along the ruins of the wall constructed by
Justinian and repaired by Manuel II. This was certainly a
useless waste of labour.

Morosini now proposed to attack Negrepont, as it was the
key of continental Greece, and its capture would have rendered the republic master of the whole country south of
Thermopylae. His plan was opposed by the generals of the
land forces, who all agreed in thinking that the season was
too far advanced for an operation of such magnitude; and
after much deliberation, it was determined to attack Athens,
where it was thought that the army would find good winter-
quarters.

The lion of St. Mark rarely made use of his wings, and the
passage of his forces round the Morea was unusually slow, but
on the 21st of September the Venetians entered the Piraeus,
and Koenigsmark encamped the same evening in the olive-
grove near the sacred way to Eleusis. The army consisted of
nearly ten thousand men, including eight hundred and seventy

cavalry. The town of Athens was immediately occupied, and the siege of the Acropolis commenced. The attack was directed against the Propylaea, before which the Turks had constructed strong batteries. The Parthenon, and the temple of Minerva Polias, with its beautiful porticoes, were then nearly perfect, as far as regarded their external architecture. Even the sculpture was so little injured by time, that it displayed much of its inimitable excellence[1]. Two batteries were erected, one at the foot of the Museum, and the other near the Pnyx. Mortars were planted under cover of the Areopagus, but their fire proving uncertain, two more were placed under cover of the buildings of the town, near the north-east corner of the rock, which threw their shells at a high angle, with a low charge, into the Acropolis[2].

In the mean time the Othoman troops descended into the plain from Thebes and Negrepont ; and Koenigsmark. as had been the case at the siege of Coron, Navarin, and Nauplia, was compelled to divide his army to meet them. On the 25th of September a Venetian bomb blew up a small powder-magazine in the Propylaea, and on the following evening another fell in the Parthenon, where the Turks had deposited all their most valuable effects, with a considerable quantity of powder and inflammable materials. A terrific explosion took place ; the centre columns of the peristyle, the walls of the cella, and the immense architraves and cornices they supported, were scattered around the remains of the temple. Much of the unrivalled sculpture was defaced, and a part utterly destroyed. The materials heaped up in the building also took fire, and the flames, mounting high over the Acropolis, announced the calamity to the besiegers, and scathed many of the statues which still remained in their original positions. Though two hundred persons perished by this explosion, the Turks persisted in defending the place until they saw the seraskier defeated in his attempt to relieve them

---

[1] The little temple of Wingless Victory had been removed to make room for a Turkish battery before the siege. The materials found when the Greek government commenced clearing away the rubbish of modern constructions, enabled Ross, Schaubert, and Hansen partially to restore the building, which Pittaki, with the assistance of a contribution from Colonel Leake, has completed as far as possible. Compare Ross, *Die Acropolis von Athen,* with Laborde, *Athènes aux XV., XVI., et XVII. Siècles,* ii. 116.

[2] See the plan of the Acropolis, by the Venetian captain of engineers, Verneda, in Laborde, ii. 182.

on the 28th September. They then capitulated on being allowed to embark with their families for Smyrna in vessels hired at their own expense [1]. On the 4th of October, two thousand five hundred persons of all ages, including five hundred men of the garrison, moved down to embark at the Piraeus. Morosini complains in his official report to the republic that all his precautions could not prevent some acts of rapacity on the part of his mercenaries. About thirty Turks remained, and received baptism. Count Tomeo Pompei was the first Venetian commandant of the Acropolis.

Athens was now a Venetian possession. The German troops remained in the town. One of the mosques near the bazaar was converted into a Lutheran church, and this first Protestant place of worship in Greece was opened on the 19th of October, 1687, by the regimental chaplain Beithman [2]. Another mosque in the lower part of the town, towards the temple of Theseus, was given to the Catholics, who possessed also a monastery at the eastern end of the town, containing the choragic monument of Lysicrates. The time of service of the three Hanoverian regiments first enrolled had now expired, and on the 26th of December, 1687, they sailed from the Piraeus. In the three campaigns in which the red uniform had taken so distinguished a part, it had lost eighty-eight officers and two thousand nine hundred men ; yet, from the recruits which the contingent had received, its number still amounted to one thousand four hundred [3].

A short time convinced the Venetian leaders that it would be impossible to retain possession of Athens. The plague, which was making great ravages in the Morea, showed itself in the army. The seraskier kept two thousand cavalry at Thebes, and, by a judicious employment of his force, retained all Attica, with the exception of the plain of Athens, under his orders. The Venetians found it necessary to fortify the road to the Piraeus with three redoubts, in order to secure the communications of the garrison in Athens

---

[1] These vessels were, an English pink, three Ragusan petraks, and two French tartans; *see* Morosini's despatch, given by Laborde, ii. 159. The negroes were kept as prisoners, and divided among the troops in the usual way. Locatelli, ii. 7 ; Pfister, 92, 94.

[2] Schwenke, 156; Pfister, 104.

[3] Schwenke, 156.

with the ships in the port. The departure of the Hanoverians weakened the army, and in a council of war held on the 31st of December, it was resolved to evacuate Athens at the end of the winter, in order to concentrate all the troops for an attack on Negrepont. Lines were thrown across the isthmus of Munychia, to cover the evacuation and protect the naval camp, which could be distinctly traced until they were effaced by the construction of the new town of the Piraeus. It was also debated whether the walls of the Acropolis were to be destroyed; and perhaps their preservation, and that of the antiquities they enclose, is to be ascribed to the circumstance that the whole attention of the army was occupied by the increased duties imposed upon it by the sanatory measures requisite to prevent the ravages of the plague, and the difficulties created by the emigration of the Greek population of Athens. Between four and five thousand Athenians were compelled to abandon their native city and seek new homes in the Morea. Some were established at Vivares and Port Tolon, on the coast of Argolis, as colonists; the poorest were settled at Corinth, and others were dispersed in Aegina, Tinos, and Nauplia. About five hundred Albanians, chiefly collected among the peasantry of Corinth and Attica, were formed into a corps by the Venetians, but no Greeks could be induced to enter the army[1].

The last act of Morosini at Athens was to carry away some monuments of ancient sculpture as trophies of his victory. An attempt was made to remove the statue of Neptune and the Chariot of Victory, which adorned the western pediment of the Parthenon, but, in consequence of an oversight of the workmen employed, and perhaps partly in consequence of a flaw or crack in the marble, caused by the recent explosion, which destroyed a considerable part of the building, the whole mass of marble was precipitated to the ground, and so shivered to pieces by the fall that the fragments were not deemed worthy of transport. This misfortune to art occurred on the 19th

---

[1] Fanelli, *Atene Attica*, 311. The greater part of the Athenians were then, as at the breaking out of the Greek revolution, small landed proprietors, shop-keepers, and petty dealers in exports and imports. Ranke (*Die Venetianer in Morea*, 437, 443) mentions the concessions granted to the emigrants.

of March 1688. Instead of these magnificent figures from the hand of Phidias, Morosini was obliged to content himself with four lions, which still adorn the entrance of the arsenal at Venice. One of these, taken from the Piraeus, is remarkable for its colossal size, its severe style, and two long inscriptions, in runic characters, winding over its shoulders [1]. The complete evacuation of Attica was at length effected. Six hundred and sixty-two families quitted their native city, and on the 9th of April the Venetians sailed to Poros.

These records of the ruin of so much that interests the whole civilized world, awaken our curiosity to know something of the character and feelings of the modern Athenians, Greeks and Albanians, who then dwelt under the shadow of the Acropolis. Neither Morosini nor his German auxiliaries, though they joined in lamenting the destruction of the ancient marbles, seemed to think the modern Greeks deserving of much attention, merely because they pretended to represent the countrymen of Pericles and still spoke Greek. Venetian statesmen perceived the same degeneracy in their national character as German philologians discovered in their language. The Greek population, from its unwarlike disposition, was only an object of humanity; the Albanian peasantry, though a hardier and more courageous race, was not sufficiently numerous in the immediate vicinity of the city to be of much military importance. Yet, to a Hessian officer, Athens appeared a large and

[1] These inscriptions long baffled the sagacity of antiquaries. Some thought they were Pelasgic, others divined they were runic. They have been at last deciphered by M. Rafn, a learned Danish archaeologist. *Inscription Runique du Pirée,* interprétée par C. C. Rafn, et publiée par la Société Royale des Antiquaires du Nord ; Copenhague, 1856. The lion is sitting up on its hind legs, and is in this position about ten feet high. The style of art is noble and severe. It is supposed to be a work of the fifth century B.C. Two runic inscriptions wind along on its shoulders. That on the left side records that four Norwegian chiefs under the command of Harald Hardrada (who subsequently, when King of Norway, fell at Stamford Bridge) conquered the port of the Piraeus, and levied contribution on the Greeks because they had revolted against the emperor of Constantinople. That on the right side records that the runes were engraved by order of Harald, though the Athenians forbade placing the inscription. Harald Hardrada served in the Varangian guard, of which he rose to be chief, from 1033 to 1043. Rafn with some probability conjectures that the insurrection at Athens occurred during the Bulgarian revolt in 1040. It appears that the Athenians were not treated very tyrannically, as their Norwegian conquerors record their protest against any memorial of their insurrection. It is strange to find runic memorials in Attica of events which the Greeks desired should be forgotten. [*See* vol. ii. p. 418.]

populous town, with its ten thousand inhabitants, and the Athenians were found to be a respectable and well-disposed people[1]. But they were so completely destitute of moral energy, that they were unable to take any part in the public events of which their city was the theatre. They had no voice to give utterance to their feelings, though Europe would have listened with attention to their words. Perhaps they had no feelings deserving of utterance. Greece was thus the scene of important events, in which every nation in Europe acted a more prominent part than the Greeks. Even my countrymen from the misty hills of Caledonia, are named among the officers who joined the Hanoverians in 1686 as volunteers[2].

Morosini was elected Doge of Venice on the death of Giustiniani, and he was invested with the insignia of the ducal rank at Poros. The senate made the greatest exertions to increase the army in the Levant, and enable the doge to perform some exploit worthy of the prince of the republic. New troops were recruited in Germany, but they arrived slowly, and a campaign, which from the nature of the climate ought to have commenced in the month of April, was not opened until the season of the greatest heat had arrived. On the 8th of July 1688 the Venetian expedition sailed from Poros to besiege Negrepont. The land forces amounted to upwards of thirteen thousand men, the crews of the fleet to about ten thousand[3]. The garrison of Negrepont consisted of six thousand men, and the place was strongly fortified. Its communications with the continent were secured by a fortified bridge over the Euripus, and covered by the strong fort Karababa. On the land face, in the island, the fortifications were strengthened by a deep and broad ditch. A strong outwork, affording space for an intrenched camp, occupied by four thousand five hundred janissaries, crowned an eminence which protected the suburbs. Koenigsmark was of opinion that the attack ought to begin from the land side, by investing Karababa and the bridge, and thus cutting off the communications

---

[1] Laborde, ii. 358 ; Pfister, 105.
[2] Schwenke, 64: 'Siebzehn an der Zahl, meistens Schotten, Schweden, und Franzosen.'
[3] Schwenke (163) gives the list of the Venetian forces.

with the Othoman army at Thebes; but the doge considered
that it would be easier to attack the place from the island,
and his opinion prevailed. On the other hand, his proposal
to make an immediate attempt to storm the eminence on
which the janissaries were intrenched, was rejected, and
the advice of Koenigsmark, to proceed against it by regular
approaches in order to spare men, was adopted. In both
cases the decision proved unfortunate. A month was lost
in the attack on the outwork, and after a succession of
bloody skirmishes it was at last taken by storm on the
30th of August. Thirty pieces of cannon and five mortars
fell into the hands of the besiegers, who were then enabled
to push their approaches up to the ditch of the citadel.
But, as the communications between the garrison and the
army of the seraskier remained open, reinforcements and
supplies were continually introduced into the place, and
the sick and wounded were withdrawn. In the mean time
the Venetian army was encamped near a pestilential marsh,
which spread disease through its ranks. Thousands of
soldiers perished, and almost all the higher officers were
unable to do duty. Count Koenigsmark died on the 15th
of September, and before the end of the month a majority
of the land forces was incapable of service. The progress
of the siege was very slow. At length, on the 12th of
October, Morosini resolved to make a desperate attempt
to storm the place. Even with all the assistance that
could be drawn from the fleet, only eight thousand men
could be mustered under arms. This number was clearly
inadequate to attack a strong fortress garrisoned by six
thousand men, for the Turkish garrison, having been strengthened by fresh reinforcements, was still as numerous, and
far more confident, than at the commencement of the siege.
After a long and desperate struggle the assault was repulsed
at every point, but not until the Venetians had lost one
thousand men[1]. All hope of taking Negrepont was now
abandoned, and it only remained for Morosini to save the
relics of the expedition. The re-embarkment of the land
forces was covered by Prince Maximilian of Hanover, and
effected without loss. On the 21st of October the army was

---

[1] Pfister, 186.

landed at Thermisi in Argolis, by no means a healthy spot, and from thence the German troops, whose period of service had expired, were embarked for Venice. The remaining battalions of the Hanoverians and Hessians quitted Greece on the 5th of November 1688[1].

Before returning to Venice, Morosini was desirous of rendering his title to the proud epithet of 'the Peloponnesian' indisputable by the conquest of Monemvasia, the only fortress in the peninsula of which the Othomans still retained possession. He made an unsuccessful attack on it in 1689; and almost immediately after its failure, the state of his health compelled him to resign the command of the fleet. His successor, Cornaro, gained possession of Monemvasia in the following year; but the place yielded to famine, and not to the arms of the republic.

The possession of the fortresses of Lepanto and Corinth gave the Venetians the command of the whole northern shore of the gulf, and the greater part of northern Greece submitted to their authority, the Turks only retaining garrisons at Zeitouni, Talanti, Livadea, and Thebes, and in the mountain-passes which connect the valley of the Spercheus with the Boeotian plains, in order to secure the communications between Thessaly and Negrepont by land. But a considerable part of continental Greece was left without either Turkish or Venetian troops, and the Greek population not venturing to take up arms to defend their property, the country was exposed to be pillaged by marauders from both sides. Several districts were occupied by bands of deserters from the Dalmatian and Albanian troops in the service of Venice. Bossina, the leader of one of these bands, established his head-quarters permanently at Karpenisi, where his authority was recognized by the primates of the surrounding country, who paid him regular contributions, for which he defended them against the plundering expeditions of the Mohammedan Arnauts and Christian armatoli. Bossina assumed the title of General of the Venetian deserters. In vain Morosini endeavoured to suppress desertion and punish the deserters, by offering a reward of ten zechins for every deserter brought back to a Venetian port. The Albanians and armatoli, who posted

---

[1] Schwenke, 177; Pfister, 195.

themselves in the mountain-passes, arrested a few, and delivered them up to be punished ; but the evil continued, in consequence of the irregularity with which the republic paid the troops enrolled in its own possessions on the Adriatic. The success of Bossina induced another corps, under Elia Damianovich, to occupy Lidoriki and the surrounding district ; and to such a state of anarchy was Greece reduced, that the peaceable cultivators of the soil found these foreign deserters more humane and effectual protectors than either the Othoman or Venetian governments, and far less cruel and rapacious than the native Greek armatoli, who were a species of Christian gendarmerie in the service of the Porte. The Greek primates furnished the leaders of the deserters with monthly pay and subsistence for their followers, and the deserters defended the country against the armatoli and the foragers from the hostile armies, and maintaincd better discipline than was observed either by the Venetian or Othoman troops [1].

The Othoman government finding that the disorders in Greece were every day becoming greater, and that the number of districts which failed to pay taxes was constantly increasing, became seriously alarmed at the defection of the Christian population, and laid aside its usual haughtiness in order to make use of its Greek subjects in opposing the progress of the Venetians. Liberaki Yerakari, one of the Mainate chiefs who had embraced the Othoman party when Kueprili compelled Maina to pay haratch, and who had assisted the Turks in establishing their permanent garrisons at Zarnata, Kielapha, and Passava, was subsequently imprisoned at Constantinople for acts of piracy. He was now liberated, invested with the title of Bey of Maina, and sent to the army of the seraskier at Thebes, where he appeared, at the end of the year 1688, with about three hundred followers. He endeavoured to bring back the Greeks who had submitted to the Venetians, to their allegiance under the sultan ; and he invited the Athenians who had fled to Salamis and Aegina to return to their native city, promising them pardon for the past, and protection against illegal exactions in future. Many availed themselves of this offer when they found it was

---

[1] Locatelli, *Historia della Veneta Guerra in Levante contro l'Impero Ottomano*, ii. 11, 156, 172.

confirmed by the seraskier. Liberaki also opened secret communications with his partizans in Maina, in order to raise a rebellion against the Venetians ; and he entered into negotiations with the deserters at Karpenisi and Lidoriki, in order to persuade them to join the Turks. These negotiations were unsuccessful, and he was defeated in an attempt to gain possession of Salona by force[1].

In the year 1690 the Othoman armies, having received reinforcements, drove the deserters from the districts they occupied, and recovered possession of all the open country north of the Dardanelles, of Lepanto, and the Isthmus of Corinth, but they were defeated in an attack on the fortress of Lepanto. The property of the unfortunate Greek peasantry continued still to be exposed to devastation by the hostile armies, and by bands of marauders who plundered on their own account. Two examples may be cited to show the miserable condition of the population in continental Greece. In the year 1692, a party of Moreot Albanians made an incursion as far as Livadea, which they plundered, carrying off many slaves, seven hundred oxen, and four thousand sheep. Again, in the year 1694, another party of the Greek and Albanian militia in the Venetian possessions invaded continental Greece, and plundered Patradjik and many of the neighbouring villages[2].

These campaigns reflected no glory on Venice. The doge believed that he could again bring back victory to the arms of Venice by taking the command in person, and in 1693 he returned to Greece. He was now seventy-five years old, an age at which it is difficult to infuse enthusiasm into the hearts of lukewarm followers, so that fortune probably treated him kindly by conducting him to the tomb at Nauplia on the 16th January 1694, before he had dimmed the glory of his former deeds by any signal failure. Francesco Morosini was the last great man who has acted a part in the public affairs of Greece; his exploits have not yet been eclipsed by those of any subsequent hero.

The new captain-general, Zeno, attacked Chios. The

---

[1] Locatelli. ii. 152, 220.
[2] In 1689 several Othoman galleys entered the Saronic gulf, and carried off three hundred and fifty Greeks as slaves from the island of Salamis. Locatelli, ii. 204.

imprudence of assailing the Turks close to the coast of Asia
Minor, and near the centre of their resources, was pointed out
to him in vain. Zeno was a party leader and a braggart.
Chios was taken without difficulty, but the Othoman government displayed all the energy which it has so frequently put
forth on the occurrence of great misfortunes. It did everything in its power to render its fleet superior to that of Venice,
by constructing a number of line-of-battle ships, for it had
observed that its line-of-battle ships were better able to
contend with the Venetians on equal terms than its galleys.
After some severe fighting, Zeno lost heart, fled, abandoned
his conquest, and was deservedly imprisoned on his return
to Venice [1].

About the same time the Othoman government made a
bold attempt to regain possession of the Morea. A Turkish
army assembled at Thebes, traversed the Isthmus of Corinth
without opposition, and encamped in the plain of Argos ; and
Liberaki, who accompanied the Turks, availed himself of his
secret correspondence with many discontented Greeks to
plunder the interior of the peninsula. The capitan-pasha,
Mezzomorto, sailed from the Dardanelles to assist the invading army. The German corps of auxiliaries in the Venetian
service was concentrated at Nauplia, and, when joined with
a body of Venetians and Sclavonians, formed a small army,
which was placed under the command of General Steinau,
who attacked and defeated the seraskier before the arrival of
the Othoman fleet. The Turks were driven back to Thebes,
and Liberaki was bribed to desert the sultan and enter the
service of Venice. Molino encountered the capitan-pasha off
Scio, and two naval engagements were fought, in which, however, the Venetians gained no advantage over the Turks. It
was now evident that the Othoman government was recovering
its energy and strength, and peace was necessary to enable
Venice to retain the possession of her recent conquests [2].

After long negotiations peace was concluded at Carlovitz,
in January 1699, between the Emperor of Germany, the King
of Poland, the Republic of Venice, and the Sultan. Venice

---

[1] Gratiani, ii. 590, 626, 631, and p. 81 of this volume.
[2] The Mainate Liberaki soon recommenced his intrigues, hoping to force
Venice to recognize him as Bey of Maina ; but the jealous republic, having
secured his secretary as a spy on his proceedings, immediately arrested him,
and sent him a prisoner to Brescia, A. D. 1697. Locatelli, *Continuazione,* i. 29.

retained possession of the places it had conquered in Dalmatia, of Santa Maura, of the Peloponnesus, and of Aegina ; and it was relieved from the tribute it had formerly paid to the Sublime Porte for the possession of Zante. Prevesa, the northern castle at the entrance of the Gulf of Lepanto, and the city of Lepanto, were restored to the sultan after the destruction of their fortifications. The republic must have felt that, in spite of all the valour and ability of Morosini, and the great expense it had incurred in bringing German mercenaries to Greece to fight in its cause, still the conquests it had gained were due more to the victories of Prince Eugene on the Danube than to its own power and exertions [1].

When the Venetians conquered the Morea, they found it ruined and depopulated. At the commencement of the war the Turks distrusted the Greeks, and took every precaution in their power to deprive them of the means of combining together and assisting the enemy. The Christians were everywhere disarmed, the granaries were emptied, and their contents transported into the fortresses ; and their flocks and herds were driven into the districts commanded by Turkish garrisons. When the Turks were at last compelled to abandon the country, they carried off everything of value belonging to the Christians which they could transport, in order to indemnify themselves for what they were compelled to leave behind. The youth of both sexes were seized when they were likely to prove valuable slaves, and the property of the Greeks was destroyed on the line of retreat. The richest plains of the Morea, having been in turn the scene of military operations, were left almost uncultivated. Famine followed war, and the plague came as an attendant on famine, carrying distress and ruin into districts which neither war nor famine had visited. The roads were neglected, the bridges broken down, the towns in ruins, commerce annihilated, the administration of justice in abeyance, and the whole peninsula filled with bands of armed brigands, who seized what they wanted

---

[1] The treaty signed at Carlovitz between the Republic and the Porte, is given by Rycaut (iii. 597) ; but Hammer (xiii. 35) mentions that, when the Venetian ambassador Sorano visited Constantinople to obtain its confirmation, he concluded an additional and more explicit treaty, embodying seventeen clauses contained in the preceding treaties between the Republic and the Porte, besides the fifteen which constituted the original treaty of Carlovitz.

wherever they could find it. With these robbers the pastoral population in the mountains often formed alliances, in order to share in the plunder of the agricultural population of the plains[1].

The Venetians found that, in order to render their conquest of any permanent utility, it would be necessary to establish a decided military superiority over the whole country, in order to restore that feeling of security without which there can be no prospect of agricultural and commercial prosperity, even in the most fertile regions. The Venetian government performed its duties both with goodwill and ability. It possessed men experienced in dealing with Greeks; and the loss of Crete had taught them a lesson of tolerance and moderation. Their recent government of Tinos had been mild and judicious; and that island, which is now the most industrious and flourishing portion of the Greek kingdom, owes its superiority to the Venetian government. Still there were many difficulties in the way of establishing order in the Morea which did not exist in the islands, and these difficulties must be candidly weighed before we venture to pronounce that Venice acted either injudiciously or tyrannically during the period it ruled the Morea.

Many circumstances prevented the Venetian government from intrusting the Greeks with any considerable share in the local administration. They did not, however, so completely falsify the communal system, and render it a mere organ of the central administration, as has been done recently by Bavarian and Greek ministers. The Venetians were compelled to guard against the influence of the Othoman Porte, which continued to be great in the Morea, both over the Greek primates, who had property or connections in the Turkish provinces, and over the Greek clergy. The power of the Patriarch of Constantinople was an especial object of disquietude, as he was an instrument in the hands of the Othoman government to create opposition to Venice. The complete alienation in religious and national feeling between

---

[1] Those who witnessed the extent that brigandage attained in liberated Greece in the year 1835, during German domination, and in the years 1854-5, under the constitutional government of King Otho, can alone form any correct idea of the lawless state of society through which the peaceful agricultural population has perpetuated its laborious and suffering existence. In the present year (1855), acts of torture have been committed never exceeded by Turkish tyrants.

the Greeks and the Catholics rendered it impossible for the
Venetians to attempt amalgamating the native population of
Greece with the subjects of the republic, by conferring on
the Moreotes the privileges of citizens of Venice. The French
of Louisiana and the Spaniards of Florida, though staunch
Catholics, have become good citizens of the United States;
but no concessions have hitherto induced the Greeks to
become loyal to any foreign state. They can be industrious
in money-making like the Jews, but even when they accept
the boon of foreign citizenship as a means of increasing their
gains, they rarely, if ever, become good citizens. To judge
the Venetian government fairly, it must be compared with
the British government in the Ionian Islands, and with the
Bavarian domination in Greece, and surely it will not suffer
by the comparison.

When the Venetians found leisure to devote their attention to the civil government of the Morea, the native population had sunk, through the ravages of war and pestilence, to
about one hundred thousand souls, although, before the commencement of hostilities, the Christians alone, including
Greeks and Albanians, were estimated at two hundred and
fifty thousand, and the Turks at fifty thousand; an estimate
which does not appear to be far removed from the truth[1].
Morosini established a provisional civil administration, which
restored order, and, with the cessation of the plague,
the increased security of property enabled the Morea to
recover so rapidly from its misfortunes, that, in the year
1701, the native population, Greek and Albanian, had already
reached two hundred thousand. Morosini introduced the
municipal system of the continental possessions of Venice
into the towns he conquered. The rights he thereby conferred on the Greeks, and the improvement which took place
in their condition, soon produced a considerable immigration
from Northern Greece, where the Turks were slower in re-
establishing order. Thousands of families, with their baggage
and cattle, were conveyed by the Venetians from the northern

[1] The best authority on the administration of the Venetians is the work of
Ranke, entitled *Die Venetianer in Morea*, published in the *Historisch-Politische
Zeitschrift*, Berlin, 1835, vol. ii. pt. 3.

Cornaro, the first general proveditor, gives only 86,460 souls as the result of
the first Venetian census; yet the men capable of bearing arms were 20,123.
Ranke, 436.

coast of the Gulf of Corinth into the Morea, and the emigration became so great as to induce the Porte to order the
pashas and provincial governors to treat the Greeks with
greater consideration and justice than they had previously
received from the Othoman authorities. Thus one of the
most valuable results of Morosini's conquests was, that it
compelled the Turks to make an effort to gain the good-will,
or at least to alleviate the discontent, of their Christian
subjects[1]. Another feature which marked a considerable
change in Turkish society was the return of many families
of Mohammedan agriculturists to Christianity, which their
ancestors had forsaken in order to escape from persecution
and fiscal oppression[2]. The liberality of the Venetians at
this time is shown by the fact that they allowed these converts to join the Greek Church. At any earlier period they
would have considered themselves bound, as a Catholic power,
to force the converts to embrace Catholicism, or else to
remain Mohammedans.

The revenues derived by Venice from the Morea were
considerable. They consisted of one-tenth of all the agricultural produce, besides taxes on wine, spirits, oil, and
tobacco, and a monopoly of salt. It is needless to dwell
on the impediment which the payment of tenths offers to
any improvement in agriculture, though this tax is not to be
regarded as too heavy in amount; still the manner in which
it must unavoidably be collected renders it always a wasteful,
as well as an oppressive mode of obtaining a revenue. The
Venetians in order to avoid constant disputes between the
fiscal officers of the government and the people, found it
necessary to farm the tenths. The consequence was, that
the farmers, who were generally Greek archonts, always contrived to make their agents live at the expense of the people
in the district they farmed, and, by uniting the trade of
money-lenders and dealers in agricultural produce with their
occupation as farmers of the revenue, they employed the
great powers they received as collectors of the taxes to
enforce payment of their private debts. In order to relieve

---

[1] *See* some of the concessions to the Christians, mentioned by Hammer, xiii. 65.
For the emigration, *see* Rycaut, iii. 271.
[2] The Venetian accounts mention 1317 families of Mohammedan peasants who
embraced Christianity. *See* Rycaut, iii. 270, 272.

agriculture from these abuses, the Venetian government endeavoured to facilitate the farming of the revenues by the communes for terms of not less than five years, and the plan was attended with considerable success.

The salt monopoly was the cause of great oppression, and still greater inconvenience, though the price was only two solidi a pound (about a halfpenny). The expense of transport and loss of time in procuring salt from distant magazines were serious and just grounds of complaint against the system; for in many places where the peasant could easily have procured salt gratis on the sea-shore within a few miles of his sheepfolds, he was compelled to take a day's journey with his mules in order to purchase it at some distant depôt of the monopoly.

The Venetian government gained possession of extensive domains in the Morea; but it had sufficient experience in territorial administration to know that the State is the worst possible landed proprietor, and that the land belonging to government is often the portion least profitable to the public treasury. The patronage of the powerful, the neglect and dishonesty of officials, and the avidity of farmers, all contribute to the mal-administration of property placed in such exceptional circumstances as government lands[1].

The revenues of the Morea are stated by Grimani, the general proveditor from 1698 to 1701, at 605,460 reals: but his estimate was apparently too high; and Emo, who administered the province from 1705 to 1708, found the actual receipts only amounted to about 400,000 reals. By wise measures and liberal concessions he increased the receipts to 461,548. The good effect of a mild administration became still more visible during the government of Loredano (1708 to 1711), as the revenues rose to more than half a million of reals[2].

The regular expenses of the Venetian government amounted to only 280,000 reals, so that a surplus of 220,000 was annually paid over into the treasury of the fleet. Though it was necessary to maintain a considerable naval force in the Grecian seas to protect the country against the incursions of corsairs,

---

[1] The evil effects, both politically and financially, are strongly exemplified at present in the Greek kingdom.

[2] Ranke, 455. The Venetian real was, I believe, then valued at twenty pence, English money.

and to enforce the commercial laws and restrictions of the republic, still there can be no doubt that the revenues of the Morea under the Venetian domination were amply sufficient to pay all the expenditure both of its internal administration and of its military and naval establishments in time of peace.

The commerce of the Greeks was almost annihilated when the Venetians commenced the war. The Ionian sea and the Archipelago were so crowded with pirates, that even Greek fishing-boats could hardly venture to creep out of a harbour, lest the men should be carried off to labour at the oar in some French, Maltese, or Barbary corsair. These pirates had established many regular stations in the Levant. The Christians compelled several Greek towns on the continent and in the islands of the Archipelago to pay them a regular tribute, in order to secure their lands and fishing-boats from being plundered; while the Mohammedans had formed establishments in the Othoman fortresses in Western Greece and Albania for the sale of the plunder and slaves they collected in their cruises between the Barbary coast and the Adriatic.

The only foreign trade that existed in the Morea at the time of its conquest was that between Messenia and Barbary, and between Monemvasia and Alexandria[1]. It was very insignificant. A few boats were also employed in transporting the produce of the Morea to the Ionian Islands, from whence it was conveyed to Venice in armed vessels. The Venetian conquest quickly restored some activity to the trade of the native Greeks. The demand for good wine was soon so much increased by the number of foreigners established in the Morea, that it was for a time necessary to import the better qualities from France, Italy, and the islands of the Archipelago. But the Moreotes, as soon as they were assured that their labour would be well rewarded, made such improvements in the preparation of their own wines as to share in the profits of this trade, and supplant the foreign importers, who were compelled to confine their dealings to the finest qualities, which could only be consumed in small quantities.

---

[1] Prinokokki, a red dye, from an insect collected on the holly-leaved oak, which is used for dyeing the fez or red skull-cap, and valonia, for tanning and dyeing, with silk, oil, and fruit, were the chief articles in this trade.

The trade of the Morea was prevented from receiving all the extension of which it was capable by the severity of the restrictive commercial policy enforced by the Venetians. The possessions of the republic were regarded as valuable to the State in the proportion in which they contributed to increase the trade and fiscal receipts of the city of Venice. Instead, therefore, of allowing the inhabitants of the Morea to trade directly with the nations who might desire to consume Greek produce, and of raising a revenue by export duties, the Venetians compelled their subjects to send every article of value they exported to Venice, which, by this system of restriction, was rendered the sole emporium of the trade between Western Europe and the Venetian possessions in the Levant. The rigour with which this system was enforced injured the inhabitants of the Morea by lowering the price of every article of export, and it prevented the French, English, and Dutch merchants from purchasing many articles which they had previously procured there, while, instead of seeking them at Venice, they generally succeeded in procuring them in provinces of the Othoman empire. The trade in oil, silk, Turkey leather, and fruit, suffered particularly from this monopoly.

The Venetians at first established seven fiscal boards in the Morea, of which Patras, Castel Tornese, Modon, Coron, Kielapha, Monemvasia, and Maina were the seats; but these were afterwards reduced to four, corresponding to the four provinces into which the peninsula was divided for the facility of the civil administration. These were, Romania, with Nauplia or Napoli di Romania for its capital; Laconia or Zaccunia, of which Monemvasia was the capital; Messenia` with Navarin, and Achaia with Patras, as their chief towns. Each of these provinces had its proveditor, in whose hands the civil and military authority was placed; its Rettore, or chief judge; and its Camerlingo, or intendant of finance. The whole Morea was governed by a general proveditor. As soon as Morosini had conquered any town, he established in it a Consiglio, or municipal council, in imitation of the communal system adopted in the Venetian provinces of the terra firma. This council chose the magistrates and local officials, who were selected from the Greek inhabitants devoted to the interests of Venice, and on these magistrates considerable

privileges were conferred [1]. The council itself was generally
composed of Venetians, or Venetian subjects. The general
practice of Europe, the prejudices of the age, and the peculiar
position of the Venetians in their foreign dependencies, rendered it impossible for the republic to avoid employing
privileges and monopolies as a means of attaching partizans
and creating a revenue. But no care or prudence on the
part of the general proveditors, who appear to have governed,
on the whole, both ably and honestly, could prevent these
privileges and monopolies from nourishing intrigues and
financial abuses. All endeavours to extirpate these evils
proved vain: as soon as one abuse was discovered, and a
remedy applied, it was found that it was replaced by some
new corruption, equally injurious to the State and to society,
equally profitable to officials, and equally oppressive to some
class of the native population. The system of privileges and
exemptions has sometimes proved a powerful instrument of
State policy, where the great object has been to hold the
mass of the people in subjection, by making their own
jealousies supply the place of an active police and a large
military force; but it has invariably served as a premium for
official dishonesty and political immorality.

One of the evils of the system may be noticed as an example of its effects. The burgesses of towns were exempted
from the burden of quartering troops, which fell heavily on
the inhabitants of the country. The better class of Greek
proprietors, who resided on their property, or who inhabited
the rural districts as traders in agricultural produce, soon
contrived to corrupt the lower Venetian officials and place
themselves on the roll of burgesses in the nearest town.
They then succeeded in gaining an exemption from quartering soldiers in the house they inhabited, as being the country
residence of a burgess. This abuse made the burden fall
heavier on the poor peasantry, who having no persons of
knowledge, wealth, and influence to defend their interests,
became the victims of great oppression on the part of the
Venetian military. The soldiers were only entitled by law
to receive rations of barley bread and cheese; but they exacted dinners of roast meat, wheaten cakes, and wine. The

---

[1] Locatelli, i. 197.

assessment authorized by the Venetian government was light, for the annual maintenance of one soldier was charged on eighteen families; but laws are powerless where the government is both weak and corrupt[1].

At first sight, it would seem that the Venetian senate possessed absolute power to govern the possessions of the republic in Greece,—for there existed no nobility, no established system of laws, and no organized corporations in the Morea. But this was not really the case. The traditional maxims of Italian statesmen, the privileges of the nobles of Venice in the dependent territories of the republic, and the financial principles then deemed conducive to political power, on the one hand, joined to the restless disposition of the Greeks, who often fancied that a wider career would be obtained for their activity and ambition by the restoration of the Othoman domination, to the want of truth and conscience engendered by their servile condition, and to the violence of their orthodox prejudices, on the other hand, presented, on many subjects, barriers to improvement, which the Venetians had not strength to destroy. The Greek character seems less adapted for political order than for individual progress. Envy and suspicion have always been marked characteristics of Hellenic society; and more Greek

---

[1] At the present day, a greater abuse is universal in the kingdom of Greece, and King Otho and his ministers seem to be powerless to restrain it. The gendarmes of King Otho are only entitled to quarters, and not to rations; but they extort from the poor peasantry of liberated Greece far more abundant supplies of provisions, and exercise greater exactions, than were exercised even by the Venetian soldiers. They take turkeys and lambs, where their predecessors, the Venetians and Turks, were satisfied with fowls and bread; and when they have feasted and slept, they compel the peasant to take his horse from the threshing-floor and to quit the plough, in order that they may ride at their ease from one station to another, though they invariably report that they have marched the distance. This is no trifling hindrance to the progress of agriculture in liberated Greece, or it would not be noticed in this place. It is one of those abuses which warranted the Earl of Carlisle in describing the present government of Greece as 'the most inefficient, corrupt, and, above all, contemptible, with which a nation was ever cursed.' *A Diary in Turkish and Greek Waters*, 208. Not a day passes in seedtime or harvest that many poor Greek and Albanian peasants are not compelled to leave their work to follow their oppressors. The writer of these pages has witnessed this systematic extortion perpetuated for twenty years without any effort having been made by king, ministers, or chambers to extirpate it, though all are aware of the severe burden it imposes on the poorest and most industrious class of the population. The contrast between the conduct of the Venetian proveditors and that of a constitutional king, with native ministers, is not favourable to either German or Greek political honesty and intelligence. The Venetian governors laboured incessantly to repress the abuse; the nomarchs of King Otho do much to perpetuate it.

states have been ruined and subjected to foreign conquest at every period of history by the operation of internal vices than by the force of hostile nations. The inhabitants of the Peloponnesus, from some causes which it is difficult to detect, but which appear to have operated in the most dissimilar conditions of civilization, and in times and circumstances widely different, are considered by their countrymen as the most envious and suspicious of all the Greeks. The Venetian general-proveditors, who were extremely anxious to improve the condition of the country, complained that, though they found the inhabitants active and intelligent, they found them false from excessive suspicion, and obstinate from aversion to foreigners. It was deemed a patriotic duty to persist in native habits, even when these habits had originated in the oppression of the Othoman domination. They were so suspicious and envious that the middle classes wasted the greater part of their time in watching the conduct of their neighbours, and in taking measures of precaution against imaginary schemes of supposed intriguers. The consequence was, that all the Greeks lived together in a state of feverish excitement, wasting great energies to no purpose. They laboured with their whole attention directed towards a distant point from which they expected an enemy to issue, as the husbandman who sows a field on the verge of a tribe of nomades. The higher classes were rapacious, avaricious, and idle. They despised all agricultural and manual industry, and looked for wealth to saving rather than to industry. Their contempt for the agricultural classes was shown by their calling all who were engaged in the cultivation of the soil Albanians, and all who were occupied in pastoral pursuits Vallachians. These two classes, the cultivators of the soil and the shepherds, were unquestionably the most industrious and honest portion of the population of Greece at this period, which may be in part attributed to the circumstance that they had been less exposed to the demoralizing influence of a bad political government, and of a worse social system. One feature in the Moreote population of every rank made a strong impression on the Venetians. This was, the insuperable aversion they manifested to military service. No young men were desirous of seeking to advance their fortunes by arms. The aversion they displayed to war contrasted strangely with their unquenchable thirst for civil strife. The Mainates were the only part of the population of the Morea attached to a military life. The most noted bands of robbers in the peninsula were generally composed of Albanians from northern Greece.

It has been already mentioned that, after the conquest of Crete, the Othoman government had reduced Maina to complete submission, and compelled the inhabitants to pay the haratch like the other Greeks. The assertion that this tax was never paid by Maina, though extremely erroneous, since it had been levied by the Othomans in the sixteenth century, was now revived, and has often been repeated since. After the Othoman government had established regular garrisons in the fortresses of Zarnata, Kielapha, and Passava, in 1670, the Mainates paid this hated imposition, which was considered as the severest mark of Othoman servitude, until they were relieved from it by the victories of the Venetians.

When the Mainates joined Morosini they concluded an alliance with Venice, which conferred on them many privileges, and authorized them to establish an independent local administration throughout their mountains. The most important privilege they obtained was exemption from paying a tenth of their agricultural produce to the State. This tax was commuted for a fixed tribute, called by the Mainates *maktu.* During the Venetian domination in the Morea the Mainates succeeded in constituting themselves into a really independent people, but the use they made of their independence did not tend to improve the condition of the mass of the population, for Maina became the scene of innumerable family feuds, and petty civil wars ; and the defeated party generally endeavoured to gain a livelihood by plundering the Venetian provinces of Messenia and Laconia, or by exercising piracy. The Mainates displayed great courage and extraordinary perseverance in their feuds, though they sought rather to waylay and assassinate their enemies than to meet them in open fight. The northern and central parts of Maina were, however, valuable to Venice, which retained a monopoly of their trade, for they exported a considerable quantity of valonia, red dye, galls, cotton, and oil. The population was estimated at more than twenty-five thousand souls.

The first object of the Venetians, after they had established their domination in the Morea, was to give security to pro-perty. They recognized every existing private right, and wherever a right of occupancy was clearly established, the possessor was considered the absolute proprietor in so far as the State was concerned. To the peasants who had cultivated property claimed by the Othoman government the boon was very great, as their payments to the fisc were diminished one-half. The primates and ecclesiastics, it is true, frequently contrived to appropriate to themselves pro-perty that had belonged to private Turks and to the Othoman government; but the Venetians wisely overlooked some fraudulent gains on the part of individuals, in consideration of the great benefits which the measure conferred on the many small cultivators of the soil, who were thereby rendered the undisputed proprietors of the lands their families had long occupied.

Immense tracts of land still remained uncultivated, of which the property was vested in the State by the fortune of war. When this property was capable of being immediately ren-dered productive by some outlay of capital, as in the case of mills, cisterns, warehouses, and building-sites, it was conceded to tenants on leases for ten years, with the obligations of making the necessary outlay, and of paying one-tenth of the annual produce. But irrigable lands, gardens, and meadows, in the vicinity of towns, were let for a rent of one-third of their produce, as was customary in private leases. Pasture lands, olive groves, and vineyards, were usually let for a money rent. When peace was concluded with Turkey in 1699, and the domination of the Venetians was definitively recognized by the sultan, the Greeks began to consider their lot as subjects of Venice permanently fixed. The republic made use of this opportunity of giving additional security to its power, by endeavouring to gain the good-will of the native population of the Morea. All temporary rights of property in the domains of the State were declared perma-nent. Thus all lessees became proprietors on paying their previous rent as a perpetual duty. A complete survey of the peninsula and a census of the population were then completed.

Until the conclusion of peace the Morea had been infested

by bands of robbers; numerous exiles from the Othoman provinces, who were too lazy or too proud to work, and deserters from the army, wandered about, and when they were not employed as gendarmes, local guards, or policemen, exercised the trade of brigands[1]. The Venetian administration proved successful in establishing order and security for life and property. The municipalities were intrusted with some real power; they were authorized to form a local militia to guard their property, on the condition of undertaking the responsibility of making good any losses sustained within their limits by robbery. Even the jealous republic intrusted them with the right of bearing arms. Sagredo, the last general-proveditor who ruled the Morea in time of peace, reported the country to be so tranquil that few crimes were committed which required to be punished with death[2]. This, we must remember, was said at a time when death was the punishment universally applied to many minor offences. It forms a sad contrast with the condition of Greece in the year 1855[3].

The administration of justice in civil affairs, though very much superior to what it had been under the Othomans, was still very defective. The tribunals were presided over by young Italian nobili, whose long residence at Padua had not always enabled them to acquire more knowledge of law than a short sojourn at Venice taught them to forget; for they generally displayed great aptitude in learning the vices and corruption of that luxurious city. Their ignorance was a constant subject of complaint. The clerks of court, who possessed more knowledge, were notorious for venality and dishonesty, and the advocates, who were Ionians, were prompt agents in pointing out to the young judges how they could enrich themselves by selling judicial sentences. Wealthy suitors easily gained their causes, but the poor were exposed to delay in every process, and could find no protection from the law against acts of injustice committed by the Greek primates.

---

[1] Grimani, as quoted by Ranke, says, 'rare volte fu fermato un ladro che non fosse meidano.' At present the brigands in Greece are recruited principally by deserters from the irregular troops, by the persons allowed to escape from the prisons, and by those pardoned by King Otho.

[2] Ranke, 473.

[3] A long list of villages plundered by the brigands might be made from the Greek newspapers.

The weakness or mildness of the Venetian civil administration increased the sufferings of the peasantry, as it relieved oppressors from the fear of punishment. The feeling of impunity among the unprincipled Greek archonts and merchants, soon led them to gratify their avarice and revenge by iniquitous law-suits, which they usually succeeded in gaining by bribing false witnesses. The Venetians saw these evils gradually increase, but they were unable to suppress the false testimony which was habitually given in the courts of law. Their legislation was ineffectual to restrain the demoralization of Greek society, nourished by the bad example of their own judges. The same want of truth and honesty, which contributed for many centuries to maintain the Greeks in a servile position, baffled the partial efforts of the Venetians to improve their condition. Time alone can show whether the establishment of the national independence will efface from the Greek character these vices. The general-proveditor, Emo, describes the Moreotes in 1708 very much as the Emperor Cantacuzenos had described them in the middle of the fourteenth century. The Venetian says they were a race addicted to wrangling, unwearied in chicanery, and inexorable in revenge, who seemed to take delight in nourishing the bitterest quarrels with all their neighbours. The imperial historian mentioned the mutual hatred which the archonts of the Morea cherished to the hour of death, and the feuds which they regularly transmitted, as a death-bed legacy or an inalienable inheritance, to their children and heirs [1].

Religious liberty was not a principle of government recognized by any European state in the seventeenth century; the difference of faith consequently formed an insurmountable obstacle to an equitable administration of public affairs in all European governments. The spirit of the Italians was peculiarly opposed to toleration. Indeed, so deeply was intolerance a part of Christian civilization at this time, that even a sense of the wrong which they had suffered for conscience sake in the Old World, did not restrain the exiles, who sought religious liberty in America, from persecuting those who differed from them in their new homes. The Venetians were then remarkable for liberality, but, as sincere

---

[1] Ranke, 470 ; Cantacuzenos, 751, edit. Paris.

Catholics, they could not become the sovereigns of the orthodox Greeks without awakening strong feelings of opposition to their government, even though their conduct was marked by unusual prudence and toleration, and though they had long acted as protectors of the orthodox against papal influence at Constantinople[1].

The vicinity of the sultan's dominions, the great power of the Patriarch of Constantinople over the Greek clergy, and the general feeling which induced the members of the orthodox church in Greece to regard the sultan as their protector, created a sense of insecurity on the part of the senate of Venice, which made it avoid, with the greatest care, giving its Greek subjects any just cause of dissatisfaction. It knew well that no act of the republic could deprive the Greek clergy of their civil influence any more than of their ecclesiastical authority.

The Venetians, nevertheless, considered it their right as conquerors, and their duty as Catholics, to restore to the papal clergy all the mosques which had been Christian churches at the time of the Othoman conquest. Many of these buildings had been erected by the Frank princes. The Venetians naturally invested the Catholic Church with the fullest authority over the Catholics in Greece, but they did not permit the Pope to assume any supremacy over the Greek Church. The Catholic Church in the Morea was divided into four bishoprics, under the superintendence of the archbishop of Corinth. Catholic priests and monks flocked to the Morea from Italy and the islands of the Archipelago.

The Greek Church retained all the property and privileges it had possessed under the sultans, and was not required to make any concessions of ecclesiastical superiority to its Romish rival. The power of the Patriarch of Constantinople, however, both as being a foreigner in a hostile State, and as a political agent in the hands of the Othoman government, caused great anxiety at Venice. The Patriarch named the bishops in the Morea; his influence was, consequently, all-powerful with the clergy, who looked to his favour and protection for ecclesiastical advancement; and the power of the clergy over the great body of the people was exorbitant. The

---

[1] Hammer, *Histoire de l'Empire Othoman,* ix. 31.

Patriarch of Constantinople named also the abbots of many monasteries. One-half of the annual offerings made by the priests, and by each family in every diocese, was paid over by the bishop to the exarch of the Morea, who received these sums on account of the Patriarch. A portion of the revenues of the monasteries was also remitted to Constantinople by their abbots[1]. The bulls of the Patriarch possessed as much authority in the Morea as in any part of the Othoman empire, for his excommunications were feared by all the orthodox laity as well as clergy, and his patronage was powerful to advance the temporal interests of his partizans. The Venetians, who had deprived papal bulls of authority in their dominions until they received the sanction of the civil government, desired to exercise the same control over the bulls of the Patriarch of Constantinople. The measures adopted marked the prudence of the senate, and were carried into execution by the general-proveditors with great moderation. No acknowledged exarch of the Patriarch was allowed to reside in the Morea, and the publication of patriarchal bulls by the clergy was prohibited ; while, in order to curtail the influence which the distribution of immense patronage conferred on the Patriarch, the Greek communes were invited to select their own bishops, and an attempt was made to abolish the payment of the dues which were remitted to Constantinople. The Venetian authorities were well aware that the Archbishop of Patras acted secretly as exarch for the Patriarch, and that the bishops and abbots, in order to secure the good-will of the Patriarch and synod at Constantinople, continued to make considerable remittances of money to the patriarchal treasury ; but they were satisfied to put an end to the public payment of these dues, without forcing the Patriarch

---

[1] Ranke gives the following ecclesiastical statistics from Grimani : 'The metropolitan archbishop, who exercised the superintendence over the whole peninsula, then resided at Tripolitza. There were four other archbishops without suffragans. There were twelve suffragan bishops, and sixteen titular bishops without sees ; thirteen hundred and sixty-seven monks in one hundred and fifty-eight monasteries ; ninety-four of these were monasteries having the right of electing their own abbots ; in fourteen the nomination of the abbot was a right of patronage, and twenty-six abbots were named by the Patriarch ; twenty-four of these monasteries also were only metochia, or dependencies of other greater monasteries. Besides these, there were one hundred and fifty-one churches possessing landed property.' p. 479. Morosini had endeavoured to gain the Greek clergy by his liberality during the war. He assigned pensions to the bishops of Larissa, Thebes, Negrepont, Athens, and Salona, who all fled to the Venetians for protection in 1688. Locatelli, ii. 156.

to assail their political authority in defence of his revenue. By this conduct the influence of the Patriarch in the Morea was considerably diminished, without producing any direct collision between the Greek Church and the civil power.

Simony was too deeply engrafted on the orthodox church to admit of its being extirpated by external influence. The bishops sold the office of priest, and the communes, when they became invested with ecclesiastical patronage, followed the established usage of the church, and endeavoured to turn ecclesiastical elections into a means of increasing the communal revenues. They bargained with their nominee for a share of the ordinary ecclesiastical dues and church offerings. Thus the clerical office was rendered universally an object of bargain and sale[1]. The proveditors could not venture to interfere. They required the assistance of the Greek clergy to aid in maintaining public order, and found it politic to wink at abuses which often rendered the priesthood anxious to secure the support of the government. Thus the same policy of employing the Greek Church as an instrument of police, to watch over the people and to support the power of a foreign domination, which had been established by the Othomans at Constantinople, was adopted by the Venetians at Nauplia. The vices of the Greek ecclesiastical system made the priesthood the most efficient agents for riveting the chains of their country. The success of the Venetian policy was proved when the Patriarch sent a letter to the primates of Misithra, enjoining the community to solicit the nomination of a new bishop from Constantinople, instead of the one chosen under the authority of the Venetian government. The community of Misithra left the letter unanswered, and the bishop it had chosen remained in office[2].

The presence of the Catholic clergy in the Morea, though it caused some exacerbation on the part of the orthodox Greeks, was nevertheless productive of permanent good. The Catholics first drew the attention of the Moreotes to the improvement of the system of education then prevalent, and extended a desire for instruction more widely among the people. They also taught the Greeks that active charity,

---

[1] Ranke, 481. [2] Ibid., 483.

and a constant exercise of benevolence, are prominent duties in the office of a Christian parish-priest. The superior moral character, the greater learning, and more disinterested behaviour, in pecuniary affairs, of the Catholic priesthood, formed so strong a contrast to the meanness, ignorance, and rapacity of a large portion of the orthodox, that even the Greeks acknowledged the virtues of the papal clergy. The influence of the Catholics was greatly increased by the knowledge of medicine which several possessed, by their readiness to attend the sick, and by their liberality in furnishing medicines from dispensaries established at the expense of the church. Many schools were founded in the provincial towns, and several colleges were established, in which the education was so much superior to that bestowed on the pupils in any Greek schools then existing in the Morea, that many of the orthodox sent their children to be educated in these establishments. The college of Tripolitza was remarkable for its excellence, and for the concourse of orthodox Greeks who attended it. This declaration of public opinion in favour of morality and education produced a sensible effect on the Greek clergy. They began to exert themselves to win that personal esteem, which they saw was attained by their Catholic rivals, and a considerable improvement was soon visible in their general conduct. The torrent of social demoralization which had been rolling onward and gaining additional force as time advanced, under the Othoman domination, was now arrested.

The first productive seeds of social improvement were sown in the minds of the Greeks by their Venetian masters during the short period of their domination in the Morea. The hope, as well as the desire of bettering their condition, became then a national feeling, which gained strength with each succeeding generation, until it ripened into a desire for national independence. The obligations of the Greeks to the Venetian government and to the Catholic clergy may not be very great, but it would be an oversight in the history of the Greek nation to omit recording these obligations. The young Greeks of the Morea, who grew to manhood under the protection of the republic, were neither so ignorant, so servile, nor so timid as their fathers who had lived under the Turkish yoke. It is true that the Venetian government failed in making any great social improvements in Greece, and in gaining the good-will and gratitude of the people; but what foreign government has ever succeeded better?

Prudence induced the Venetian senate to maintain a strict neutrality during the great European war of the Spanish succession. To avoid being involved in the general hostilities, it overlooked more than one open infraction of its territory by the belligerents; and, as often happens with those who fear to make a single enemy, it soon remained without a single friend. Its policy was presumed to be dictated by the selfishness of the ruling class, whose members were more anxious to preserve their large salaries and sinecures than to support the dignity of the republic. Rather than encounter the slightest risk of diminishing their own incomes, they allowed Venice to be despised as a spiritless state. The consequence was, that when the Treaties of Utrecht and Rastadt re-established peace in Western Europe, Venice remained without an ally. France, whose success in placing a Bourbon on the Spanish throne had given her a predominating influence in the Mediterranean, was the ancient ally of the Othoman Porte, and was supposed to be especially envious of the great extension which Venetian commerce had gained by a long neutrality. The French government, seeing no hope of their merchants recovering the share they had formerly enjoyed of the Levant trade, as long as the possession of the Morea enabled the Venetians to enforce their system of monopoly, was suspected of urging the Porte to commence hostilities with the republic.

In the mean time Russia had taken its place as a first-rate power in the international system of Europe, and already threatened the power, if not the existence, of the Othoman empire. The statesmen of Venice were too traditional in their policy, and too conservative in their views, to appreciate the full value of an alliance with the Czar Peter at this crisis. The moment was one when all thoughts of neutrality ought to have been laid aside, unless Venice was convinced that she possessed singly the strength necessary to defend the Morea against the whole force of the Othoman empire. A considerable change had taken place both in the internal condition of the Othoman empire and the state of its relations with Russia at the commencement of the war with Peter the

Great in 1710. The Russian empire was strong in the feeling of progressive improvement and increasing power. Peter was elated by his victory over Charles XII., the military hero of the age. The Othoman empire showed visible signs of decline and weakness. The defects in the financial administration and in the dispensation of justice became every day more apparent, as the necessity for order and security of property were more generally felt in consequence of the progress of social civilization. The military organization, which had given power to the sultan's government, was ruined: the janissaries, instead of being, as formerly, the best infantry in Europe, were little better than a local militia of armed burghers; the institution of the tribute-children, which had long been the firmest support of the Othoman empire, no longer supplied the sultan's army with a regular influx of enthusiastic neophytes and well-disciplined soldiers; the timariot system was weakened by the poverty and depopulation of the provinces and the luxurious manner of living of the large landed proprietors. War was no longer the normal condition of Othoman society. The difficulty of recruiting the armies of the sultan was constantly augmenting. An inferior class of men was received into the army; and it was generally believed that the Mussulman population was everywhere decreasing in number. On the other hand, it was said that the Christians were rapidly increasing, and there were many proofs that the Greek population was acquiring a new degree of importance. Wherever the Greeks enjoyed some degree of security, whether under the protection of Venice or of Russia, they began to exhibit signs of mental and commercial activity.

Sultan Achmet III. was despised by Peter the Great as a weak prince; and the Othoman ministers were considered both worthless and venal. The Czar was persuaded that a single campaign would enable the Muscovite army which had gained the battle of Pultowa to sweep from the field any force the Sultan could assemble to oppose it. Russian agents had visited every part of European Turkey, in order to instigate the Christians to revolt. The Greeks were reminded of ancient prophecies said to have been found in the tomb of Constantine the Great, which declared that the time had arrived when the Byzantine empire was to be

restored by the Russians. The Sclavonians were flattered
with the assurance that they were destined to become the
dominant race in a new eastern empire, as the sovereignty
of Constantinople was about to pass into the hands of the
Czar of Russia, the head of the Sclavonian race and the
emperor selected by Heaven to rule all the orthodox nations
of the earth. In short, the Czar Peter had good reason to
believe in 1710 what his successor Nicholas said in 1853,
'that the affairs of Turkey were in a very disorganized condition; that the country itself seemed falling to pieces; and
that he had to deal with a sick man—a man seriously ill,
whose constitution afforded little hope of recovery[1].' To
increase the internal fever which threatened the existence
of Turkey, Peter augmented the exacerbation by constructing several forts on its frontiers. Repeated infractions of the
Othoman territory by his subjects were left unredressed; and
the hospodar of Moldavia, Demetrius Cantemir, was gained
over to betray the interests of his sovereign the sultan. Peter
apparently expected that the sultan would not venture to
resist his encroachments, and he was surprised when a declaration of war anticipated the progress of his clandestine
schemes. It found him, however, fully prepared for carrying
out his plans by force of arms.

Peter led the Russian army forward in person to invade
the Othoman empire; but his expectation of being welcomed by a general rising of the Christian population in
Moldavia and Vallachia was disappointed. The presence
of a numerous Turkish army soon showed him that he was
not likely to find it a very easy task to plant the cross over
the dome of St. Sophia. The campaign of 1711 confounded
all Peter's hopes, and astonished Europe. The Christians
remained everywhere quiet: in every province of the Othoman empire the Mohammedans flew to arms, with all their
old warlike energy. Peter the Great advanced incautiously,
and was surrounded by the Tartars of the Crimea, and by
the army of the grand-vizier. Cut off from all hope of
escape, except by daring manœuvres and the most desperate
valour, he despaired of being able to force his way through
the Othoman army, and preferred signing a disgraceful peace

---

[1] Parliamentary Papers, 1854. Secret correspondence of the Emperor of Russia
with the British government, No. 1, dated 11th January, 1853.

to encountering the risk of entering Constantinople as a prisoner. By this treaty the czar engaged to demolish the fortifications which he had recently constructed at Kamiensk, Samara, and Taganrog; to yield Azof to the sultan, and to abandon all his artillery to the grand-vizier as a trophy of victory. The czar also bound himself not to meddle in the affairs of the Cossacks, nor to send ambassadors to reside permanently at Constantinople. This humiliating treaty was signed in July 1711, on the banks of the Pruth.

The credit of the Othoman arms was restored by this unexpected display of strength. The Christian subjects of the Porte were reconciled to their allegiance by the increased profits of an extended trade in the Sea of Azof, the Black Sea, and the Levant, and by somewhat milder treatment on the part of their masters. The sultan subsequently renewed his treaty of peace with Poland; and at last, by the treaty of Adrianople in 1714, finally regulated his disputes with Russia concerning the execution of the treaty of the Pruth, and arranged the frontiers of the two empires. At the same time the Porte prosecuted its warlike preparations both by land and sea with unusual vigour. The object of these preparations was generally supposed to be the reconquest of the Morea; yet Venice alone would not believe in the danger which threatened her power; and when war was declared by the Othoman government, the republic was unprepared to meet the enemy, and the military and naval forces of Venice were far too weak to offer a successful, or even a prolonged resistance, to a serious attack on the part of the Turks. The Venetians believed that the object of the sultan's preparations was to conquer Malta. If they had displayed the same energy and determination as the Order, they might perhaps have saved the Morea. For as soon as the grand master, Raimond Perellos, was informed of the extent of the naval armament fitting out at Constantinople, he summoned all the knights in Europe to the defence of the island, provisioned the fortress for a long siege, and strengthened the fortifications in every possible way. The Porte declared war with Venice in the month of December 1714, making use of some disputes concerning the conduct of Venetian cruisers to Turkish ships and of the protection granted to bands of insurgents on the

Dalmatian frontier by the Venetian authorities, as a pretext for an appeal to arms.

The grand-vizier who took the command of the army destined to invade the Morea was Ali Kumurgi, the son of a charcoal-maker in the village of Soloes, on the southern bank of the Lake of Nicaea. He had been received as a child into the serai, and educated as an imperial page. The favour of Sultan Mustapha had raised him to the rank of chamberlain, and Sultan Achmet III. treated him with even greater favour than his brother. At an early age he was appointed selictar-aga, and his counsels exercised considerable influence on the sultan's conduct, even before he became a minister of the Porte. His first public office was that of grand-vizier; but when placed at the head of the government, though he was destitute of experience, he displayed considerable talents as a statesman, and great energy as a general[1].

The Othoman army assembled at Adrianople in spring, and after the cavalry had remained some time encamped in the rich plains of Serres and Saloniki, in order to feed the horses on green barley, according to the invariable usage of the East, the grand-vizier marched southward[2]. On the 9th of June he reviewed his troops at Thebes, and according to the official returns, the army then assembled amounted to 22,844 cavalry, and 72,520 infantry. If this estimate be reduced one quarter, which is not too great a reduction for so large a body of men, consisting of many irregular bands under almost independent officers, the army of Ali Kumurgi may still be estimated at 70,000 men.

The fleet sailed from Constantinople under the capitan-pasha, Djanum Khodja, and the grand-vizier received the news that it had conquered Tinos before he quitted Thebes. This island, of which the Venetians had retained the sovereignty for five centuries, and which had repeatedly foiled

---

[1] Hammer, in his *Othoman History,* always calls the grand-vizier Damad Ali. Keumur means coal.

[2] The army crossed the river Vardar at a fine bridge recently constructed by Mohammed Pasha at his own expense. Mohammed had been kiaya of the Sultana Validé, and was then kaimakam at Constantinople. Brue, *Journal de la Campagne que le Grand-Vizier Ali Pacha a faite en* 1715, *pour la Conquête de la Morée,* p. 1.

the attacks of powerful Othoman fleets, was surrendered by the proveditor, Balbi, without striking a blow [1].

From Thebes one division of the army was sent forward to the isthmus, with orders to proceed along the southern coast of the Gulf of Corinth, and besiege the Castle of the Morea, at the Straits of Lepanto. The Asiatic troops were employed in the mean time in rendering the road over Mounts Cithaeron and Geranea suitable for the transport of the artillery and baggage which accompanied the main body of the grand army.

During the period which followed the peace of Carlovitz the Venetians had employed much time and large sums of money in strengthening the fortifications of Nauplia, Modon, and the fort at the Straits of Lepanto, called the Castle of the Morea. They were surrounded by deep ditches and augmented by such new works as the modern system of defence rendered necessary; and when the war broke out these three places were made the chief military establishments of the republic in the Morea. The Hill of Palamedi, which commanded Nauplia, was crowned by a well-planned series of works, consisting of three closed forts and four detached batteries, amply supplied with water from large cisterns constructed in the rock. The most elevated of the three forts commanded the whole defences, and was furnished with bomb-proof buildings. Corinth and Monemvasia were considered impregnable from their natural position. It was the plan of the senate to confine all preparations for defence to these five fortresses, which were well furnished with artillery, ammunition, military stores,

---

[1] [Tournefort, who visited Tenos just at the commencement of the eighteenth century, remarks on the undefended state of the island, in case of an invasion. *Voyage into the Levant*, Engl. Trans. of 1718, p. 277. The principal Venetian fortress and town was called Exoburgo, and was situated on the central ridge of the island, where a steep rocky peak rises to the height of 2000 feet above the sea. Considerable ruins remain, both of the fortress and of the town at its foot. It is remarkable that this island should have remained so long in the hands of Venice, when the surrounding islands were held by the Turks. The results of this protracted occupation are seen at the present day in the large number of Roman Catholics in the island, comprising more than half the population, and in the appearance of the houses, which, from their flat roofs, trim gardens, and battlemented enclosures, forcibly recall those of parts of North Italy. Indeed, throughout the islands of the Archipelago the most striking feature is the absence of Byzantine influence; for whereas on the mainland of Greece the Byzantine style of architecture is universal in ecclesiastical buildings, in the islands it is hardly ever seen, and the Italian mode of building and corresponding architectural features are predominant. ED.]

and provisions. The other fortified places in the peninsula were dismantled. But fortresses are of little use without strong garrisons; for insufficient garrisons and bad troops really facilitate the progress of an enemy. The whole military force of Venice in the Morea when the war broke out only amounted to eight thousand men, and the Venetian fleet in the Levant, under the captain-general Delfino, consisted of only forty-two ships, large and small, some galleys with oars, a few galleasses, and some galliots carrying mortars. The captain-general counted much on the attachment which he supposed the Greek population felt for the Venetian government, and believed that the Greek militia would display great valour in the field, and impede the advance of the Othoman army by hanging on its flanks and rear[1]. Against these forces the grand-vizier advanced with seventy thousand men, and the capitan-pasha with a fleet of sixty ships, besides galleys and galleasses.

On the 25th of June, 1715, Ali Kumurgi passed the wall across the Isthmus of Corinth, which was far too extensive for the Venetians to think of defending it, and, advancing through the lines they had constructed to connect Corinth and Lechaeum, leaving the fort on the sea-shore on his right and the city on his left, he encamped near the Gulf of Corinth. On the 28th the trenches were opened against the outer wall guarding the ascent from the town to the Acrocorinth, and the proveditor, Giacomo Minoto, was summoned to surrender the place[2]. The summons was rejected, and Sari Achmet

---

[1] In a letter from Delfino to Bono, the proveditor of Nauplia, intercepted by the grand-vizier, the captain-general cautions Bono against allowing the Greeks to expose themselves too much from their great zeal. So completely had the hypocrisy of the archons and priests, and the vaunting of the irregular Greek soldiers, deceived the Venetians. Brue, *Journal*, pp. 11, 12.

[2] Lord Byron's *Siege of Corinth* having given a classic interest to the events of this siege in English literature, I subjoin the summons sent by the grand-vizier, and the answer.

'I, who am the first minister and generalissimo of the most powerful emperor of the universe, and the most high among the monarchs of the earth, inform you, who are the Venetian commandant in the fortress of Corinth, that if you surrender the fortress, which from old time belongs to our most powerful emperor, the inhabitants shall be treated in the same manner as we treat all the true and faithful subjects of the empire; that they shall enjoy in perfect liberty all their possessions and property; nor shall their wives and children be ill used. And with regard to you, the Venetian commandant, you and all your garrison shall be treated according to the articles to be stipulated on surrendering the fortress. But if, in consequence of an ill-timed obstinacy, you resist the invincible arms of our most powerful emperor, know, that with the assistance of God, we will take your fortress, and put every man within it to the edge of the sword, and we will

Pasha (by whose advice, in the following year, the grand-vizier lost the battle of Peterwardein and his life) was ordered to press forward the siege. The Venetian garrison consisted of four hundred soldiers, assisted by two hundred armed Greeks; but the place was crowded with Greek families, who had retired with all their most valuable property within its walls. These non-combatants were all eager for a capitulation, believing that they would be able to save their property by a speedy surrender of the fortress. The Turks directed their attack from a hill to the south. Their batteries were too distant to produce much effect, but they protected the advance of the janissaries, who contrived to effect a lodgment under the walls; and it was resolved to attempt storming the outer gate, when Minoto hoisted a flag of truce. The Reis-effendi was sent into the place to settle the terms of surrender, and a capitulation was concluded, by which the grand-vizier engaged to transport the Venetian garrison in safety to Corfu.

On the morning of the 3rd August, while preparations were going forward to convey the garrison to the Othoman ships at Kenchrees, on the Gulf of Aegina, the janissaries, who were enraged at being deprived of the immense booty supposed to be accumulated in the fortress, contrived to escalade an unguarded part of the wall, and commenced plundering the houses. About noon a great smoke was seen from the Othoman camp to rise over the Acrocorinth, and a loud explosion announced that from some unknown cause a powder magazine had blown up. The grand-vizier was soon informed that the janissaries had forced their way into the place and broken the capitulation. The cause of the explosion was never known. The Turks accused the Venetians of setting fire to the powder, and commenced a massacre of the garrison. The troops, who were hurried up to the Acrocorinth, by order of the grand-vizier, in order to arrest the disorder, could only save the lives of a part of the Venetians, and conduct them to

---

make slaves of the women and children, and you shall be responsible to Heaven for the blood and slavery which will ensue, the crime being in no way to be attributed to us.' The seal of the grand-vizier was affixed to this document. The reply was in these words: 'To you who are the minister of the Othoman Porte, know that we, and all the troops and inhabitants of the fortress of Corinth, are determined to defend it; therefore your menaces are useless, for we are prepared to resist all your attacks, and, with confidence in the assistance of God, we will preserve this fortress to the most serene Republic. God is with us. (Signed) GIACOMO MINOTO, Proveditore Generale.'

a place of safety in the camp. The janissaries made slaves of the Greeks, men, women, and children ; nor did the grand-vizier venture to put a stop to these captives being sold publicly in his army. It was reported by the prisoners that Minoto had perished in the confusion ; but it was afterwards known that a soldier of the Asiatic troops had taken him prisoner, and concealed him in order to profit by his ransom. He was secretly conveyed to Smyrna, where he was released by the Dutch consul, who advanced his ransom money[1]. Bembo, the second in command, and about one hundred and eighty Venetian soldiers, with a few women, were saved, and sent on board the vessels at Kenchrees, from whence they were conveyed to Corfu, according to the terms of the capitulation. The grand-vizier, though he feared to attempt depriving his troops of their plunder in the camp, sent orders to all commandants of ports, and captains of defiles in the mountains, to secure and send back any Venetians who had been clandestinely enslaved ; but he took no measures to deliver the Greek captives, whose sale in the camp was legalized by regular certificates issued by the proper officers.

The mutinous conduct of his troops chafed the pride of Ali Kumurgi, who, in order to make a display of his power, calculated at least to make individuals tremble, ordered Suleiman Pasha of Selefke (Seleucia in Cilicia) to be beheaded, as a punishment for his delay in bringing up his troops to head-quarters. This pasha prayed in vain that he might be strangled privately in his tent, instead of being publicly executed before the whole army.

As soon as the capture of Corinth was generally known, the Greeks crowded to the Othoman camp, and gave the grand-vizier the strongest assurances of their attachment to

---

[1] Hammer, xiii. 270 ; Brue, *Journal,* p. 19, *note.* M. Brue mentions the following circumstance in this part of his Journal :—
' June 29. Five Janissaries brought to the grand-vizier the head of a man with a long beard. They said they had fallen in with seven soldiers who had made a sortie from the fortress, and that they had killed one. and carried off his head. The others had escaped into the place. The grand-vizier gave two hundred and fifty crowns to the janissary who said he had killed the bearded soldier, and divided two hundred and fifty more among the other four.
' July 4. The prisoners informed us that Minoto ordered a Greek who wore a long beard to be beheaded, and his head to be thrown from the walls, because a petition from the Greeks in the Acrocorinth to the grand-vizier had been found in his possession, which he was suspected of endeavouring to deliver. This we supposed was the head which the janissaries had carried to the grand-vizier.'

the Othoman government, and of their eagerness to see the Venetians expelled from the Morea. Ali promised them protection, and issued orders that they were to be treated as subjects of the sultan, and on no account to be molested in their persons nor injured in their property. These orders were obeyed, for the grand-vizier enforced the strictest discipline in his army during its march, and effectually protected the property of the rayahs in all the districts through which he had passed. This conduct secured to his numerous army regular supplies of provisions and forage; the peasants brought their produce in abundance to the markets which were established in his camp according to the system of earlier times, when liberal payment for provisions filled the Othoman camps with plenty, and excited the astonishment of Christian Europe[1]. The Moreote peasantry welcomed the grand-vizier whose cavalry paid for their barley, as they considered this conduct a proof that he would be a better master than the Venetians, who allowed their mercenaries to extort wine and meat gratis. Either from carelessness or from weakness and fear of causing dissatisfaction among the rural population, the Venetian authorities neglected to destroy the supplies in the country between Corinth and Nauplia. The army of the grand-vizier found the houses filled with provisions, the threshing-floors covered with grain, and the pastures stocked with cattle[2]. It met with no obstacle in its advance, and on the 11th of July, Ali Kumurgi encamped in the plain between Tiryns and Nauplia. On the 14th the janissaries, by a daring attack, effected a lodgment in the covered way of a tenaille on Palamedi, but suffered great loss in an obstinate and rash attempt to storm the tenaille itself. On the 15th the Othoman fleet arrived, and on the following day seventeen heavy guns and some large mortars were landed, and placed in the batteries prepared to receive them. Little impression, however, had been made either on the fortifications of the town or on the works of Palamedi, when, on the 20th of

---

[1] *See* above, p. 53.
[2] Daru (iv. 684) says, 'Delfino se détermina à faire ravager tout le pays et brûler les moissons, pour ôter à l'ennemi les moyens d'y subsister.' But Brue (*Journal*, p. 24) contradicts this, saying expressly, 'Le pain et la viande étoient très rares, aussi bien que l'orge pour les chevaux; et si les Vénitiens avoient eu la précaution de brûler tous les grains de la campagne de Corinthe, d'Argos, et de Napoli, au lieu de les laisser comme ils avoient fait, on auroit eu bien de la peine à faire subsister la cavalerie.'

A.D. 1684–1718.]

July, a mine was sprung against the tenaille where the former assault had been repulsed, and the janissaries, rushing forward over the ruins, carried the work by storm. The Venetians in the works behind were seized with a panic, and the whole of the Palamedi was abandoned in the most cowardly manner, for the forts were in a state to have made a long defence, and to have secured an honourable capitulation, even after the loss of the tenaille. The janissaries followed so close on the steps of the flying garrison as to enter the town of Nauplia by the gallery which descends from the Palamedi, without encountering any opposition. The troops in the plain, seeing the confusion on the ramparts and a Turkish standard in the town, plunged into the muddy ditch and escaladed the walls in the most exposed position. The proveditor Bono no sooner heard that his troops had retreated from the Palamedi than he hoisted a white flag ; but the janissaries were already in the place, and the Othoman troops had commenced pillaging the city before the grand-vizier was aware that it was taken. It is said that twenty-five thousand persons were either slain or reduced to slavery. About a thousand Venetian soldiers were brought to the grand-vizier, who paid their ransom to their captors, and then ordered them to be beheaded before his tent. Balbi, who commanded the insular fort called the Burdgé, immediately surrendered, and eight thousand sequins were found in his possession. When Nauplia fell, the garrison consisted of nearly two thousand regular troops, amply provided with every means of defence [1].

Nauplia was at this time a well-built town, as well as a strong fortress. Its fortifications were excellent ; its public

---

[1] The military stores found in Nauplia consisted of 96 brass guns, some very large, 55 iron and 10 large brass mortars, 6 iron and 18 smaller brass mortars, and 4 iron mortars for stones, 15 field pieces, 1664 cwts. of lead, 34,697 cannon-balls, 12,115 bombs, 2930 iron hand-grenades, 2320 glass grenades, and 20,000 cwts. of powder. Many of the glass grenades of different colours were found in Nauplia when it was taken by the Greeks in 1822. I knew a Philhellene who used one as an ink-bottle.

The Greeks attribute the fall of Nauplia to the treachery of a French officer in the service of Venice, the Colonel Lasala ; but there seems no reason to adopt their version of the causes which led to the Turks entering the place with facility. See a letter of Antonio Zara, one of the chief officers of the garrison, dated from the bagnio of Constantinople, 15th March, 1716, in which it appears that Lasala succeeded to the charge of the works on the death of Cardosi, and that he quarrelled with Colonel Stade, and was put under arrest by the proveditor Bono. Hammer, xiii. 376. Συμφορὰ καὶ αἰχμαλωσία Μωραίως στιχολογηθεῖσα παρὰ Μάνθου Ἰωάννου τοῦ ἐξ Ἰωαννίνων, 8vo., Venice, 1800.

and private buildings large and solid structures; its population numerous and wealthy. Its feeble defence afforded
strong proof of the incapacity and worthlessness both of
the civil and military authorities of the Venetian republic.
But, on the other hand, the grand-vizier and the Othoman
generals are not entitled to attribute the conquest of the
place either to their valour or military skill. The whole
merit of the rapid success is due to the courage, or rather
temerity, of the janissaries, who, by a succession of rash
attacks, and a gallant defence of every step of ground they
acquired, though maintained with severe loss, gained possession of the Palamedi, the key of the fortress, in nine days.
Ali Kumurgi, who did not pretend to possess any knowledge
of military affairs, remained in the camp during the whole
siege, and never once visited the trenches of the janissaries on
Mount Palamedi. Sari Pasha, who commanded there, no
more expected to see the place fall, by the explosion of a
single mine, than the proveditor Bono.

From Nauplia the grand-vizier marched through the Morea
by Akhladokampo, Tripolitza, Veligosti, the Lakkos of Messenia and Nisi, from whence, proceeding towards Navarin, but
leaving that place on his right, he encamped before Modon on
the 11th of August[1]. Coron and Navarin were abandoned by
the Venetians, and their garrisons withdrawn to Modon, into
which the greater part of the Venetian property in both towns
had been conveyed, though articles of great value had been
previously transported to the Ionian Islands and to Venice. The
fortifications of Modon were commanded by a rising ground in
the vicinity. The grand-vizier, who wished to save the valuable
property in the town from pillage, summoned the governor to
surrender, declaring that, if he refused the terms offered, he
should not be admitted to any capitulation, but must surrender at discretion. This summons was rejected; for, as the
captain-general Delfino was anchored at Sapienza with a fleet
of fifty sail, the garrison felt sure of support. The Turks
opened their trenches, and the capitan-pasha arrived with
the Othoman fleet. Delfino then declined the engagement
offered, lest, as he himself says, disasters by sea should

---

[1] It is interesting to find Veligosti and the Lakkos of Messenia mentioned as
stations in the itinerary of the grand-vizier. The site of Veligosti is now deserted,
and its feudal celebrity forgotten.

accompany defeat on shore, and Venice should find that her only fleet had been sacrificed in vain[1]. The garrison of Modon, seeing that it was abandoned to its fate by the captain-general, after a feeble defence offered to capitulate. Sari Achmet, the beglerbey of Roumeli, wished to save the place, but the grand-vizier refused all terms; and the janissaries, availing themselves of the truce, approached the walls, and found an entrance into the town, which they immediately commenced plundering. The greater part of the inhabitants were reduced to slavery, but the wealthiest had employed the preceding night in conveying their money and jewels on board the ships in the port, and the capitan-pasha allowed many of them, with the soldiers of the garrison, to escape on board the Othoman fleet. All the males in the place would probably have been put to the sword, and their heads heaped up before the tent of the grand-vizier, to obtain the usual head-money, had his kihaya not declared that, the place having surrendered at discretion, the law of the Prophet forbade the massacre of the inhabitants, and, therefore, the grand-vizier was not authorized to pay any head-money under such circumstances. The troops grumbled at what they called the avarice of the kihaya, for they knew the liberality of the grand-vizier too well to attribute the decision to his love of money; so they made the most they could by the sale and ransom of their prisoners whose lives were spared[2]. The Venetian general Pasta was protected and well treated by the capitan-pasha, who, when a slave at Venice, where he had passed seven years in the galleys, had been treated with kindness by that officer[3].

The Castle of the Morea surrendered to Kara Mustapha, the pasha of Diarbekr, after only three days of open trenches. The Venetian troops, six hundred in number, were transported to Cephalonia, but the Sclavonians and Greeks of the garrison were reduced to slavery. The janissaries, however, violated the capitulation, and detained many of the Italian soldiers until they were ransomed by the pasha. Kielapha and

---

[1] Ranke, 495.

[2] Brue, in his Journal (p. 49), directly contradicts the account of Hammer (xiii. 274) that on this occasion the grand-vizier paid thirty imperial dollars for every Christian who was brought to him, in order to have the pleasure of seeing them beheaded before his tent.

[3] Hammer, xiii. 274.

Zarnata, though well prepared for defence, surrendered on the first summons.

From Modon the grand-vizier marched by Leondari and Misithra to Elos, where he awaited the capitulation of Monemvasia, which took place on the 7th of September. This impregnable insular rock was supplied with provisions for more than two years; but the Greek inhabitants who possessed property in the Morea were eager to exchange the mild domination of the Venetian republic for the stern yoke of the Othoman sultan—as at the present day we see the inhabitants of the Ionian Islands eager to transfer their allegiance from Great Britain to King Otho.

The grand-vizier, having completed the conquest of the Morea, returned to Adrianople, where Sultan Achmet III. then resided. Before the end of the year the Venetians abandoned Santa Maura and Cerigo; Suda and Spinalonga were taken by the capitan-pasha.

The surviving Turkish exiles who had been driven from the Morea by the Venetians were now re-established in possession of their landed property, and many of those Mussulmans who had embraced Christianity to preserve their estates were condemned to death, though they had always continued to wear white turbans, and affected to retain as much attachment to Mohammedanism as the Venetian and the Greek people would tolerate. This system of compliance in religious matters at the dictation of the civil power was borrowed from the Greeks, and most of these compliant Mussulmans were of Greek descent; but the votaries of Islam had no sympathy with those measures of dishonourable conformity which, under the name of economical arrangements, make so prominent a figure in the history of religious opinion in the Byzantine church[1].

The Emperor of Germany was alarmed at the facility with which the Othoman army had conquered the Morea, and he feared that the sultan would follow up his victory by an attempt to re-establish the Othoman power in Hungary, where the tyrannical government of the house of Austria had, as usual, filled the country with discontent. The court of Vienna, alive to its true interests, did not show the same

---

[1] *See* vol. ii., *History of the Byzantine Empire*, p. 121; Neander, *History of the Christian Religion and Church*, by Professor Torrey, iii. 541.

supineness as the Venetian senate. It had an able minister, as well as an experienced general, in Prince Eugene of Savoy. An offensive and defensive alliance was concluded with the republic, and the Porte was invited to re-establish peace on the basis of the treaty of Carlovitz. To this demand the natural reply was an immediate declaration of war; but the divan was anxious to avoid hostilities, and the grand-vizier had some difficulty in getting war declared. He however took the command of the army destined to invade Hungary; and on the 5th of August, 1716, the battle of Carlovitz or Peterwardein was fought. The Othoman army was completely defeated by Prince Eugene, and Ali Kumurgi was among the slain. Another Othoman army, under Kara Mustapha Pasha, in conjunction with the fleet under the capitan-pasha Djanum Khodja, besieged Corfu about the same time. That fortress was valiantly defended by Count Schulenburg, whom Prince Eugene had recommended the republic of Venice to appoint general of its troops, with the rank of field-marshal[1]. The energetic defence of Schulenburg, and the news of the defeat at Carlovitz, forced the Turks to raise the siege of Corfu on the 19th of August. The events of that siege belong to the history of Venice, and have very little connection with that of the Greek nation. It was the last glorious military exploit in the annals of the republic, and it was achieved by a German mercenary soldier. The defeat of the Othoman expedition enabled the Venetians to regain possession of Santa Maura.

The following year was distinguished by the siege and capture of Belgrade, which surrendered to Prince Eugene on the 18th of August. The operations of the Venetians were confined to the conquest of Butrinto, Prevesa, and Vonitza, and to several indecisive naval engagements in the Archipelago.

The victories of Prince Eugene disposed the sultan to peace, which was concluded, after long conferences, at Passarovitz, on the 21st of July 1718. Venice was compelled to cede the Morea, Tinos, Aegina, Suda, and Spinalonga to the sultan; but the republic retained possession of the places it had conquered in Dalmatia, as well as Santa Maura, Butrinto,

---

[1] The Duchess of Kendal, mistress of George I., was the sister of Schulenburg.

Prevesa, and Vonitza, and it received back Cerigo. Austria acquired the fortresses of Temesvar, Belgrade, and Semendria.

The facility with which the Othoman arms had conquered Greece, and the feeble resistance which Venice offered to an invading army, after the care with which the administration of the Morea had been organized during a period of eighteen years, affords an instructive lesson in the history of the government of foreign dependencies. There is no sure basis of the subjection of any foreign nation, unless there be a decided superiority of military power on the part of the rulers; and no scientific administrative combinations can secure good government and an equitable dispensation of justice, unless private individuals are courageous, honest, and deeply imbued with a love of truth and self-respect. No moderation and no political art alone will ever reconcile a subject people to foreign domination, unless the sovereign authority connect its power with the existence of popular municipal institutions. Indeed, no government can properly fulfil its duties, nor rightly aid the progress of social civilization, which does not leave the population of each village, town, and district to exercise an active share in the administration of its local affairs, in the management of its local improvements, and in the control of its local finances, responsible only to the public opinion of the country and to the law of the land. The fear which the Venetians entertained of the Greek population of the Morea induced them to centralize all power, and the corruption of the Venetian nobles made that centralization the cause of general discontent. It was the venality, rapacity, and cowardice of the ruling classes and of the wealthy native archonts, far more than the defects of the government, that destroyed the power of the republic in Greece.

Venice, like all governments which persist in a traditional system of administration during a long period of tranquillity, stood greatly in need of administrative reforms at the commencement of the eighteenth century. Her system of commercial restrictions and monopolies was so hostile to the interests of every Christian power engaged in the trade of the Levant, that it prevented any State from becoming her friend and ally. All foreign governments regarded her with jealousy, and she was utterly destitute of all generous or progressive social impulses from within. The government offices were regarded as provisions for younger sons of the nobles. The military career was abandoned to the provincial militia or to foreign mercenaries, for it entailed years of service in distant garrisons, and offered slow promotion. Long service alone could bring rank; and if wealth came, it came when age had deprived its possessor of those passions which, at Venice, rendered wealth valuable for their gratification. On the other hand, the civil and judicial service admitted of rapid promotion through favour and intrigue, while means could be found of making them conducive to the accumulation of illicit gains. The universal practice of corruption, bribery, and peculation had dulled the force of conscience, and all sense of honour appeared to be wanting in the civil government during the eighteenth century. The young nobles who had it in their power to share in a contract, or to sell a judicial sentence of importance, might hope to return to Venice with wealth to enjoy those pleasures which rendered her inhabitants notoriously the most luxurious, debauched, and idle population in Europe. In a State where suspicion was the characteristic of the government, dissipation the occupation of society, and where the feelings of the people were systematically suppressed, it is not surprising that selfishness and cowardice marked the conduct both of the government and of individuals, nor that the republic of Venice was unable to resist the forces of the Othoman empire.

CHAPTER V.

THE CAUSES AND EVENTS WHICH PREPARED THE GREEKS FOR INDEPENDENCE.—A.D. 1718–1821.

Improvement in the condition of the Greeks during the eighteenth century.— Condition of Chios.—Comparison of Chios with Tinos and Naxos.—Religious contests of the Catholics and Orthodox in the Othoman empire.—Character and influence of the Phanariots, or Greek officials in the service of the sultan. —Treaty of Belgrade, A.D. 1739.—War between Turkey and Russia concluded by the peace of Kainardji, A.D. 1768–1774.—Operations of the Russians in the Morea.—Naval operations and battle of Tchesmé.—Defeat of the Russians at Lemnos.—Hassan Ghazi exterminates the Albanian troops in the Morea.— Establishes the authority of the capitan-pasha in Maina.—War between Turkey and Russia, A.D. 1787–1792.—Insurrection of the Suliots, an Albanian tribe in Epirus.—Lambros Katsones and piracy in the Grecian seas.—Ionian Islands subject to the French Republic, to the Russians, and to the English. —Change in the social position of the Greeks at the commencement of the nineteenth century.—Influence of the Phanariots and of commerce on national consolidation.—Improvement of the modern Greek language a powerful instrument in advancing national centralization.—Change in the nature of the sultan's power, and decline of the Othoman empire.—Conclusion.

AFTER the treaty of Passarovitz, the material and political position of the Greek nation began to exhibit many signs of improvement. The cultivators of the soil obtained everywhere the rank of freemen, and emancipated themselves from the peculiar condition, partaking of slavery and serfage, which they had occupied until the complete extinction of the tribute of Christian children. About the same time the increasing importance of money as the representative of the value of all services, as well as of every kind of produce, introduced the system of commuting the personal labour of the rayah, whether it was due to the timariot or to the government, for a determinate portion of the produce of the land, or for a fixed pecuniary payment. The agricultural population of

Greece, in consequence of these changes, became, in great part of the country, the legal as well as the real proprietors of the soil; and even where the Christians remained as labourers of land belonging to Mohammedan landlords, instead of working a fixed number of days on the land of the aga, they now hired the land, and paid rent, in determinate proportions of produce and money, according to agreement. The pashas, also, instead of compelling the people, as formerly, to supply the materials for public works, and to labour in person at their construction, now exacted payment of a sum of money, and employed a contractor to execute the work. As the demoralization of the Othoman government increased, this manner of collecting and paying money became a means of enriching officials and impoverishing the people, while the public works of all kinds throughout the Othoman empire were allowed to fall into ruins. Mussulman landlords also began to find so great a difficulty in obtaining slaves, that slave-labour could no longer be profitably employed in agriculture. Before the end of the seventeenth century, predial slavery had disappeared in the European provinces of the Othoman empire south of the Danube. The Greek peasant was everywhere a free labourer, and began to feel the sentiments of a freeman. No power could now have long enforced the collection of a tribute of Greek children, for the lowest class of the Greek population had ascended so far in civilization, that, by enforcing such a tax, the Othoman government would have condemned the Greeks to apostasy, exile, or extermination. Those who remained true to their religion would either have ceased to perpetuate their race, or would have escaped from their native land, and Hellas would have no longer been the dwelling-place of the Greek race, any more than Palestine is that of the race of Israel. To preserve their national existence, the Greeks would have been compelled to become a people of exiles like the Jews.

The decline of the military system and the corruption of the civil administration in the Othoman empire fortunately coincided with the improvement in the condition of the Greek agricultural population. The conquest of the Morea by the Venetians, and the increasing power of the Christian states whose territories bordered on Turkey, forced the Othoman government to conciliate the good-will of the rayahs, and the sultan's ministers began to recognize the necessity of granting the Christians a public guarantee for the security of their personal liberty, and for the protection of their property. But the practical concessions of the Porte were tardily granted, and were generally obtained by the force of accidental circumstances and of social changes, rather than by the progress of political intelligence and a sense of justice. They were, consequently, too restricted in their operation to remove many galling marks of subjection, or allay the national opposition which increased communications with western and northern Europe were spreading among the sultan's Christian subjects. The opinion that the power of the sultan possessed a divine sanction, because he was the protector of the orthodox church, though taught by the Greek clergy, was no longer implicitly admitted by the people. The English Revolution of 1688 caused the people over all Europe to discuss their own rights. Other claims to political authority were recognized as more valid than the legitimacy of princes, and apostolical succession was no longer held to be an indispensable requisite in a teacher of Christianity. The doctrine of the supremacy of parliament invested the people with the right to make its own laws, while the principles of religious liberty flowing from Protestantism emancipated the human mind from ecclesiastical intolerance. In estimating the effect produced on the Greeks by the new doctrines which began to ferment in European society at the commencement of the eighteenth century, we must remember that they were placed in closest contact with those classes of society that had suffered most from feudal oppression and religious bigotry, and that were most inclined to question the authority of existing institutions.

The good intentions of the Porte towards its orthodox subjects were displayed in several measures tending to improve their material condition. The inhabitants of the Morea were exempt from the land-tax for two years after the conquest of that province; and as soon as peace was established, the Porte invited colonists to settle on the lands which still remained uncultivated, by exempting the settlers from taxation for three years.

The island of Chios had always retained the social

superiority which it possessed under the prudent administration of the mercantile company of the Giustiniani. Until
the peace of Passarovitz, its inhabitants preserved their old
system of collecting their land-tax by the local authorities,
and annually remitted to the Othoman government a fixed
amount of tribute. But, after the peace, the grand-vizier
Ibrahim modified this system, and subjected the island
to most of the ordinary fiscal arrangements adopted with
regard to the other Greek islands. In 1727 the haratch
was extended to the twenty-one villages engaged in the
cultivation of mastic, and three thousand and thirty-six additional tickets were added to the capitation-tax of Chios [1].
Still the inhabitants were the portion of the Greek people
which suffered the fewest evils from the Othoman domination
during the eighteenth century. The causes of their happiness
and prosperity during a long period, while the rest of their
countrymen were poor and discontented, deserve to be
examined with attention. The first fact to be observed is,
that they were more honest and industrious than the other
Greeks. It was their moral and social superiority which
enabled them to secure to themselves the enjoyment of
the fruits of their industry. Their island, it is true, possesses
some remarkable physical advantages. Almost every article
it produces is of superior quality, and when exported,
obtained the highest price then paid for such commodities
in foreign markets. In the town of Chios, and in the rich
plain to the south, many remains of well-built houses may
still be seen, which bear on their ruined walls dates proving
that they were constructed during the eighteenth century,
yet they rival in size and solidity the massive structures of
the Genoese domination. The mastic, the almonds, the
lemons, the preserved citrons, the conserve of roses, and
the orange-flower water of Chios, were highly esteemed by
the luxurious in every province of the East. The manu-
factures of silk and cotton, of which large quantities were
exported, as well as several rich varieties of lace, were
produced by the labour of private families in their own
dwellings, and embroidery of every kind was executed on
scarfs and handkerchiefs by the same hands which had
already dyed them of the richest colours.

---

[1] Hammer, *Histoire de l'Empire Othoman*, xiv. 6, 33.

The superior moral character of the Chiots was acknowledged throughout the Levant. They were alike destitute
of the insolence and rapacity of the Phanariots, and of
the meanness and fraudulency of the trading Greeks of
the continent. The marked difference which existed
between them and the rest of their countrymen was observed by every traveller and foreign merchant. It was
generally attributed to the great privileges they possessed.
This explanation was suggested by the other Greeks, as
an excuse for their own vices and dishonesty, and it was
adopted by strangers without sufficient examination. It
was said that Suleiman the Great, or rather his son Selim
II., after the island had been subjected to the Othoman
administration by Piali Pasha in 1566, had granted a
charter to the Chiots, by which their previous local usages
were confirmed. But this does not appear to have been
the case. The supposed charter was nothing more than the
toleration of the fiscal system of the Giustiniani, obtained
by the payment of an augmented tribute[1]. The true explanation of the moral superiority of the Chiots must be
sought in their family education. The boasted privileges
which they enjoyed from the time of Selim II., and which
were so much envied by the other Greeks, were the permission to repair their churches, the right to carry the
cross in procession through the town, and to perform many
ecclesiastical ceremonies publicly, besides the highly-valued
privilege, retained by the wealthy, of riding horses and
wearing spurs. Their other privileges were the continuation
of the fiscal arrangements established by the Giustiniani,
and the election of the magistrates who conducted the
local administration. Sultan Selim II. may have confirmed the existing system when he abolished the authority
of the Giustiniani, and his successors appear to have
frequently issued ordinances, on their accession to the
throne, enumerating and guaranteeing these concessions.
The oldest of these charters, which was preserved in the
archives of the municipality of Chios previous to the
Greek Revolution, was that of Suleiman II., the son of
Ibrahim, who ascended the Othoman throne in 1687, and

---

[1] The Giustiniani became tributary to Mohammed II., and his successors
claimed the suzerainty of Chios.

his name gave rise to the opinion that the privileges of Chios dated from the time of Suleiman the Great[1].

The civil advantages conceded to the Chiots applied rather to the city than to the agricultural population of the island: they were chiefly fiscal; and similar concessions were enjoyed by other Greek communities in the islands of the Archipelago, and on the continent of Europe, sometimes even in a higher degree. The following were the most important: The commutation of all taxes for a fixed sum of money, paid to the Othoman authorities by Greek magistrates, who partitioned the quota of each family and collected the amount. The right of electing these magistrates by universal suffrage, and of electing in the same way native judges to decide all commercial questions. The municipal government of Chios consisted of five primates, of whom three were chosen by the Orthodox, and two by the Catholics; the commercial tribunal consisted of four judges, three of whom were Orthodox and one was a Catholic. But perhaps the practical usage most conducive towards perpetuating the mutual good faith of the Chiots, was the existence of notaries-public, whose acts were written in Greek, and were received as official documents by the Othoman government[2]. The morality of the Chiots was not a consequence of these privileges; on the contrary, it was that morality which gave them their value. Other Greek communities enjoyed equal immunities. The Greeks of Constantinople, Rhodes, and many islands of the Archipelago, were never subjected to the tribute of Christian children; and the inhabitants of Tinos and Naxos were governed by their own laws and usages, like those of Chios, with the additional advantage of not having a body of Mussulman proprietors resident in their islands.

The condition of the people in Tinos and Naxos may be instructively compared with that of the Chiots. In the three islands a part of the inhabitants had joined the Catholic Church, and they had all three been long under Catholic domination. In Tinos, as in Chios, the Catholics were as

---

[1] Vlastos, Χιακά, ii. 84. Suleiman the Great, or the Legislator, is sometimes called Suleiman II. by historians, who include Suleiman, the son of Bayezid I., in the list of Othoman sultans.

[2] For details relating to the municipal administration of Chios, see Vlastos, Χιακά, ii. 152, 180.

remarkable for their industry and honesty as the Orthodox, but in Naxos they were distinguished by their idleness. Though the island of Tinos was destitute of a good port, and far removed from any advantageous market for its produce, and though its inhabitants had been long cut off from many branches of trade with their immediate neighbours by the commercial monopoly of the Venetians, still they were industrious and contented. The soil of Tinos is not fertile, and the population was so great that many young persons of both sexes quitted the island annually to lighten the expenses of their family, and gain a small capital for themselves by a few years of domestic service at Constantinople, Smyrna, and Saloniki, where their probity insured them liberal wages and kind treatment in the families of wealthy Christians. At home and abroad the Tiniots were remarkable for their good conduct, frugality, and industry.

Naxos offered a complete contrast to Tinos. Though it enjoyed all the advantages of a municipal government, the influence of a small number of privileged landed proprietors, remains of the ducal aristocracy, rendered the local administration a scene of intrigue and dissension. The Catholic nobles were proud and luxurious; the Greek primates malicious and rapacious; the people of both churches lazy, superstitious, and false. This rich island only contained about two-thirds of the population of the smaller and more barren surface of Tinos; and it paid little more than half the amount of taxation to the Othoman government. The superiority of the Tiniots, like that of the Chiots, was evidently caused by the moral education they received in their earliest youth. The superiority was equally remarkable in the Catholic and the Orthodox population, when compared with the general mass of the Greek race[1].

Chios did not possess all the advantages of Tinos and Naxos, for it contained an Othoman fortress with its garrison, and a considerable Turkish population. The prosperity of Chios, under Othoman domination, must consequently be considered as entirely due to the excellent education the inhabitants received for many generations in the bosoms of

---

[1] For some information concerning the state of Tinos and Naxos at the end of the eighteenth century, see Olivier, *Voyage dans l'Empire Othoman, l'Egypte, et la Perse*, ii. 149, 163.

their families, and not to any extraordinary fiscal privileges and immunities the island enjoyed, nor to any peculiar favour with which it was treated by the sultans. Had the Chiots displayed the same spirit of envy and dissension, and followed the same course of selfish intrigues as the greater part of the Greeks, their peculiar privileges would only have become an additional incitement to dispute, and would have entailed greater misery on them than the direct operation of Turkish oppression. It was by union in their municipality, and good faith in their private dealings, that the Chiots rendered their ancient usages a blessing to their island, and their fiscal system an advantage to the people, instead of converting them into a means of gratifying the ambition of the wealthy archonts, and of enriching a few primates, as was the case in most other Greek communities. Among the Chiots industry was honoured, and the honest and active citizen, whose personal exertions had gained him the respect of his fellow-countrymen, was selected to conduct the municipal affairs and to fill the local magistracies. Idleness was so universally despised that in Chios alone, of all the Greek cities, there was no class of young archonts who considered it ignoble to be usefully employed, and who spent their time in soliciting from the Turks the post of tax-collectors, or in intriguing to be named primates by the influence of a pasha, in order to obtain the means of enriching themselves by acting as the instruments of fiscal extortion. The superior morality of the Chiots in all the relations of life, their truth and honesty, rendered their island for several centuries the most flourishing and the happiest portion of Greece, alike under the Othoman as under the Genoese domination.

But the Chiots cannot be expected to have been free from the social errors of the age in which they lived. Religious sincerity was then too closely united with bigotry for any Greeks to have learned that toleration was a Christian virtue. In religious bigotry neither the Orthodox nor the Catholics of Chios yielded to other Greeks, and their mutual animosity was repeatedly shown in violent and unjust proceedings towards one another. But the fact that this bigotry was cherished and aggravated by foreign interference must not be overlooked. The Greek clergy were continually alarmed by the attempts of the French ambassador at Constantinople

to extend the authority of the Catholics, and to obtain for
them a superiority over the Greeks. In the year 1719, the
intervention of Count Virmont obtained for the Catholics
the restoration of the privileges which they had lost, after
the expulsion of the Venetians in 1695. Sultan Achmet III.
issued a firman, recognizing the rights of the Catholics to
participate in the privileges granted to all the inhabitants
of the island by the firman of Suleiman II., and reinstating
them in the possession of the church of St. Nicholas [1]. This
concession was undoubtedly an act of justice; but as it was
conceded to the influence of a foreign power, whose object
was to obtain indirect authority in the Othoman empire,
through the instrumentality of the Catholics, and not to
secure toleration for religious opinions, to which it was more
decidedly hostile than the Greeks themselves, it was natural
for the Orthodox to fear an invasion of their rights as a consequence of the success of the Catholics. The religious pretensions of the Papal Church, and the ambitious projects of
the King of France, warned the Orthodox to prepare for
defending themselves against political aggression. In 1724,
the French ambassador obtained permission from the Porte
to build a new chapel in the consulate at Chios; and under
his protection the Catholic missionaries displayed a degree
of activity which alarmed the bigotry of the Greeks, and
roused their opposition. To counteract the eloquence of the
missionaries and the political influence of France, the Greeks
in 1728 succeeded in persuading the Othoman government
to defend orthodoxy by prohibiting proselytism [2].

The restless activity of the French ambassadors at Constantinople sought to extend the influence of France by
circumscribing the rights of the Greek Church at Jerusalem.
The custody of the Sepulchre of Christ, and of the other
holy places in and round Jerusalem, has been long a subject
of dispute between the Catholics and the Orthodox; and
from the time that both have been admitted to a share of
this custody, by the toleration of their Mussulman conquerors,
these two sects, instead of exercising their respective privileges in a Christian spirit, have made the toleration of the
Othomans a ground for intrigues to encroach on each other's

---

[1] Hammer, *Histoire*, xiv. 23.   [2] Ibid., xiv. 109, 200.

rights. The aggression of the Catholics, being protected by France, was more open and daring than that of the Orthodox, until the Greeks obtained the protection of Russia. At the period of which we are treating, the proceedings of France created a feeling of fierce hostility against the Catholics among the Greeks, even more than among the other orthodox nations, and a contest of intrigue was commenced at the Porte, which tended greatly to lower the Christians in the opinion of the Mussulmans. Several French ambassadors, in order to obtain the credit of establishing a permanent influence in the Levant, induced the Porte to grant concessions to the Catholics, which were subsequently neglected, or were again abrogated by other concessions to the Orthodox. The court of France displayed little delicacy, and no sense of justice, in these intrigues. Constantinople, Jerusalem, Chios, Crete, Cyprus, and the islands of the Archipelago, were made the scenes of public tumults as well as of incessant discord[1]. At last, after the great diplomatic success which the Othoman government obtained over Austria and Russia, by the treaty of Belgrade, the sultan, to mark his satisfaction with the conduct of the Marquis of Villeneuve, the French ambassador who acted as mediator during the negotiations, inserted articles in the French capitulations, on their renewal in the following year, which were supposed to authorize the Catholics to take possession of several of the Holy Places previously in the custody of the Greeks. These concessions,

---

[1] D'Ohsson, *Tableau Général de l'Empire Othoman*, v. 115. Hammer (xiii. 184, corrected by p. 228) mentions the banishment of the Armenian patriarch to Chios, for opposing the influence of France, and asserts that he was kidnapped by order of the French ambassador, and carried to the isle of St. Marguerite. near Antibes, where he died. But it appears that this patriarch, whose name was Avedik, was not in reality taken to St. Marguerite, but was secretly transported from Marseilles to the abbey of Mont St. Michel, where he was intrusted to the safe keeping and zealous teaching of the monks, in whose custody he remained completely secluded from the world for three years. He was then removed to the Bastille. The terror of imprisonment for life in that celebrated place overcame his fortitude, and he declared himself a convert to Catholicism, yet he remained in France until his death. The complaints of the sultan against this outrage on the law of nations caused the French ambassador at Constantinople to deny the transaction, and he even attempted to persuade the Porte that the Spaniards were the man-stealers who had kidnapped the unfortunate Avedik. At last, to avoid a rupture with Turkey, Louis XIV. formally announced that Avedik was dead, though he was still languishing in a French prison. His death was universally believed to have taken place long before it actually occurred. See a communication to the 'Athenaeum Français,' 5th January, 1856, by G. Depping.

On the subject of these disputes concerning the Holy Places, compare Hammer, ix. 283, 406; x. 67, 113; xi. 425; xii. 305, 461, 542.

whatever they were, appear never to have been carried into execution, and the Greeks were subsequently confirmed in their previous rights by more than one firman.

It is needless to observe that religious zeal was not the principal cause of the activity of French diplomacy, and it is evident that pecuniary interest, as well as ecclesiastical authority, urged the Orthodox to maintain rights which were extremely profitable to the church. The Orthodox, however, sincerely believed that the most sacred ties of religion bound them to resist what they deemed to be unjust attacks on their church by the Catholics. The rashness and levity with which French diplomacy has attempted to make the question relating to the custody of the Holy Places a criterion of political influence in the Othoman empire at different periods, and the utter neglect, and even contempt, with which it has treated the subject at other times, afford a just measure of the religious zeal of the French government. After treating the subject with scorn for a considerable time, in the year 1850 France thought fit again to open the question. The history of the negotiations which ensued is not more edifying than the record of earlier and equally futile pretensions; but on this occasion Russia, availing herself of the proceedings of France, mingled in the dispute as protector of the Orthodox. New complications were introduced into the discussion concerning the relations between the Porte and its orthodox subjects, and the Emperor Nicholas, deeming the moment favourable for a new encroachment on Turkey, plunged into a bloody war [1].

The ecclesiastical privileges which Mohammed II. granted to the Greek Church, and to the Patriarch as the chief of the Greek nation, enabled the laity gradually to acquire a recog-

---

[1] A report of the English consul at Jerusalem to the Secretary of the Foreign Department, dated 27th October 1852, shows how far diplomatic intrigue can lose sight of true dignity, and how much France must have degraded the Christian character in the opinion of the Mussulmans. 'After the Corban Bairam festivals were over, and ceremonial visits fully exchanged, the commissioner, Afif Bey, with a suite of the local effendis, met the three patriarchs, Greek, Latin, and Armenian, in the Church of the Resurrection, just in front of the Holy Sepulchre itself, and under the great dome; there they were regaled with sherbets, confectionary, and pipes, at the expense of the three convents, who vied with each other in making luxurious display on the occasion. M. Botta, the French consul, was the only consular person present.' *Correspondence respecting the Rights and Privileges of the Latin and Greek Churches in Turkey, presented to Parliament* 1854 (part i. p. 45).

nized position in the public administration of the Othoman empire. The importance of ruling their Greek subjects with justice as well as firmness, was felt by the most powerful sultans, and by the ablest grand-viziers; while the complicated fiscal relations of a numerous population widely dispersed, and possessing a monopoly of many necessary branches of industry, induced the Porte to employ Greeks as useful subordinate instruments in the fiscal administration. Soon after the conquest, Greek archonts and primates were employed by the Turks as collectors of the land-tax, and as custom-house officers. At length, during the seventeenth century, the increased importance of the diplomatic relations of the Porte with the Christian powers opened a new political career to the Greeks, and gave rise to the formation of a class of officials in the Othoman service called Phanariots, from their making the quarter of Constantinople around the Patriarchate, called the Phanar, their place of residence. The higher clergy and wealthy Greek primates had long dwelt in this quarter, in order to enjoy security under protection of the immunities granted to the Patriarch. The wealthiest and most influential Greeks generally acted as fiscal-agents of the church, as well as tax-gatherers for the Porte[1].

Before the administration of the celebrated grand-vizier Achmet Kueprili, the Greek officials employed as secretaries in the Othoman service were ranked as little better than literary menials. But after the conquest of Candia, Achmet conferred on his secretary, the Chiot Panayotaki, an official rank in the Othoman administration, by creating for him the post of Dragoman of the Porte. Panayotaki's devotion to the grand-vizier, and his fidelity to the interests of the sultan, enabled him to render his place one of great political influence. The Porte subsequently created a second officer of a similar nature, attached to the capitan-pasha, called the Dragoman of the Fleet, who exercised direct authority over the Greeks employed in the naval service, and great influence in the islands and continental districts where the taxes were farmed under the capitan-pasha. The existence of these two offices

---

[1] Zallony, *Essai sur les Fanariotes*, 157 (note concerning the Patriarchal Treasury).

laid the foundation of the power of the Phanariots in the Othoman empire.

The successor of Panayotaki was Alexander Mavrocordatos, also a Chiot. He distinguished himself by his able conduct during the conferences preceding the treaty of Carlovitz, and thereby added much to the influence of his office[1]. These two Chiots gained the confidence of the grand-viziers they served by displaying more truth and honesty than the Othoman ministers had ever found in the false and intriguing Greek officials who were educated under the immediate influence of the patriarchate in the Phanar. The moral superiority, imbibed from the family education of Chios, did more to gain a political position for the Greeks in the Othoman administration than the learning of the Byzantine archonts and the privileges of the orthodox clergy. The servility and acuteness of the Constantinopolitans could not gain the authority readily conceded to the truth and fidelity of the Chiots.

The office of Dragoman of the Fleet became the first step towards obtaining the highest offices granted to Christians. His duty was to act as secretary to the capitan-pasha, and to see that the tribute of the Greek islands was regularly paid. His favour, and the extent of his political influence, depended on his activity and ability in obtaining large presents and illegitimate profits for the capitan-pasha, and in enforcing the regular payments due to the imperial treasury. His own interest, and even his personal security, made him the oppressor of the Christians, whom he might secretly wish to protect. Unless he accumulated money for himself, he could never hope to purchase the dignity of Voivode of Vallachia or Moldavia, where he could feel a greater degree of security.

---

[1] Alexander Mavrocordatos was the son of a silk-merchant of Chios, who married the daughter of Skarlatos, who had made an immense fortune as purveyor of beef for the sultan's palace and the public markets. Mavrocordatos studied medicine in Italy, and wrote a treatise in Latin on the circulation of the blood, which has been much praised, as well as several works in Greek. He was a proficient in the Greek, Latin, Italian, French, Sclavonian, Turkish, Persian, and Arabic languages. Before his appointment as Dragoman of the Porte, he exercised the charge of grand logothetes or treasurer of the patriarchate of Constantinople. Vlastos, Χιακά, ii. 93. The families of Mavrocordatos, Kallimakis, Hypsilantis, and Karadjas, which received the title of Prince from holding the office of Voivode in Vallachia or Moldavia, are all descended from doctors in medicine. The protection of Turks of rank, whom they had served professionally, opened for them an entrance into the political career. Hammer, *Histoire*, xvi. 188. Zallony (239) gives the origin of several Phanariot families, I know not on what authority.

His power as agent of the capitan-pasha was almost absolute. His accusation was alone sufficient to send any Greek to the galleys without trial. Such power has never been possessed by a slave without being abused.

The extension of the power of Greek officials in the Othoman administration was attended with both good and bad consequences to the nation. The desire of literary instruction became more general, the sphere of Greek ideas was enlarged, and the bigotry cherished by the exclusive power of the higher clergy was diminished. But, on the other hand, the great profits gained by the illegal exercise of the power intrusted to the higher Greek officials increased the corruption of the class, and made the name of Phanariot a byword for the basest servility, corruption, and rapacity. A numerous body of Greeks became interested in supporting the Othoman domination, since, by acting as the instruments of Turkish oppression, they could live luxuriously and accumulate wealth.

In the year 1716 a new career of wealth, influence, and power was opened to the Phanariots. The Porte, in order to strengthen its authority in Vallachia, when it was about to commence war with Austria, determined to subject the native population to the domination of Greek officials, who were found to be servile instruments of Turkish tyranny. Nicolas Mavrocordatos, the eldest son of Alexander the dragoman, was appointed the first Phanariot voivode of Vallachia. He had already filled the office of voivode of Moldavia, to which he had been appointed in 1709. The government of Phanariot voivodes, or fiscal-agents of the Porte, in these two principalities, dates from this period. Like the Phanariot influence in the Othoman administration at Constantinople, it was founded by a Chiot family. Two sons of Alexander Mavrocordatos, Nicolas and John, and a grandson, Constantine, held at different times the offices of dragoman of the Porte, of voivode of Moldavia, and of voivode of Vallachia. The Greeks gained no honour and little permanent advantage by their power in the Transdanubian provinces. Their administration was more corrupt and oppressive than that of the Turks in the adjoining pashaliks. The Phanariots, intent only on accumulating money and enjoying their power, rendered the native inhabitants of the Principalities the most wretched portion of the sultan's subjects. No other Christian

race in the Othoman dominions was exposed to such unmiti-
gated extortion and cruelty. The Othoman Turks were
better masters to the various races they conquered, than the
Phanariot Greeks to the fellow-Christians committed to their
care and protection. A detailed examination of the vices of
the Greek administration in Vallachia and Moldavia does not
lie within the sphere of this work; but it would form an
important object of inquiry in any complete history of the
political condition of the Greek race[1].

A considerable portion of the Greek population was drawn
within the corrupting influence of official employments under
the Turks. In this career, fraud and violence were short
paths to wealth, and wealth generally secured impunity for
crime. The four great Phanariot offices were those of
Dragoman of the Fleet, Dragoman of the Porte, Voivode
of Moldavia, and Voivode of Vallachia. Each of these officers
was surrounded by a crowd of minor officials, who looked
to him for protection and promotion. Many offices which
insured large profits were always at their disposal. They
appointed their dependents collectors of taxes, farmers of
public revenues, fisheries, and salt-works, and secured to them
the profits of many local monopolies and government con-
tracts. To such an extent had the corruption nourished by
this system proceeded, that, in the earliest years of the nineteenth century, the sums extorted by Phanariot officials from
the Greek population illegally, were supposed to equal the
whole haratch paid by the inhabitants of Greece. The profits
of this iniquitous service invited the Greeks, from the most
distant provinces, to enter the households of the leading
Phanariots, who became virtually princes of the nation; for
even their domestics might look forward to attaining the very
highest honours conferred on Christians. In a government
where purchased slaves were habitually elevated to the rank
of grand-vizier, a Greek pipe-bearer, or household doctor,
might, without presumption, aspire to become Bey of Vallachia. The Phanariot instruments of the Othoman administration extended their influence over all Greece, and connected
the interests of a numerous class with their own; which was
identified with the Turkish domination. Political feelings,

---

[1] See the list of the Phanariot voivodes of Vallachia and Moldavia, in Appendix, III.

hostile to Greek independence, and to all sympathy with the Christian powers of Europe, were thus created in a numerous class of civilians at the time when the ecclesiastical authority, which had previously propagated these dispositions, began to decline. This Greek official aristocracy, accidentally formed by the carelessness of the Turks, was quite as anti-national in its policy as the ecclesiastical hierarchy established by Mohammed II. While the Greeks continued to be dependent on the patriarchate in all matters relating to their ecclesiastical and religious rights, everything connected with the civil and fiscal administration was addressed either to the Dragoman of the Porte, or to the Dragoman of the Fleet: the first acting as a general secretary of state, and the second being especially charged with the business of the navy and the Greek islanders.

Though the influence of the Phanariots is acknowledged to have exercised a demoralizing effect on the character of the Greek nation, some persons have considered that the nation was fully indemnified for this evil by the impulse which it gave to education. They appear strangely to undervalue morality, and extravagantly to over-estimate the advantages of knowledge. Some degree of literary instruction was necessary to enable the dependents of a great Phanariot official to attain many offices in his gift. The desire of learning was consequently extended among the people, but, unfortunately, the very object for which it was sought prevented its producing any moral improvement on the national character. Fortunately for the Greeks, other contemporary causes tended also to disseminate education from a purer source, and by revealing to the people some idea of the vicious nature of the society by which they were governed, whether Christian or Mohammedan, awakened a conviction that, until the national independence was established, no permanent improvement could be effected in the moral condition of the people.

The misfortunes which attended the wars of Sultan Achmet III. against Austria and Persia, and the additional weight of taxation caused by the disorder that pervaded every branch of the administration during his reign, produced at last an insurrection of the janissaries and populace of Constantinople. The great successes over Russia and Venice, which had marked the early years of Achmet's reign, were forgotten,

and in the year 1730 he was compelled to cede the throne
to his nephew, Mahmoud I. This revolution modified in
some degree the government of the empire. The influence
of the officers of the sultan's household on the public administration became more direct, and was more openly exercised.
The power of the grand-vizier was controlled by the authority
of the Kislar-aga (chief of the black eunuchs). The decisions
of experienced statesmen, and the guidance of traditional
maxims of policy which moderated the action of arbitrary
power, were set aside by the rash ignorance of slaves, whose
secluded position deprived them of patriotic feelings, and
whose nature and occupation rendered them insensible even
to the ordinary sympathies of mankind. This change was
not disadvantageous to the Christian subjects of the sultan.
The Phanariots and the clergy found it easier to purchase
the support of a menial in the serai than to gain the esteem
of a pasha.

In the year 1739 the successes of the grand-vizier against
Austria enabled the Porte to conclude the treaty of Belgrade,
which restored that frontier fortress to the sultan[1]. A treaty
concluded with Russia at the same time obliged the Empress Anne to restore Chozim and destroy the fortifications
of Azof. These treaties, concluded under the mediation of
France, were followed by fiscal arrangements in Vallachia,
established by Constantine Mavrocordatos, which greatly
increased the influence of the Phanariots in Vallachia and
Moldavia, added to the number of Greek officials in these
provinces, and prepared the way for the corrupt influence
of Russian diplomacy on the Greek population[2]. From this
period the court of St. Petersburg began to make use of
Greek agents for thwarting the Othoman administration, and
undermining the sultan's power, in every province of his
empire inhabited by the orthodox.

As early as the reign of Peter the Great, the statesmen

---

[1] See the opinion of Marshal Munich on this treaty, so dishonourable to
Austria, in his letter to Prince Lobkovitz; *Mémoires Historiques, Politiques, et
Militaires sur la Russie*, par le Général de Manstein, ii. 32; compare also p. 6,
note, and p. 10.

[2] Some of the measures of Constantine Mavrocordatos were beneficial to the
people, but their advantages were neutralized by the rapacity of the Greek
officials and tax gatherers with whom he filled the province. Kogalnitchan,
Histoire de la Valachie et de la Moldavie, 390; *Mémoires Historiques et Géographi-
ques sur la Valachie*, par Général B. (Baur), 43.

of Russia employed the religious prejudices of the Greeks as a means of creating a political attachment to the Czar. The disastrous campaign of Peter on the Pruth checked for a time the extension of Russian influence; but the government of the empresses Anne and Elizabeth employed agents in various parts of European Turkey to prepare the Christians for taking up arms, should the court of St. Petersburg consider it advisable to carry into execution the plan of attack on the Othoman empire, which Marshal Munich recommended before the conclusion of the treaty of Belgrade, and to which he subsequently directed the attention of the Empress Catherine II.[1]

The vanity and ambition of Catherine II., the hope of conquering Constantinople, and the wish to gratify her lover Gregory Orloff, who expected to gain a principality for himself in ancient Hellas, all operated to revive the projects of Russia in favour of a Greek insurrection. Agents were employed to examine the resources of the country, and to prepare the Greeks for acting in subserviency to the policy of the court of St. Petersburg. Unfortunately for Greece, the intrigues of Catherine II., and the wild enthusiasm of a few adventurers, involved the nation in a course of conduct which has too often diverted it from the steady pursuit of its own advancement. The extension of the local privileges of the people, the development of a system of moral as well as literary education, and the improvement of agriculture and commerce, were neglected in order to pursue schemes of visionary sovereignty, which were to be attained by the conquests and to depend on the generosity of Russia. Much capital was diverted from profitable employment, many active citizens were turned away from occupations of honest industry, the attention of the provincial Greeks was distracted from the local spheres of action in which they were beginning to control the power of the Othoman administration, and an artificial national ambition was fostered with objects so vague, that it could only act as subservient to the more definite plans of Russian policy.

---

[1] Helladius, *Status praesens Ecclesiae Graecae; Epistola dedicatoria,* 4; Rulhière, *Histoire de l'Anarchie de Pologne,* Œuvres, i. 158, edit. of 1819.

Before the peace of Belgrade, Munich aspired at being appointed hospodar of Moldavia, by means of the influence of the Empress Anne. *Mémoires Historiques, Politiques, et Militaires sur la Russie,* par le Général de Manstein, tom. ii. 96.

The intrigues of Russia, which have inflicted many misfortunes on the Greeks, were actively commenced in 1764. Chandler, who visited Greece in 1767, heard the people frequently talk of their approaching deliverance from the Othoman domination through the assistance they were to receive from Russia.

In order to render a successful revolution of the orthodox subjects of the sultan subservient to her project of transferring their allegiance to herself, Catherine II. sent a large naval force to the Mediterranean. Her agents prepared the maritime population to take up arms when this fleet should appear in the Levant. The inhabitants of Montenegro, a Sclavonian tribe to the north of Albania, did not wait even for this support. A Greek captain of artillery in the Russian service, named Papasoglou, was sent by Gregory Orloff to establish relations with Maina in 1766[1]. One of his agents, a young monk named Stephen, soon acted a conspicuous part in Montenegro, where he obtained extraordinary influence by his eloquence and enthusiastic demeanour, and contrived that a vague and mysterious report should be spread, which designated him as Peter III., the murdered husband of Catherine II. In consequence of his exhortations and promises, the Montenegrins took up arms against the Turks in 1767, but before any support arrived from Russia, they were assailed by the forces of all the neighbouring pashas, and the insurrection was suppressed. The monk Stephen, laying aside his imperial pretensions, succeeded in making his escape on board a Russian ship, which arrived too late to assist the insurrection[2].

[1] The Greek name of Papasoglou was Gregorios Papadopoulos. He is also known by his Mainate synonym, Papapoulo. For the events in Montenegro, and the extent of the Russian intrigues in the Levant at this time, see Rulhière, vol. iii. pp. 294, 358.
[2] [If we can trust Cyprien Robert, who in *Les Slaves de Turquie* (vol. i. pp. 152 foll.) relates this story at some length, though he gives no references, Stephen the Little, as he was called, was a mere adventurer, and Prince Dolgoruki was sent from Russia to Montenegro to denounce him as an impostor. He maintained his position there, however, for four years; but ultimately, having lost his sight in the springing of a mine, he retired into a convent, where he was said to have been murdered by his Greek servant at the instigation of the Pasha of Scodra. Zinkeisen also (*Osmanisches Reich*, v. 853) speaks of him as an adventurer; while Von Hammer (*Geschichte*, viii. 300; 10 vols. Pesth. 1827-35) regards him as acting in the interests of Russia: but both the last-named writers mention him in a very cursory way. It would certainly seem strange, if an agent of the Russian government gave himself out as Peter III., when Catherine II. was suspected of complicity in his murder. ED.]

INTRIGUES OF RUSSIA.

The visit of Papasoglou to Maina had been productive of mutual promises only, for the Mainates had little to gain by taking up arms, unless Russia would pay them, or assist them to plunder the rest of the Morea. At Kalamata he had more success. He there drew into his plans Benaki, the richest Greek in the Morea, an influential kodja bashi or primate, who was habitually consulted by the pasha, and generally respected by the Mohammedans. Benaki also possessed considerable influence in Maina, from being one of the largest purchasers and exporters of its produce. Moved by ambitious hopes, and ignorant of the relative military power of the nations interested in the fate of the Othoman empire, his patriotism made him the dupe of his vanity. He persuaded himself that a primate of Messenia was a man of importance in the scale of nations. Through his influence several Greek primates were induced to form a conspiracy to aid the projects of Russia, and they were persuaded to sign, and place in the hands of Papasoglou, an engagement that, as soon as the Russian forces appeared in the Morea, they would call to arms one hundred thousand Greeks. The value of this engagement was magnified by Papasoglou in his communications to the cabinet of St. Petersburg, and active preparations were made for supporting the insurrection in Greece. Alexis Orloff, his brother Feodor, and Tamara, a young officer from the Ukraine, who had increased the Philhellenic enthusiasm he had imbibed with a classical education by a tour in Greece, were sent to Italy to direct the conspiracy, and prepare for the arrival of the Russian forces. Maruzzi, a Greek banker of Venice, was made a marquis, and intrusted with the monetary transactions in the Adriatic and Greece. The hopes of Catherine II. rose so high in 1768, that even Voltaire contemplated the probability of Constantinople soon becoming the capital of the Russian empire [1].

The Porte was aware of the rebellious disposition of its Greek subjects ; nor was it entirely ignorant of the intrigues of Russia, though it obtained no knowledge of the conspiracy of Benaki. With its usual carelessness it neglected to take any precautions ; partly from its contempt for the cowardice

[1] Rulhière, iii. 334; Voltaire, *Correspondance avec l'Impératrice de Russie*, Nov. 15, 1768.

of the Greeks, and partly from a conviction that it was impossible for Russia to send any force from the Baltic into the Mediterranean. The Venetian senate understood the danger better; and when the Orloffs withdrew the veil from the Russian schemes, the republic recommended them to remove their residence from Venice, as the republic was determined to preserve its neutrality. Nothing but the insolence which characterized the intercourse of the Othoman government with Christian powers prevented it from obtaining proofs of the complicity of Russian agents in exciting the Greeks to rebellion, and even when its suspicions were awakened, it long allowed itself to be deceived by the assurances of the Russian court that the empress desired to maintain peace. But when the Russian armies openly violated the engagements contracted by the treaties of the Pruth and of Belgrade, the sultan perceived that the peace did not prevent the czarina from making conquests in Poland. The sultan declared war with Russia to defend the integrity of Poland; but the Christian population of his dominions felt that the question really at issue was the integrity of the Othoman empire.

The commencement of this war affords an example of the imprudence with which European diplomatists compromised their official character, and the political interests of nations intrusted to their care, in order to indulge the prurient curiosity which is a common vice of their profession. The sandjak-sherif, or sacred standard of Mahomet, was unfolded at Constantinople on the 27th of March 1769[1]. When this banner is displayed, the Mussulmans deem it unholy for a Christian to gaze on it; but the Austrian internuncio, Brognard, thinking that his impertinent curiosity would be protected by his diplomatic character, resolved to gratify it by a sight of this sacred banner of Islam. To effect his object, he placed himself, accompanied by his wife, four daughters, his secretaries, and interpreters, in a house which overlooked the line of the procession as it passed to the Top-Kapousi, by which the Othomans had stormed Constantinople. From this house the party was driven by the Imam of the quarter, but persisting in its object with Teutonic obstinacy,

---

[1] D'Ohsson, *Tableau de l'Empire Othoman*, i. 261, fol. edit.

it retired into the house of an Armenian in the neighbourhood, hoping to secure a view of the procession by creeping
from thence into a barber's shop which overlooked the public
street. The Turks watched the proceedings of the Austrians,
for they were determined to prevent any Christian from
seeing the sandjak-sherif unless flying in their face on the
field of battle, and when the cry arose that the holy standard
approached, their enthusiasm was inflamed with indignation.
Superstition led many to fear that the Christians might use
enchantments which would cause the defeat of the Othoman
armies, and their bigotry persuaded them that it was a duty
to punish the insolence and malice of the infidels. The tumult
was commenced by the Turkish women, who had assembled
in great numbers to see the procession pass. The populace
of the quarter needed little excitement. The doors of the
barber's shop were burst open, the minister and his secretaries
severely beaten, the veils and scarfs were torn from the necks
of his wife and daughters, and the party, after being robbed of
their jewels and gold lace, were allowed to escape with their
clothes hanging about them in rags. All the shops belonging
to Christians in the same street were broken open and plundered[1]. The Othoman police had some difficulty in saving
the inquisitive diplomatist from death, and his wife and
children from being turned into the street without clothes.
The internuncio informed the court of Vienna that one
hundred and fifty innocent persons were killed, and one
thousand wounded, in consequence of his foolish conduct;
but his misplaced vanity is said to have exaggerated the
results of his imprudence[2].

The first division of the Russian fleet under Spiritoff, a
brave officer, but without much naval experience, arrived in
the Mediterranean towards the end of 1769, and passed the
winter at Port Mahon refitting and embarking stores and
provisions. Early in 1770 one squadron of the fleet visited
Leghorn, to embark a number of sailors collected by the
Orloffs and their agents; while another, under the command
of Feodor Orloff, having been refused entrance into the port
of Malta, sailed on to Greece. This division, consisting of
three ships of the line and two frigates, with five hundred

---

[1] Hammer, *Histoire*, xvi. 203.   [2] Ibid,

troops on board, anchored at Port Vitylo in Maina. The
Mainates, who expected to see ten thousand Russians open
the campaign, were disconcerted on seeing the small corps
which was disembarked to commence an invasion of the
Othoman empire. The defective armament of the large
ships, the absence of small vessels, the want of all means
of transport, and the neglect to bring a supply of field
artillery and ammunition proper for the wants of a Greek
army, discouraged the Mainates so much that they displayed
a decided aversion to take up arms. But a sum of money
judiciously divided among the chiefs, the hopes of obtaining
plunder in the rich plains of Messenia and Laconia, the
distribution of a small supply of arms and ammunition to
volunteers, the confidence that they could defend their
mountains against the Turks whatever might happen, and
the assurance that Alexis Orloff would soon arrive with a
powerful fleet and numerous army, at last induced a body
of Mainates to join the Russians, on condition that Feodor,
following the example of Morosini, should immediately
lay siege to Coron, which was not prepared to offer a long
resistance.

The first acts of the Russians in Greece awakened feelings
of distrust. Feodor Orloff would only subsidize and arm
those who swore allegiance to the Empress of Russia and
engaged to become subjects of Catherine II. The Greeks,
who aspired at forming an independent state, perceived that
even a successful insurrection would only make them the
slaves of the czarina, instead of the rayahs of the sultan;
and they knew that materially they would be no gainers by
the change. The Othoman yoke was not so universally
galling as to cause a revolution, and national feelings had
not yet prepared the Greeks to make great sacrifices in the
cause of liberty, so that those classes who took up arms were
moved generally by local animosities or personal views. In
Crete the Sphakiots flew to arms, and sent a body of men to
Maina. Some recruits also joined Feodor from the Ionian
Islands, but his army remained insignificant in number in
spite of all his exertions and promises. The unarmed
Moreots were overwhelmed with terror when they compared
the force of the Russians with that which they knew the
Turks were preparing to pour into the peninsula. Benaki

crept secretly to the Russian camp, and when he had seen the force on which he was to rely for expelling the Turks from the Morea, returned to Kalamata in despair, and attempted to conceal the part he had taken in the conspiracy, at least until the arrival of the main body of the fleet.

The Russians had counted on the assistance of a Greek army, but they found some difficulty in collecting three thousand men. These recruits were divided into two legions. The command of the eastern or Spartan legion was conferred on Antonios Psaros, a young supercargo of Mykone, who showed some military aptitude[1]. He marched to Passava, which he found deserted, plundered the Mussulman district of Bardunia, and took possession of Misithra, where the Mainates massacred numbers of the Turkish population, and plundered a part of the town, without respecting the houses of the Christians. Psaros succeeded with difficulty in establishing order; he protected the Mussulmans, and formed what he called a Spartan Senate, composed of the bishop and the primates, which acted as a governing commission. The legion was increased by enrolling three thousand Laconians, to whom he promised regular pay, and among whom he attempted to introduce regular discipline. A chosen body was clad in Russian uniforms, which had been brought to make the Turks believe that a Russian force had already arrived in the Morea.

The western or Messenian legion, under the command of Prince Dolgoruki, marched into Kalamata without opposition, and ravaged the property of the Turks in the plain of Messenia. All the Mohammedans who fell into the hands of the Greeks were put to death, and Dolgoruki advanced to the town of Arkadia, which was surrendered by the Turks, and made the head-quarters of this legion.

In the meantime Feodor Orloff, with his four hundred Russian troops and a motley army of Mainates, Sphakiots,

---

[1] Antonios Psaros was one of the proprietors of a vessel from Mykone which visited Taganrog before the war broke out, and was drawn to St. Petersburg by the general encouragement given to adventurers in Greece. Eton says he was a livery servant, but Orloff soon took him under his protection, and he probably only wore a livery while attached to Orloff's household. In the memorial of the Greek deputies to Catherine II. in 1790, he is called a man sprung from the dregs of the people, and abhorred by the whole Greek nation. Calumny, however, has always been too prevalent in Greece for us to attach much importance to such phrases. Eton, *Survey of the Turkish Empire*, 359.

Ionians, Montenegrins, and Sclavonians, besieged Coron. His operations offer a discreditable contrast with the exploits of the Venetians; but he was not a Morosini. The batteries were ill-constructed and inefficient. The fleet was anchored too far off to aid the attack, and the Othoman garrison, though consisting of only four hundred men, soon perceived that they could watch the proceedings of their besiegers and wait for succours without alarm. Two months were wasted in futile operations. Dissensions broke out between the Russians and the Greeks. Feodor accused Mavromichalis, the leading Mainate chief, who had entered into the pay of Russia, of want of courage; Mavromichalis replied, by ridiculing the pretensions of Feodor as a general, and exposing his ignorance of the art of war. Alexis Orloff arrived towards the end of April, and finding that his brother had made no progress in the siege, deemed it advisable to abandon this first enterprise of the Russians in Greece, and concentrate his forces at Navarin, which had capitulated to a Russian force under General Hannibal[1].

The war, so far, had only been remarkable for the incapacity with which the Russian officers had acted. Bands of armed Greeks from the Venetian islands had landed in the Morea, where their conduct had been that of robbers, not soldiers. Defenceless Turks had been murdered, villages had been plundered, but no battle had been fought. The first success obtained by the Greeks alone was at Mesolonghi, and it was not stained by any act of cruelty. A report reached the inhabitants that Coron had capitulated to the Russians. They immediately flew to arms, and the primates ordered the few Turks who resided in the place to retire to Patras. They then took possession of the small insular town of Anatolikon, and sent a deputation to Feodor Orloff, to place themselves under the protection of Russia, and request assistance. Feodor neglected their solicitations. In the mean time a band of Dulcigniot corsairs, hastening to the assistance of Patras, and observing the defenceless condition of Mesolonghi, attacked the place, massacred a part of the inhabitants after a desperate resistance, regained possession of both Mesolonghi and Anatolikon, and entered Patras in triumph. The greater

---

[1] General Hannibal was a mulatto; his father was a negro slave of Peter the Great.

part of the Mesolonghiots had embarked their families in small vessels, with which they escaped to the Venetian islands.

The operations of Alexis Orloff were planned on a more extensive scale than those of Feodor, but they were not carried into execution with greater vigour. He published a proclamation, calling upon the Greeks to take up arms in defence of their liberty and religion, yet he treated those only as friends who would swear allegiance to Russia; and he showed so much indifference to truth in his conduct, and so little humanity and judgment in performing his duty as a general, that he gained few friends[1]. Prince Dolgoruki was ordered to besiege Modon, Psaros to march on Tripolitza, and a third corps was pushed forward from Messenia by Leondari, to join Psaros in the great Arcadian plain. The junction being effected, Psaros found himself at the head of an army of fifteen thousand men, and a single battle was expected to give the Russians possession of the centre of the Morea.

The Othoman government had been more active than the Russian generals, and the measures adopted for defending the Morea were better concerted than those for its conquest. The native Mussulmans were ordered to retreat on Tripolitza, where they formed, when united, a strong body of cavalry, which commanded all the communications. The vizier of the Morea was Mehemet Emin, who had been deprived of the office of grand-vizier for advising Sultan Mustapha to avoid war with Russia[2]. He was now eager to prove that his wisdom in counsel did not diminish his energy in action; but as he was not a soldier, he could only direct the plan of operations, the execution of which he was compelled to intrust to others. He established his head-quarters at Nauplia, in order to facilitate the transmission of military stores to the interior of his province, and to hasten the arrival of succours, particularly of a powerful body of Albanians, which was rapidly advancing towards the Isthmus of Corinth, and for which he took care to prepare provisions at every station of their march, that they might reach Tripolitza without delay. On the western coast the corsairs of the Adriatic

---

[1] Rulhière, iii. 402.   [2] Hammer calls him Mouhsinzadé.

were ordered to transport troops from Albania direct to
Patras, and then to cruise off the Ionian Islands to prevent
the Russians receiving supplies from the Greeks under
the Venetian flag. The tardy proceedings of the Orloffs
allowed the vizier to complete all his arrangements before
he was attacked. The vanguard of the Albanians, six
thousand strong, entered Tripolitza about the time Psaros
concentrated the Russo-Greek army to attack the place.
He had lost much time in transporting across the mountains
a few pieces of artillery, and the ammunition required to
breach the feeble wall round Tripolitza. The whole force
under his command was said to amount to fifteen thousand
men; but it was dispersed over much ground, from the
difficulty of supplying it with provisions. The greater part
consisted of half-armed peasantry, and the only force on
which any reliance could be placed in battle was a corps
of four hundred Russians, and about four thousand Greek
irregulars and half-disciplined recruits. The Albanians,
supported by the native cavalry of the province, attacked
his army as soon as it encamped. The Greeks offered
little resistance : the greater part fled when they saw the
Albanians rushing forward in spite of the first volley of
musketry. The Russians alone defended themselves valiantly,
and perished almost to a man in their ranks. Three thousand Greeks were slain in the pursuit, and the day after
the battle the metropolitan of Tripolitza and several bishops,
who had entered into correspondence with the Russians,
were hanged by order of the pasha.

Another corps of Albanians advanced from the Isthmus
of Corinth along the southern shore of the Gulf of Corinth,
to relieve Patras from the attacks of the Ionian Greeks
who had besieged it; but the enemy had been dispersed
by the Dulcigniots before the arrival of the Albanians.
Fresh reinforcements soon joined the main army at Tripolitza, which then advanced in two divisions. One descended into the plain of Laconia, retook Misithra, and
drove Psaros and the relics of his army beyond Gytheion
into the fastnesses of Taygetus. The other marched into
the plain of Messenia, drove the Mainates back into their
mountains, defeated the Russians before Modon, and captured all their siege artillery and stores. The successes

of the Albanians were marked by the greatest cruelty: the country was ravaged, the people massacred without mercy, often merely to find a pretext for carrying off the young women and children to be sold as slaves. The pasha of the Morea endeavoured in vain to put a stop to these atrocities. He proclaimed an amnesty; and, as far as his power extended, his humanity restored order and confidence; but the Albanian irregular bands remained for some years masters and tyrants of the greater part of the peninsula.

Towards the end of May another Russian squadron, under Admiral Elphinstone, an excellent naval officer, but a man of a violent character, arrived at Port Vitylo, where he landed six hundred troops to support Psaros. The news of the appearance of a Turkish fleet in the Archipelago, carrying supplies to Nauplia, made Elphinstone put to sea immediately, in order to thwart the operations of the Othoman squadron that might enter the Gulf of Nauplia, or engage any ships separated from the main body of the capitan-pasha's fleet. He despatched a courier to Alexis Orloff, as high admiral, informing him of his movements, and requesting his support. Orloff, despairing of any success by land after the recent disasters of his troops, abandoned Navarin with precipitation, and, embarking only Papasoglou, Benaki, and the bishops of Coron, Modon, and Kalamata, with a few primates of wealth, sailed away to join Elphinstone, leaving all the other Greeks who had taken up arms for the cause of Russia, and sworn allegiance to the Empress Catherine II., to procure the means of escape from others. In vain the Greeks, and their friends among the Russian officers of rank, urged Orloff to allow a small garrison to retain possession of Navarin until the issue of the expected naval engagement should be known. They pointed out that the island of Sphakteria was covered with refugees, that more than ten thousand Greeks of all ages were assembled round the walls of Navarin, that the fortress was strong enough to resist the attack of the Albanians for some months, and that the command of the port would enable the Greeks to distract the attention of the Turks, and keep up a mountain warfare, by furnishing supplies of provisions and ammunition to armed bands on every inaccessible mountain near the coast. Alexis Orloff was deaf to entreaties and advice.

The Othoman fleet was commanded by Hosameddin, the grandson of Djanum Pasha, a man destitute of courage as well as of naval knowledge[1]. On quitting the Dardanelles, he sailed with ten line-of-battle ships to land reinforcements and stores at Nauplia. The vanguard of this squadron was led by Hassan the Algerine, and it encountered the squadron of Elphinstone at the entrance of the Gulf of Argolis[2]. After some desultory fighting, which enabled the capitan-pasha to enter the gulf without loss, the whole Othoman fleet anchored under the cannon of Nauplia. Elphinstone was anxious to attack them in this position, but the Russian captains refused to engage in so desperate an enterprise before effecting a junction with Alexis Orloff, who was commander-in-chief. Elphinstone, therefore, returned to seek Orloff; but meeting four line-of-battle ships and a frigate under Spiritoff, it was determined to pursue the capitan-pasha, who had also quitted the Gulf of Argolis. Feodor Orloff persuaded Spiritoff to allow Elphinstone to retain the command of the united squadrons. The capitan-pasha was overtaken in the channel of Hydra; but the Russian captains paid so little attention to the admiral's signals, that the Othoman fleet had no difficulty in avoiding an engagement.

On the 23rd of June 1770, Alexis Orloff and Admiral Greig joined Elphinstone, and Spiritoff was ordered to act as admiral of the fleet under Orloff. The capitan-pasha had selected the Bay of Tchesmé, in the Channel of Chios, as the position in which to await the attack of the Russians.

---

[1] Hammer (*Histoire de l'Empire Othoman*, xvi. 244) says that the post of capitan-pasha was conferred on Hosameddin on the 26th April 1770; and at p. 254 he mentions that he was dismissed after the battle of Tchesmé, when Djaffir was appointed his successor. But in the biographical sketch of Hassan in his *Staatsverfassung und Staatsverwaltung des Osmanischen Reichs* (ii. 355) he follows the common error of calling the capitan-pasha who commanded at Tchesmé, Djaffir.

[2] Hassan, called commonly Djesairli or the Algerine, until he received the title of Ghazi, or the Victorious, is said by Hammer (*Staatsverwaltung*, ii. 350) to have been the son of a Christian of Rhodosto, or from the neighbourhood of the Dardanelles. By Rulhière (iii. 417) he is said to have been born in Persia, and sold as a slave to an inhabitant of Rhodosto. He served when young at Algiers, where he acquired rank and wealth. The vicissitudes of his eventful life are recounted with many variations, and they warn me against the danger of implicit confidence in facts even as recorded by contemporary historians.

His fleet consisted of fourteen sail of the line and several frigates, and was anchored in the form of a crescent, with one horn defended by rocks and shallows, and the other by the mainland. The capitan-pasha, and perhaps most of his captains, were too ignorant of naval tactics to perceive the great disadvantage of rendering his superior force stationary, and exposing its parts to be overwhelmed by a smaller movable force. Hassan the Algerine, the ablest officer in the Othoman fleet, who acted as flag-captain of the capitan-pasha's ship, endeavoured in vain to point out the disadvantages of the position. His representations succeeded only in convincing Hosameddin that it would be safer for himself to land and issue his commands from a place of perfect security. He therefore went on shore, under the pretext of completing a battery, and remained there, leaving each captain to defend his own ship. The Russian fleet consisted of ten line-of-battle ships and five frigates; but one of the large ships had only her main-deck guns on board, and was therefore called a frigate. The battle was fought on the 7th of July 1770. Spiritoff led the vanguard; Alexis Orloff, in Greig's ship, occupied the centre; and Elphinstone, in consequence of the jealousy of Orloff, was placed in the rear. About noon the engagement commenced. Spiritoff bore down on the ship bearing the capitan-pasha's flag, which Hassan commanded; but as he was exposed to the fire of several ships during his advance, he lost nearly one hundred men, killed and wounded, before he could close with his enemy and open his own fire. His losses were replaced by boats from the other ships. When he was within musket-shot of his opponent, he poured his first broadside into the hull of the capitan-pasha, which was promptly returned. The firing of both ships was kept up with vigour, and the loss in both was great. At last a ball from a very large Turkish gun carried away the rudder of Spiritoff's ship, and rendered it unmanageable. As he neglected dropping his anchor, he drifted close to his enemy and the Turks immediately rushed, sword in hand, on his deck. To repulse this attack of the Turkish boarders, the Russians made use of hand-grenades, threw combustibles into the enemy's ship, and sent a party of marines to board it from the yards. The decks of both ships became the scene of pitched battles, and fresh combatants hastened from the other ships to aid both parties. Hassan, seeing that the riflemen in the tops of the Russian were thinning his men, ordered the sails, which the Russians had left hanging loosely from the yards, to be set on fire. In a moment the whole rigging was in flames, and before the Turks could cut their cable, their own ship took fire. Spiritoff, Feodor Orloff, and the Russian officers abandoned their ship, but Hassan suspended the combat to get all his boats afloat and save his crew. The two ships soon separated ; but both being driven into the line of the Othoman fleet, the Turkish captains cut their cables, one after another, and the line-of-battle ships crowded into the narrow harbour of Tchesmé, where their position rendered them defenceless. The blazing ships blew up. The gallant Hassan plunged into the sea, and, though severely wounded, succeeded in swimming until he was taken up by one of his boats. His first care was to send a message to the capitan-pasha, recommending him to seize the moment for ordering the fleet out to sea before the Russians could attack it in its defenceless position, where its guns were useless. Hosam-eddin was such a coward that he feared to embark, and as he did not venture to send the fleet to sea while he remained on shore himself, he pretended to believe that the ships were sufficiently protected by the batteries of Tchesmé.

The Russian admirals immediately held a council of war, to decide on the manner in which they should attack the Turkish ships, and it was resolved to burn them before they could change their position. Three fireships were prepared without loss of time, and, shortly after midnight, everything being ready, several Russian line-of-battle ships stood in towards the port, and opened a heavy cannonade, under the cover of which the three polaccas fitted out as fireships were steered into the midst of the Turkish fleet. Two of the fireships were commanded by English officers, Dugdale and Mackenzie ; the third was under the command of a Russian. The crews consisted chiefly of Greek and Sclavonian sailors. Dugdale, who led the way, was deserted by his crew, but he carried his ship alongside the enemy, fired the train himself, and then jumped into the sea and swam to the boat of one of the other ships. Mackenzie and the Russian were well supported, and the attack was completely successful. The three fireships drove into the midst of the enemy's fleet, and the whole harbour was soon enveloped in flames. The Turkish line-of-battle ships blew up, one after another; and when the fire ceased, one only remained afloat. This was captured, and Alexis Orloff conferred the command of it on Dugdale, as a reward for his distinguished valour. Tchesmé was abandoned by the Turks and occupied by the Russians. The fugitives spread the news of the destruction of the fleet in every direction; and the Russians were expected to make their appearance before Constantinople. At Smyrna the Mussulmans, seized with frenzy, murdered all the Greeks they met in the streets. At Constantinople the foreign ministers were in danger; and perhaps the plague, which raged at the time with extraordinary violence, alone moderated the fury of the populace.

After the destruction of the Othoman fleet, Elphinstone urged Alexis Orloff to sail immediately to the Dardanelles, force the entrance, and either dictate terms of peace at Constantinople, or lay the capital of the Othoman empire in ashes. Orloff was incapable and selfish. He feared that Elphinstone would reap all the glory of an exploit which he felt that he could not himself direct; and, as a plausible reason for rejecting so great an enterprise, he declared that his instructions directed him to support the Greeks, but did not warrant his venturing to treat for peace, consequently he did not feel himself authorized to risk the destruction of the fleet of the empress merely to have a chance of setting fire to Constantinople. Ten days were wasted in vain debates. The projects of attacking Chios and Smyrna were rejected; and at last it was determined to occupy Lemnos, as a station from which it would be easy to maintain a strict blockade of the Dardanelles. The castle of Lemnos offered an unexpected resistance, and three months were consumed in fruitless endeavours to take it. In the mean time the Russian fleet was weakened by the recall of all the officers who held commissions in the British navy; and the dilatory proceedings of Orloff gave the Turks time to assemble fresh forces. Baron de Tott was employed to fortify the Dardanelles, and Hassan, as soon as he recovered from his wounds, was appointed

capitan-bey, and intrusted with full power to collect a force
to relieve Lemnos. Hassan assembled four thousand chosen
troops at the Dardanelles, which he embarked in twenty-three
small vessels. This flotilla, escorted by two line-of-battle
ships, landed the troops on the east side of Lemnos on the
9th of October, and stormed the Russian camp sword in hand.
The Russians escaped to their ships with the loss of all their
artillery, military stores, and provisions. A naval engagement
took place a few days later, in which Hassan manœuvred
so well as to keep the sea without any loss; and Alexis
Orloff, finding that his vessels had need of repairs, sailed
to Paros, leaving Hassan the highest personal honours of
the campaign of 1770, in spite of the catastrophe of
Tchesmé[1].

The Russian fleet remained in the Levant until peace was
concluded in 1774, but it performed nothing further worthy of
notice[2]. The harbour of Naussa in Paros was its naval station;
and the scale of the buildings constructed by the Russians induced the Greeks to believe that the empress had determined to
retain permanent possession of the island. Batteries were
erected to defend the port, extensive warehouses were built
to contain naval stores, and the village of Naussa became
a populous city; but the place was unhealthy, and the crews
of the ships suffered severely from fever. After the conclusion of the first campaign, Alexis Orloff hastened to St.
Petersburg to enjoy his triumph as the victor of Tchesmé.
Elphinstone soon followed, disgusted with the inactive service
to which he was condemned; and the Russian navy ceased
to display any activity.

The war in the Levant was now neglected by Catherine II.,
whose attention was absorbed by the project for partitioning
Poland. Voltaire, who watched the changes in the sentiments
of the empress, with prompt servility altered the tone of his

---

[1] Hammer, *Histoire*, xvi. 256 ; Baron de Tott, *Mémoires sur les Turcs et les
Tartares*, ii. 247, 284, edit. Amst. De Tott must be read with caution. Vanity
and a spirit of exaggeration often make him misrepresent details. He pretends
that Hassan, who had fitted out line-of-battle ships, directed considerable works
in the arsenal of Constantinople, and visited the dockyards of Barcelona and
Naples, did not know how to mount a heavy gun.

[2] [An interesting account of the condition of the Greek islands at this
period will be found in the *Breve descrizione dell' Arcipelago* of Count Pasch van
Krienen, who visited them under Russian auspices in 1771 and 1772. It was
originally published at Leghorn in 1773, and was reprinted at Halle in 1860 from
an edition prepared by Prof. Ludwig Ross, who died before it appeared. ED.]

correspondence concerning Greece. He began to defame the Greeks, in whose favour he had previously affected great enthusiasm. Perceiving that Catherine was no longer eager to support their cause, he now spoke of them as unworthy of freedom, which, he says, they might have gained had they possessed courage to support the enterprises of the Russians. The French philosopher, in the fervour of his adulation, declared that he no longer desired to read Sophocles, Homer, and Demosthenes. Voltaire expected the Greeks would fight like heroes to become serfs of a Russian favourite[1].

The Greeks who had been cajoled and bribed to rebel, were abandoned to their fate as soon as their services were useless to Russian interests. The Sphakiots of Crete were attacked by the Turks, pursued into their mountains and compelled to pay haratch, like the Christians in the plain. The Albanians who had entered the Morea formed themselves into local companies, and collected the taxes of the province on their own account, besides extorting large sums by cruel exactions, as arrears of pay due to them by the Porte.

The successes of the Russian armies on the Danube forced Sultan Abdul-hamid, shortly after his accession to the throne, to sign the peace of Kainardji, on the 21st July 1774. This memorable treaty humbled the pride of the sultan, broke the strength of the Othoman empire, and established the moral influence of Russia over the whole Christian population in Turkey, which henceforth regarded the sovereign of Russia as the legal protector, if not as the legitimate emperor, of the orthodox. Yet in this treaty the Greeks of the Morea and the islands were sacrificed by Russia. The Porte, indeed, engaged by the seventh article to protect the orthodox Greek church ; but Russia allowed the sultan to interpret the article as he pleased, until she deemed it for her interest, many years after, to make this engagement a pretext for claiming a right to watch over its fulfilment, in order to paralyse the government of Turkey and extend her own dominion. Though the seventeenth article contained the promise of an amnesty to the rebel Greeks, the court of St. Petersburg, even when it

---

[1] He adds: 'Je détesterais jusqu'à la religion grecque, si votre majesté impériale n'était pas à la tête de cette Église.' *Correspondance avec l'Impératrice de Russie*, No. 107, 6 Mars 1772. Certainly no Phanariot ever addressed Sultan Mustapha in baser language.

restored the islands of the Archipelago to the sultan, never gave itself any concern about the execution of this article. It is strange that the Greeks, who were saved from oppression and mildly treated by the Venetians, should always have hated and calumniated the republic, while, though they have been frequently deceived and generally despised by the Russians, they manifest the warmest devotion to the Czars. The bigotry of Orthodoxy is more powerful than the feeling of patriotism, and effectually stifles all gratitude to Catholics. Enthusiastic orthodoxy, and an eager desire of vengeance, rendered them the ready dupes of Russian policy; and though they were severely punished on this occasion, they have ever since been ready to serve the interests of Russia and sacrifice those of Greece, from the same motives, with similar blindness. The peace with Russia could not make the Turks forget the cruelty with which their countrymen had been massacred in the Morea; and for several years the Greeks were everywhere subjected to increased oppression. The cruelties of the Albanians were tolerated even after their rapacity became so great that many Turks as well as Greeks were ruined by their exactions, and compelled to abandon their property, and escape to other parts of the empire.

Policy at last induced Sultan Abdul-hamid to protect his Greek subjects. The reiterated complaints of the disorders perpetrated by the Albanians in the Morea, both on Mussulmans and Christians, at length determined him to restore tranquillity to that valuable province. Hassan, whose victory over the Russians at Lemnos had gained him the title of Ghazi (the Victorious), had been raised to the rank of capitan-pasha. In the year 1779 he was ordered to reduce the Albanians to obedience, and re-establish order in the Morea. With his usual promptitude in action, he landed a considerable force at Nauplia, and marched with a body of four thousand chosen infantry, and the cavalry collected by the neighbouring pashas, to attack the Albanians, who had concentrated a large part of their troops at Tripolitza. The Albanians, confident in their numbers and valour, marched out to engage the little army of the capitan-pasha in the plain, and were completely defeated by the steady valour of the infantry and by the fire of the artillery. After this victory Hassan hunted down their dispersed bands over the whole peninsula, and exterminated them without mercy. The heads of the chieftains were sent to Constantinople, and exposed before the gate of the serai, while a pyramid was formed of those of the soldiers under the walls of Tripolitza, the remains of which were seen by travellers at the end of the last century[1]. Hassan remained in the Morea for a few months, uniting the rank of pasha of the province with his office of capitan-pasha. His administration restored order and re-established justice in such a degree, that most of the fugitives returned from Roumelia, Asia Minor, and the Ionian Islands, and the greater part of the deserted lands were again culti-vated. Mavroyeni, a Greek of Mykone, who was dragoman of the fleet, enjoyed the confidence of Hassan, and employed the influence he possessed to improve the position of the Greeks.

The Mainates, who feared the Albanians more than the Turks, had deputed Zanet Koutouphari, one of their chiefs, to wait on Hassan at Rhodes in 1777 to solicit an amnesty for the part they had taken in the Russian war, to assure the capitan-pasha of their devotion to the sultan's govern-ment, and to claim his protection. Hassan, having received the sanction of the Porte for separating Maina from the sandjak of the Morea and placing it under the jurisdiction of the capitan-pasha, now organized the administration, and arranged the payment of its taxes, on the same plan as the other districts under his command. Zanet, as chief primate, was invested with the authority of governor and the title of bey[2]. The bey was charged with the duty of collecting the tribute ; and to facilitate the operation, where topographical difficulties and the feuds of hostile tribes rendered the task dangerous, he obtained a monopoly of the export of oil, silk, and valonia, which was easily enforced at the few points from which produce could be exported. In 1780 Hassan visited Maina with the Othoman fleet. He landed a body of Turkish troops, and arrested some of the chiefs who had plundered in Messenia or committed acts of piracy. Murzinos, who had distinguished himself both as a Russian partizan and a pirate,

---

[1] Pouqueville, *Histoire de la Régénération de la Grèce*, i. 52.
[2] Pouqueville (*Voyage de la Grèce*, v. 559, edit. 1827) gives the firman of in-vestiture ; see note 1 at p. 135, which corrects a common error of confounding Zanet Koutouphari and Zanet Gligoraki, beys of Maina.

was taken after a vigorous defence, and hung in his Russian uniform from the main-yard of Hassan's ship [1]. Hassan then compelled the Mainates to compound for the arrears of tribute due to the Porte, and to give hostages for their fulfilment of the obligations into which he forced them to enter.

The favour which Mavroyeni enjoyed, and the influence of the Phanariots on the general policy of the Porte towards the rayahs, alleviated the oppression of the Othoman administration in Greece. The people enjoyed greater security for their lives and property, new paths were open to them of acquiring wealth, and their commercial intercourse with the Western nations became more frequent. Education, also, became more general, and less exclusively ecclesiastic. In the Morea, particularly, the government of Sultan Abdulhamid was so much milder than that of his predecessors as to be ascribed by the Greeks to the influence of his favourite sultana, whom they imagined to be the daughter of a Moreote priest; but the fact is, that the same improvement in the manner of treating the Christian subjects of the Porte is observable in the other provinces of the empire [2]. Had the Greeks been fortunate enough, at this period, to have passed a generation in the tranquil enjoyment of the commercial, political, and moral advantages which they began to enjoy in the year 1780, it is probable they would have succeeded in giving their local institutions such a development as would have placed a large part of the communal and provincial administration in their own hands, and served ultimately as the basis for the establishment of a Greek government on sound principles of civil liberty, which, while it secured the national independence of the Greeks where they form the majority of the population, might have enabled the different Christian races in the Othoman empire to combine in forming a powerful federal state.

The influence of Russia unfortunately withdrew the attention of the Greeks from local improvements to schemes of conquest. The court of St. Petersburg did not wish to see the Greeks in a condition to gain their independence by their own unassisted efforts. As discontented subjects of the

[1] Pouqueville, *Voyage*, v. 588.
[2] Rizo Néroulos, *Histoire de l'Insurrection Grècque*, 93.

sultan, they were useful instruments of Catherine's policy; but, in possession of local privileges which, as in Chios, would enable them to improve their own condition, they might become useful subjects of the sultan, and ultimately the recognized heirs of the Othoman empire. At all events, they would be interested in opposing the progress of Russian despotism, and perhaps capable of making both the czarina and the sultan treat them with justice. In a few years the leading statesmen of Russia renewed their attacks on Turkey from motives of selfish ambition, and the Greeks again aided them from avarice and bigotry. Potemkin revived the projects of Marshal Munich; and the Greeks were urged to rebel merely to distract the attention of the Othoman government from the northern provinces of the empire, and facilitate the schemes of Catherine II. to extend her dominions on the shores of the Black Sea. The measures adopted by Potemkin with regard to Greece did not, however, originate so entirely from selfishness as those of Orloff. Men of talent were invited to Russia, employed, trusted, and promoted. A military school was formed, in which many young Greeks received their education. The pupils were selected from the principal families in Greece by the Russian consuls in the Levant; the expenses of their voyage to Russia, and of their maintenance in the establishment, were defrayed by the empress; and when their education was finished, they were employed in the army or navy, or as dragomans and consuls in Turkey. If want of talent or health rendered it advisable to send a pupil home, he was assured of Russian protection, and taught to consider himself a subject of Russia. The patronage of Potemkin drew considerable numbers of Greeks to Russia, where most of those who conducted themselves with prudence gained wealth, and some obtained high rank.

In 1783 Catherine II. renewed her encroachments on the Othoman empire by assuming the absolute sovereignty of the Crimea. About the same time she obtained a treaty of commerce from the Porte, by which the Greeks of the Archipelago were allowed to make use of the Russian flag[1]. The project of conquering Constantinople became again the ordinary subject of conversation at court; the Grand-duke

---

[1] This treaty, dated 10th June 1783, enlarged the privileges conceded by that of 1779.

Constantine was taught to speak Greek; and Catherine II. seems to have expected that she would be able to place the Byzantine crown on his head, and thus gain for Russia a legitimate title to bear the double-headed eagle of Rome on its escutcheon. The proceedings of Russia forced Sultan Abdul-hamid to declare war in August 1787, which he commenced according to the established usage of the Othoman empire by sending the Russian minister to the Seven Towers. The military operations of the Turks were most disastrous. The fleet under Hassan Ghazi having entered the Liman at the mouths of the Bug and Dnieper, was defeated by the Russians with the loss of five line-of-battle ships, three frigates, and many smaller vessels. Hassan's proud title of Ghazi was forfeited, but he lost neither his courage nor his energy; and when he collected the remains of the powerful fleet with which he had left Constantinople at Sinope, the greatness of his misfortune tended to increase his influence over the minds of his countrymen, and did not diminish his favour with Abdul-hamid. When Selim III. mounted the throne, his disgrace seemed inevitable, but the new sultan raised him to the post of grand-vizier, and intrusted him with the command of the army on the Danube. Before the opening of the campaign of 1790 death closed his long and brilliant career at Shumla.

As soon as war was declared, the agents of Russia scattered manifestoes in all parts of Greece, inviting the Christians to take up arms, and co-operate with the armies of the empress in expelling the Turks from Europe [1]. Phrases concerning ancient liberty and national independence could not, however, entirely efface the memory of Orloff's flight from Navarin. Catherine also was persuaded that the unwarlike Greeks of the Morea and the islands of the Archipelago could render no effectual assistance to her cause. Her agents were now instructed to rouse the warlike Albanian tribes in Epirus to attack their Mussulman neighbours. Their intrigues were successful with the Suliots, a Christian tribe which had always retained its arms, and preserved a degree of semi-independence, like the Sclavonians of Monte-

---

[1] Eton, *Survey of the Turkish Empire*, 354. See the memorial of some self-elected Greek deputies, who rendered homage to the Grand-duke Constantine, as representatives of the Greek nation.

negro and the Greeks of Maina and Sphakia. Instigated by Russian emissaries, the Albanians of Suli quitted their barren and almost inaccessible mountains, and invaded the plains, carrying off the cattle, and plundering the farms of the Mussulman landlords and of the Christian rayahs who lived peaceably in the plains under Turkish domination. They defeated the attempts of Ali Pasha of Joannina to invade their mountains; but as it was soon evident to the court of St. Petersburg that their power was insufficient to produce any diversion of importance, they were abandoned by Russia, and left to carry on the war they had commenced by their own unassisted exertions. The Empress Catherine II. had great reason to be dissatisfied with the results of her policy in Greece. She deceived the people of the country to serve her own political views ; her Greek agents cheated her to serve their private interests. They embezzled large sums of money, and transmitted to her ministers exaggerated accounts of victories achieved by small bands of Suliots, and absurd projects for future campaigns. Convinced at last that there was no hope of extending the insurrection, either by the forays of the Christian Albanians, or by the intrigues of her Greek emissaries, Catherine ceased to nourish the war in the Levant. The Suliots, abandoned to their fate, were compelled to conclude a truce with Ali Pasha, which their activity and valour enabled them to do on favourable terms.

The naval operations of this war in the Grecian seas were every way dishonourable to Russia. Catherine II. had fitted out a fleet at Cronstadt, under Admiral Greig, which was destined to act in the Archipelago, but a declaration of war against Russia by the King of Sweden prevented its quitting the Baltic ; and the maritime warfare in the Levant was confined to privateers under the Russian flag. Lambros Katzones, a Greek, who received the rank of major in the service of the empress, partly by the aid of Russia, but principally by the subscriptions of Greek merchants, fitted out an armament of twelve small vessels at Trieste. Lambros possessed more enthusiasm and valour than naval skill. He imprudently engaged an Algerine squadron, cruising off the coast of the Morea, and after a gallant but ineffectual fight, the greater part of the Greek ships were sunk, and he escaped with difficulty in the vessel he commanded (May 1790).

The system of privateering to which Russia lent her flag was carried on with great energy, and the crews engaged in it were collected from every European nation. The cruisers being virtually released from all control, and being often manned by those who had long acted as pirates in the Levant, perpetrated the most horrible acts of cruelty. The unprotected and industrious, Greek population of the islands and sea-coasts of the Othoman empire never suffered greater misery from the slave-dealing pirates, than were now inflicted on them by pretended friends under the orthodox banner of Russia. Greeks were on this occasion the principal agents in the sufferings of Greece, but those who have left us any memorials of this period were so ashamed of the barbarity of their countrymen, that they have sought to bury every record of these privateering expeditions in oblivion. Few accounts of the scenes of bloodshed enacted by the pirates have been preserved ; the wail of the murdered has found no echo, while infatuated *literati* have deemed it patriotic to represent every privateersman as a Themistocles and every klepht as a Leonidas. The journal of an English sailor is among the few authentic records of the horrible exploits of these privateers [1].

In December 1788, William Davidson, a young seaman from the north of England, sailed from Leghorn in a privateer, under the Russian flag, mounting twenty-two guns, and carrying two hundred and fifteen men. This vessel returned to Leghorn in August 1789, and during a cruise of only eight months, it captured upwards of forty vessels, and about fifteen hundred men perished; a few were slain in battle, but far the greater part were murdered in cold blood on the deck of the privateer, after they had surrendered prisoners of war. Several Greek islands were plundered, the defenceless town of Castel Rosso was taken, all the Turks in the place were murdered, though they offered no resistance, and half the houses were wantonly burned. The plunder collected

---

[1] Davidson's narrative in a *History of Shipwrecks*, edited by Cyrus Redding, second series. When the author first visited Greece in 1823, it was his fortune to meet with individuals whose testimony confirmed the fearful narrative of Davidson.

from the Greek inhabitants was very considerable, and even the churches were robbed of their gold and silver ornaments, images, and candlesticks. On some occasions the privateers spared Greek ships under the Turkish flag when they were the property of Greek merchants, but the cruelty with which they generally treated their prisoners requires to be described in the words of one of the murderers. The circumstances attending the capture of a Turkish galley with eighty-five men on board are thus narrated. The prisoners were confined all night in the hold. Many of them must have been Christians compelled to work at the oars. In the morning they were brought on deck one by one, and 'their heads were cut off as ducks' heads are cut off at home,' says the narrator, 'and then we threw them overboard.' This was the first time the whole crew were obliged to take their turn in murdering the prisoners, and the English at first refused ; but when the captain told them they were cowards, and that he could not believe they were really Englishmen, they did the same as the rest, and afterwards were even worse than the others, for they were always first when such work was going on. Yet even these privateers were not the worst robbers in the Grecian seas. On the coast of Maina piracy was openly carried on, and the pirates treated the Russian flag with no more respect than the Othoman, if they supposed it covered a rich prize. The privateer in which Davidson served fell in with a large ship to the west of Cerigo. It was pursued, and did not refuse to fight, for 'to our misfortune,' as Davidson says, it proved to be a celebrated pirate with thirty-two guns and three hundred and seventy-eight men. A severe engagement took place, which lasted more than four hours, and when the pirate struck to the superior discipline and the heavier weight of metal of the privateer, it was found that he had lost fifty-four men killed and forty-three wounded. The success of the victor was in part attributed to the confusion which was caused on board the pirate by the variety of nations composing the crew. The wounded were immediately put to death. Next morning the prisoners were examined, and when they confessed that, like their captors, they were in the habit of killing the crews and sinking the ships they took, the captain of the Graeco-Russian privateer, forgetful of his own conduct, told them they should

all die by the cruellest death.   He was as brutal as his word;
for next day he murdered them in so horrible a manner, that
it is necessary to record the fact in the words of the eye-
witness.   His diary says: '*August 5th.*—We got whips on
the mainstay, and made one leg fast to the whip, and the
other to a ring-bolt in the deck, and so quartered them,
and hove them overboard[1].'   The lure which enticed the
crews of the privateers to act these scenes of horror was the
immense booty they obtained.   Each of the English sailors
received, as his share of prize-money after the eight months'
cruise, the sum of nine hundred and fifty dollars, about £200
sterling.

The infamous cruelties and open piracies committed under
the Russian flag at last induced the court of St. Petersburg to
refuse all further countenance to the privateers.   Lambros,
who had succeeded with the assistance of some Greek merchants at Trieste in fitting out a few vessels, was nevertheless
allowed to carry the Russian flag until the end of the war;
but when peace was concluded, he also was compelled to
strike it.   Though disavowed by the empress, he continued to
cruise against the Turks.   Peace had turned adrift a number
of daring seamen, and as many of these joined him, he
resolved to hold the sea as an independent cruiser.   Unfortunately, he soon found it impossible to pay his men without
committing acts of piracy on the flags of nations who had
it in their power to punish his misdeeds, and vengeance
quickly followed his piracies.   He made Porto Quaglio in
Maina his naval station; and having secured the assistance of
the Kakovouliots, the poorest and most desperate portion of
the population of Maina, he plundered the flag of every nation
off Cape Matapan.   Emboldened by a few months' impunity,
he had the audacity to attack two French ships near Nauplia,
which he burned in May 1792.   As soon as the French ambassador at Constantinople heard of this outrage, he sent
information to a French squadron then cruising in the Levant,
which immediately joined the fleet of Hussein, the capitan-
pasha, and sailed in pursuit of Lambros.   The Greek piratical
squadron consisted of eleven vessels.   It was found anchored
at Porto Quaglio, under the protection of batteries, which

---

[1] Davidson's narrative, p. 204.

Lambros supposed would be sufficient to keep the Turkish fleet at a distance. On the 19th of June, he was attacked by the Othoman fleet, assisted by the French frigate La Modeste. The batteries in which he had trusted were soon destroyed, and the pirate ships, abandoned by their crews, were all captured by the Turks, and conducted in triumph to Constantinople. Lambros escaped into the mountains, and reached the Ionian Islands.

Austria joined Russia in the war against Turkey, with the expectation of sharing in the spoils of the Othoman empire. The Emperor Joseph commenced the war unjustly; his brother Leopold terminated it disgracefully. He concluded a separate peace at Sistova in 1791, which, like that of Belgrade, was calculated to destroy the influence of Austria in the East. Russia was more successful. Her arms were crowned with victory, but the treaty she concluded with the sultan at Yassi in 1792 only extended the frontier of the empire to the banks of the Dniester. The partition of Poland arrested the fall of the Othoman empire.

The French Revolution now began to exert a direct influence on every nation in Europe, and to modify the position and policy of every government. France invited the people in every country to declare itself free and independent. These revolutionary principles found an echo in the breast of every Greek ; but the different classes composing the Greek nation were not yet united by common feelings which could produce simultaneous action. The restless presumption and envious disposition of the Phanariots and archonts, the noisy cowardice of city mobs, and the lawless conduct of the armed mountaineers, afforded the Greeks little hope of being able to emulate the French in their devotion to liberty and equality. Rhiga of Velestinos was one of the warmest partizans of the new revolutionary ideas. His patriotic songs and his personal energy have made his name dear to his countrymen. His enthusiasm deluded him into the belief that he could guide the events of his time, and avail himself of the aid of France as an instrument for framing Hellenic republics, and gratifying the dreams of ambitious pedants. The confined sphere of his political vision made his schemes degenerate into mere conspiracies. The plots of Rhiga were betrayed to the Austrian police by one of his own countrymen, and the Austrian government delivered him up to the Turks, who put him to death at Belgrade in 1797[1].

The treaty of Campo Formio in 1797 placed the Ionian Islands under the dominion of France, and the Greeks became the ready instruments of French policy, as they had formerly been of Russian. Venice had protected her possessions in Epirus by forming alliances with the various tribes of Christian Albanians who preserved their independence; and the republic had systematically supported these tribes, particularly the Chimariots and Suliots, against the neighbouring pashas. The French adopted a different policy; they sought the alliance of Ali Pasha of Joannina, because he possessed a numerous army of hardy irregular troops, from which they hoped to derive assistance in their schemes of conquest. They allowed him, therefore, to consolidate his power by destroying the local independence of the dispersed and disunited tribes of armed Christians who had long successfully resisted the Othoman power. Ali, availing himself of these views, obtained permission from the general commanding at Corfu to send troops by sea to Chimara, in order to reduce to obedience the inhabitants, whom he called rebel subjects of the Porte. The district, of which Novitza-Bouba and Aghio-Vasili were the principal villages, contained six thousand Christians, who enjoyed the same degree of partial independence as the Suliots. The young men were in the habit of entering the military service of Venice and Naples, and when they had saved a small sum of money, they returned to their native mountains and married. Their privileges had been protected by Venice. France allowed them to be exterminated by Ali Pasha, whose troops landed in the bay of Lukovo, surprised the population during the Easter festivals, and massacred most of those able to bear arms[2].

In 1798 the treacherous invasion of Egypt by Napoleon Buonaparte caused the sultan to declare war against the French republic. Ali Pasha availed himself of the opportunity to gain possession of the dependencies of the Ionian Islands on the continent. The French garrison at Prevesa

---

[1] The traitor was Demetrios Oikonomos Kozanites. Philemon, Δοκίμιον ἱστορικὸν περὶ τῆς Φιλικῆς Ἑταιρίας, p. 92.

[2] Perrhaevos, Ἱστορία τοῦ Σουλίου καὶ τῆς Πάργας, p. 1; Emerson, Modern Greece, ii. 436.

was defeated. Vonitza, Gomenitza, and Butrinto surrendered, and Parga alone, of all the ancient Venetian possessions on the continent, repulsed the forces of the pasha and retained its local immunities. Even before the declaration of war the sultan obtained proof that the French government had sent emissaries into Roumelia, the Morea, and the islands of the Archipelago, to distribute publications inviting the inhabitants to revolt[1]. Russia, as well as Turkey, became alarmed lest the fanaticism of liberty should overpower the bigotry of orthodoxy. A common fear of French influence in Greece united those apparently irreconcilable enemies, the czar and the sultan, in a close alliance. The first object was to expel the French from the Ionian Islands. In 1799 a combined Russian and Othoman force took possession of Corfu, and by a convention between the court of St. Petersburg and the Porte in 1800, the Ionian Islands were constituted a republic, while, as if to make the mockery of liberty more complete, this nominally independent republic was prepared to undergo the fate of Poland, by being placed under the joint protection of the two most despotic sovereigns in Europe.

By the same convention all the Venetian possessions on the continent were ceded to the Porte. It was stipulated that their Christian inhabitants were to enjoy every religious and judicial privilege possessed by the Christians of Vallachia and Moldavia ; a vague stipulation, which was calculated chiefly to authorize Russian interference and to extend Russian influence, but which proved of no avail as a protection to the inhabitants of Prevesa[2]. The Emperor of Russia, though the avowed champion of the orthodox, was thus the last Christian sovereign who voluntarily placed an orthodox population under Othoman domination. As the sultan was already, by the success of Ali Pasha, in possession of all the territory ceded by the convention, except Parga, Ali Pasha expected to gain possession of that place. But neither Russia nor the Porte wished to see that strong position fall into his hands. The people of Parga were encouraged to resist his attacks, while the combined fleet refused to blockade them,

---

[1] Rizos Néroulos, *Histoire*, 171 ; Alison's *History of Europe*, vol. iv. p. 188 (People's edit.), where an extract from the Turkish manifesto is given.
[2] This convention is dated 21st March, 1800. The 8th article cedes the continental possessions of Venice to the sultan.

as they proclaimed their devotion to the sultan. Parga, from these circumstances, was allowed to retain its municipal independence, though it was regarded as henceforth forming a part of the Othoman empire. Russia did not take any trouble to exact the observance of the article in the convention which reserved their religious liberties to the inhabitants of the other Venetian possessions.

By the treaty of Tilsit in 1807, Russia ceded the Ionian republic to France, and though England conquered the other islands, the French retained possession of Corfu until the peace of 1814. In 1815 the Ionian republic was revived, and placed under the protection of the sovereign of Great Britain. The convention of 1800, relating to the continental possessions of Venice, including Parga, was regarded as part of the public law of Europe, for the jealousy of Russia and Austria feared to leave England in possession of a fortress which might serve as a key to Epirus and Greece.

When the French garrison of Corfu found that it would be necessary to deliver up Parga to the English, they resolved to prevent it falling into their hands by ceding it to Ali Pasha. But an English force from Zante arrived in time to occupy it before the arrival of Ali's troops. The sultan, however, called on the British government to execute the Russian convention of 1800, and after much negotiation it was at last resolved in 1819 to deliver up Parga to the Turks. As the hated Ali would, however, become master of the place, the inhabitants declared they would rather emigrate than become subjects of the sultan. They asked to be indemnified for the full value of all the property they abandoned; and, by the persevering exertions of the English authorities, the Porte paid to them the sum of £150,000, which was divided among them according to the valuation of their property. There is no doubt that the pecuniary indemnity was most liberal, but many of the poorer classes, possessing no property, received no indemnity, and all who emigrated were loud in their complaints of English policy, which had condemned them to become exiles. In vain they enjoyed protection and the liberty of complaint in the Ionian Islands; every tongue in Europe was loud in reproaching England for consenting to fulfil the convention of 1800, and compelling the inhabitants of Parga to forsake the tombs of their ancestors, and change their municipal existence and ancestral name, for the rights and the name of citizens of the Ionian republic[1]. Perhaps public opinion is not unjust when it blames the acts of a free government for violations of the principles of abstract justice, which it would praise as wise and politic measures if they were adopted by a despotic prince. Men habitually arraign the free before the tribunal of equity; slaves and despots they judge by the exigencies of expediency and policy. Truth and justice ought always to penetrate to the hearts of freemen, but they are not expected to find an echo in the breasts of princes and statesmen. The severe criticism of English policy is the eulogy of English liberty. The conduct of the English government in the Ionian Islands has, however, neither been wise nor liberal: though it has administered justice with equity and protected industry and commerce, it long opposed the liberty of the press. The chief ground of its unpopularity nevertheless is, that it has checked the movements of those who desired to cause an insurrection of the Greeks in Turkey. This duty has rendered it unpopular with every party in Eastern Europe. The Ionians themselves cared little for trade, but they were zealous partizans of Russian policy and of orthodox bigotry. But the inhabitants of the Ionian Islands have no good reason to complain, for if the English government has not performed its duty, the nobles and the people of the Ionian Islands have completely neglected theirs. They have not availed themselves of the liberty they have so long enjoyed for improving their moral condition, and for attaining a moral and intellectual superiority over the other Greeks who were subject to the sultan. All foreign domination appears to have exerted a baneful influence on Greek morality. It has always found them ready to become servile instruments and secret traitors. In the Ionian Islands the moral condition of the people, when they passed under the protection of the sovereign of Great Britain, was much worse than that of the Greeks

---

[1] The enemies of England endeavour to make her conduct appear more odious, by representing Parga as a free republic, which it never was. Foscolo, *Delle fortune e delle cessioni di Parga.* [Some of the details of this cession, which were of the most tragical character, and must always be painful to an Englishman, are given in the account of the proceeding in Alison's *History of Europe from* 1815 *to* 1852, vol. iii. pp. 86-88. The feeling of the inhabitants is well expressed in the Greek ballads on the subject; Passow, *Popularia Carmina Graeciae recentioris,* Nos. 222-224. ED.]

under the Turkish domination. Their communal institutions were only administrative facilities modelled by a foreign central authority. When the islands were first occupied by the French, assassination was the commonest crime, and it was a popular saying that there was a murder for every day in the year[1].

A great improvement took place in the material condition of the Greek nation after the peace of Yassi. Great social changes were exerting their operation on the Othoman government as well as on the Greek people. The sultan was impelled, by the necessity of self-defence, even more than by the desire all sovereigns feel to centralize power in their own hands, to destroy the ancient fabric of the Othoman state institutions, which time and individual corruption had already undermined. The cruel use the pashas made of the absolute power delegated to them ; the rapacity of the fiscal agents of government; the venality of the Ulema ; the selfishness of the timariots, and the anarchical insolence of the janissaries, rendered these classes equally hateful to the sultan and to the people, and marked them out for destruction. The Othoman sultans had to attempt the double task of saving their empire from dismemberment, and of destroying the institutions which had long formed the barriers against its dismemberment. The Greeks caught some of the enthusiasm in favour of liberty, independence, and the rights of man, propagated over Europe by the French Revolution. A reminiscence of Hellenic glory was revived ; the educated classes taught the people that they were Greeks and not Romans, and began to inculcate the duty of laying aside the national appellation of Romaioi and resuming the name of Hellenes. The project of regaining their political independence was no longer circumscribed to a few thoughtful and aspiring men ; it became the very object of existence to numbers engaged in the pursuits of active life, in every rank of society. The social position of the mass of the Greek population explains the facility with which it was influenced by the revolutionary ideas of the French. The Othoman government, though in some respects the most tyrannical in Europe, was in others the most tolerant. It fettered the body, but it left the mind free. The lower

---

[1] Holland's *Travels*, p. 23.

orders of its Christian subjects were in general possessed of more intellectual cultivation than the corresponding ranks of society in other parts of Europe. The Greeks were neither industrial slaves nor agricultural serfs; their labour was both more free and more valuable, and their civil rights were as great as those of the same class, even in France, before the Revolution. The Othoman government corrupted the higher classes of the Greeks more than it oppressed the lower. The cruelty and injustice of the Turks were irregularly exercised, and were more galling than oppressive. Towards the end of the eighteenth century the burden of the Othoman domination was so much lightened that the Greeks became ·an improving nation. They possessed a numerous body of small peasant-proprietors of land, whom circumstances often enabled to better their condition; and in the towns an industrious population of labourers and traders was supported and protected by a body of wealthy merchants often enjoying foreign protection. A numerous maritime population of Christians, partly consisting of Greeks, and partly of Albanians, also tended to give the Greeks a considerable degree of personal independence. The Turkish peasant and trader suffered quite as much from fiscal exactions as the Greek, and the political obstacles to his rise in the social scale were generally greater. Few native Turks of the provinces ever acquired as much influence over the public administration as was systematically and permanently exercised by the Phanariots. The local authorities of the Mussulman population in the rural districts rarely possessed the same power of defending the people from injustice as, and they certainly possessed fewer rights and privileges than, the Greek communities. It is not, therefore, surprising that the Greeks were superior in social and political civilization to the Turks. The fact was generally perceived, and a Greek revolution was consequently regarded as an event which must occur at no very distant date, both by the Christian and Mussulman population of the Othoman empire, at the commencement of the nineteenth century. In the ordinary course of human affairs it was inevitable.

But unless some closer bonds had united the dispersed members of the Greek nation than those by which they had hitherto been connected, it may be questioned whether the revolutionary movement could have proved successful. Some spiritual tie was required to infuse a common feeling of national enthusiasm more powerful than the formal cere- monial of the orthodox church, or the ecclesiastical influence of the clergy, which had too long been an instrument of Othoman domination, and which seemed more inclined to transfer the allegiance of the people from the sultan to the czar, than to aid a struggle for liberty. The future prospects of a Greek Church in an independent State did not offer an inviting field for clerical ambition, compared with the magnificent vista opened to episcopal imaginations by an orthodox hierarchy under Russian domination. Various causes, however, tended to centralize those feelings of nationality which the church neglected to cultivate. We have already mentioned that the corrupting influence of the Phanariot system tended to this object. The hope of attaining the high rank to which the Chiot Mavrocordatos, and the Mykoniot Mavroyeni, had risen, drew aspirants for political employ- ment to Constantinople from every corner of the empire where Greek was spoken. The direct dependence of a considerable portion of Greece on the capitan-pasha united a large popu- lation by common interests and ideas in administrative affairs. It is true that the centralization thus formed tended to corrupt the higher classes as much as to unite the people; but the influence of the Phanariots was not more demoralizing than that of the patriarchate, while the separation effected between the political and ecclesiastical classes caused collisions of interest and personal disputes, which awakened the attention and enlightened the minds of the many. The Greeks were thus taught to perceive that their interests as a nation were not always identical with the policy of their clergy.

The extension of Greek commerce tended also to develope the feelings of national union. The active trade which the Greeks and Albanians carried on over the whole surface of the Mediterranean, nourished a healthier spirit of central- ization than the allurements of Phanariot protection, and the profits of office in the service of the sultan. This influence of Greek commerce dates from the conclusion of the commercial treaties between Russia and the Porte in 1779 and 1783, which enabled the orthodox subjects of the sultan to obtain the protection of the Russian flag. Even

before the conclusion of the first of these treaties, ten Greek
vessels, laden with wine from the islands of the Archipelago,
had entered the Russian ports in the sea of Azof in one year.
The treaty of Yassi enabled Russia to increase still further
the number of her protected subjects in Turkey, and even to
secure to Greek subjects of the sultan the fullest protection
for their property under the Russian flag [1].

Fortunately for the commerce of the Greeks, the Othoman
government was enabled to maintain its neutrality during the
greater part of the wars in which the French Revolution
involved the powers of Europe. Greek merchants visited
ports in the Mediterranean closed against every flag but
that of the sultan, and the profits of their commerce were
immense. The manufacturers of Adrianople, and of the
mountain village of Ambelakia on Mount Ossa, sent cotton
fabrics, dyed with the rich colour called Turkey red, even
to England [2]. The Greeks of the island of Psara, and of
the town of Galaxidhi in the Corinthian Gulf, and the
Albanians of the islands of Hydra and Spetzas, carried on
an extensive commerce in their own ships. Many of the
sailors were part proprietors both of the ship and cargo,
and united the occupations of capitalists and sailors. All
shared in the profits of the voyage. Their extensive commercial enterprises exercised a direct influence on the great
body of the Greek population, which dwells, in general, near
the sea-coast. Tales of distant lands visited, of dangers

---

[1] Rizos Néroulos, *Histoire*, 125; Castera, *Histoire de Catherine II.,* ii. 210.

[2] At the end of the last century there were twenty-four dyeing establishments at
Ambelakia, and the population amounted to four thousand persons. For a time
the inhabitants, capitalists and workmen, formed a general stock company, with
several subordinate branches, but the family education of Chios was wanting, and
the selfishness which is a prominent characteristic of the modern Greek, induced
many who had more money or more skill to separate their interests from the rest.
Dissensions and intrigues arose even in this mountain-village society, and the
mutual envy of the Greeks themselves ruined this once flourishing spot. Beaujour,
Tableau du Commerce de la Grèce, i. 274. [Other accounts of the remarkable
manufacturing communities of Ambelakia will be found in Clarke's *Travels,* vol. iv.
p. 285, and Leake's *Northern Greece,* vol. iii. p. 385. Both these travellers, as
well as Beaujour, visited the place when it was at the height of its prosperity.
Colonel Leake, with his accustomed admirable accuracy, has given details respecting the process of dyeing pursued there, and statistics as to the exports and the
system on which the trade was managed. Other causes besides home dissensions
contributed to ruin the community—the increasing scarcity of madder, commercial
failures in Germany, the spinning-jennies of England, and the Greek Revolution.
But the speedy collapse of such a community is not so much a cause of wonder as
the fact of its having existed at all in a place which possessed no natural advantages, and under a system which presupposed extraordinary disinterestedness and
concord. ED.]

successfully encountered, and of wealth rapidly acquired, were repeated even in the secluded villages of the mountains. Examples of penniless adventurers becoming richer than pashas were daily witnessed. The ideas of the people were enlarged; they knew that order reigned in many countries; their hopes of improving their condition were awakened; they heard that security of property prevailed, and justice was impartially administered, in most Christian states; and the determination to vindicate for themselves these advantages was silently formed. Gradually the conviction was everywhere felt that this could only be effected by recovering their national independence.

The corruption of the Othoman government introduced many vices into the commercial system of the Levant, which nourished fraud, and invited the Greeks to degrade their character by habitual dishonesty. A Greek subject of the sultan was subjected to higher duties than a foreigner, or a Greek enjoying foreign protection. To carry on his business profitably, he was consequently compelled to find some means of cheating the Othoman government out of the differential duty imposed by its ignorance and injustice. The fiscal corruption of the Othoman administration introduced the practice of the sultan granting special exemptions from extraordinary taxes to many of his subjects. This privilege was conceded to Christians who enjoyed the favour of the sultan or his ministers, and was gradually extended until it placed them in fiscal matters in the same position as the subjects of Christian princes most favoured by their commercial treaties with the Porte. Firmans, in this sense, were granted to rayahs, called barrats[1]. The abuse was carried so far that it became customary for the Turkish government to bestow forty of these barrats as a gift on every new ambassador when he arrived at Constantinople. The ministers of the sultan, and the Phanariots in high office, made a traffic of these immunities. The dragomans of foreign embassies, the consuls, and even the ambassadors themselves, were accused of selling these barrats to the Greeks. The Russian legation systematically extended its

---

[1] The privilege most valued by the vain Phanariots was that of dressing like Mussulmans and wearing yellow slippers.

EDUCATION.

influence by availing itself of this corruption of the Othoman administration. It procured as many barrats as possible, it granted passports to Greek subjects of the sultan as if they were Russians, and it authorized Greek vessels to hoist the Russian flag.

The capitan-pasha, Hussein, who effected great reforms in the Othoman naval administration after the peace of Yassi, always protected the Greeks who sailed under the Turkish flag. During his long and liberal administration, the Albanians of Hydra and Spetzas found it more advantageous to sail under the Othoman flag than under the Russian. Hussein had two hundred Christian Albanian sailors from Hydra on board the three-decker which carried his flag in the year 1797 [1]. He was particularly attentive to the shipping of Hydra, which increased and prospered under his protection. After Hussein's death, the disorder that prevailed in the naval administration revived the exactions of subordinates and local pashas, and the Christians in Turkey again endeavoured to protect their property under the Russian flag. It is needless to dwell on the evils of a political system in which corruption alone afforded the means of escape from oppression.

In the darkest periods of their national existence the Greeks continued to feel the influence of literature. The greatest of the Iconoclast emperors feared John Damascenus. Yet the influence of Greek literature was for ages unfavourable to the progress of society. It is reasonable to complain of its nature during many centuries, but it is an error to suppose that learning entirely failed among the Greeks at any period of their history. The Greek clergy always kept up a competent knowledge of the ancient language, though their schools conveyed very little instruction to the mass of the people. During the Othoman domination, it is probable that the proportion of Greeks who could read and write was as great as in any other European nation; and every Greek who could write had some faint knowledge of Hellenic literature. When the Greek mind, therefore, began to emancipate itself from ecclesiastical trammels, education became the purest and most powerful instrument of national centralization. Schools

[1] Antonios Miaoulis (son of the admiral), Ὑπόμνημα περὶ τῆς νήσου Ὕδρας, p. 11.

were very generally established, and the difficulties which both the founders and the scholars of these schools met with in their pursuit of knowledge increased their zeal. The progress of the modern Greeks in intellectual culture does not require to be traced in detail. A chronological enumeration of the schools established, and a list of the names of individuals who devoted their lives to teaching, would cause a grateful throb in the heart of every patriotic Greek, but the history of the nation only requires us to record the result. That result is attested by the formation of a common literary dialect of the modern language, which served.as the means of uniting the ideas of the people. The literary progress of the modern Greeks must not be measured by a comparison with the standard of knowledge of Greek literature in Western Europe. The Greeks were unable to throw light on the topography of their native land, or to extend the interpretation of the language of their ancestors ; but they made their written language an instrument of national centralization distinct from all provincial dialects, yet intelligible and harmonious to every Greek.

Every fact relating to a language which has given its form and character to the literature of Europe and America, must be deeply interesting to the student of Greek political history ; but the subject demands a chapter, not a paragraph. The great feature of the revival of modern literary cultivation was the emancipation of the Greek mind from ecclesiastical subjection. To effect this it was necessary to abandon the language of ecclesiastical literature, and give a literary character to the language used by the people. Two individuals, Eugenios and Koraës, distinguished themselves as active instruments in this great and noble undertaking. They united the Greeks by intellectual ties far stronger than the bonds which Turkish domination had laid on the clergy [1].

Eugenios Bulgares of Corfu was the first reformer of the ecclesiastical system of education, which had perpetuated Byzantine pedantry in the schools, and ecclesiastical servility

---

[1] Some interesting observations on the living language of the Greeks have been published by Professor Blackie of Edinburgh, the translator of Aeschylus, who unites sound sense with profound learning. I must also refer to the admirable little dissertation, entitled *Romaic and Modern Greek compared with one another and with Ancient Greek*, by Dr. James Clyde, from whom I borrow the selection of Eugenios and Koraës as the prototypes of modern Greek literature.

in politics. He taught at Joannina, at Mount Athos, and at Constantinople; but his reforms in the ancient system of education, and his pleadings in favour of religious toleration, alarmed the clergy[1]. He was silenced by the ecclesiastical and Phanariot influence, which supported the sultan's authority. In 1775 he was invited to Russia, and raised to the bishopric of Sclavonia and Kherson. Eugenios was the first scholar who employed a style generally intelligible, in a serious work, addressed to all classes[2]. His tract on religious toleration was considered a revolutionary production by the ecclesiastical party, which maintained its supremacy at Constantinople under the sultan's protection. Anthimus, the patriarch of Jerusalem, accordingly endeavoured to apply an antidote, and in 1798 he printed a work at the Greek press of Constantinople, in which he congratulated the Greeks on having escaped the artifices of the devil, who had enticed the Catholics, the Lutherans, the Calvinists, and various other sects, into the path of perdition. He told them, that when the last emperors of Constantinople began to subject the Oriental Church to papal thraldom, the particular favour of Heaven raised up the Othoman empire to protect the Greeks against heresy, to be a barrier against the political power of the Western nations, and to be the champion of the Orthodox Church.

Koraës, a native of Chios, but who fixed his abode at Paris, was the great popular reformer of the Greek system of instruction, the legislator of the modern Greek language, and the most distinguished apostle of religious toleration and national freedom. He was a firm opponent of the Orthodox bigotry which would have enslaved Greece to Russia, and of the Phanariot servility which supported the Othoman domination. His residence in France protected him from those whose interests he assailed, and he was personally endowed with all the qualities which gave authority to his teaching. He was indifferent to wealth, honest and independent, a sincere patriot, and a profound scholar. Unlike

---

[1] [On Mount Athos Eugenios Bulgares established a large school with extensive buildings, the ruins of which remain on a hill above the monastery of Vatopedi. For some time it was attended by numerous scholars, but the atmosphere of monasticism proved unfavourable to it. Ed.]

[2] See the passage in Leake, *Researches in Greece*, 193; and compare the notice of Eugenios in Clyde, *Romaic and Modern Greek*, 48.

his countrymen, the Chiots, who are generally as remarkable for avidity as for industry, he passed his life in independent poverty, in order that he might consecrate his whole time, and the undivided strength of his mind, to improve the moral and political feelings of the Greeks. His efforts have not been fruitless. He methodized the literary language of his countrymen, while he infused into their minds principles of true liberty and pure morality. His influence on the men who participated in the Greek Revolution was so great, that no political history of Greece would be complete which omitted to name Adamantios Koraës as one of those who contributed to establish the national independence [1].

The fact that the Greeks have hitherto made greater progress in regenerating their language than in improving their moral condition, must be attributed to the superiority of the material on which they worked. The language retained its ancient structure and grammar; the people had lost their ancient virtues and institutions. Literary eminence may be attained in retirement, where feeble men can write under the guidance of reason alone; but moral superiority can only be displayed and acquired amidst the temptations and the duties of active life.

We have seen that the two earliest institutions tending to national centralization after the Othoman conquest—the patriarchate of Constantinople and the official aristocracy —were employed by the sultan's government as instruments for enslaving the Greeks. Even the centralization effected by the cultivation of the language and the creation of a modern Greek literature might have been pressed into the service of bigotry and despotism, had the influence of the French Revolution not counterbalanced that of orthodox Russia, and infused the love of freedom into the popular mind. The Greek language was saved, by this alliance with mental liberty, from becoming an instrument of priests and princes, and perpetuating an existence, which, like a national dress or a national music, might form an interesting subject of study for an antiquary, but could add little to the strength, virtue, or political improvement of the people.

---

[1] See the Biography of Koraës, also the sketch of his philological influence, in Clyde, 49.

Indeed, had a large part of the Greek population not enjoyed municipal rights which enabled them to feel the spirit of independence, and to labour to better their own condition, the improvement of the language would have remained a barren fact. It was the municipal activity which displayed itself at Chios, at Ambelakia, at Galaxidhi and at Psara, that gave to the literary centralization of language its political power. The same municipal institutions and religious feelings drew the Albanian population of Hydra and Spetzas within the circle of Greek centralization, though they remained long without the sphere of Greek literary influence. The local energies and local patriotism of all the Christian municipalities in the Othoman empire could readily unite in opposition to Othoman oppression, whenever a connecting link to centralize their efforts could be created. In these local institutions the foundation was laid for a federal union of all the Orthodox races in European Turkey, which time may perhaps consolidate if they can escape from the bureaucratic power of Continental centralization. The vigorous Albanians of Hydra, the warlike Albanians of Suli, the persevering Bulgarians of Macedonia, and the laborious Vallachians on the banks of the Aspropotamos, embarked in the struggle for Greek independence as heartily as the posterity of the ancient inhabitants of the soil of Hellas. Ecclesiastical ties greatly facilitated this union, but they neither created the impulse towards independence, nor infused the enthusiasm which secured success. The first step to national liberty in modern Greece, as in every country which has made any considerable advance in improving the condition of the mass of the inhabitants, was made in the municipalities. They were the political soul of the nation.

Too great influence has been generally ascribed to the clergy and to ecclesiastical literature in preserving national feelings, and too great merit is attributed to the popular songs, as well as too much influence, in forming the character of the people. Ecclesiastical learning was so deeply tinctured with pedantry as to be generally unintelligible; it spoke in a language which few understood. The popular songs neither possessed the poetic feeling nor those general expressions of human sympathies which exert a strong and permanent influence on every rank of society. The Greeks had no poetry which the mother taught her child alike in the palace on the shores of the Bosphorus and in the cottage on the banks of the Alpheus[1].

In the mean time the most striking feature in the political state of Greece, at the opening of the nineteenth century, was the decline of the Othoman empire. The sultan's administration was every day growing weaker and more exclusively fiscal. The Turks were dwindling away under the operation of social and political corruption. The primary object of the government appeared to be, to draw money to Constantinople without reference to the manner in which it was to be expended. The most oppressive exactions of pashas were winked at, in order to share the profits of their injustice. Yet while the authority of the sultan was weakened and the power of the empire declined, the influence of the central executive administration was absolutely augmented by the social changes which time had produced in the Mohammedan population. Every barrier which privilege and class had once opposed to the exercise of arbitrary power had vanished. The Ulema, by corruption and venality, had forfeited all influence over the people, and formed no longer a systematic check on the executive. The janissaries had ceased to be regular troops. They were a mere Mussulman city-guard, an ill-organized militia, without discipline or tactics. The old Turkish feudal militia, the provincial timariots, were too poor and dependent to oppose the pashas and the central government. They had fallen so completely from their ancient position, that they generally sought employment as farmers of the public revenues, or as mere tax-gatherers. The only manifestation of their former

---

[1] [Throughout these histories the Author has spoken of the poetical compositions of mediaeval and modern Greece in depreciating terms, which, if they are estimated, as they ought to be, apart from a classical standard, I think they hardly deserve. Many of the popular songs are beautiful (Goethe, at least, thought so), and many have had a very wide oral circulation throughout the country, and have certainly exercised great influence. This has been the general opinion ; and the latest writer on modern Greek history, Karl Mendelssohn Bartholdy, in his *Geschichte Griechenlands von der Eroberung Konstantinopels durch die Türken bis auf unsere Tage* (vol. i. p. 22) says of the popular poetry—' *Sie war es, die den Protest gegen die bestehende Knechtschaft nie verstummen liess.*' They were, however, of spontaneous growth, and must not be regarded as a product of education, though they are an evidence of the intelligence of the people. ED.]

influence was displayed in their readiness to join any pasha or local leader in rebellion.

The increase of the power of the pashas is the characteristic of the period immediately preceding the Greek Revolution. The progress of society had swept away the mediaeval privileges of Mohammedanism, and the pashas intrusted with the sultan's delegated power enjoyed the fruits of the change, and were absolute monarchs in their provinces. This phasis of administrative government repeats itself in all despotisms, and generally leads to the dismemberment of large empires. The caliphates of Damascus, Bagdad, and Cordova, the Seljouk empire of the Great Sultan, and the Seljouk empire of Roum, all fell to pieces from this cause. The weakness of the central authority enabled the governors of provinces to found independent States. The Othoman empire, towards the end of the eighteenth century, had reached this crisis of its existence. Many pashas seemed on the eve of founding independent dynasties. A succession of rebellions, though they were all eventually suppressed, seemed only to open a field for new and more powerful rebels. Not to speak of the deys of Tripoli, Tunis, and Algiers, who rendered their governments virtually independent, Pashvan Oglou at Vidin, Djezzar Pasha at Acre, Ali Bey in Egypt, long ruled almost as independent sovereigns. At a later period, Ali Pasha of Joannina was rather a tributary prince than a dependent pasha ; and Mehemet Ali of Egypt at last became the founder of a dynasty.

This feature in the state of society must not be overlooked in examining the social and political causes which produced the Greek Revolution. The tendency to dismember the Othoman empire was shown by the Arab population in Syria and Egypt, and by the Albanians in Epirus, as well as by the Christians in Greece and Servia. The increased authority of the central government enabled the sultan ultimately to crush his rebellious pashas, and restore the integrity of the Othoman empire. But in Greece and Servia, where the struggle was one for national independence and religious liberty, the cause of the people was victorious, the Othoman empire was dismembered, and two new States were added to Christian Europe.

The career of the Othoman conquerors in Greece was

now terminated. They were themselves involved in a struggle to maintain their national existence against political anarchy and external attacks. But their domination in Greece had not been without its use; it had accomplished a task which neither the Roman power nor the Orthodox Church had effected; it had nationalized the Greeks, and compressed their various communities into one body. A great cycle in the history of Greece was completed. The tribe of Othman had fulfilled its mission in Hellas, and it was now to depart from the land, like the Romans, the Crusaders, and the Venetians.

On the other hand, the desire of civil liberty had already germinated in the modern Greek nation which the Othoman rule had formed. Political institutions of a permanent character existed, and were rapidly giving a new organic form to Greek society. Communities and municipalities, governed by established laws and usages, secured a basis for popular self-government. Provincial assemblies for fiscal purposes, though used only as instruments of Othoman oppression, afforded the means of connecting local liberties with national centralization. Throughout the East it was felt that the hour of a great struggle for independence on the part of the Greeks had arrived. The Greek Revolution was a social and political necessity. National sovereignty is an inherent right of the people, as civil liberty is of the individual. Men know instinctively that there are conditions and times when the rebellion of subject nations and of disfranchised citizens becomes a duty. 'The liberties of nations are from God and nature, not from kings and governments.' The whole history of the Othoman domination in Greece attests that the Greeks were perpetually urged, by every feeling of religion and humanity, to take up arms against their tyrants. The dignity of man called upon them to efface the black stain of their long submission to the tribute of Christian children from the character of the Hellenic race by some act of self-sacrifice.

Though the Othoman government had relaxed its fetters on the minds and bodies of the Greeks at the commencement of the nineteenth century, it was still a powerful and dangerous enemy. The sultan was engaged in a struggle to centralize the administration of his empire; and if his endeavours had been crowned with success before the Greeks succeeded in establishing their independence, new bonds would have been imposed on them, which would have restrained their movements as effectually as their former chains. The patriarch and the synod, the princes of the Phanar and the provincial primates, were always ready to serve as the agents of the sultan. It is therefore needless to justify the Greek Revolution. The time was well chosen. The act was the natural result of human sympathies. The growth of popular intelligence, and the development of moral, political, and religious feeling in every class of society, made the yoke of the Mohammedans insupportable. To others the increased strength of the slave might make the fetters which he wore appear light ; but it was his growth that really rendered them the cause of intolerable torture. The Greeks arrogated to themselves the highest rank among the Christian races under Mohammedan domination. It was consequently their duty to stand forward as the champions of civil liberty and Christian philanthropy.

APPENDIX.

I.

	A. D.	A. D.
Mahmud I., son of Mustapha II. . . .	1730 to	1754
Othman III., son of Mustapha II. . . .	1754 —	1757
Mustapha III., son of Achmet III. . .	1757 —	1774
Abdul-hamid, son of Achmet III. . . .	1774 —	1789
Selim III., son of Mustapha III. (dethroned) .	1789 —	1807
Mustapha IV., son of Abdul-hamid (dethroned) .	1807 —	1808
Mahmud II., son of Abdul-hamid . . .	1808 —	1839
Abdul-Medjid, son of Mahmud II. . .	1839 —	1861
Abdul-Aziz, son of Mahmud II. . . .	1861 —	1876

II.

LIST OF SIGNORS OF MYTILENE OF THE FAMILY OF GATTILUSIO.

A.D.

1. Francis I. 1355

2. Jacobus, son of Francis I., was Signor in 1395.
   Ducas, p. 52, edit. Bonn. *Le livre des faicts
   du bon Messire Jean le Maingre dit
   Boucicaut*, Pt. i. c. xxviii. Paul Jovis,
   Turcic. rerum comment.; Bajazetes I.
   A brother of Jacobus, named Nicolezo, was
   Signor of Ainos. Codinus, *De officiis
   et officialibus curiae et ecclesiae Constan-
   tinopolitanae*, 415, edit. Paris.

3. Francis II. Codinus, 415, edit. Paris.

4. Dorinus, brother of Francis II. (?) . . . 1455
   Signor of Mytilene (Lesbos), Lemnos, and
   Phocaea. Ducas, 328, edit. Bonn.
   Chalcocondylas, 249, edit. Paris.

5. Dominicus or Kyriakos, son of Dorinus . 1455 to 1458
   Murdered by his brother Nicolas. Ducas,
   328, 346; Italian translation, 503, 511,
   edit. Bonn. Chalcocondylas, 277, edit.
   Paris.

6. Nicolas, brother of Dominicus . . . 1458 to 1462
   Surrendered Mytilene to Mohammed II.;
   embraced Islam, and was soon after
   strangled by order of the sultan.

See Memoir on the Coins of the Gattilusii, by Julius Friedländer, in
Beiträge zur ältern Münzkunde, by Pinder and Friedländer; Berlin,
1851.

III.

LIST OF PHANARIOT VOIVODES OR HOSPODARS OF VALLACHIA AND MOLDAVIA.

VALLACHIA.	MOLDAVIA.
A. D.	A. D.
1716. Nicolas Mavrocordatos I.	1709. Nicolas Mavrocordatos I.
1717. John Mavrocordatos I.	1716. Michael Rakoviza I.
1719. Nicolas Mavrocordatos I.	1727. Gregorios Ghika the elder.
1731. Constantine Mavrocordatos I.	1733. Constantine Mavrocordatos I.
1733. Gregorios Ghika I.	1735. Gregorios Ghika I.
1735. Constantine Mavrocordatos I.	1741. Constantine Mavrocordatos I.
1741. Michael Rakoviza I.	1743. John Mavrocordatos II.
1744. Constantine Mavrocordatos I.	1747. Gregorios Ghika I.
1748. Gregorios Ghika I.	1748. Constantine Mavrocordatos I.
1752. Matthew Ghika I.	1749. Constantine Rakoviza I.
1753. Constantine Rakoviza I.	1753. Matthew Ghika I.
1756. Constantine Mavrocordatos I.	1756. Constantine Rakoviza I.
1758. Skarlatos Ghika I.	1757. Skarlatos Ghika I.
1761. Constantine Mavrocordatos I.	1758. John Th. Kallimaki.
1763. Constantine Rakoviza I.	1761. Gregorios Kallimaki I.
1764. Stephen Rakoviza.	1764. Gregorios Ghika II.
1765. Skarlatos Ghika I.	1766. Gregorios Kallimaki I.
1766. Alexander Ghika.	1769. Constantine Mavrocordatos I.
1768. Gregorios Ghika II.	

Military occupation of the two provinces by the Russians from 1770 to 1774.

1774. Alexander Hypsilanti I.	1774. Gregorios Ghika II.
1778. Nicolas Karadja.	1777. Constantine Mourouzi.
1783. Michael Soutzo I.	1782. Alexander Mavrocordatos I.
1786. Nicolas Mavroyeni.	1785. Alexander Mavrocordatos II.
	1787. Alexander Hypsilanti I.

Military occupation of Vallachia and Moldavia by the Russians, 1788 to 1789.

1791. Michael Soutzo I.	1792. Alexander Mourouzi I.
1793. Alexander Mourouzi I.	1793. Michael Soutzo I.
1796. Alexander Hypsilanti I.	1794. Alexander Kallimaki.
1798. Constantine Handjerli.	1799. Constantine Hypsilanti I.
1799. Alexander Mourouzi I.	1801. Alexander Soutzo I.
1801. Michael Soutzo I.	1802. Alexander Mourouzi I.
1802. Alexander Soutzo I.	1804. Skarlatos Kallimaki I.
1802. Constantine Hypsilanti I.	1806. Alexander Mourouzi I.
1806. Alexander Soutzo I.	
1806. Constantine Hypsilanti I.	

Military occupation of Vallachia and Moldavia by the Russians, from 1808 to 1812.

1812. John Karadja.	1812. Skarlatos Kallimaki I.
1818. Alexander Soutzo I.	1819. Michael Soutzo II.

Insurrection at the commencement of the Greek Revolution, 1821.

Printed in Great Britain
by Amazon